WITHIN THE WALLS

The Epitome of a Sheriff's Deputy

To Sheila & Tyrone,
I'd rather light a candle
then curse the darkness

Krasne

7-31-1999

Krasne V. Taylor

to my dearest mother:
Ora Christine Ross Taylor-Johnson
I'll always love you. You will *never* be forgotten

Acknowledgements

THE ARTWORK, WRITING, AND TEXT WORK OF THIS BOOK WAS not completed due to my efforts alone. It could not have been accomplished without the dedication, patience, wisdom, and understanding of many people. To all those who assisted me, and gave me encouragement to stick with it, I would like to extend my deepest appreciation for helping me reach this endeavor.

I would like to especially thank Telitha Cumi Bowens, who drew the book cover collage and poster with pastel chalk. This gifted lady is a world class talent by all means. Her patience, guidance, and discerning spiritual involvement with each project makes every one of them unique in stature.

Thank you, Mr. McArthur Stuckey, for taking the pictures for Ms. Bowens to do her excellent work. Mr. Stuckey is president and CEO of A & M Photography Studios in Detroit and Pontiac, Michigan. Thank you to my Aunt Betty, who had faith and believed in what I was doing (she notarized my first "poor-man" copyright).

I want to give my warmest thanks to several people whose patience and creative ideas were instrumental in helping me in the initial stages of *"Within The Walls."* They are: Allen Watts, and Herbert Metoyer from Detroit's Black Writer's Guild. Lesley Anderson for her editing assistance and help. But most of all thanks go out to Jim McGowan of Akashic Press in Ambler, Pennsylvania (a suburb of Philadelphia) for his formatting and typesetting, and Jay Wade of Visual Images, for his expertise and ideas in designing the front and back cover illustrations.

To my dearest friend Sylvia Winbush, I love you very much for all your patience, genuine love, in helping me reach my endeavors. Many thanks go out to Dian Sims of Dian's Miracle Bazaar in Little Rock, Arkansas, for her many years of loving friendship through our college years and beyond. Thanks go out to Mr. Cordell "Cash" Kelly, for all the help you've given me as I struggled to complete this book. To Garth Wisdom and his wife Kim, thanks for your inspiration and forever upbeat mentality every time we talked.

To all the *"Bombers,"* but especially to Byron Ramsey, I'll always love you for your timely thoughtfulness and eagerness to lend an ear to help me in the time of need.

I can't forget to give thanks to the many members who attend the Bally's Health Club in the suburban city of Southfield, Michigan. Many of them saw me in the initial stages of writing, promoting, and editing my manuscripts while taking take out between those grueling workouts. Many of those members gave me encouragement to continue throughout those years. I want to thank the many residents of the Riverfront Apartments, down on the Detroit River, who in the summer of 1991, saw me reading manuscripts everyday out by the marina.

Thanks go out to my friends Ed, Stephanie, and Terry of *Hands of Precision Barber Shop* for keeping my facial hair, and hairline up to code over those law enforcement years.

Oh yeah, I would *never* forget to give thanks to those many mediocre politicians (**politricksters**), judges, county commissioners, institutionalized state and federal entities, and so-called civil rights organizations, who have blatantly proven time and time again to me and the people, how their political agendas, bias favoritism, and ever growing ineptness created this vehicle, *Within The Walls.*

Dedications

WITH REVERENCE TO GOD, I DEDICATE THIS book to Our Lord and Father, and to my loving mother, Ora Christine Taylor, who, to me I feel, is closer to God than anyone I know. She always be the biggest, most influential person in my life. Before her retirement from the Detroit Board of Education in 1987, she taught and supervised well over 100,000 students, and teachers in her 33-year career.

My mother endured a lot of stressful conditions over her life: a divorce, diabetic illnesses, high blood pressure, heart problems, two amputations (toe and below the knee of the right leg), cataract surgery, dealing with all those naughty kids in school, and non-supportive relatives. Although she trusted everybody and was an ill senior citizen, white male contractors, banking lenders, mortgage companies, pharmacists (the Good Ol' Boys Network in Arkansas), and illiterate step-relatives took advantage of her generosity and naivete, but despite all that she still had love in her heart and *still praised God*.

After ten years of residence in El Dorado, Arkansas, Ora returned to Detroit in July of 1997; I started taking over her care at home with me, and I gained great strength from her. However, on the morning of Saturday, January 10, 1998, she had a massive stroke, which paralyzed the left side of her body and brain, and she went into a coma. The next day she had to have brain surgery to relieve the massive swelling, and was put on a ventilator that was on her for almost eight weeks. Everyday was a constant struggle on whether I should take my mother off this machine that kept her alive throughout her suffering. I had to give her a chance at life.

On March 1, 1998, the day that I had decided to remove the ventilator, she made her transition right in front of many family members and friends at the hospital. I can't begin to tell you how much I loved my mother, *__PLEASE__* pray for her. If there is any human who should've be cloned, it should've been *Ora Christine Taylor*, and this world would have definitely been a better place to live. My mother was truly *A PROFILE IN COURAGE*, and this two-part sequel is being dedicated entirely to her.

I also want to give honor and dedicate *Within The Walls* to the many Black officers (male and female), who have either been killed off duty or in the line of duty, committed suicide, or died of an illness while employed with the Wayne County Sheriff's Department. The sacrifices some of those officers made for the betterment of the department, will *never* be told. I would have loved to have printed those Black officers' names on this *Dedication* page (some are characterized in the book), but since there was difficulty getting those family's permission in writing, I neglected to do so. However, I must in some way honor their service.

And... to my father Tillman Taylor, who passed away September 9, 1992, he longed to see this project completed, but his health also wouldn't permit him to. Mom and Dad, *finally, it is done*. May God bless and keep you both.

Table of Contents

Introduction

BEING A POLICE OFFICER CAN BE ONE OF the most dreaded professions on this earth. At times it can be an enlightening experience, especially when the work of helping or saving someone from imminent danger is appreciated and acknowledged. There are times, however, when officers wished it was a job that was completely nonexistent. And the task (some call it *duty*), becomes even more of a drudgery when society and its citizens don't realize how much pressure, stress, and negativity an officer encounters while executing his official duties.

If you are contemplating employment in the arena of law enforcement, you must first consider these *five* important criterias, that affect the potential success of a police officer or jailer in the corrections arena.

The first *three major elements* that are very important in the institutional incarceration setting are 1) an *individual's temperament*, 2) *their adaptability*, and 3) a term called "*vocational personality*" which describes the personal characteristics of a worker as they relate to success on a job. Many of these institutionalized systems *ignore* "adaptability," and *enforce* "conformity," in an attempt to change an individual's temperament and talents by using aggressive, marginalization tactics, that will ultimately lead to one's rebellion, and with rebellion, how can you achieve adaptation?

The other *two* are an individual's *environmental conditions* and *physical surroundings*. These place specific demands on an officer's physical and mental capacity, which are grossly affected by the mismanagement of overzealous officials. Management's actions can create untold havoc and stress for officers on and off the job. In many cases, these conditions erupt in acts of workplace violence especially when an unfair, egotistical member of management becomes unwilling, unreachable, unyielding, and uncreative in using officer's talents and interacting with their subordinates.

In Detroit and its surrounding communities, numerous stories are heard from former and current Black sheriff's deputies, and workers who have worked, and who are still working for Wayne County. For the most part, the Department continues to inflict severe and unnecessary suffering, severe chastisement, and other counterproductive conduct that devastate the careers and ambitions of its Black officers. The Wayne County Sheriff's Department scourged vengeance and perpetrating influence, has historically been tolerated without any opposition from the leaders of Detroit's Black community, or more importantly, without any intervention from state, county, or federal judicial officials.

The majority of the public tends to forget that police officers are human, too. They are prone to sins, silly mistakes and failures just like everyone else. They are also required to perform dangerous, dirty, and sometimes seemingly stupid, mundane, unnecessary things, at a so-called *higher standard* (in the face of loyalty) and occasionally, a few are seduced into criminal and perverted acts.

I dreamed of being a policemen when I was a child. However, once I began my training, the reality of this challenge hit me like a ton of bricks. And now, after experiencing both sides of the coin as a civilian and a law enforcement officer, I can only say with honesty, that I'd rather stay a civilian, because in retrospect, a police officer's job is totally *"reactionary"* in their response to violent situations. So, in many cases, citizens are compelled to protect themselves. You can't have a police officer on every corner to stop crime, or from just someone that just wants to mess with you.

To be a police officer in an urban community like Detroit, and many other troubled urban inner cities in this nation, requires courage, and those who have undertaken this task are to be commended. Yet, there are some *"bad apples"* and *"gun slingers"* in each group. In the beginning, most cops (like those on cop TV shows) will say "it's the best job they have ever had" and that they want a safer environment that is free of crime, corruption, drugs, and other types of criminality. While most pursue that ideology and tenaciously try to combat these vicious elements, many become a fixed part of a racial, bureaucratic system of injustices perpetrated against Black people and other so-called minorities. In doing so, they either create or join an already existing feudal system that gears itself on underlying schemes of greed, collusive power, manipulation, fabrication, and perpetration.

My parents *never* taught me about the evils of racism. However, when I became an adult it was demonstrated, and solidified through on the job and hiring discrimination (favoritism), court injustices, and the news media. Only blatant acts of racism and discrimination are reported and used as media tools to incite public reaction. My story is merely *one of those* that was pushed aside, and a prime example of the undermined separatism that the department devised. In part, I don't consider myself a prejudice person, I just tell it like it is. I always—and will continue to pick my friends for what they stand for; the content of their character, quality and zest for righteous living. Not for the color of their skin, but the humanitarian realism in their heart.

Living rather carefree, I never worried or thought about the white and Black issues of this country—not until the assassination of Dr. Martin Luther King, Jr. on April 4, 1968. Until that time, I didn't know anything about the lives and history of Malcolm X, Medgar Evers, Rosa Parks, or Marcus Garvey, to name a few. Guess I was too young and my parents just weren't into that. It wasn't until that terrible day that I realized that there was something

Introduction

terribly wrong with this country. I was 13-years old at that time, watching television, troubled by seeing the tears in the eyes of many international dignitaries at Martin Luther King's funeral, and suddenly, I was aware. Aware with a consciousness that grew daily as I watched the many ensuing riots that erupted in the urban cities around the country—definitely, something was wrong. This was a major turning point in my life. The experiences I encountered at the Wayne County Sheriff's Department were many, and it also was another turning point in my life. That experience was so impactful, that I *had to* write a sequel about it.

Within The Walls attempts to provide an open forum for discussion about mismanagement, favoritism, nepotism, cronyism, and provide solutions regarding the same in the law enforcement arena. It also attempts to increase the public's awareness of the critical role a jailer plays, its many nuisances that one faces, and by blending humor with profundity.

Within The Walls is an historical and chronological account of a Black male sheriff's deputy's experiences while working as a jailer from 1985-1989, and his many years of frustrated attempts to obtain redress for a gross injustice.

Within The Walls alerts others of a law enforcement agency's tactics of shrouded secrecy, policies of hypocrisy, collusion, poisoned mentality, lies, and fixed destruction to not obtain retribution through the arbitration process.

On June 22, 1989, I wrote over *twenty* congressional figures: both Democratic senators, the NAACP, the Urban League, several state representatives in the Black caucus, a AFL-CIO secretary\treasurer, and even a preacher of a prominent Detroit church who was a former Detroit Police Commissioner. I even submitted a civil rights complaint with the Michigan Civil Rights Department which was forwarded to the Equal Employment Opportunity Commission... none of which was enough to warrant a favorable response to thoroughly investigate. I also wrote *four* Black Wayne County Commissioners, who thought nothing of my plight (I got pacifying replies from two).

This book is surely written to reveal some of that bigotry and preferential treatment by the white structures. I don't anticipate that everyone will agree with such a sequel, but if one person is positively informed, then this mission is a success. As developments changed through this project, several Black officers who worked or have worked for the department, kept me abreast of the continuing bigotry displayed there, often pressuring me to expedite the publication of this book. Once I was taken seriously, many Black officers even wanted me to add some of their experiences in **my** book too! Many of these Black officers refused to speak up about the injustices, but would rather fall on the heels of someone who would, in this case, me.

The cliques and supporting groups are well known, and anyone who has worked for the sheriff's department or under Wayne County's administration know of these existing problems. During my employment with the Wayne County Sheriff's Department, I felt the scourge of the racist hammer. I was persecuted for speaking up and defending my rights. This persecution included false charges and write-ups to destroy my character, and any possibility of any future employment with another law enforcement agency.

Let me make this perfectly clear. **Within The Walls** <u>_was not written_</u> to gain fame, riches, or notoriety. It was merely written to help others avoid such calamities of deceit, heighten the consciousness and awareness of persons who are contemplating a career in law enforcement, and to provide an open forum for years of discussion relative to overcoming the difficulties of imperialistic, arrogant, people of power who invented "**The System**," and who continually revise it to meet _their_ needs.

I must also address the geographical preference of **Within The Walls**, which is Wayne County, which is in Detroit, Michigan. For those readers outside of Detroit or the State of Michigan, I'm sure that **Within The Walls** will have a correlation that anyone out-of-state can relate to their own locale and its politics. To my readers, I must also say, that there is some realistic cursing and vulgar language **Within The Walls**, and I hope it doesn't offend too many readers. I mean... this is the jail, **and if it does offend someone, so be it! I'll tell _my_ story the way it happened and the way I see it.**

In the optimistic words of Black author, James Baldwin, he stated, "even the most **incorrigible** maverick has to be born somewhere." In the realistic, most simplistic statement by Malcolm X, he stated, and said it all, "The most powerful tool in the hands of the oppressor are the minds of the oppressed."

Remember that a person who stands for nothing, will fall for anything. God has a purpose for all of us, and we must seek Him to endure and discover that gift. I've written a poem entitled, "**The System**," that I'd like to share with you... my readers. It goes a little-something-like-this:

Yes, I know that ignorance is bliss,
And the world has heard it all,
But who are we to blame?
Some people will always have their own cause.
There are so many injustices and lies,
Proportionally... they say caused
Because this world is in a hateful pause
Could it be from human premeditated fraud?
For there seems to be no prevention
Either untold, and yet we're all appalled.
Everyday the world is becoming savagely clawed
Into a Devils' Brawl
The truth that's flawed to make you feel small
Lies hidden—**Within The Walls**.

Introduction
Never give up, no matter how hard the task
Never give up, because that's what some want
You must fight for your rights and take a firm stand
for what is right is close at hand
If not, we all will take a fall
Buried deep, *Within The Walls*.

PRAYER OF SERENITY

God grant me the serenity to accept the things I cannot
change. The courage to change the things I can,
and the wisdom to know the difference.

EPHESIANS 6:10-14

Finally, my brethren, be strong in the Lord, and in the power of
his might. Put on the whole armour of God, that ye may be able to stand
against the wiles of the devil. For we wrestle not against flesh and blood,
but against principalities, against powers, against the rulers of the darkness of this world, against spiritual wickedness in high places. Wherefore
take unto you the whole armour of God, that ye may be able to withstand
in the evil day, and having done all, to stand. Stand therefore, having your
loins girt about with truth, and having on the breastplate of righteousness.

PROVERBS 3:5,6

Trust in the Lord with all thine heart; and lean not
unto thine own understanding. In all thy ways
acknowledge him and he shall direct thy paths.

PROVERBS 13:20

He that is walking with wise persons will become wise, but he that is
having dealings with the stupid ones will fare badly.

ORA'S PUBLISHING'S
MISSION STATEMENT

What is a Vision?

A *Vision* is a directive that is commissioned from
the *Almighty God*, that requires patience, obedience,
commitment, foreseeability, loyalty to a cause, and
pride in what you're doing, no matter how long the
time frame it takes to complete it, and no matter
what the obstacles may be.

Thank you *Heavenly Father*, for giving me a
Vision, in order that I may please you
by doing *Your Will*.

1

The Sheriff is in Town: My Early Childhood

A S A CHILD I ADMIRED POLICE OFFICERS. To me, these unwavering and valorous civil servants were fortitudinous warriors: bold, fearless, faithful, courageous, faultlessly decisive, with immeasurable devotion, someone prestigious and highly respected in the community. This precipitated my decision to become involved in law enforcement.

I was also inspired by watching and emulating "law and order" cartoon characters like Quick Draw McGraw, and his alias El-Kabong, who smashed villains with a guitar. Q-T Hush and Yosemite Sam were also subtle influences.

Consequently, I spent many hours playing in the cowboy or sheriff regalia, feeling proud and assured. Like the Rifleman Chuck Connors, I wore a shiny silvery badge affixed over my heart, while rapidly cocking my plastic, double-barreled Winchester rifle, with a trusty six-shooter loaded in a side holster, and spinning spurs glittering on highly polished black patent leather cowboy boots.

In the 1950s, 60s, and 70s, *Shoot-'em Up* had an entirely different meaning. As the "Lawman," I kept my pistol loaded with paper caps: long narrow rolls of paper lined with a row of tiny dots filled with gunpowder. The dots exploded with vigor when struck by the hammer of my toy pistol, although some were ineffective duds and failed to pop. These were my bullets!

Lots of playing time was spent trying to master the hula hoop, playing *Engine, engine-number-nine...*, tag, the stupid and infamous

Pattycake, pattycake-baker's-man... (every kid in the world was taught that game), hopscotch, shooting marbles, and *Mister Fox, what time is it?,* one of my favorites. We kids also played a lot of "cowboys and Indians," but back then I didn't know that the first "cowboys" *were* "Indians," and that most cowboys in the Old West were Black, not white: and all this in the face of Roy Roger's reputation.

Another game of choice was *Hide and Seek,* better known in the Black community as *Hide and Come Get It.* We kids also played *Spin the Bottle.* When I would spin the bottle, it often stopped at the uglier but more educated girls in the neighborhood: but back then who worried about smarts? However, the best liked game was *Doctor* or *House.* We boys could examine the anatomies of various girls in the neighborhood or play the father in the family.

When it was time for we kids to play, I would always suggest *Cops and Robbers* games, and always preferred playing the sheriff: All criminals **BEWARE**, Sheriff Taylor is in town. As the sheriff, I apprehended and nabbed friend and foe, anyone who played the criminals, and sternly enforced my own totalitarian rule: making arrests without provocation or any kind of lip.

Forcefully I wrestled those who resisted to the ground, initiating restraining holds around the neck, arms, head, legs, in order to sub-due them. I then took, or dragged, my prisoner to jail after securing them with plastic toy handcuffs bought from the neighborhood dime store. Never was I without at least three pairs. For a jail I used the family garage, big cardboard boxes from household appliances, or the front porch of the house, for detention. The garage could be locked, which made detention more realistic, but the cardboard boxes and the front porch had imaginary doors and bars, making escape easy. Because of this, instead of training or teaching some formal-ized rehabilitation, I spent more time apprehending escapees than maintaining their confinement.

It seemed that the majority of kids wanted to play the bad guys. I had no idea *why* everybody else wanted to play the criminal. Could it be because the general wisdom is that nice guys finish last? In essence, I was forced to have a one-man sheriff's department. As a kid I accepted that responsibility; I always liked challenges!

On one occasion I had to use lawman ingenuity: the use of force.

Cornelius Porter, one of the hardest criminals to keep in check, was an 11-year old bully in the neighborhood, who had a reputation for terrorizing any kid he wanted to terrorize. Even at the age of eleven he had a bald head and was big, weighing about 130 pounds. I was eight years old and weighed about 90 pounds. One day, on my way home from the candy store, we got into it.

"Hey you, boy, you better give me some of that candy, or get your butt whipped," Cornelius demanded, angry, reaching back and balling his fists. "Buy your own dibbies," I responded, afraid. Without another word, or further hesitation, Cornelius jumped on me and we fought a few minutes. I got a bloody lip. Fighting back, I held my own, even though Cornelius was much bigger and stronger than I was.

Completely frustrated, I vowed to get revenge. Now, I had never joined a gang, one way of getting revenge. I was too individual and independent-minded for that. It seemed like there was a gang on every street: the Vancouver Vipers, the Oregon Hawks, and the Spokane Spider gang—Cornelius' gang. So one day I tried to convince Harold Alston to join me, so together we could capture Cornelius Porter.

Now, when we played, none of the kids in the neighborhood wanted to be deputized except Harold Alston. He was my ace booncoon. Harold was one year older than me, a sneaky kid, spunky but fearful at times, and he stuttered a lot. His antics reminded me of Don Knotts, as Barney Fife, from *Andy of Maybury:* always screwing up by chunkin' and hitting rocks in the alley with a baseball bat. So I tried to convince Harold to become braver, so we could apprehend and capture Cornelius.

"Come on, Harold, he's a lot bigger than me; I need some help. If we can both get him down, I think I can handcuff him, and we can bring him back to the garage, lock him up for awhile, and teach him a lesson."

"I don't know, Khaki, that boy is pretty big."

"Come on, Scaredy-cat, I'm sure if we work together, we can do it. You a chump! What's the matter, you scared?"

"Yep."

"Well, if you're *that* scared, don't be asking me for no more favors. Don't ever ask me to help you any more for anything, ya hear?"

"Well, alright, but we might get in trouble with the Spiders; they might come back and beat us up."

"They ain't gonna beat us up. Some of them don't even like Cornelius. Come on: we got to get him."

To capture Cornelius, Harold and I knew we had to devise a good game plan of attack and surprise. We knew, from previous experience, that Cornelius walked down Spokane St. a lot, past Ms. Bostic's summer school camp to mess with the kids on the playground. The scheme was, once he reached the alley we'd use the element of surprise, knock him down, and handcuff him. And we'd use whatever force was necessary to subdue and bring him back to the garage for detention.

Ms. Bostic's summer school camp was the summertime haven for recreational activity for kids out of school. Many parents in the neighborhood sent their kids there. There were swings and stationary animal and train figures to climb and play on. Camp activities included baseball, arts and crafts, shuffleboard, checkers, boy and girl scout troops, dodge ball, camping retreats, and government-supplied hot lunches. For a half hour after lunch everyday, all the kids were required to gather around inside the house to play *Pattycake...* and hear Ms. Bostic play the piano. She and the camp coordinator led the children in singing, *Old McDonald...*, *Mary had a little lamb...*, and other kiddie songs. Those summer camp activities taught kids about togetherness, and taught them to respect the feelings of others: keeping throngs of them out of trouble.

The next day, while summer camp was still in progress, our plan to capture Cornelius worked perfectly, just like clockwork. As Cornelius crossed the alley Harold and I, hiding behind a garage bin, ran up behind Cornelius, knocked him to the ground, and, embedding our knees in his neck and back, swiftly secured his wrists with a pair of plastic handcuffs. When we stood him on his feet, Cornelius laughed and sneered: "You two little punks better let me go!"

"We just gonna teach you a lesson and lock you up for awhile. When we decide to let you go, you must promise us that you are gonna leave all the kids alone."

Eleven-year-old Cornelius was just a-cussin': "When I get out of these cheap handcuffs, both of you are gonna get your asses kicked." "Well, it won't be the first time," I commented, as Harold looked frightened at the prospects.

Not too far away, the garage was in the next alley, so transporting Cornelius wasn't as difficult as we had projected, though he fought valiantly: kicking and jumping up and down. Hearing all the commotion, several kids on the campgrounds looked on, as did several neighbors. The kids yelled gleefully, "Ahhh-ha," happy that someone had paid Cornelius back for his evil deeds.

Mrs. Vera Love, a neighbor in the house behind my house, peered out her front screened door and yelled, "Oh, y'all got that bully, huh? It's about time someone stood up to that little punk; but you need to do something about that damn hardheaded Harold for breaking out my back window with them damn rocks. Harold, when you gonna get yo mama to come down here and pay for it?"

"Damn hag, why don't she just shut the hell up. I didn't break her damn window," Harold uttered under his breath.

"Yes, you did, Harold. You ought-ta pay Mrs. Love her money. You know she's been real good to us, and always helps us out a lot."

Jobs were generally in abundance back then, but Mrs. Love, an elderly Black woman, was even more fortunate than others in the neighborhood because her family had invested in real estate in the South. They had hundreds of acres of farmland in Mississippi: full of soybeans, corn, peas, and watermelon. Three of her six sons were into agriculture, devoted farmers. Of the other three, one was a carpenter, one a science teacher at Howard University, and a third worked at the Ford factory, making 1964 Mustangs.

Mrs. Love customarily had the nicest looking house in the neighborhood: seemed like every two weeks she was having some remodeling work done, or something to enhance the property. She had a nice, manicured lawn, aluminum siding, not one piece of dried out or rotted-out wood on the garage. Nearly everybody else's garage needed work, or was severely falling apart.

Without another word, Harold ran ahead to open up the gate to my yard. While approaching the garage Cornelius began frantically kicking, and put up another valiant struggle to escape. Harold quickly rushed back to help, and again we had to use excessive force to restrain Cornelius' second escape attempt. After a brief struggle, finally getting control of the situation, we placed Cornelius inside the garage; I locked the door with an old skeleton key. For four hours Cornelius was unable to get out. Dusk was approaching fast.

Savoring our capture of Cornelius, Harold and I celebrated by sitting on the front porch and toasting to a glass of grape Kool-Aid. We had worked up a sweat. Ms. Nellie Porter, Cornelius' mother, a single Black woman raising such a bad boy, came walking down the street, appearing worried, looking for her son. In those days single-parenting was rare. She had already asked several Spokane gang members where he was, but they didn't know.

"You boys wouldn't happen to have seen my son Cornelius?"

"Ah, yeah," I responded hesitantly. Harold remained silent. I continued: "The other day we had a fight because I wouldn't give him my candy, and that wasn't the first time, so my friend and I captured him and locked him up in my garage."

"Let me out of here." We could faintly hear Cornelius yelling from the garage, all the way to the front of the house.

At first Ms. Porter looked at Harold and me, kind of mad, but soon she broke into a smile: "Yeah, he needs a lesson anyway. Please take me to him, OK?"

While the three of us walked between the houses, before reaching the garage, we heard the yells getting louder and clearer. When I opened the garage door, Cornelius, with streams of tears coming down his cheeks, vowed: "The next time I see you, me and my boys are gonna beat you and your friend's butt!"

"Now son, that's enough of that," Ms. Porter interrupted. "You were wrong in the first place for fighting this boy for not giving you some candy. Don't I give you enough money every day to buy your own? What are you doing with that money?" Cornelius said nothing.

"If I hear of you or your so-called boys ever messing with these boys again, you're going to reform school in Lansing. I'm sick and tired of you disobeying me and not going to school. See this damn report card? Child, I work too hard for you, and you're messing up like this?"

Ms. Porter had Cornelius' report card in her pocket, and this was one reason why she was looking for Cornelius: she wanted to give him a whipping for getting a "C" in gym and the rest all E's. Mainly she was after him for skipping school thirty-four days in one semester.

There was no ten percent bond, so after taking off the handcuffs I released my prisoner to his mother. She grabbed his arm and forcefully pulled him along.

Two days after the incident several Spokane gang members approached Harold and I as we left Ms. Bostic's summer camp: "We're glad y'all did that; we're tired of him anyway. He was getting to be a problem. You two young fellas are pretty tough; y'all wanna join our gang?"

"Nope," I answered, "Plus we stay on Vancouver and the Vipers might not like that. I don't like gangs, and my parents would whip me anyway. Somebody around here has to keep some *law and order,"* I added, hesitating. Harold remained on pause, ready to run.

"Well, y'all is cool with us, alright," a gang member concluded.

Whew, Harold and I had escaped trouble. We looked at each other in relief. We worried for several weeks about the prospects of those hoodlums coming back to beat us up, but they never did: it never happened. Cornelius never bothered us again either, and the kids in the neighborhood were freed from his hooliganism.

In the summer of 1967, when I was twelve, I migrated to my grandmother *Big Momma's* house in Arkansas for summer recess. I watched the national newscasts on television show Black people in Detroit and many other urban cities rioting, looting and killing across America because of the escalating racial tensions, which still, today, continues to destroy America and the world. The Civil Rights movement was going strong back then, and many Blacks were inspired by a surge of ethnic pride and awareness. Would I ever be able to go back home? Crying hysterically, I sought answers from relatives.

When summer vacation was over and I returned to Detroit, my homecoming was marred by the ever-present national guardsmen, army, and police units. There were nearly 30,000 armed service units camped out at several inner city high schools. Two of these were set up at Northwestern and Central High Schools: each deep in the Black urban ghetto areas of Detroit. There was an eerie, unsettling strangeness riding down the streets in those areas, armored tanks riding alongside, manned as they were by itchy-fingered tank gunners ready to rapid fire automatic weapons. Camouflaged infantrymen rode in jeeps and carried M-1 carbines. It looked like these were the new sheriffs in town.

Sadly, in 1970, Harold Alston was killed in a car accident, at age fourteen, on a fishing trip to Northern Michigan. I'll never forget the day I was informed of that accident: it was one of the most difficult days of my youth. I couldn't sleep, couldn't eat, and hardly spoke to anyone for two weeks after that.

The day after Harold's death I was at Sunday School, given the job of child monitor: I would watch to see if kids or teenagers violated any church ethics while classes were in session. I looked for things like gum chewing, talking, that sort of thing.

Just before a collective discussion of the lesson I was asked to go up in front of the congregation and point out which persons violated church ethics: "In Mrs. Johnson's class, Tony was chewing gum and popping it; Sheila and Tina were talking a lot in Deacon Quarterman's class." Proudly I spoke, and everyone looked in the direction of the violators and said, "Amen."

I didn't get great satisfaction telling on people but it was my job. Then Harold came to mind. I wasn't finished, there were more violators, but at that moment I became very sad and began talking instead about my friend's death:

I started: "Yesterday my best friend was killed in a car accident." Suddenly I began trembling, felt very sad, and broke into uncontrollable tears. I couldn't finish, and had to be consoled by my mother and a few other church ladies. I knew my manpower was gone and "Sheriff" Taylor would have trouble finding any other kid to deputize and trust when we played cops and robbers, because I could count on Harold: he was my *ace boon-coon*.

2

The A.C.B.D.C., What Happened to the "E" Conspiracy? The Acquisition of the New Jail

ETROIT, WITH A MOMENTOUS CRIME RATE that continuously grew out of proportion to its population, sorely needed another jail. In the early 1970's, the acquisition of the new jail was an everlasting bureaucratic and orchestrated battle amongst city commissioners, community leaders, city coalition organizers, state legislators, and the many predominantly white, suburban rural communities of Wayne County. As expected, there was the usual spontaneous, lingering civil uproar and political bickering: how would monies to build the new jail be appropriated, and where should this new monstrosity be built?

In May, 1971, six months before a special committee was formed, a panel of three Wayne County Circuit judges ruled that incarceration in the old jail constituted cruel and unusual punishment and was in clear violation of inmates' constitutional rights. *New Detroit Incorporated,* a nonprofit community group formed after the 1967 riot to establish better relations between businesses and the community, provided $150,000 for the special new committee. The money was mainly used to generate other monies to apply for federal grants.

There were also several subcommittees formed to give advice to the commissioners on the most practical location for the new jail, its size, design, recreational facilities, and the standard for determining what constitutes *"better general treatment"* for inmates. In my opinion, these needless expenditures cost Wayne County taxpayers an arm and two legs.

In November, 1971, the special committee: Wayne County Jail

Advisory Committee, formed when members of New Detroit Inc. expressed their concerns about jail conditions to the New Detroit President Stanley Winkelman. Winkelman met several times with Wayne County Commissioners to discuss the horrible conditions in the old jail. Armed with $150,000, this committee of sixty influential citizens held its first meeting in January, 1972, and announced a willingness to help facilitate construction of the new jail, and improve the inhumane conditions of the old jail.

After careful deliberations, the cochair of that committee, along with a Wayne County Commissioner, commented: "There are many citizens of this county who do not have the slightest idea of what is really needed." The city of Westland, considered *then and now* to be white suburbia, was initially the county's first geographical choice for a new jail site. From day one, Westland's all-white city council didn't like the idea and consistently fought the proposal of this site for the new jail. The majority of Wayne County officials wanted the new jail built on Westland's county-owned acreage; whereas most of the Detroit City Council wanted the new jail built in the city of Detroit, right in the "dat-blain" center of a tri-county, high crime area.

In 1972, Westland's mayor notified the council that this action violated its city charter, which stated that "... the city council must unanimously approve an issue. But if one member abstains because of a conflict of interest, then the vote is nullified." Unprecedented but not unexpected, two councilmen from Westland abstained from voting to put the new jail in Westland because of conflicting interests. One owned stock in a weekly Westland newspaper, *the Heritage,* and the other was the Council President, who abstained to fall in line with the weekly paper.

The "N" Building, just south of the Wayne County General Hospital in Westland, was one area under serious consideration, and the Detroit House of Corrections (De-Ho-Co) in Plymouth was another alternative. Both structurally sound and usable Wayne County Historical Landmarks had sat abandoned for over two decades, and remained dilapidated eyesores and *negative fiscal reminders* for anyone driving on the major throughway. Many Wayne citizens felt that the barren, undeveloped, spacious and vacant prairie land surrounding the "N" Building and "De-Ho-Co" should have been the first and only choice for a new jail.

Detroit citizens always wondered why the Detroit House of Corrections was so called when it wasn't even actually in the City of Detroit. Now it's true most of its prisoners were from Detroit, but it's one thing to associate the name of the city with sports teams' logos, and another to say it in the same breath as *jail*, especially when the house of corrections wasn't even within Detroit's city limits. The move was *only* suitable financially, and it was politically motivated.

In 1985, "De-Ho-Co" was taken over and controlled by the state, and named Western Wayne Correctional Facility. Prisoners sentenced there had offenses against them ranging from third offense drunken driving to murder. They were no longer double-bunked in the old cell block, but were housed in small dormitory-type rooms. It took more than two decades for Wayne County to decide to renovate those buildings for their original use: to jail prisoners.

After months of constant political bickering, a consulting firm was hired by the county, and recommended the elimination of the sheriff's role as Wayne County's chief jailer. They next recommended the creation of a county corrections department to replace him. These recommendations, like shifting the pieces around in a shell-game, were made in a preliminary report to Wayne County Commissioners about specific *needs* for new jail facilities as part of a restructured, county criminal justice system. This type of railroading, presented as *recommendations,* surfaced often at the Department of Corrections and continually threatened the sheriff's role.

Although the study's recommendation was clearly to eliminate the sheriff's responsibility for the jail, a white male Wayne County official insisted loudly it was *not* aimed at Sheriff Kenneth Barrett or jail administrator Frank Wilkerson, both Black. Finally, after all the consultations, recommendations, and stagnation, the firm decided unanimously that the new jail should be built downtown, behind the Detroit Police headquarters, on city-owned land bounded by Beaubien, Clinton, St. Antoine and an alley north of Monroe. The decision was to close Macomb between St. Antoine and Beaubien. The old Recorder's Court had to be demolished, and the old Detroit Police garage was left untouched.

Meanwhile, on November 7, 1972, Wayne County voters acted

on two tax proposals: one to pay for a new county jail, and the other to expand the Juvenile Court and the County Youth Home. The Wayne County Board of Commissioners decided to seek voter approval of a six-tenths of a mill tax increase (60 cents per $1,000 of state equalized valuation) to finance a new jail.

The passing of Proposition F would have authorized this assessed valuation for five years to raise $40 million for a new jail. The passing of Proposition G would have approved fourteenths of a mill levy to raise about $28 million to build youth home facilities in Detroit and western Wayne County. Both millage proposals would have made it possible, for the first time, to adequately house adult county prisoners, and isolate youthful offenders from older, more dangerous criminals. For the first time, the new facility would provide for a prisoner dining room instead of requiring the inmates to eat in their cells or wards. It would also provide educational and recreational facilities.

At the same time, commissioners authorized a separate ballot proposition asking approval for five years in order to build a new juvenile facility. The projection was that nearly $65 million would be raised over five years if both taxes were approved by Wayne County voters. A one mill increase would have cost homeowners an additional twenty dollars a year on property worth $20,000. There was a heated 90-minute discussion, after which the county commissioners voted 15 to 4 to place the new jail millage proposal on the November 7th ballot. Several commissioners questioned the need for a new jail in light of a recent, sharp reduction in the prisoner population and a permanent increase in Recorder's Court judges from thirteen to twenty.

To push for the passage of both millage proposals the county needed a reputable booster and, in October 1972, there was an unlikely political alliance of former teamster president Jimmy Hoffa and Wayne County Sheriff Kenneth Barrett. Hoffa, just released December 23, 1971, from federal prison after serving nearly five years of a 13-year jury tampering and mail fraud conviction, joined Barrett in a press conference on the stage of the Fisher theatre. Hoffa spoke in favor of public action to gain prison reform, and stood with Barrett: both men urging passage of the November millage proposals for construction of a new county jail and two youth detention homes.

Hoffa described prison life and asked the audience of five hundred, primarily women, "to destroy prison conditions that take away the desire of a man to return to society" and dehumanize him. "If you fail to take action on prison reform, each one of you may be the victim of a person who was disturbed, raped or beaten while in prison," Hoffa added. He also suggested convicts be taught practical skills and paid union wages for working in prison industries. Room and board, Hoffa reasoned, could be deducted from prisoners' wages and the rest sent to the prisoners' families, significantly reducing welfare rolls. Hoffa also noted that letters should be written to legislators, urging them to support prison reform proposals, and to ease prisons tensions by formation of prisoner unions, which could arbitrate grievances with prison officials.

In the Wayne County jail there was never a legal right regarding inmates' self-government, or an inmate grievance council. There has never been an inmate legal right to have representation on jail disciplinary tribunals, although such matters are at the discretion of and within administrative and legislative jurisdiction. Departmental officials might give an opined inmate complaint as much weight as *they* deemed reasonable, but not necessarily proper protocol.

The courts could not and would not, under constitutional principals of separation of powers, order the sheriff to give inmates the influence sought (1971 opinion; also 8/7/71, order #43). This fixity of separation of powers also has comparison and explains why senators, congressional figures, and civil rights groups (NAACP, Urban League, CORE, SCLC, Michigan Civil Rights Commission, and the EEOC) seem to historically ignore the many complaints from Black people against law enforcement agencies, and corporate entities. The separation of powers rule is regarded as *take care of your own problems*. This is ironic because law enforcement is known for ineptitude and severe management problems, including discriminatory practices, just like any other business. Law agencies are no different, but are considered exempt from investigation or persecution by the federal government: only because they are controlled and mandated primarily by white-male ruling officials.

Many in the Detroit political arena thought the most likely method of financing the new jail would be construction by the Wayne County

Building Authority. The Authority could issue bonds to finance construction. With this method, the county had to pledge full faith and credit of its general fund to the bonds. The county could lease the jail from the Building Authority with rental payments going to pay off the bonds.

The other alternative was to build a new jail with money from the county's general fund. Part of the county's 1972-73 budget contained a seven million dollar surplus, and could have been used for a new jail. Instead, the County Board Chairman blamed *improper means* to explain the proposal to the general public: a likely political excuse. The seven million dollar surplus for a new jail was considered a likely source in light of the defeat of the two jail millage proposals, but the county board took no action to use the surplus monies, feeling that the seven million dollar fund would allow ground breaking as early as Spring of 1973.

Construction of the new jail was delayed for years because the county's federal, revenue-sharing funds did not live up to expectation. County officials learned that their federal grant would be $11.7 million instead of the $15.5 million estimated earlier by the U.S. Treasury Department. The slash in revenue-sharing money raised new doubts about the scheduling for a new jail and dimmed any prospects for an early start on jail construction. The county president called on Wayne County's seven U. S. representatives and Michigan's two U.S. senators to help find out "... why the county's original revenue-sharing figures were lowered."

The county board chairman sent a letter to the legislators to protest the Treasury Department's refusal to tell the county's Washington lobbyist the reasons for such a significant cutback in money. He also believed that the sharp reduction could have been caused by a computer, or human error: totally preposterous because the government, of course, wanted the county to fund its own jail-building project.

Since the general public wasn't naive enough to burden itself with the funding of upwards of $40 million plus dollars, it was the commissioners' electoral duty to find other viable resources to fund the construction. The chairman also asked legislators to help the county force the Treasury Secretary to release the population, tax and per capita income figures in order to show the citizens of Wayne

County how their tax dollars were being used. According to the chairman: "The federal government can't continue to deny the people of the county their equity in the redistribution of their tax money."

The county chairman tried every conceivable tactic to put the burden of financing the jail on county residents. As the process continued, county officials discovered a significant cut in revenue-sharing money when they received a check for $5,852,176, only half of the county's 1972 allocation. Based on that amount, however, county officials still expected the county to collect the usual $11.7 million for 1973. It is interesting to note that the county government's $11.7 million grant did not apply to communities within the county, which received individual allocations under a federal revenue-sharing plan. This was another way of holding back allocating monies that should have been appropriated accordingly: for example, Census Bureau counts determine how much money a city should be allocated by the number of city residents counted.

The county commissioners' cop-out, no surprise, came at the same time they were appealing a decision by the three-judge Circuit Court panel, which ruled that the commission "must act promptly in remedying the deplorable jail situations." For over a year the commissioners *ignored court orders* and vied for the best excuse instead of complying with the judges' orders. In addition, reluctant to foot the twenty-five million dollar expense in an election year, the commissioners tried to pass the buck-to-build-a-new-jail to the voters in the November, 1972 millage test rather than issue bonds. The commissioners were banking on the fact that prisoners and their families don't command many votes. The commissioners' political careers were more important, we can assume, than correcting the deplorable conditions inside the old jail, where humanity and proper rehabilitation standards should have come first and foremost.

Meeting guidelines, county commissioners and auditors were directed to submit objective plans to the court: providing details, a timetable and financial arrangements. In 1971, to see those regulations met, the court ordered the county to pay for a court monitor within the jail. This was met with stiff resistance from the commissioners, who twice *ordered* the county treasurer and auditor *not to* pay for the monitor, relenting only when rebuked by the court.

In 1986, the courts again ordered a monitor to view various internal and administrative problems in the newly built jail. Superiors were always very meticulous, making sure all jail or departmental paperwork was in order, thus keeping the jail fairly free of possible scrutiny. The jail was always in full compliance when the court appointed monitor stalked the floors to detect court violations. In 1990, a permanent monitor was appointed, authorized, and instructed by the courts to oversee jail operations and report any new findings.

In 1995, because of years of continuous reports of mismanagement, overcrowding, contaminated food, danger to inmates from violent jailers, roach and rodent infestation and an all-around filthy environment, Wayne County's Juvenile Detention Center had to choose either to stop violating civil rights or face federal monitoring from the Justice Department when a youth home-detainee complained to the Detroit News of an outbreak of a sexually transmitted parasite and unsanitary conditions.

Once again, showing a bold reluctance, the commissioners, claiming that *"separation of governmental powers prohibits a judicial body from ordering a legislative body on how to spend its monies,"* refused to pay for the additional jail personnel ordered by the courts. The court had ordered that *"it has a right to protect the judicial process, including the well-being of defendants waiting in jail to go to court."* The courts noted that conditions in the old jail were so bad that some defendants pled guilty just to hasten their removal to relatively more humane conditions at Jackson State Prison and other maximum state prisons in Michigan.

The court also denied the inmates' motion to have the county pay the fees for outside attorneys, who helped court-appointed attorneys with their class-action lawsuit of 1971. Two lawyers, representing the inmates, argued that in filing and litigating the jail case, they were acting in a public capacity. One asked for $21,700 and the other for $7,000: fees based on the minimum allowed by the State Bar of Michigan. The fees were to cover both investigative and in-court work during the yearlong case.

A Wayne County corporate counsel opposed the payment, arguing: "There were other lawyers involved in the case... paid by the public agencies [who] could have handled the case rather than private lawyers." Other lawyers contributing to the inmates' case were either law students or employees of Michigan Legal Services, funded by the Federal Office of Economic Opportunity.

Several inmate complaints surfaced concerning the court-appointed lawyers: pressuring inmates to plead guilty to lesser charges, tricking inmates into waiving preliminary examinations, and never thoroughly consulting inmates on their own cases. The two lawyers who represented the inmates claimed "that in filing and litigating the case they, in effect, acted in place of the Attorney General." Their basis for this claim was that "The Attorney General was once asked by the State Corrections Commission to file his own lawsuit over the conditions at the old jail but he delayed doing so."

The judges, who heard the original jail case, replied that they "would rule on the fee requests after the Wayne County corporate counsel had filed a written reply." The University of Detroit Law School was ordered by the judges in February 1972 to halt jail advice to inmates in their selection of lawyers for their lawsuit. The Law School also tried to show the inmates how to fire their court-appointed lawyers. Taking their case seriously, the inmates wanted more experienced lawyers than the by-n-large inexperienced lawyers the county commissioners tried to appoint.

While many were bogged down in this political quagmire, a Detroit Recorder's Court judge accused an assistant professor at the Law School of stirring up the inmates. The judge said, "He would find the assistant professor in contempt of court if he or any of his students talked to any inmates who already had an attorney." The assistant professor reacted: "his students were not stirring up the inmates, but rather informing them of certain constitutional rights." Court-appointed attorneys have always been suspect in the minds of many. The professor and his students were just telling the inmates that "they had a right to petition the court and how to prepare that petition."

Another political squabble took place on October 4, 1972, when a Wayne County Circuit judge told jail officials they must allow inmates voting privileges. The order came after a Detroit attorney tried to get permission from jail officials to conduct a massive voter registration drive among inmates. To thwart that attempt jail officials claimed,

"We don't have the security nor the manpower to register inmates to vote."

The Detroit attorney wanted to get the inmates registered before he filed a suit testing the constitutionality of Michigan's election laws, which forbade sending absentee ballots to anyone in jail. The attorney claimed it was unconstitutional to deny voting rights to people awaiting trial in jail because *they had not* been proven guilty of anything. A sheriff's legal advisor stated in rebuttal, "I'm concerned about what would happen in the jail if the inmates were registered and the court refused to overturn the state electoral laws." One of Detroit's longest-acting City Clerk's claimed "he was eager to register the inmates," and he could do it by himself, if necessary, to comply with the 8 p.m., October 6, 1972 deadline.

A day before the deadline two deputies were indicted by a federal grand jury and charged with the alleged beating of a prisoner in the county jail. One deputy was Black, the other white, and they beat a white inmate who refused to be put in a cell with a Black prisoner. Both officers were suspended from duty when the indictment was announced. Asked why *federal* law enforcement agencies handled the case, jail administrator Frank Wilkerson declined to make a comment, stating that "he had little information about the incident."

Assaults in the county jail are normally handled by local law enforcement officials. It was never clear why this case was handled by the FBI. After all this political commotion, the county board chairman charged the three-judge Circuit Court panel with meddling and for criticizing the board's action in setting up a bond issue for the new jail.

Historically, there have been many internal problems between Wayne County and city of Detroit governments. In March 1972, one of the most notorious and unforgettable occurred, involving a fatal shootout between officers of the Detroit Police Department and sheriff deputies of the Wayne County Sheriff's Department.

A former member of the Detroit Police STRESS unit was involved in a shooting that left one sheriff's deputy dead. The STRESS member testified that a man with a gun walked into an apartment building, so three Black male STRESS cops followed him and fired shots into the apartment. One emptied his gun and killed the man. The victim turned out to be a Wayne County Sheriff's deputy, who the STRESS cops thought was a criminal.

Rumors circulated throughout the neighborhood and through both Departments that the fight was about drugs and the control of drug money. None of this was either proven or dis-proven because the case was never investigated fairly or thoroughly. A former Black, male member of STRESS was cleared of the charges and later assigned to the Homicide Section, where he worked on many of Detroit's highest-profile murder cases. In 1991, that same Black, male cop was accused of securing and protecting drugs at the airport.

STRESS, which means *Stop The Robberies, Enjoy Safe Streets*, was a special surveillance, police tactical unit in the early 1970s. Because of its many Civil Rights violations, and lawsuits pending against the Detroit Police Department, it was disbanded by mayor Coleman Young after his election in 1972.

STRESS accounted for a third of the killings by the Detroit Police Department, and conducted an estimated five hundred raids without search warrants. One particular cop, known as Mr. STRESS, gained his reputation by committing nine killings and three nonfatal shootings in his first two years on the squad. Before Coleman Young was elected mayor, the Detroit Police Department *was not* racially balanced, and STRESS, mainly composed of white, male officers, was responsible for twenty deaths in thirty months, seventeen of them Black citizens of Detroit.

Since the killing of the Sheriff's Deputy, the Detroit Police Department and the Wayne County Sheriff's Department were pitted against each other territorially, administratively, fiscally, and morally; and the city and county jurisdiction was always in question. The shooting of the Sheriff's Deputy also caused divisions between city and county officials. Feuds over who should have authority over jail operations continued long after Sheriff Barrett's reign. Removal of the sheriff's responsibility for the jail left him in charge only of the road patrol, which provided police services primarily in western Wayne County.

The study's Project Director for the new jail stated: "We are fortunate now to have a Sheriff who is an expert in law enforcement, but since he's in an elected position, we might not always have one of his expertise in the job all the time."

This problem still existed in the 1980's and 90's. The popularity of the candidate seemed more important and took precedence over qualifications and experience in law enforcement. The primary duties of the Sheriff's Department included security; canine and bomb disposal units at Metropolitan Airport; a marine division, which, with the Coast Guard, patrolled western Wayne County waterways; security at Juvenile, Circuit and Recorder's Courts; and a DEA Department, which has jurisdiction over all Wayne County communities.

There was also an Auto Theft Department; a program to counsel kids about drug education; and an alternative work force program, which gave convicted criminals a chance to hold a job while serving their sentence. The alternative work force program is unique and a good idea: it gives a convict an opportunity to show the judge, courts, and community that he or she has become a responsible individual, who can take care of him or herself and, perhaps, a family, while spending time in jail.

Sheriff Jacob Carmeno and Wayne County Executive James Sterling had fought each other politically since 1986 for control of jail operations. Mutual agreements, though sparse, were eventually made, and jail operations were split appropriately to their liking. In the early 1990s, however, Sterling seized complete control. The judge who made this bureaucratic and politically motivated decision was Recorder's Court Judge Bob Grossman, himself considered noncontroversial. It is interesting to note that on January 15, 1994, Judge Grossman was suspected of marijuana usage when two white male, Plymouth Michigan police officers claimed they "smelled marijuana odor in the judge's car" during a routine traffic stop. In grand, Good Ol' Boy style, no charges were filed because the judge and his car weren't searched.

Carmeno and Sterling had battled to control the jail and police the airport, to give you only two examples, since Sheriff Carmeno had taken office in 1984. In April, 1993, their relationship heated up again when a second judge temporarily blocked Carmeno from firing deputies, who had switched allegiance to Sterling's new vision of a Detroit Metropolitan Wayne County Airport Police force, by granting a request by their union (Local 502) to prevent any disciplinary action against the deputies.

Now, Carmeno believed wholeheartedly that Sterling's move was in retaliation for Carmeno's defeat of handpicked, Sterling sheriff-hopeful Lawrence Dornan, a county commissioner with no law enforcement experience. Hoping to thwart and sabotage Sterling's attempt, Carmeno sent several of his loyal minions (commanders, lieutenants, and sergeants) to the airport to harass officers involved in the transition. He also threatened to fire all transferring deputies who didn't report directly to him.

To add to Carmeno's worries airport officials backed Sterling's claim by insisting that the move was needed to ensure that deputies were never pulled from the airport to cover either emergencies or just short-handed parts of the county. But his biggest problem, however, was how to afford to replace the one hundred or more deputy positions lost to the airport's new police force.

Carmeno continually applied to the county commissioners. He stated: "It would cost about $5.6 million to replace equipment and personnel taken for the new Airport Police, including canine and bomb disposal units that were sometimes needed in other parts of the county. If they [the new airport police] want to be their own department and they have a right to do it, let them do it. But don't raid the Sheriff's Department. Don't take our people, don't take our equipment, don't take our training in order to do it. They should pick up the cost of training of all the officers. They are getting certified officers. This is going to be a very costly divorce."

Sheriff Carmeno also wanted the new airport police force limited in jurisdiction to inside airport duties only, with no authority to make felony arrests outside airport territory. He also wanted the Department to patrol the airport's exterior. The familiar yellow hexagram, the Wayne County Sheriff's Department's patch and badge, were changed entirely for the new airport police.

Continued court proceedings and Judge Grossman's incomplete decision to make the transition permanent also created a stressful situation for the officers affected. Also, officers already working at the airport were given no prior notification of the move. Deputies were once again caught in a personal and political quagmire: All deputies had reported to Carmeno since 1984, but the airport's budget covered their eight million dollars' annual expenses.

A commission subcommittee was formed to decide the matter of Carmeno's and the union's positions. The union wanted the agreement, outlined in their contract, honored. This allowed for transfers between the Department and airport police. Jim Morely, the union President, commenting that his men and women were once again caught in the battle trenches between the sheriff and county executive, lamented: "I would like to see our men and women taken out of this battle. I wish the sheriff would have said... You'll be more than welcomed back in my department because you are fine people."

Court proceedings dragged on for months. After final settlement, some joint agreements between the two governments were for new patrol cars, communications equipment, joint jurisdiction, and a new gun range by the airport.

The downtown location for the new jail was a fair choice, but without question it should have been built at the old Detroit House of Corrections and "N" Building sites in Westland, which were clearly more suitable, especially since the hospital was only half a mile north. For many years Wayne County General Hospital was the county jail's primary medical facility for inmates and, because of the downtown Detroit location, the Department wasted time, gas, person power, and taxpayers' money; all because politicians squabbled about choosing a site where inmates could receive adequate medical attention.

A costly, 170 page study was prepared by Hellmuth, Obata and Kassabaum, of Washington, which envisioned construction of a new $21.3 million downtown jail next to Detroit Police Headquarters. The new jail was originally to be composed of two connecting, six-story buildings housing only 750 prisoners. It would provide a medical dispensary, separate facilities for close observation of potentially violent, suicidal, and mentally disturbed prisoners, treatment for drug addicts and alcoholics, and recreation areas for daily exercise.

As the final plans for the new jail were being worked out, the old jail had $2.2 million of renovation with an additional $3.3 million recommended to further rehabilitate the 46 year old jail. The consultants also recommended: "Although the incumbent sheriff (Kenneth Barrett) and his jail administrator (Frank Wilkerson) are well qualified to administer the jail, the diverse correctional functions... recommended for consolidation should be the responsibility of a professional director and staff independent of law enforcement authority."

There were several questions that kept popping up. Could Carmeno have been elected sheriff of Wayne County because, though he had no prior law enforcement experience, higher-ups felt he had enough managerial experience to put the proper staffing together to manage a diverse corrections functions? Why did many Wayne County citizens believe that Carmeno wanted to be sheriff only to enhance his future political ambitions? This was also true of the former Undersheriff Carlton Vance, an attorney like Carmeno, who hoped to advance on the judicial level. This was not unusual, for historically law enforcement has been used as a stepping stone for those people who survived the country's racial, political, bureaucratic shambles. Many went through the revolving door of law enforcement or other politically conducive professions.

After Carmeno became sheriff of Wayne County, Kenneth Barrett ran unsuccessfully for governor of Michigan in 1986. To the complete surprise of most Democrats and all Black citizens of Michigan, Barrett decided to run on the Republican ticket. Formerly a member of the *donkeys*, Barrett felt that the transition to the *elephant* side would inevitably increase his popularity among Michigan voters: at least enough to be victorious.

Oddly enough, his running mate was an Irish Catholic white woman, the former wife of a Michigan governor, and unacceptable to many voters. Kenneth Barrett thought that switching parties would improve his chances, but many Blacks didn't take too well to his crossing over; Black women in particular. It was clear to many that there was something deceitful, almost sinister, in Barrett's intentions, and many people saw the move as *closet* desperation instead of honest, wholesome politicking.

Barrett's decision to run as a Republican also caused division among Black civil, civic, and charitable groups, and produced an array of power struggles within the infrastructure of Wayne County's government, law enforcement, and organized labor. Some staunch Barrett supporters, most of them old-line Democrats, turned the other cheek: not by joining another party or showing loyalty to their race, but by continuing to support the party they had supported all their long lives. One who was dissatisfied with Barrett's decision was U.S. Senator and incumbent John Conyers, Detroit's 14th District representative and Chairman of the House Committee on Government Operations. Conyers was also a two-time, unsuccessful mayoral candidate in 1989 and 1993. Conyers considered Barrett's position on Civil Rights a clear and total disregard of the Afrikan-American struggle, regardless of Barrett's successful, four-time election as sheriff of Wayne County, and one term as undersheriff.

Barrett had a worthy record: a poor orphan from Harlem, a first-generation American, who worked his way up; an ex-New York City cop, who studied law at Manhattan College and Fordham University, taking night classes. He was Black: an Afrikan-American in the FBI, a former Wayne County Executive. A splendid record indeed, but switching parties definitely hurt Barrett's reputation with both Black and Democratic voters in Michigan.

Well, Kenneth Barrett was whipped soundly in the 1986 governor's race by an astounding 878,491 votes, and his nomination as an assistant attorney was rejected by a Senate Judiciary Committee made up of Senate Democrats. Several Civil Rights groups also opposed the nomination, and President Bush's relationship with Senate Democrats didn't help matters any. Barrett was eventually appointed by the President to a job in the Justice Department. It seemed to the majority that Barrett was given the job in Justice for attempting to swing Black votes the Republican way. His theory seemed to be *if you can't beat 'em, join 'em.*

Many considered the gubernatorial election of 1986, truly a political farce: there was no competition for the incumbent. Despite Barrett's respectability and longevity, a Black man elected Democratic sheriff of Wayne County four times, he was all of a sudden tempted and bought: an untenable position on a suspect Republican ticket. While Barrett tried to woo Black voters with color, his already dubious reputation in the Black community fell into worse repute. Without fanfare, Barrett left for Washington, abandoning Wayne County and Michigan politics altogether: ostensibly, never to be heard from again.

In 1993, the Republican governor unceremoniously announced Kenneth Barrett as his new appointment to Detroit's Recorder's Court after a seven-year hiatus and total alienation from Wayne County and Michigan politics, and to the complete surprise of everyone.

Barrett was sworn in Wednesday, March 24, 1993, and started work in Frank Murphy Hall of Justice on Monday, March 29th. Ironically, Frank Murphy Hall of Justice is next to the old and new jails of Wayne County, Barrett's old stepping grounds.

In a March 27th, 1993 news article in the Detroit Free Press, a political writer emphasized the continuing hysteria over Kenneth Barrett's political agenda:

"That's right! It's been seven years since Barrett did his big party flip-flop from Dem to GOP, ran for governor as a Republican and got massacred by Charles Poshard by 878,491 votes. And nobody's about to let him forget it. Democrats still treat him like a pariah, and Republicans still talk about him like he's a charity case. To be sure, Barrett contributed to that 1986 mess. He was dreadfully naive, for example, about the heavy mean-spiritedness that accompanies big-time partisan politics, and never quite understood why his obvious charm and Horatio Alger accomplishments weren't enough to get him elected. But lots else was at work too. Democrats cast him as a villainous turncoat even though many of them, including Poshard, had, by snubbing him for years, helped run him off. The snubs resulted in part from turf wars and from the fact that Barrett, in trying to run a tight Wayne County ship, and offended both hizzoner Coleman Young, and the big magoos in organized labor. The Republican establishment, including then-president Ronald Reagan, slobbered all over him to get him to switch, milked it for maximum propaganda with Black voters and, once Barrett was nominated, largely walked away. Some of them even snickered openly about how easily he's been manipulated. And so on."

In 1990, as the job market plummeted and the crime rate increased, the Federal Law Enforcement Officers Association, in a briefing for freshmen legislators in Washington, pointed to the "shortage of jail and prison space" as a reason for construction of regional prisons. They suggested turning several military facilities into half way houses, and building prisons in blighted urban areas. This is a questionable practice.

When a prison was built in a Missouri town of only 3,000 citizens, the economic developer commented, "This prison will be the cornerstone for economic growth in the town." Whenever prison growth becomes the major catalyst for economic empowerment, however, Afrikan-Americans and other people of color are in deep trouble: especially as long as Republican congressionals continue to legislate unfair constitutional changes and budget cuts that disenfranchise the poor, the hungry, children, seniors, and the disabled.

Adding new jails to solve crime is only a slight deterrent anyway because eventually that criminal, who hasn't gotten an ounce of rehabilitation, or learned a trade, not to mention being psychologically warped by "*The System's*" lack of compassion or love, is released back into the same underdeveloped and unempowered environment they came from.

Without permanent job skills, periodic social and sexual satisfaction with the gender of choice, self-esteem and awareness programs, testing for hidden ability, and savvy about the etiquette of a job search, the ex-convict is likely to renew a life of crime. The recidivism rate is at a level of 70 to 80 percent, or higher, for untrained graduates of "*The System*" described in the previous three paragraphs.

It is clear that no one is ever really willing to welcome a jail into their neighborhood. It's basic and simple reasoning: having a jail in the community tends to lower property values. This is least affordable in a poor neighborhood. The possibility of inmate(s) escape and thus potential hostage situations is also a fear. A child, elder, or entire family could be held hostage by a barricaded gunmen seeking to negotiate a release to getaway. Traffic in the neighborhood is also likely to increase as vans and buses transferring inmates and the cars of jail employees drive through the streets each day.

The overall environmental and structural change necessary to facilitate just the building of a jail complex could adversely damage the stability and peace of any neighborhood. Even the commonly-used argument that having a jail in the neighborhood prevents crime in its immediate vicinity is only marginally valid because crime would likely continue in the larger community. The traditional myth that building more jails reduces crime is naive and historically unsound.

The primary elements in crime reduction are, rather, education, jobs, morality, community involvement, justice, spiritual belief, and self-awareness. The most important, rooted element—totally essential and approaching nonexistence in any future change in criminal-

ity—is a well-structured and nurturing, wholesome family upbringing.

3

Applying for the Job:
How did I get This Job Anyway?

ANY BELIEVED THIS LOCATION WAS A MEDIOCRE choice considering all of the other possible sites, and it took many Detroit and Wayne County citizens some time getting used to another jail right in the thick of downtown. Because the location was in the downtown area, the only landscaping surrounding the new jail was of concrete. That, coupled with the many grayish, bland, old-looking buildings already part of the downtown area, had an injurious psychological affect on many officers and their coworkers, and caused stressful emotions even before one entered the new jail's lobby. Detroit desperately needs to adopt a beautification commission and initiate a program to spruce up and maintain its downtown area. The city also needs to hire some world renowned architects.

Frank Murphy Hall of Justice, a fairly new building used for criminal trials, is adjacent to both the old and new jails. The old jail, needing renovation, always had the look of ancient, medieval ruins. Working in this kind of incarceration setting has a tendency to change the mindset of its employees in some form or fashion. Many aspects of this work are similar to the drudgery of an assembly line: the majority of the people are under-educated, underachievers such as you would see in an auto plant, for example. The jail's sullen atmosphere had that same slave psychogenesis.

Probably the greatest advantage of the downtown location was its excellent transportation access to major freeways, which were virtually seconds away. Another unique advantage was the accessibility of underground tunnels to transport inmates to the jails and the courtrooms of Frank Murphy Hall of Justice. Transportation by tunnel also reduced the threat of escapes, rescues, and attempts of revenge. The third advantage was that the County's governing bodies, who amend municipal legislation, were within minutes of both the old jail and the new jail.

In December 1995, despite protest from community members over parking and safety, and the building of another detention facility so close to a heavily residential area, the Detroit City Council approved a measure for the construction of a juvenile-detention facility near Greektown, in downtown Detroit. City officials said the location makes it easier to transport youths to and from nearby courts.

In the Spring of 1983, just months before the new jail was completed, Wayne County jail officials placed several ads in the *Detroit News* and the *Detroit Free Press,* the city's two largest newspapers. They later merged into a collective effort called the J.O.A., ***Joint Operating Agreement.*** The ad was looking for persons who wanted to apply for the job of deputy in the new jail. For me, and many others like me, applying for the job of deputy was an easy decision because of the chronic Black male unemployment problem in Detroit. It was and still remains in dire straits.

In June 1992, the unemployment rate for Black inner city teenagers in Detroit rose to crisis levels of almost fifty percent, up from forty-four percent in 1991. The overall unemployment rate for Black Americans was 14.2 percent, twice that of white Americans, that same year. The Urban League estimated that when jobless Black workers, missed by the survey, were included, the jobless rate for Blacks in 1992 rose to 25.5 percent.

It wasn't my cup of tea to work for the automotive industry as an assembler, because of the tedious, dangerous, and unhealthy conditions on the assembly line. It was corporate slavery. Why do you think they call those huge warehouses filled with steel and machinery *plants?* It's just an acronym for PLANTATION! Also many factory workers are illiterate, untrustworthy, their behavior scandalous.

Robotics has replaced a high percentage of the human work force in auto plants because a human physique is not built for the kind of punishment assembly line work requires. Work in a plant is also depressing, the atmosphere negative. Many laborers, who have spent decades working in the auto industry, experience health problems, many of them psychological. I refused to become either a human guinea pig or a robot for greedy, white male auto industry executives.

Previous to applying for the corrections position, I had worked as a secretary, a CETA worker, library assistant, and duplication operator, all with the Detroit Board of Education. I had also worked as a clerk and CRT operator at Michigan Bell. Over the years I had worked periodically as a security guard, and I had been a brakeman for the railroad. All this diversity prepared me for just about any task I was given an opportunity to perform. I've had many other jobs, and some occupations, but those mentioned were the most significant and worthy.

On the average, corrections is a profession that changes sane human beings into senseless, wasteful pawns of deceitful, departmental officials. White jail officials' main game plan was to prepare strategies of *great* negative proportions, never attempting positive reform. In many cases, Black officers were treated as badly as the Black inmates, sometimes, worse. Inmates seemed to have more rights than officers.

Working for a law enforcement agency is not for everyone, the stress is tremendous and constant in the jail. Many applied just for the challenge of attending a police academy and becoming a state-certified police officer. They never realized they would be stuck working in the jail for years, regretting it.

One job I had that I liked, and would have chosen to stay there if I could, was with the railroad. This job let the worker control his own managing capabilities, and handle various dangerous situations without constant harassment from supervisors. I started at the railroad at the tender age of eighteen and never gave any thought to racism, let alone the possibility that anyone would hold a grudge against someone else *just* because of the color of their skin. But there was pervasive racism at the railroad, and one such experience came after only sixty-five days on the job.

We were traveling from Toledo, Ohio, in subzero temperatures, with a 120-car freight train loaded with autos, auto parts, produce, and furniture. Frank Olzark, an old white engineer rumored to be a Ku

Klux Klan member, stopped the train on purpose three times in emergency so our crew could get four hours of overtime. Not yet ninety days on the job, and still a relatively naive brakeman, I was forced to walk by the train tracks in snow up to my knees, carrying a 25-pound alligator wrench and two air hoses. The three tools together weighed forty to fifty pounds.

The first time Olzark stopped the train I walked twenty cars; the second time about sixty cars; and the last, third trip I walked the entire train. I walked four hundred freight cars, about three miles, including the three trips back again to the engine. It turned out that the problem was in a air hose, only ten cars from the caboose. By the time I located the problem car, the two white men in the caboose were already tying the broken air hose together with a rag instead of changing it. The two white males didn't care that they were endangering my health or potentially promoting a case of frostbite. I was furious. Of course I didn't mind the overtime, but not at the expense of my health. I was sent out blindly three times in emergency, while Olzark and the conductor, who were in constant radio communication with each other, knew what the problem was and never told me it was only ten freight cars from the caboose. They had used me as their guinea pig, and cause of justification to get the extra, four-hours overtime.

When the train finally reached the relief crew at the railroad depot in River Rouge, I ran inside, called a cab, and sat by a radiator to wait to go to the hospital. My hands and feet were numb, and I had a persistent, bad cough. We were still about ninety minutes short of our twelve-hour shift. When the relief engineer took over the train, Olzark came into the depot and, learning that I had already called a cab, looked at me out of his red, stern face and fumed loudly: "Nigger, who told you to call a cab for us?"

I jumped up and pounced on Olzark's ass immediately, intent on choking him to death, until the station master and a coworker pried me off. I faced a stiff reprimand from a railroad regional superintendent, but after talking with him in depth about the incident, I was satisfied when Olzark got reprimanded instead. I was vindicated. By the way, Olzark died several weeks after that incident.

Railroad work dealt with the outside elements, and occasionally there was work in the despised auto plant, switching out freight cars for delivery. I prefer working outdoors with some element of independence. It is too easy to become bored when you are cooped-up all day in some office full of gossip and administrative red tape.

It was a very cold, rainy day in November, 1983, when I applied for the position of deputy. There were nearly fifteen hundred applicants for the several hundred jobs in the jail. I arrived at the Wigle Recreation Center at about seven in the morning; there must have been at least six hundred people already in line, all waiting patiently in the downpour of frigid, freezing rain. To speed up operations, a man hurriedly handed out applications to be filled out before reaching the receptionist, who had set up in the Center's basement. We were each required to show a valid Michigan driver's license, a police sheet showing each individual's driving and criminal records, a social security card, birth certificate and, if over eighteen, a high school diploma or equivalent G.E.D. You had to be a Michigan resident for at least one year.

I believe wholeheartedly that hiring eighteen to twenty year olds to work in the jail is not a good idea. It involves many variables, both social and maturity-related. For example, a minor can't vote on sensitive political issues; but can be sent off to fight a war and die for his country; yet he or she has their drinking privileges regulated by State and Federal governments. Several states mandate that citizens be twenty-one years old to drink alcohol. Most officers agree that this age group is not mature enough to deal with a jail setting, in particular, young white males, bred by their families to embrace a socialist attitude and unaccustomed to authority, especially authority over Black males. Eighteen year olds are also malleable, not ready to deal with habitual criminal minds, nor should they be thrust into or trusted to deal with dangerous people and environments before they can handle them.

A large majority of the white officers working in jails are insensitive to Afrikan-Americans. They see stereotypes and know little about socializing with or handling Black males. Many come from downriver, out-of-state, and Wayne County suburban communities where there are few or no Blacks; many don't know how to handle street-wise white inmates either. There is also a gender-separation issue because of the number of *young* Black men incarcerated. Jail is much like the Armed Forces without the guns!

The Department of Corrections had started recruitment drives before. As a matter of fact, on many occasions in the past community leaders complained about the Department's lackluster attempts to recruit more minorities. With the opening of the *new* William Dickerson Detention Center in Hamtramck, community leaders saw an opportunity to increase the numbers of Hispanic, Native American, and Arab-American citizens hired. After all, this projected seventy-one million dollar jail was dedicated to, and named for Sergeant William Dickerson, a Black officer with twenty-three years of service, who was killed while transferring a Black male prisoner, sentenced to life for murder in the first degree. He was the first Wayne County Sheriff's officer killed in the line of duty since the Department's inception.

Sheriff Jacob Carmeno saw the new job openings as a way to bridge the *trust-gap* between the community and law enforcement. He also noted that the only way the Department could get ethnic groups to respond to law enforcement was to have them apply for the jobs and be accepted. Carmeno worked closely with various ethnic groups in hopes of increasing minority representation. In 1991, about half the nine hundred, fifty Sheriff's Department employees were Black, but there were too few Hispanic, Native American, and Arab-American employees. As of 1991, there were seven Arab-Americans, one Native American, and eleven Hispanic Americans employed by the Department.

The percentage of Black officers would have been higher if the Department hadn't targeted and railroaded so many of them. Many disgruntled Black officers left for other occupations as a result. It is fair to say that a career with the Sheriff's Department required much patience and will power because minorities were and still are wantonly discriminated against *Within The Walls*.

After a four-hour wait in the freezing rain I finally reached the stairway leading down into the basement of the Recreation Center. After reaching the receptionist, I was informed that "the county would contact...[me] through the mail, concerning a date to take the next step," the physical agility test. Little did I know then, that it would take over a year and a half before I received that notification. Realizing the county was looking for physically fit people, I stepped up a regimen of jogging, weightlifting, swimming, and bicycling to make a better physical impression.

The physical agility test was held on another very cold day in February, 1984. Many applicants had on several layers: sweat shirts, sweat pants, thermal gloves and mittens, to stay warm while waiting for their turn at several different tests. This all took place at the Michigan State Fairgrounds, in a big agricultural barn normally housing hogs, cows, and horses for display at the annual fair. Once inside the barn, I noticed the lingering stench of manure and animal urine, even though the fair had been held several months before.

Observing the wide physical array of applicants, who ranged from obese to very thin, midget to tall, and of every conceivable shape and size imaginable, I was somewhat amused overhearing two applicants as they walked around searching for their group: "Damn, man, look at some of these big fat ass people. I know they ain't gonna be able to do some of this shit."

The first test was for handgrip strength. You use a small device called a grip dynamometer that gauges your handgrip strength as you squeeze the handle, while keeping one arm extended parallel with your leg. Both right and left handgrips were tested, and the dynamometer recorded the pressure in kilograms. I always needed extra work on my hand strength, and would cringe when someone shook and squeezed my hand too forcefully. Some handshakers go so far as to grab four fingers and squeeze, never allowing the recipient of this shake a chance to grab the entire palm of the hand.

Whoever started this thing about giving a strong handshake must have had a powerful macho problem with their ego. When shaking hands, I always give a firm shake, but never one that competes for who is the strongest. Handshaking is *not* a test to determine who has the strongest grip or the most power, but rather a gesture of greeting to show the cordiality of one's character. But of course this test was to determine if an applicant's hand strength was sufficient enough to secure and neutralize an irate inmate.

After the hand strength test, we were tested for the number of pushups done in one minute. A staffer placed a soft, audible beeping device under the upper torso of the applicant. This registered the pushup with a ring when there was enough pressure from the chest. From a straight-up position, this device made sure that the applicant went all the way down, making it possible for the staffer to determine a complete pushup. Some female applicants with large breasts actually got away with a few because they didn't have to go down as far as everybody else. I did thirty-seven pushups, good for me because I'm mainly a situp man.

In my opinion, a regulated, timed exercise proved nothing because it wasn't a *no pain, no gain* mentality. Why not give a test on how many pushups an individual can do before getting completely tired out? That would reveal *their* real guts and fortitude. Sixty seconds just isn't long enough to show *any* real endurance.

Our next test was an obstacle course with a total distance of about ninety feet. The applicant had to first run twenty feet, then crawl six feet through a two-foot-six-inch tunnel, which had wired ovals completely surrounding the body and connected to each side of a rubberized platform. The idea was for that applicant to crawl through the tunnel without touching the sides. The wired ovals looked like the barbed wire used at the tops of fences and in sections of certain strategic areas of prison camps.

The key to this obstacle was keeping the body straight and directly in the middle of the rubberized platform. Then one had to crawl straight through with the elbows in front of the body. Extending too far from the middle of the platform, one would get frustrated because the rubber slowed the attempt, or clothes got entangled in the wire.

Once out of the tunnel, the applicant had to run twenty feet to a six-foot-six-inch wooden barrier braced by two by four footholds and handholds on its sides. After climbing the barrier, a large table, centered about twenty feet away was placed on the other side. You then had to run around this table, and in that twenty feet, gather up enough steam to scale the barrier a second time. Finally you ran to the finish line to a stop position.

Just before it was my turn, Beulah James, a heavyset, Black woman: about five feet, four inches tall, weighing at least two hundred, eighty pounds, tried to scale the wall. At first it was humorous, watching Beulah at the starting line, gauging herself by rocking back and forth like an Olympic high jumper trying to gather up enough speed to at least grab the top of the wall with both hands. In chagrin, Beulah came up short every time. Finally, she used the wooden planks on the side, built for stabilization, to climb over. Although this method was *never* used by anyone else, the staffer grew tired of watching her numerous, useless attempts, and made her an exception.

As corpulent as Beulah was, we all had to admire her tenacity, for she must have spent at least three minutes trying before she finally got over that wall. It was also sad watching Beulah try so hard, but she should have put herself on some kind of conditioning; exercise and diet program. She knew months in advance that the physical testing was coming up. An escapee or fugitive, could have achieved a mile cushion by the time Beulah got over that wall.

Some applicants, awaiting their turns, snickered at and joked about those experiencing difficulties. I saw it differently and admired the courage to even attempt a feat one found so difficult. The determination I saw in several applicants' faces was fiercely focused; yet they could not scale that formidable wall no matter how hard they tried. Even those who sniggered had to eventually clap in acknowledgment of some spirited efforts. Anticipation and impatience were getting to me. My attempt over the wall resembled that of a hunted steenbok, dodging some trigger-happy explorer's bullets in Afrika.

After defeating the wall, one had to drag a one hundred, sixty-pound dummy for fifty feet. The most efficient and proper method for this test was to grab the dummy from behind, secure both arms underneath the dummy's arms and torso and, coupling the hands, swiftly drag it while peddling backwards. Another method was to pick the dummy up and run as fast as you can using good arm strength.

Next was the ninety-five pound bag carry. The bag had handholds on each side and the exercise was timed. You had to run sixty feet with the bag and place it on top of a thirty-two inch high platform. These last two test, the dummy-drag and the bag carry, required lots of energy and exertion, with an extreme pull on the back muscles. If the applicant lacked physical stamina and a strong back, arms and legs, these two events proved particularly tiring. This was never a problem for me because of my six-month bicycling, jogging, and swimming regimen.

The dummy and bag obstacles came prior to a half-mile shuttle run, where applicants ran back and forth between two pylons, stationed ninety feet apart. The way the course was set up caused participants to slow down in order to encircle each pylon and then have to speed-up again. This was done fifteen round trips for time, and was the only obstacle that tested endurable strength. Eventually, someone whose body wasn't accustomed to running, or accustomed to cardiovascular conditioning, would lose steam. After completing the half-mile run, many participants coughed and gasped for air.

An enduring and confident attitude was a necessity for the shuttle run, as staffers looked for a completion of under three minutes. I did well, finishing in two minutes, twenty seconds. "Good time, Taylor, that was one of the better ones," a staffer complimented. Luckily, this was the last test of the day. I was exhausted and my low energy level wouldn't permit me to do much of anything else. After I had completed the test, I felt confident that my physical agility scores were excellent enough to pass and gain acceptance to the next phase. There were two more bureaucratic steps to go through before being accepted for the jailers' training course: the dreaded oral interview, which in many cases is racially bias regardless of one's character, credentials and physical stamina of the applicant, and the doctor's checkup.

The oral interview was held at a gas company's building. Walking through the lobby doors, I came upon Yvette Gordon, a sexy, mid-twenties, young, brown-skinned, Black female receptionist. She wrote down my name and accepted back the notification I had received in the mail, stating the date and time of the interview.

It was almost impossible to keep my mind on the interview: Yvette was stunningly beautiful, a golden glow about herself. She was a pretty brunette with long, down-the-back hair, five-foot, seven inches tall, and about one hundred, twenty-five pounds. She had a shape so gorgeous, it would tame any beast. Striking up a conversation, I told Yvette how nervous I was, and we talked for a few minutes more and exchanged phone numbers; but a friendship was never established.

Other applicants, waiting in the lobby, looked familiar from the physical agility test taken many months ago. I turned around to scan other sections of the lobby and discovered that several people, who had encountered trouble getting over the wall, Beulah included, were granted the oral interview. I couldn't believe it, but at the same time my confidence grew tenfold.

After waiting over an hour, Yvette called me: "Krasne, it's your turn; good luck and I hope to talk with you soon." She directed me to the elevators and I went up to the third floor, where the interviews were being held. Getting off the elevator, I saw several large placards with black arrows, placed near the elevator and in the hallway, directing applicants to the interview room.

I opened a squeaky door and, upon entering, saw two elderly baldheaded white men sitting down: one named Frierson, the other Webster. Both were high-ranking officials in the Sheriff's Department. Sitting between them was a Lieutenant Peterson, a very large Black woman in high command. They all sat very erect, with pen and paper handy.

A slight chuckle broke the tension. I assumed that initially, at least, my attire fit the image of the typical, clean-cut, conservative stereotype of a model police officer: you know, the image one often seen on TV. I appeared honest, but really was in need of some money, ready to do the right things: be a *Yes, sir* type. I was one of the many generalizations and stereotypes of what a police officer should be like.

After conferring quietly with the others, peering at my application for a few minutes, Frierson asked me the first question: "You have a very unique first name; what is the correct pronunciation?" "Kras-ne," I replied. Frierson tried to pronounce it a couple of times, but kept messing it up. I immediately interrupted to correct him. "No, sir, you've got it all wrong. It's Kras-*knee*, not Kras-zy, Kras-be, or Quasze. Kras-*knee*! You know, the *knee*, that joint on your leg." I kept pointing to my knee so Frierson could visually see where he was wrong.

Webster interrupted: "But where did you get a name like that? How do you spell it?" "Sir, I have no idea how or where my mother got the name. But it's spelled K-R-A-S-N-E. When I was young, I didn't like it because the kids in my neighborhood and in church made jokes about it. But as I grew older, I got accustomed to its uniqueness and began to really like it. I'm very proud of it now."

I had made up some kind of story, but in reality I never really knew where or how my parents conjured up my first name. I knew my father didn't make it up because he didn't have such imagination. My mother told me all kinds of stories about how she thought of the name:

"Your dad and I were expecting, praying, and hoping for a girl. We had our minds set on using the name *Karen*. However, since you came out a boy, I just used the letter 's' and changed the letters around a little." "Yeah, right, Mom." My mother told me stories like that all the time. Back in the 1950s, hospitals didn't have technology like ultrasound to predict gender.

Sam, the tailor, an old Polish man, about seventy-five years old, told me my name was Polish and meant *pretty*. To my knowledge, I have no Polish relatives or ancestry. I had no idea what my mom was thinking about when she named me, but I finally got used to my unique name. One thing that's for sure—when the teachers at school, or anyone anywhere, called out "Krasne," only *my* hand went up, only I answered!

Frierson continued with his general, quite typical questions: "Why did you apply for the deputy position with the Wayne County Sheriff's Department?" "Sir, I've always wanted to become a policeman: help my community, get rid of crime, help build civic pride..." My answers were also general and typical, but I wasn't telling them what I thought they wanted to hear, but rather sincerely explaining and expressing my innermost feelings about being an asset to law enforcement.

Throughout the proceedings I felt the panel acknowledged my honesty in my answers; but one particular question *stood out* from the others. Peterson calmly took a deep breath, peering over the top rim of her glasses. Staring directly, firmly, and quizzically, she asked this question: "Mr. Kras-knee Taylor, Ah, say, for instance, you were walking in and around the jail cells, just observing, not expecting anything to happen. Then, all of a sudden, out of the blue, an inmate throws some urine and shit on you—you're covered with it and have no extra uniform. What would you do?"

I wondered if the panel expected to hear me say, *I'd open up the inmate's cell and try to dismember his punk-ass face.* Choosing instead the conservative route, I answered this way. "Well, first I'd call a supervisor and get some assistance to take this disturbed individual from his cell for further evaluation in hope of having him transferred and placed in the psychiatric department. Because really, you know, this inmate has got to be crazy. Then I'd ask my supervisor if I could go get some soap and a rag to clean the mess off my clothes."

Judging from the panel's body and facial expressions, they approved of *that* answer. After all, it was reasonable and professional, and surely better than *I'm going into that cell and try to beat the living shit out of him.* I never experienced that scenario personally, or knew of any officer who did. Surely it happened in the past, or why would Peterson ask? I must say it wasn't a monthly occurrence, or something that even happened on a yearly basis. Then again, I never worked on the jail floors occupied by abnormal or acutely suicidal inmates either.

At the time of this oral interview my parents were on the verge of finalizing their divorce. Surprisingly, and to my dismay, Webster asked a question concerning my parents. "What kind of relationship do you have with your parents?" This probing inquiry took me completely by surprise. I was defensive and said to myself: *Why would this white man ask such a personal question? That's none of his damn business.*

I could only guess that Webster wanted to find out what kind of parental guidance and upbringing I had experienced at home. It was also possible that Webster had already gotten that information from a background investigator, who had come to my home eight months before this interview. He had also spoken to several of my neighbors, gathering irrelevant information about my character, my parents' characters... In light of this, Webster's question seemed one of pure effrontery.

My parents came from very different family upbringings. "Well, my father and I aren't that close anymore, because of the way he has treated my mother for many years." I said it with no hesitation, completely honest in its affirmation. Frierson and Webster frowned, perhaps because I was putting down a *male* figure, even a Black one. Did they want me to assume that they had experienced the perfect family setting at home with *their* sons and daughters? Peterson, on the other hand, with a hidden, conspiratorial wink, gave me one of those reassuring, *Aunt Jemima,* motherly-type smiles, which seemed to convey her approval of my answer.

My feelings, as I left the conference room, were of accomplishment rather than hopelessness. I believed the questions had been asked randomly, because they didn't appear to be read from a selective, standardized list. Generally, one might expect nervousness in such an intimidating situation, but I was gratified that I had remained calm, cool, and collective throughout. This interview took place in the Fall of 1984. Just before Christmas I received a confirmation notice in the mail stating that I had passed the oral interview and that "I had been accepted to attend the jailers' training class," which started Monday, January 7, 1985.

I was ecstatic; jubilation was in my heart; I was overjoyed. I finally had the kind of employment that appropriately fitted my cherished desires: being someone who wasn't afraid to be heard; who would defend citizens from criminals; who would be a true civil servant in my community. I was sick and tired of escalating crime statistics, demoralization and community decay from drug-infestation, habitual criminals offending without apprehension, nothing changing the negativism that nationally damaged Detroit's reputation and image.

Months later I would see this rookie attitude as gung-ho and naive, because most officers really don't give a damn about civic pride. Most just want the paycheck, retirement benefits for themselves and their families: understandable but selfish. Back in the early days of the Sheriff's Department, 1940s to the 70s, many people were hired because they knew someone who already worked there (nepotism). A recommendation from a relative, friend, or even acquaintance was the norm. You could say that this was still in effect in the 1980s and 1990s, but to a lesser degree, and it was now what many call the *Good Ol' Boys'* network.

To obtain the position of Sheriff's deputy in 1985, the requirements were: being eighteen years of age, a high school graduate or G.E.D. equivalent, and a U.S. citizen. A college degree, fluency in more than English, mathematics skills, all seemed unimportant. On the application, however, it did ask for some skilled experience. Occasionally the Department needed someone to interpret and speak several languages (Arabic, Spanish, or Polish, preferably).

The doctor's physical was the last obstacle before total acceptance to the jailers' training class. There was a cough test, a reflex test, testing of peripheral vision, urinalysis, and x-rays. The physician squeezed my testicles too hard: instead of coughing I sounded like I was yelling. The reflex test went okay, however. This is the famous test where the doctor hits the patient's knee cap with a small rubber, triangle hammer to see if the leg involuntarily reacts with a slight kick. My peripheral vision was fine, but bending over to touch my toes really frightened me because the physician was too close to my rear end. Then the urine test was conducted and I passed that too.

Everything was fine until it came to the x-rays of my back. "Mr. Taylor, judging from the x-rays taken, your back shows symptoms of degenerative change," the doctor pronounced. When he said this my mind went blank. What are degenerative changes? Old Age is one. The definition is: *a condition that says your body is deteriorating or having progressive loss in normative biological or psychological characteristics.* I was in great physical condition, just having passed a grueling physical agility test, without any back complications. Unbelievable that the doctor would say something like this. My mental and physical health was excellent. I went to the spa frequently and jogged five to seven miles a day. I had no back problems except for an occasional strain.

In the Department, I learned later, back-related problems were the main reasons for officers taking days off from work. Many officers complained about the chairs they had to sit in. Unfortunately, the Department was insensitive to health concerns, using uncomfortable, cheap chairs rather than more comfortable, anatomically correct ones. Thus the Department itself unilaterally sped up the inevitable process of *degenerative change* in its officers.

When the jail was first opened in 1984, the Department initially provided comfortable, cushiony, padded foam chairs with attached armrests. The chairs were on casters to prevent scratching along the floor or to keep from carrying them from place to place. As the better chairs became worn out, mainly because of abuse by overweight, out of shape, sedentary deputies, many were discarded and destroyed. The few remaining in decent shape took sudden and permanent refuge only in command offices, Master Control, and most white officers' stations.

The good chairs were replaced with the hard plastic kind that stacked: no armrests, no cushioned support for the lumbar region, coccyx or pelvis. In truth, the entire skeletal structure was never compensated when these chairs appeared and, after several months, deputies started experiencing chronic back and posture problems. Imagine sitting in a hard plastic chair for several years, sometimes up to sixteen hours a day. Some officers, myself included, occasionally wore waist and back support belts to strengthen our posture.

One day several white male officers stole and hid all the cushioned chairs from the seventh floor, a floor usually manned by Black officers. The chairs were never returned. Fortunately, the Black officers, including myself, had scratched identifying marks on the chairs, so the day when all four chairs came up missing, we immediately knew the white male officers from the ninth and tenth floors had taken them. But we never made a big deal about it.

The Department never gave its workers any consideration for their backs. It was commonplace to see deputies folding and using fire retardant blankets from the guard stations as cushions for those hard, plastic chairs. The Department spent money on many unnecessary items, however: freezers, office equipment, file cabinets, cold food serving machinery. Many of these purchases were rarely used, or were deemed obsolete in no time at all. Some machinery was stored in misappropriated rooms, and some equipment stayed plugged in for months, wasting electricity, before the Department thought to use the rooms more efficiently.

All this, of course, wasn't even in my consciousness while I was sitting in the doctor's office, being made aware of my degenerative back changes. "Hey, Doc, you mind if I review my records?" "Sure, go right ahead; help yourself." I leaned over and took a look at my medical evaluation: It was expansive. The laboratory results for barbiturates, marijuana, cocaine, alcohol, amphetamines, venereal diseases and viruses, all read *negative.* And this doctor was going to keep me from getting the job because of this *"degenerative changes"* routine.

Of all the diseases, the serious ailments in the world, a back problem I wasn't even aware of was to be the basis for a possible rejection. B.S.! I tried to reassure the doctor: my stamina, a routine of back exercises. After eighteen months of administrative red tape, I wasn't about to accept a medical rejection in such simple terminology.

After hearing me out, the doctor eventually called Theresa, executive secretary for the personnel department. He talked with her for a few minutes and handed me a number to call Theresa later that day. I called, continuing the conversation about the delicacies of *degenerative changes* more in-depth and extensively. I retrieved a medical journal and even went to the extreme of reading a page to Theresa to clearly interpret the term. "Yes," she admitted, "That does seem rather stupid, to reject a person for that; especially, when it's considered a natural process."

It wasn't until after that productive phone conversation that I was admitted into the jailers' training class. I had even contemplated taking the matter to court to prove a point and get the job. Much later I saw the situation as pathetic and stupid. I saw a number of officers, who worked in the jail, walking around with real, chronic back and neck problems: not responding to codes that signaled inmate fights because they were afraid to permanently injure their backs.

Theresa was quite understanding and cooperative as she listened to my complaints about the diagnosis. Most of the women, who worked in the offices of the Department's higher command, were well aware of the politics involved, of the civil rights violations that occurred there. They were the ones, after all, who typed up the lengthy paperwork for their bosses. Every day they read the methodical and systemized *paper lynchings* of many Black officers.

If Black supervisors did occasionally express displeasure and concerns, their voice was unheard because of their unified, unilateral involvement with the bigwigs. Some people just take whatever is dished out to them. Those Black people who achieved authority and tenure during the Barrett era, and because of affirmative action, should have said something about the injustice, but they *never* got involved. They could have alleviated, brought problems to the surface, to the proper authorities.

Everyone has his or her own reasons for not voicing outrage

when their moral or civil rights are violated, especially rights in the work place. Inmates have rights; so should law enforcement officers. But violations of those rights occur every day. Considering the civil rights struggles of the 1950s, 60s and 70s, I believe that Black people have a moral obligation to fight the power of prejudiced establishments, that treat people of color in a different way than they treat *whites,* the so-called majority.

Every day the Department violated and ignored constitutional and civil rights laws in dealing with officers and citizens alike. Many superiors had a freewheeling, *do-what-cha-like* attitude, and did literally whatever they felt like doing, while the general public and *proper* authorities ignored the violations or acted unaware. The public is rarely told of what happens in the jail setting.

One example of this is the cop-out that took place regarding a collective bargaining issue. This issue was used as a manipulative tool by the unions and the county's elite for personal schemes to get rid of contentious fellow officers. It was an issue filled with fabrications, improvisations, and unproven sensationalism. Many former workers of Wayne County and officers from the Department knew of the injustice and racial prejudice, but never addressed the issues squarely and collectively. This was especially true of the older officers from the Kenneth Barrett era.

In April, 1989, while I sat and waited outside Commander Steve Maloney's office for my final Trial Board hearing, Carla Fountain, a tall, very light-skinned older Black woman, who resembled the lovely Lena Horne, paced the floor and headed towards the copier. She spoke. "Officer Taylor, why are these people being so ridiculously petty with you?" I answered sullenly, slowly raising my head. "Ma'am, I really don't have no idea." I just looked at her with tearful, streaming eyes. I couldn't reply; that was all I could muster.

"Don't worry about it Sweetheart," Carla continued, "You have my prayers, Officer Taylor, and you seem to be a very nice young man. Keep the faith and stand up for what you believe in. Believe me, you can do a lot better for yourself; this place is for the birds anyway." I had endured Departmental wrath for almost five years, and at that given moment I really appreciated Carla's encouraging words of sympathy.

I have to say that the women who worked in the Administrative Building were fair, even though payroll had shorted me, and many other officers, money from our Holiday pay. Christmas 1986 and New Years 1987's pay wasn't handed over to officers until the second week in February, 1987. When my Holiday paycheck turned up short, I circulated a petition to correct the problem. It was signed by nearly every officer on the afternoon shift. Only the officers who feared reprimand and reprisals from superiors declined to sign the petition. I sent the petition to payroll through interdepartmental mail.

A few days after the petition had reached payroll, I was singled out at the start of Roll Call by Sgt. Jergenson, an older Black male. "Everybody will be getting their Holiday pay soon, and all those signatures aren't necessary, Taylor," Jergenson quipped. This comment meant little because many officers routinely gave up their Holidays to make extra money, but it was often delayed by the County for a month or more. By the time officers got their Holiday pay, Martin Luther King Jr.'s Day had passed: officers had to wait until after *that Holiday too* for their pay. Through the years, the Department continued to blame pay delays on Holiday short-handedness of County and Departmental payroll personnel.

During my tenure at the Wayne County Sheriff's Department, I was *never* given an opportunity for an informal meeting with the Sheriff, Undersheriff, or Commanders about write-ups for infractions, many of them trumped-up. Because I spoke-up, I was harassed by shift Commanders, even after I requested conferences in writing and through calls, going so far as to ask for investigations into various allegations made by officers who propagandized to make *brownie points*. After many attempts, I still hadn't succeeded in obtaining an informal meeting or discussion with even one white, male jail official, whose needs for machismo and egotism masked perhaps only fear.

This kind of treatment and the stonewalling of my efforts to confer about the harassment made me both querulous and disinterested in the job. I was *never* granted the opportunity to voice my complaints, but was shut out by white, male jail officials, whose historical treatment of nonwhite peoples, repeated here, in the jail, has always been either genocide or, barring that, to ignore others and their rights.

Over the years many white officers committed high misdemeanors, and had reputations for drunk driving, with many accidents on their records. In one instance, a white officer had a disagreement with an auto mechanic and pulled a gun on the man, threatening and abusing him with it. When the man didn't testify against him, the officer received only a thirty-day suspension.

Unbelievable as it seems, inmates escaped on *three* separate occasions while in one white male officer's care, although he was *never* suspended for negligence. A Black female officer, however, was terminated when *one* inmate, who was supposedly already handcuffed to the bed, escaped while under her watch.

A Black male officer was terminated, supposedly for neglecting to ask for permission to use a Sheriff's van, while a white male officer committed the same offense and was only suspended. After long years of judicial wrangling, that Black male officer was finally reinstated. A Caucasian officer held his family hostage at gunpoint, and yet another forged the documents of a white, female prisoner (that he knew), just so she could be transferred to more pleasant quarters at the Wayne County Jail.

A couple of intoxicated white male officers, involved in an automobile accident, simply walked away from the scene; a third got his job back after a six-month suspension for kicking a Black female nurse on the rump. In April, 1990, two white male officers hung a Black female doll by its neck in the classroom of a pretty, light-skinned, Black female instructor who for years taught sewing to inmates. The doll had been hung from the ceiling, with a tampon, saturated with a crimson liquid, stuck between its legs. The two, white male officers responsible continued to work for the Department without skipping a beat, despite this blatant racial intimidation and sexual harassment, supposedly because the Black female was coerced or coaxed by jail officials out of pressing charges—even though she had ample support for litigation from Black fellow-officers. Fearing both loss of job security and the aggressive litigious approach backed by fellow-Black officers, she fell prey to the divide and conquer strategy of the white bosses.

In a case like this, of sexual and racial harassment, it would have been important to impose severe disciplinary sanctions on the two, guilty officers. The Department, however, wasn't willing to change its policy of preferential treatment for white officers, so the Department showed their "*true colors*," and swept the misconduct of those two white officers under the rug. The Black officers knew all this, but grew complacent and, said no more about it, encouraged in their silence by the constant harassment of command officials.

Many Black officers acted like Anglo-Saxons. It seems that when Black people get a little authority they disengage from the Black causes and struggles that got them where they are, and turn to communism. The injustice in the treatment of Blacks just goes on and on. Intellectuals or not, Black people are very communistic in their approach to the betterment of Black people. Neither communism nor capitalism can really help our cause.

Haki R. Madhubuti, in his book *Black Men: Obsolete, Single, Dangerous?: The Afrikan-American Family in Transition,* emphasizes America's movement toward two separate and unequal societies: one white and one Black. In 1978, *The Kerner Report,* a major investigation of racism, published in *the New York Times,* proved this theory true. These two important works and Robert Blauner's *Racial Oppression in America* are references for discussions of the movement towards two separate race-based societies in America.

Meanwhile, smug, pretentious white male jail officials oppressed Black officers, to keep them **in their place**. The white officials spent their time quibbling over officers' pay, managerial ability, bravery, and even who they dated and what kinds of cars they drove. The politics were overbearing; imperialistic tactics were constant; pompous acts of ascendancy over others and hegemony continued as a way of life.

Whites continued to control careers and aspirations through institutional bias, justified by race-based quarterly officer evaluations and collusive report writing. This kind of leverage rendered Black political or economic clout helpless in the jail and useless in the nation at large. Blacks continue to lack the necessities to control their own destiny: education, the military and, indeed, crucial survival skills.

4

Ethnic Diversity: Undermining the Afrikan-American Economy

ETROIT IS A MELTING POT of various ethnic groups beyond just Black and white, many having gained a monopolistic control over particular businesses. Although the majority of its residents are Black, Black unemployment rates are high, and Black-owned businesses are minimal. Much of this is due to continued race prejudice in the North since, and before, the Civil War. Long-time Black residents established themselves in professions and businesses, only to be ousted by each successive wave of white immigrants, who were helped to displace Black citizens by the second of third generation white immigrant groups that had come before them. Ironic, because in a country where membership as a Daughter or Son of the American Revolution is esteemed, more Blacks than whites have roots old enough to qualify them for membership.

This displacement continues today. Coney Island restaurants are primarily owned by Yugoslavians or Albanians; barber and beauty supply shops, the fingernail business, and most laundries are being bought from economically struggling Afrikan-Americans by Chinese or Korean citizens. Koreans, Korean-Americans and other Asian groups dominate stores that sell inexpensive womens' clothing, tee shirts, wigs, cosmetics, hair care products, gold and costume jewelry, hats, lingerie, and shoes.

Nearly every convenience store—twenty-four hour gas station is owned by Middle Easterners; food markets and party supply stores are in the hands of Chaldeans, who are Iraqi Christians and Arabs.

Pawn shops, the supporting financial institution for many drug addicts, are owned primarily by Middle Easterners, or whites in general. Many of these places have installed the same thick acrylic bulletproof windows you usually see in banks.

The products carried by these stores are sold at a great profit because most are supplied to the owner from the country of his or her origin where hourly wages on the assembly line are far lower than they are in the United States. Many of these countries also engage in child labor, widely denounced by the United Nations and others.

Blacks, formerly *Negros,* (Spanish for *black*) being designated by a color alone and deprived of the true historical record of their contributions to this country, are often given jobs in these businesses as liaisons or middlemen to the community. Many handle security, and most watch the store while the owner is away at home, which is out of the neighborhood, or visiting other store locations.

In Detroit, the only viable, Afrikan-American businesses still in Afrikan-American hands are **mainly** funeral homes, churches, floral shops, printing companies, bars, night clubs, beauty salons, barber shops, car collision and accessory shops, cleaners, soul food or deli restaurants, sportswear and record shops, cellular phone and pager outlets, car washes, and afrocentric bookstores selling cultural and religious materials.

In the Spring of 1992, Detroit had only one Black-owned car dealership, an appalling figure considering the number of Black Detroiters who have worked for the *Big Three* auto industry. Historically, many Blacks migrated from the South to fill the industrial and automotive jobs that were plentiful in the North during the 1950s to the early 1980s.

There are Black people at all professional levels: dentists, doctors, realtors, architects, attorneys, accountants, and judges, etc. Still, we lack ownership of city businesses. As much money as Black people spend in Detroit: over one billion dollars annually, and in the suburbs: over four billion dollars annually, very few own their own businesses.

In 1989, Afrikan-Americans in the United States spent in excess of $300 BILLION dollars! Only five percent (5%) of this money reached the economic base of Black neighborhoods. The establishment of a viable economic base is essential for the political, social, and economic survival of Afrikan-Americans in the United States of America. The Black populace in Detroit, as in other urban communities, must finance its own businesses: particularly the food market industry in Black neighborhoods, where local people shop, spending dollars as well as food stamps. These markets are almost all owned by Middle Eastern people, who have also capitalized on the petroleum industry throughout Detroit and its surroundings suburbs. The money spent by Black Detroiters is taken out of Black neighborhoods, the capital going elsewhere, sometimes back to those store owner's country of origin.

A former president of the Detroit NAACP, also a former police commissioner, commented: "Economic and cultural differences will always cause tension between merchants and the residents of struggling neighborhoods. People in the neighborhood might feel tied to the stores because they don't have automobiles to go shopping elsewhere."

In 1993, there were about five hundred, fifty Korean-American owned businesses in southeastern Michigan, compared to about three thousand businesses owned by Arab-Americans. This is according to the American Arab Chamber of Commerce and a directory put out by the Michigan Korean Chamber of Commerce. According to the directory, there were about two hundred, seventy Korean-American owned businesses in Detroit alone. In that same year, according to the census, approximately six thousand, seven hundred Korean-Americans lived in Detroit's tri-county area.

Also in 1993, about half of the twelve hundred food stores in Detroit were owned by Arab-Americans. Black ownership also suffered because fifty Black merchants were killed in robberies from 1980 to 1993. A 1993 mayoral candidate and former president of *New Detroit Inc.* commented: "In the early 1980s New Detroit worked to improve relations between store owners and their predominantly Black clientele. Merchants who want good relations with the neighborhoods they serve should support the communities by hiring area youth and providing good products at a reasonable price."

Regardless of a few harmonious interpretations of Arab/Black relationships in Detroit, Afrikan-Americans need to realize that their money is basically filling Middle Eastern coffers, and increasing Arab influence around the world. One cannot deny that the United States government has also always exploited Afrikan-Americans: denied their contributions to the larger society and its history, withheld educational opportunities—that tool to power and knowledge, and corralled them into social, mental, and physical ghettos.

Churches, particularly Black churches, should start a national campaign to get their members to look in the direction of support for their own neighborhoods. Instead of preaching false religious hope and prophecy, positive values should be instilled and practical programs started to create jobs in Black communities. Church contributions and tithes are consistent and sometimes build large edifices, but business entrepreneurs have never come together in a coalition to solidly establish an economic base for the neighborhoods. This is morally wrong and culturally suicidal for Black people.

One way to begin would be to save an endangered segment of the human population in the United States: the Black farmer. In many rural areas property taxes are being raised to drive the farmers into foreclosure and off the land. The farmers' survival is contingent on the support of the Black consumers everywhere. In 1983, Michigan's agricultural income was estimated at over three billion dollars, placing Michigan fifteenth in agricultural production among the entire fifty states. Of this fifty-nine percent were crops, and the rest livestock and livestock products. Dairy, cattle, corn and soybeans were principal commodities, according to the *Worldmark Encyclopedia of States,* 1986.

From 1970 to 1985, Afrikan-American farm ownership declined a staggering eighty-three percent in the state of Michigan. Detroit has traditionally endorsed and supported Afrikan-American organizations important to the community, and its population in 1990 was eighty-five percent Black, the third highest among northern states, according to the *Statistical Abstract of the United States.* The support of organizations like the Afrikan-American Ministers' Alliance of Detroit is essential to the Black American farmer, and this and other Afrikan-American organizations must put their support behind the Black farmer and other Black enterprise in Michigan.

Before the new farm automation, Black Americans routinely cultivated acres of different kind of crops. People of color have always had a reputation for having **green thumbs**: Southern Blacks slaved from dawn to dusk, tilling the fields for their white, male slave masters. Some of this land wasn't good for tillage, but Blacks made something out of it anyway. Just about every Afrikan-American in the United States today has a relative somewhere who has grown a garden full of vegetables: corn, collard greens, onions, okra, peas, beans, lettuce, tomatoes, cucumbers, and, oh yeah, even watermelons.

Long before the farm crisis of the 1980s Black farmers were riding a long road to extinction. Black farmers were going out of business at 3.24 times the rate of white farmers. White operated farms in the 1980s declined 63%, while Black operated farms declined 97.5%. There were 925,710 Black-operated farms in the United States in 1920, and only 22,954 in 1987. In 1910, Black Americans owned a collective 15.6 million acres nationwide. Since 1910, Black land ownership has declined to approximately 3 million acres.

In 1997, a third generation Black farmer, who raised poultry and some grains on his Virginia farm explained the plight of Afrikan-American farmers by stating, "the USDA forecloses on farms owned by Afrikan-American at an accelerated rate, delays the issuance of certain types of loans and generally, makes life miserable for Afrikan-Americans who earn their living from the land. The National Black Farmers Association, believed that there is a 1,500-case backlog of complaints against the USDA, with 163 occurring in the state of Virginia." To his knowledge, only one of those complaints had been resolved.

According to this Black farmer and others, "in 1940 there were approximately one million Afrikan-American farmers. In 1997, that figure was down to 1,800." History has taught us that a landless people is indeed a powerless people. We as a people must train our youth to enroll in classes of agriculture and become interested in cultivating crops and raising livestock to feed our Afrikan-American communities.

In 1994, the United States Census Bureau reported fewer than 2 million farms in the United States, the lowest figure on record since 1850. Although the number of working farms keeps decreasing, in 1992 total crops were worth a record $163 billion. More and more land is in the hands of fewer and fewer people. Between 1987 and 1992 farm ownership decreased nationwide by 162,459 farms. Of these,

22,954 were Black owned in 1987. By 1992 that figure had dropped to 18,816—a loss of 18% Black ownership in five years.

Blacks face formidable obstacles in efforts to retain ownership of land, increase land holdings, engage in profitable land use development, and operate viable farming enterprises. Unfair discriminatory lending practices, taxation issues, inheritance and estate planning problems, real estate issues, marketing inequities, and lack of access to legal assistance regarding these matters are just a few.

Land ownership has always been the major source of wealth and status in the United States. Land ownership provides economic and political power. A close examination of the loss of Black-owned land in the United States shows that it is closely connected to the lack of empowerment of Blacks who reside in smaller cities and towns. Many Black urban residents have ownership interests, often unknown to them, in land located in rural areas: the land gets passed down from one generation to another without proper estate planning. This land is referred to as *heir property*.

Urban Blacks can look at their immediate environment and understand the negative effects of lack of ownership of apartment buildings, businesses, commercial property, in the ghetto. This lack of ownership in the cities is just one factor that leads to poverty and a host of other social ills for Afrikan-Americans.

It is of the greatest importance that Black land ownership is increased and the Black farmer revitalized. This will lead to business development, industrial clout, and more farming enterprises for Blacks in a country that *feeds the world*. Revitalization of the Black farmer also offers the opportunity for networking among Black consumers, farmers, brokers, advertisers, and entrepreneurs of all kinds.

Economic clout leads to decision-making power regarding, among other things, the location of businesses, industrial facilities, schools, zoning decisions, residential development, and increased markets for Black farmers. This, in turn, enhances the quality of life in the community for all its residents.

Job security and opportunities are the answer to the problems in Detroit and other urban cities. Instead of building jails, however, to create more jobs for Black people to oversee other Black people in a cycle of ethnic destruction, keeping Black business in business and keeping the monies generated in the community where they were originally generated is the more practical solution. After all, it's pretty ironic that the state builds a jail in a neighborhood to, in part, employ the residents of that neighborhood, and then when funds are low, decides it's time to hand out pink slips to Black jail guards.

I became very depressed after I had worked in the jails for about two years, upon seeing Black brothers and sisters constantly railroaded, systematically deprived of their freedoms, and subconsciously willing to commit crimes out of dire economic necessity.

As a seven year old, I would ask my parents: "What country did we come from?" They would look at each other, searching for the correct answer. "What do you think? The United States. Isn't that what you're taught in school?" In essence all this is true, but I wanted to know where my family *really* came from. My parents seemed to be ashamed to discuss the subject. Later, while reading through the pages of a Black history book, I was shocked to discover that Blacks were historically linked with great kings and queens of Afrika, and the great Nile civilizations of Nubia and Egypt.

My great-grandmother's ancestors were slaves from the continent of Afrika, and my family had some Indian, tribal blood connections. I was infuriated, while turning the pages, to discover European, white men hunting the Afrikan people like wild game, shipping them across the vast oceans to Cuba, then to the United States, or third world countries of Latin America and Arabia, to be sold and resold as slaves.

In 1991, an industry survey showed that Metro Detroit was among only three urban areas, with a population of a million or more, that ranked in the top twenty-five most affordable housing markets. Also in 1991, however, Detroit's public housing was called the worst, according to Federal officials who toured several dilapidated, boarded-up projects in the city. It was estimated that there were nearly forty thousand abandoned houses in Detroit, not including the tri-county areas of Oakland and Macomb.

A HUD audit in the Fall of 1990 reported that forty-one percent of Detroit's available public housing was vacant: a total of 3,634 units. The audit also indicated that 1,300 eligible clients were on the city's waiting list. This condition is responsible for what is termed *states of vagrancy.* The public housing issue is the main reason for homelessness increasing tenfold in Detroit. Many believe Detroit's housing department has squandered Federal money. HUD provided most of the $33 million dollar annual budget and, supposedly, monitored how it was spent.

A survey released on December 15, 1997 by the U.S. Conference of Mayors found hunger and homelessness in America's cities on the rise. The survey, taken in 29 cities, found that the demand for emergency food and housing increased in 1997, the 13th consecutive year. The demand for food rose by 16%, the largest increase in five years. One in four of those seeking shelter, and one in five seeking food were turned away. Sixty percent of the hungry and 36% of the homeless are in families. According to the report, the economy had little effect on hunger. Almost half the homeless are single men; Nearly four in 10 people seeking food aid were working; and six of every 10 cities say homelessness is increasing. Nearly nine in 10 cities say hunger is on the rise, and seven in 10 are forced to turn away those seeking aid.

While the media focuses on stories of decaying neighborhoods and abandoned houses, they never report the growing number of boarded-up Black businesses and storefronts in Detroit. Suburbanites talk about *how scared they are to come into the city,* but wouldn't you be too? if your white race knowingly ran away with the loot into the suburbs? People have a right to live where they can afford to live, but whites and Blacks who leave the city and yet still work in the city, help diminish tax revenues.

Since the 1990 census, analysis has shown Detroit to be one of the most segregated cities in the nation. There is a chasm dividing Blacks and whites on all sorts of issues. An associate professor of political science at Wayne State University and a principal investigator, found that Blacks who left Detroit, "moved to another city for personal reasons such as better schools, job opportunities, lower taxes." The professor's survey was the first to look at significant numbers of Blacks and whites in racially diverse neighborhoods. Between July and November of 1992, Wayne State University researchers interviewed 1,124 whites and Blacks in Detroit and it's suburbs.

The survey showed differences—and some startling similarities—

among Blacks and whites across a variety of neighborhoods: from nearly all-Black parts of Detroit to mixed city neighborhoods to mixed suburbs to all-white suburbs. The attitudes of Blacks about race differed to some degree depending upon where they lived, but on several key issues differences were not great. For example, an overwhelming majority of Blacks, no matter where they lived, believed that Blacks were discriminated against getting both jobs and pay raises. There was greater diversity among whites about this issue, and it seemed to depend on where they lived. One-third of whites in mixed city neighborhoods agreed that Blacks *do face* job discrimination, but in all-white suburbs fewer than one in ten whites agreed that this was so.

On June 14, 1993, a *Detroit Free Press* newspaper article, *Black Views Shared Widely,* published the Wayne State University survey findings: "A virtual apartheid separates Black Detroiters and white suburbanites. Half of the white in all-white suburban neighborhoods said they had no Black friends or acquaintances, and half of the Blacks in all-Black city neighborhoods had no white friends or acquaintances.

Whites and Blacks still view race relations from very different perspectives. For example, 51 percent of the Blacks felt that whites don't want Blacks to get ahead. Only 18 percent of the whites agreed with that. And while just 10 percent of whites said Blacks were discriminated against in the job market, 78 percent of Blacks felt that way.

Racial experiences of Blacks differed depending on the kind of neighborhoods in which they resided. For example, while one-fourth of Blacks from Black city neighborhoods said they'd been mistreated in stores, more than two in five suburban Blacks from mixed neighborhoods reported such mistreatment.

Moving to the suburbs didn't reduce Blacks' interest in ending discrimination, or in improving the lives of the less fortunate. Blacks in mixed suburban neighborhoods were more likely to be members of the NAACP, Urban League or similar groups than Blacks in the city.

Integration does not appear to be a primary motivation for Blacks who move to the suburbs, though whites in mixed neighborhoods seem strongly committed to integration."

To create job opportunities, Detroit's "M.O." is to continually give tax breaks to big corporations, which are given preferred locations while Afrikan-American businesses remain relegated to facing empty lots in crime-ridden inner city neighborhoods. Also the tax breaks are not shared by relatively smaller in size, minority businesses. Most government grants do not go to enhance the infrastructure of Black neighborhoods and create business opportunities.

Looking at the billboards in urban neighborhoods and along the city's main thoroughfares; there are many advertisements for tobacco products, alcoholic beverages, hair care products, radio stations, political candidates, sportswear, autos, drug-awareness campaigns, and the threat of AIDS. A 1987 study in St. Louis found three times as many billboards in the Black community as in white communities. In the Black community 62 percent of the billboards were found to advertise tobacco and alcohol compared to 36 percent in the white community.

A similar pattern was found in Detroit, where nearly 43 percent of all billboards in the city advertised alcohol and tobacco; only 24.7 percent did so in surrounding white areas. Marketing strategies aimed at the Black community reflect an adjustment to the national trend of a decreasing consumption of tobacco, hard liquor, and cheap wine among whites and the affluent.

In 1965, 40 percent of the population smoked. By 1987 that number had dropped to 29 percent overall. In the Black community, however, use of these substances continues to rise, a significant factor in choosing the Black community as a site for billboards advertising cigarettes and alcohol. A disturbing example of increasing health problems among American Blacks is that the lung cancer rate in the United States has grown four times faster among Black Americans than whites.

In Detroit there is even self-advertising scrawled on the plywood used to board-up the many abandoned buildings in the city. Advertisements tell you *where to get a job,* including a number to call. Gang slang or graffiti is ever present to demarcate gang territories where drugs are to be sold. Prostitutes might advertise *where you can call to get a head job,* while locals might want to know *who in the neighborhood has herpes.* Highway overhead passes announce gay revolutions, white supremacy, left or right wing revolutionary groups vying for support, or perhaps some communist organizations struggling for acceptance in their struggle to liberalize their native land.

A major reason millions of unskilled, Afrikan-American laborers can't get meaningful jobs is that there are technicalitics and restrictions on programs to retrain laid-off workers. Although welfare recipients and laid-off workers are theoretically considered for retraining programs, in reality many aren't applying for them: some don't know about them and others are disqualified because they have a high school diploma, or are over the age of twenty-one.

Those sufficiently uneducated and young enough to be accepted in a job training program in office automation, for example, are not mentally of functionally educated enough to begin to think about being diversified or learning various skills. Most have no real social skills. This transition is made more difficult because many poor, disenfranchised people have been subjected to and spellbound by the political science of brainwashing: tuned only to subservient work.

But change is inevitable, and the comfort zones of many people must be extended so that they can learn and work independently to make a living. It could be said that the *Contract For America,* however questionable its methods, was initiated to bring about this result.

The need for change was never more evident than at the Sheriff's Department. Here, many officers grew indifferent to a stultifying routine of sitting and watching inmates all day and night: being paid to be professional baby sitters. Deputies became lazy, overweight, many lost their creativity, and were increasingly stressed-out. And seniority meant nothing, because officers employed there for twenty or thirty years never gained in authority; only their pay scale went up. Promotion for skill, wisdom, or expertise was rare. Torpor was everywhere in the jail brought on by both a lack of skills and the knowledge that promotions could be achieved only through favoritism, racism, personal loyalty to buddies and higher-ups, or a dedicated longevity.

Detroit is a prime example of what happens when the economic base of a neighborhood is not in the hands of the people who live there. The urban rebellions of 1966, 1967, and 1968 forced the city's white power structure to accept a Black mayor (the late Coleman A.

Young) and create social programs. Job training and community-based social services, all administered by Blacks, were established by a new alliance between white corporate power brokers and moderate Black elected officials. When the auto industry collapsed in the late 1970's, corporate handouts to the city abruptly ended and Detroit started its apparently endless economic decline. Nearly all the gains won by Blacks in the late Sixties were lost.

In Black communities across the nation economic and social decay has resulted as Black leaders have been unable to win concessions from government and corporate sources. Suburban areas around Detroit and elsewhere continue to sprawl with new office buildings, malls, highways and retail businesses. As America's urban cities lose their economic base, they are also losing vitality and hope.

In some suburban communities red-lining is common in regard to taxes and insurance to destroy the cities' economic dependency and further increase the economic base and population of suburbia. Such governmental, institutionalized neocolonialism, designed to polarize along racial, gender and economic lines, demonstrates an easy disregard of fair treatment or job equity.

One way to gauge how suburbia thrives as the cities decline is to survey morning rush-hour traffic. Traffic coming in to Detroit from the suburbs is always bumper to bumper in the morning, and equally heavy leaving the city at the work day's end. It looks like a mass exodus from a war torn land. Traffic leaving Detroit for the suburbs at the beginning of the workday is light on the uptown beltways and similarly light coming into Detroit as the sun goes down. This was the main reason my first choice at the Sheriff's Department was the afternoon shift. When I left home at 2:15 p.m. to come to work the traffic coming downtown was light; it was similarly light traveling home at 11 p.m.

The issue of transportation is getting new attention around the country as an overlooked cause of massive unemployment. This is especially true in Detroit, where a traditional neglect to solve the mass transit problems broadens the gulf between city and suburbs. Also the influx of Canadians who work in Detroit, gain easy access to American jobs by traveling through the Windsor-Detroit tunnel, or across the Ambassador Bridge.

A study of Metropolitan Affairs Corporation, a private Michigan research group, found that more than half of southeast Michigan's unemployed people live in Detroit. Thirty percent of Detroit's families have no car and forty percent have only one. More profoundly, the study said that, *"three-fourths of the region's new jobs were being created in outer suburban areas, served poor public transportation or none at all."*

Because of that, nonprofit and for-profit agencies began transporting Detroiters to suburban work places in van pools, with employers paying fares in some cases. This was one of the main reasons many employers ask, "if applicants have transportation, the year and make of the car."

Transportation is a major factor in securing and maintaining gainful employment, but still Blacks are discriminated against when they go to the suburbs looking for work. Most employers figure if someone has some old beat up jalopy, or have to rely on public transportation, they can't make it to those abundance of slave-paying jobs for only minimum wage of five plus smack-a-roos an hour, somewhere in the *boonies.* Many city dwellers who have become suburban workers spend upwards of $80 to $100 or more on transportation a month alone, just to get to those jobs. The labor mobility problem has its roots in the urban decay and *"white Flight"* of businesses to the suburbs that began after World War II. But it has long been overshadowed by other causes of chronic unemployment, like substance abuse, poor education, welfare and lack of child care. Most of the experimentation with van transit and other labor mobility projects decades ago failed, because suburban labor needs were not sufficient enough to sustain the programs. But the 1980's brought labor shortages in many suburban areas as the country's aging population provided fewer workers to the low-paying service jobs, usually provided by temporary services. This shift revived the concept of transporting the urban jobless to the suburbs. With the help of federal grants, a number of cities undertook major, labor mobility projects.

But not all white business groups believed that Black urban workers are the solution to suburban labor shortages, because the jobs going unfilled in those areas were those requiring skills that many of the chronically unemployed lacked, and were not willing to train for. Most employers in the suburbs believe transporting employees to work sites, cuts down in absenteeism and turnover. It is a known and accepted fact, that even in the Southern towns of this nation, the structure of the community changed once crossing the railroad tracks, which usually housed Blacks on one side, whites on the other. Sanitation and all city services were better on the whites' side of the tracks. Those railroads tracks were the emphasis for red-lining and redistricting.

An article in The Detroit News entitled, "Racism a fact, but not always the culprit," by William Raspberry, a Washington Post columnist, told how racism is both a fact of life and an overworked explanation for Black America's problems, and the vital distinction between the two. The article expounded on job and hiring discrimination, and matched pairs of Black and white job seekers who visited personnel offices in Chicago and Washington, D.C. The results removed any doubt that racial discrimination still exists and is "widespread and en-trenched" in the job market.

Researchers took Black and white college students specially trained for the experiment, matched them for age, speech, demeanor and even physical build, then gave them identical resumes and had them apply individually for five hundred, seventy-six entry-level jobs that had been advertised in the want ads. In twenty percent of the cases, the white man advanced further in the hiring process than did the Black. That is, the white person was asked to submit an application, told to report for a formal interview, offered a job, while the Black applicant was not. The Black applicant got further into the process only seven percent of the time.

In an editorial from the Journal of the American Medical Association, the author/editor, argues that a key reason for unequal access to health care is "long-standing, systematic, institutionalized racial discrimination." He suggested that Blacks are refused health services, overcharged, or otherwise denied medical care on the basis of their race. Blacks, because of historic employment discrimi-nation, are more likely to be unemployed or to work at jobs that do not provide medical benefits. Racism is the direct culprit—a barrier to Black employment. In the other, the effect is indirect. Job discrimination, to state the obvious, has implications that go far beyond the immediate loss of income: to housing, to education, to social mobility and, of course, to health care.

The point is this: In the case of job bias, a race-specific approach makes sense. Stronger laws and penalties against discrimination, tighter enforcement of existing laws, public policy toward workplace diversity—all these things would help move Blacks beyond the fact-of-life racism discloses. But when it comes to the inadequate health care that has become a national scandal, the solution purely lies in adopting a national health-care policy. Blacks need to attack racism, and help white America come to grips with its ethnic biases.

Racism has become such a universal explanation for everything that has gone wrong in Black America that it is in danger of losing its power source to influence that national debate even in those cases where it is the critical factor.

Afrikan-Americans need to focus their attention on the skyrocketing cost of a college education, the death of moderately priced housing and the continuing decline of inner city schools, the health-care crisis that has millions of Americans (most of them white) without any health insurance whatsoever, decreasing the crime rate, building up their communities, learning a variety of different skills and trades for self-esteem instead of depending upon "*The System*" and, of course, taking care of their family. Considering all of this, the charges of racism are more diversionary than helpful.

In this everlasting cycle of racist intent plaguing America, people of color with great potential, continually try to withstand social infringements and endure prejudices. The malicious deployment of white, structural, institutional racism continues, through the establishment of large companies making relocations to other countries for lower wages, inadequate educational opportunities, and thus giving constant denials of gaining consistent employment to make a viable living.

5

Jailers' Training:
The Epitome of Boredom

WELL, AFTER GOING THROUGH ALMOST TWO YEARS of administrative processing, the stage was finally set for attending the Department's version of jailers' training. The two week course started on Monday, January 7, 1985, and was taught in the basement of the Administration Building, adjacent to the new jail.

Upon entering the building's electronic front doors, visitors were confronted by officers working in a square acrylic cubicle, who took incoming phone calls and checked the credentials of visitors. Then, after going through another set of electronically controlled doors, guests were greeted by a picture of Sheriff Carmeno hanging on the wall. The sheriff's department's familiar cornered hexagram badge and a picture of the state seal (Coat of Arms), adopted in 1911, also hung on the wall. The State of Michigan seal features an elk and a moose. Between the elk and moose is the national bird, the eagle, and there's a man standing with a gun just below the eagle and the Latin word *Tuebor*, which stands for peace: the gun is for his defense. The state motto, also in Latin, translates, *If you seek a pleasant peninsula, look about you*. Also on the wall were a couple of snapshots of officers standing together, proud, their chests stuck out, posing by a patrol car and several other departmental modes of transportation: a customary and typical pose. On another wall in the lobby was a rehearsed, training action picture of the members of an elitist swat team, jumping out of the back of a police step van, simulating a lively response to a terrorist act. For special effects, hovering clouds of smoke accompanied the background. This picture appeared to have been subjected to censorship and dramatized with choreography. Though the action appeared very dangerous, I thought about how interesting it would be to train for dangerous tactical maneuvers.

Before attending the jailers' training class, cadets were constantly told that the only requirements were to bring a spiral notebook and two black ink pens. Instead of identifying cadets by name, we were given numbers: mine was 41. All class materials and tests had to have our number on it. Some of the names in the class were as follows: Stallings, Frances, Starling, Holt, Stark, Kramer (who mysteriously died in the fall of 1989), Agerton, the Biddell's (an hilarious sister-brother combo), Fromley, Cooley, Brockley, Overton, Romanowski, Loom, Lindsay, Grimes, Peabody, McLean, McInnis, Steed, Frowns, Lovett, and Mary Coyle (who later became very negatively instrumental in my tenure). The chemistry of the class was rather unique.

I sensed gratification from the instructors, who were officers: they seemed to enjoy sharing their valued opinions and expertise. Some of their teaching methods, phrases, and statements seemed so traditional without any variance, that trainees could tell they were spoken repetitiously from previous classes. Receiving pay for attending the classes made the subjects a little more tolerable and interesting; we were paid about $400 for two weeks of training. This was the second time I received pay to attend a training course: the first was for a railroad safety class with the Penn Central Railroad. Getting that first check from the sheriff's department made me feel as though I was really a part of a class organization. Boy, was I mistaken!

It took a lot of patience from the cadets to sit and stay attentive in class because some instructors were monotonous and lacked creativity in their teaching approach, except for one: his name was Sergeant James Shoulders. Later, in the fall of 1985, he was promoted to lieutenant. Debonairly, Shoulders walked into class with a smooth, cool demeanor, like a Black Eliot Ness, but with a more assured savvy than the famed, televised, white male FBI detective. I really liked Shoulders. Just imagining the kinds of prejudices Shoulders, or any Black, had to endure to get to his position in the command structure was astonishing in itself. Before he died in the fall of 1989, Shoulders unsuccessfully tried to bring attention to the problems with pollutants in the drinking water and contaminants in the air of the new jail. Many times when subjects grew boring, Shoulders cracked a few jokes about the many characters in the Department to keep cadets interested and our awareness heightened. He possessed a certain calmness, not naturally inherited, but trained. He had a military sense of authority that was easy going and smooth, when dealing with people. As the days in class went by, I nicknamed him "Smooth," and that name continued to spread throughout my tenure.

A rumor circulated that some of the instructors were ordered to teach the class as a disciplinary measure, but there were some who taught because they enjoyed the experience. I can tell you from experience that many officers would rather teach a class than work in the jail and hear inmates complain, seek favors, and talk *"boo-coo"* shit all day. Shoulders' attitude showed the cadets that he cared and had a flair for instructional, constructive teaching.

One day, there was a break in class and Shoulders completely caught us off guard by unleashing what would later become his motto and most recognized statement. It was a stern, serious warning that was surely directed to all of the Black cadets: "Always remember the initials, C.Y.A... that means "Cover Yo Ass," because shit at this sheriff's department always rolls downhill when you have riled the feathers of the wrong people," Shoulders constantly reminded us. My own favorite acronym is C.C.C., which means Cool, Calm, and Collective

Relatively, I adhered and took heed to those principles in my tenure, but this plausible method was never respected: subsequently, it instead seemed to fuel communism and non-compromising approaches from white superiors. Many times I thought of Shoulders' warning, though I was already quite aware of the secret underhandedness of whites. In reality Shoulders was warning the incoming Blacks of the Department's racial prejudices: its tactics of degradation and calumnious defamation, the animosity of naive propagandized rumormongers, and the jealousies of the envious and back-stabbing officers who spread them.

Shoulders was also telling us that the perpetration of conniving and collusive schemes of white jail officials was in forms of class action at its best. Even when officers did so-called cover their asses, it didn't matter: the Department still manipulated, and carried out a misdirected and misused dictatorship with a totalitarian mentality.

There was hardly ever a dull moment in Shoulders' class, which mainly dealt with the intricacies of an inmate class action suit in 1971. The lawsuit was against Wayne County Sheriff Kenneth Barrett, the Wayne County Board of Commissioners, and the Wayne County Board of Auditors. Inmates alleged that there were multiple violations of their civil rights: the conditions in the old county jail were so bad that being housed there constituted cruel and unusual punishment. The inmates' class action suit focused on ten primary areas of concern: recreation, jail sanitation, suicide prevention, jail population and overcrowding, medical services and facilities, jail rules, methadone detoxification, vermin control, inmate towels, clothing, bedding, and plumbing maintenance. Yes, those are all inhumane violations, clearly legitimate reasons for someone to pursue litigation. Who wants to sit up in a cell block all day only playing cards, watching TV, seeing the same hoodlums, only able to exercise or walk around in proportioned limited space without an outlet to improve their physical or mental stimulation?

Of course that would drive anyone totally batty and, in essence, it was a *total disregard of rehabilitation*. Things are already bad enough when inmates are restricted from having sex, which is one reason why many men and women released from jail become homosexuals: while incarcerated they are only engaging and surrounded by their own gender. The only time an inmate *does* see the opposite sex is as a visitor, nurse, or officer; but of course there is no activity. More tragic, some inmates become totally confused by confinement and become transvestites and bull dikes. The court ruled in favor of the inmates and ordered Wayne County and the sheriff to *correct all ten areas or be held in contempt of court*.

Historically, the court orders usually weren't very specific as to what action the sheriff should take, and many times the sheriff neglected certain requirements through stipulations. In most cases, the sheriff's department themselves proposed plans and procedures that were in close compliance with court orders. Many times the Department's plans and procedures were approved by the court and thus became *in fact* court orders. The court orders pertained to all employees of the Department having or exercising inmate custodial care and responsibility, however slight. The courts periodically issued more orders that affected jail operations. When and if further rulings were issued, the Department provided the information to officers in the form of directives, orders, memoranda, and the like. It was the total responsibility of officers to adhere to such information and keep it up-to-date. Violations of court orders could have resulted in criminal, civil, or departmental actions, or any combination thereof against employees.

Court orders required the sheriff to take some action. Whenever civilian employees performed duties for the Department, they were also under those same court orders. Trying to concentrate on the boring study of rules and jail policies, I (and surely some of the other trainees) began to wonder whether or not this was the career we truly desired. Some of the teaching modes of the instructors were not conducive or relevant to work in the jail. The same holds true for the Department's version of a police academy (M.L.E.O.T.C.—Michigan Law Enforcement Officers Training Council), which gave more attention to a lot of irrelevant classroom training, rather than to tactical, racial and social sensitivity training that many officers truly needed. Those officers who saw work in the jail as only a career, needed extensive training in dealing with the psyche/mentality of criminals.

After two weeks, the cadets were practically burned-out from all the boring, non-apposite subjects. It was like going to school and taking algebra, trigonometry, and calculus; subjects that seem never to apply to the basic necessities of living, which seem to require primarily reading, writing and arithmetic. Shockingly, to our astonishment, the training class didn't have a course in first aid, which *should have definitely* been taught. Officers in the jail rarely used or performed emergency medical techniques, and it was uncommon for them to attempt CPR or other medical resuscitative methods to save lives. When medical staff arrived on the scene, officers gave way to doctors and nurses to initiate life reviving processes.

The training class also focused on Constitutional Amendments and the Bill of Rights: all police officers need to become knowledgeable about citizens' individual, given rights. The basis and intricacies of these basic rights are usually handled by a lawyer, judge or prosecutor, *__not a police officer__*. If these protective rights were handled exclusively by police officers, you'd see more of them in jail, because the majority of them are not trained thoroughly enough to rely, expound, and interpret the laws.

The class was given several definitions to study: words like *responsibility, authority, liability, causation, negligence, conspiracy* (there was a lot of that), *omission,* and the phrase *color of law.* The five elements of liability were taught: 1) Standard of Care, 2) Breach of Standard of Care, 3) Causation, 4) Foreseeability, and 5) Damages: all of these are typical of the underlying mischievousness of law enforcement agencies. The class learned the three main objectives of the jail: no escape, no contraband, and no disorder. We also learned the four goals of corrections: rehabilitation, protecting society, deterring others from committing crimes, and retribution. After seeing the continuous failure of the prevailing system, all this seemed highly insignificant.

During one of our periods of *undivided attention,* Shoulders informed the class about the dreaded medieval days when jail wardens didn't use lengthy prison sentences. He talked about the *Pennsylvania System,* which meant that rude inmates could not have any social interaction with other inmates: no recreation, no telephone calls, total confinement until that inmate's conformity and attitude improved. The *Auburn System* allowed inmates to work only during the day; they were locked up at night. If an inmate worked hard enough, and in doing so got a superior's approval, he could interact with other inmates and receive rehabilitation and certain privileges not given to the general inmate population.

Both of these systems of jail incarceration are primarily used today and are in sharp contrast with the practice of sending inmates to the *hole*: a cell with no telephone, no television and no interaction with other inmates. Many times the inmate was put there because of personality conflicts with spoiled, disgruntled officers. Many white male officers acted very irritable when handling throngs of Black male inmates. Some white officers were quite intimidated: just *one* conflict, *one* disagreement, *one* obstacle facing a white officer, usually meant going to the *hole* for a Black inmate. Some white officers even had it out for white inmates who acted like or congregated with Black inmates.

"Call the sarge, dep; I ain't going to no damn 'hole', I ain't did nothing," Clyde Robinson, a Black male inmate, yelled, feeling no compromise from Officer Lee Wallop, a white male officer. Some inmates asked me to plead for the reason, but white male officers rarely ever repent. When the above kind of situation got out of hand, it usually required calling a sergeant, who'd beckon his specific goons from different floors to show signs of force. If the show of force lacked fear or intimidation, officers would just rush in and remove the inmate from the ward with physical brutality, and in any restraining fashion necessary, to instill fear in the other inmates and keep them from doing the same.

Whenever the class took a break, it was spent in a small lunch room next to the classroom. Here were several vending machines filled with coffee, candy, potato chips, pop, and a microwave oven for officers who brought their lunch. Sometimes I had to drink three or four cups of caffeine coffee a day in order to stay awake through the boring and tedious classes. I love Reese's peanut butter cups, so the candy machine always got plenty of business from me. The Department or vendor made at least $80 a day from a class of forty plus.

A block from the vicinity of the jail is a place called Greektown. It's an ethnic neighborhood consisting of several restaurants in a four block radius, serving Greek, Italian, Cajun or American cuisine, but not much soul food. Having the convenience of Greektown close by, tempt many trainees to walk over for lunch to eat gyros, pizza, lamb, chicken, or hamburgers. The food aromas coming from Greektown were alluring at that juncture of employment, but later, as deputies grew immune to the scent, and seeing the filthy alleys rampaged by fat rats next to the Administration Building, many began to stay away. Sometimes the food seemed to upset the stomachs of, and induce headaches in many Black trainees, who became sleepy, drowsy, irritable, and remained alert only when another trainee pinched them. Trainees with a sense of comradeship whispered to one another, trying to keep each other awake.

The class learned about psychiatry from Instructor Walridge, who was very interesting and helpful in that field. Superfluously, because of that training, some officers really started to think they had the knack to clinically evaluate the minds of criminals and even some officers.

There was a session on report writing, which is considered the most tedious job of police work: basically that's what police work is all about. Writing responsive reports is essential so that the judge, jury, lawyers, or whoever, can read and interpret an officer's recollection of what he or she *thought* really happened. More important, a well written report can also determine the charge(s) of the defendant.

Every once in a blue moon the Department would let a few of its officers attend seminars sponsored and conducted by other police departments. The only problem: the seminars seemed to always occur outside of Wayne County's jurisdiction, and mainly white officers were given the opportunity to attend individual session or additional training, which sometimes only lasted a few hours. Many times I attempted to matriculate into one of those classes because writing an unclear report can bring additional bias suspicions and litigation against an officer. I didn't have that problem because I *never* believed in writing many reports anyway. Some officers got-off writing unnecessary, trivial reports, only because they lacked the social intelligence to solve and handle intricate situations themselves. This was especially true of white officers, who resided in nearly all white communities and never experienced any interaction with or authority over the "street-ish," Black male mentality.

To my recollection, during my tenure, the sheriff's department never held classes in report writing at its own jail. They could have easily hired someone to teach classes in report writing to new deputies, but chose instead to send its officers, traveling on their own time, to learn a skill that's mandatory and considered essentially necessary if law enforcement is to evaluate truth.

There are two basic kinds of police report writing: the *inductive* and *block* styles. The inductive style starts where the incident occurred and leads to some kind of solid conclusion, whereas the block style is usually out of sequential order, but tentatively the report still should make some sense. I felt very comfortable with both writing styles.

Using *I* a lot in a report isn't considered proper protocol for police report writing. It's more appropriate to say *this writer* more than *I*. All person involved in the incident should have their whole names printed in the report. Abbreviations are never acceptable, except for the defendant's and complainant's names. In sections of the report, some words are commonly abbreviated: the drivers license (DL), Black male (B/M) or white male (W/M), Black female (B/F) or white female (W/F), date of birth (DOB), and social security number (S.S.#). Information from the complainant and the defendant should be written on top of the report before the inductive style starts. Names of complainant, defendant and witnesses should be in block style.

In college, I had extensive experience in business writing courses that helped me in the art of police report writing, even though I refrained from writing many reports. During those four-and-a-half years I worked in the jail I may have written a total of twenty reports on inmates. The vast majority of my reports dealt with maintenance neglect: repair work of inoperative cells and doors, and plumbing. But mainly I wrote rebuttal reports about write-ups from harassing minions within the Department. In all probability *"this writer"* could have easily written sixty reports or better, if I was a real antagonistic, momus, petty person, but that wasn't *my style*! I believed in handling situations with wits and intelligence, rather than resorting to a report that, in most cases, would be taken out of context by some bias, authoritative, protagonist figure, who didn't have firsthand knowledge of the incident.

White male jail officials had a *sick sense* of prejudging officers without ever consulting them. Black officers were notoriously put up to back stab one another, while white officers snitched and collaborated with other white officers and superiors because of their dislikes. The sheriff's department skillfully used naive Black officers in their schemes against strong-minded Black officers. Many times a white officer would turn in a report to a white superior, who would immediately, without investigation, "rubberstamp" and write-up an even more stringent, dictatorial report, and then send *this* to another higher-up white male, imperialistic supervisor. But when Black officers did the same, many were severely harassed. This form of deceitful degradation harmed departmental esteem, and that professional stigma that the public has been led to naively believe for decades, proved suspect. In secrecy, Black officers never trusted white superior's institutionalized judgment regarding racial equality. As the county's political bureaucracy continued, departmental morale grew nil and the atmosphere was that of a continuing racial dilemma of dangerous implicating proportions.

The training class learned how to operate computers that were in every center station on each jail floor, and in each departmental function of the jail. Trainees only spent a couple of hectic hours on just two computers because the Department was unable to furnish, and supply ample computer equipment for the class to learn the many jail systems and codes. Considering the size of the class, and the importance computer literacy plays in the jail, this was ridiculous pre-planning. Actual computer training only occurred when officers learned through trial and error (hands-on experience) of working on the computers in the center station on the jail floors. Sergeant Metoyer taught the computer class and he was very helpful, but understandably could not teach each trainee individually because of the class size and lack of sufficient equipment.

Speculation was that in 1991 the Department, in conjunction with the Detroit Board of Education, purchased $60,000 worth of state-of-the-art computer equipment to rehabilitate and train inmates. Think about it—now blue collar inmates were getting ready for the high-tech world of white collar crimes, such as forgery, counterfeiting, computer hacking, feloniously using the Internet for porn and sending out messages over the E-mail, and fund tampering: undoubtedly, you can rest assured that there will be significant increases in these types of criminality in the future.

To me, the computer training was the most interesting segment of the class because I type well. Many times I brought my typewriter from home and carried it up to my assigned station. At first, instead of handwritten submissions I preferred to type all my reports and letters, but that practice was stopped when shift command officers spontaneously hashed a jail rule about carrying certain implements onto the floors. I felt more professional when typing my reports than just writing them in black ink. Some superiors even threatened to discipline officers for submitting reports written in any ink color other than black. Being in a guard station for eight or sixteen hours with a typewriter gave me a sense of having my own executive office.

Though my printing and handwriting are excellent, still I preferred typed reports: they had a more profound impact on the reader and, in the jail, storage and memory are essential. There were numerous special codes that revealed inmate information: a code telling officers what floor and where an inmate was housed, codes that showed an inmate's charges, bond amount and specific information concerning height, weight, and race. The computer also showed the inmate's birth date, address, aliases, and the judge that was handling, or would handle, the case. Aliases were also listed on an inmate's floor card. Inmates faces always showed a look of astonishment when an officer called out a couple of their aliases.

If an inmate was being transferred from a floor, officers simply typed "/OFF," the inmate's number, and the computer screen showed the inmate as *off the ward* until that inmate reached another floor destination in the jail, or returned from court. When the inmate arrived at another floor, then *that* officer was supposed to use "/ON" and "FC" (floor change), the inmate's number, his or her appointed cell, the station where he would be housed, what floor he was previously on, and the bunk number (1-upper, 2-lower). If the inmate was being transferred from either the old jail or the new, the receiving officer was required to change the jail divisional number (1-new, 2-old). Because so many inmates are habitual and recidivistic, with multiple charges, the officer, after entering the right code, could bring up their additional charges by entering "P/2" or "P/3." This would show all the inmate's past crimes, some of which were probably still pending.

Computers in the jail always seemed to malfunction when the weather was damp, rainy, cool, or the humidity was relatively high: weather conditions that also made it stuffy and difficult for officers to breathe. Many officers assigned to center station rejoiced when these conditions existed because they knew eventually it might effect computer operations, and that meant no computer entry work, just recording entries in the logbook. Many officers hated typing: were unaccustomed to the keyboard and feared learning future automation. Putting numerous entries in the computer seemed tedious and uninteresting to unskilled, disorganized officers, who couldn't type efficiently or weren't business oriented.

With regularity, just minutes before shift change, Male Registry officers brought up elevators full of inmates. This resulted in the **Trickle Down Syndrome**, because the center station officer, who was ready to go home, suddenly had to log and enter late incoming inmates into the computer as "/ON." The reluctance to do so puts that burdensome task up to the incoming officer, thus creating a negative and complaining attitude.

The creativity and endless possibilities of the computer often intrigued me, especially when boredom set in. When the days became monotonous in center station, as they so often did, to find cures I sent messages to friends or female officers I admired; but I could only send messages to them if they were working in another center station or department that had a computer. Daily, a schedule of assignments were issued to each center station to inform officers of who was working in what locations. Out of the five stations on each jail floor, center station was the only one supplied with a computer. There were different codes for every department in both new and old jails. In the new jail, messages could be sent to the medical department, RDC (Reception Diagnostic Center), shift command offices, male and female registries, front lobby desk, trustee services, bond office, inmate clothing, and Master Control.

Sending a message to the wrong station or department could be very embarrassing. The receiving station could find out where the message came from by reading the top of the computer screen's first reply. You can imagine what kind of ramifications occurred when a sexy, tantalizing note was accidentally sent to the wrong floor or person. But if an officer was dumb enough not to double-check where the outgoing message was sent, than they deserved whatever was coming. Several officers took this common mistake for granted. Sending the wrong message to some ambiguous, deceitful person, like many of the Sambos, and white command officers, meant your ass was theirs, even though the message may have been sent to the proper station and wasn't meant for them. If such insensitive persons, without a sense of humor, happened to read it, many would use it derogatorily.

It was even once rumored there was a computer that transcribed all messages sent through both jails' computer system. If so, surely this super computer had a few of my most treasured, sensual thoughts. Whoever read those messages specifically sent to female officers surely got the hots immediately! Sometimes the officer the message was sent to may have gone to the rest room, to lunch, or was being relieved. In most cases this situation didn't have to occur, it happened unexpectedly because calling the person in advance about an incoming message spoiled the surprise. When Black officers displayed continuous acts of humor or joy, they were usually cast down by harassing superiors. White male officials hated to see Black officers enjoying themselves.

The job really became boring, especially if you were on a floor full of **Robocops***:* an officer who **never** had any authority at any level, and when county or state commissioned authority is granted, uses it tacitly with every rule interpretation, little diplomacy, and far too much aggression.

After the computer class, trainees watched a movie about different types of contraband and the various techniques inmates use to smuggle it into jail. Contraband are any goods smuggled into jail, not issued by the institution, which are also a means of escape, and intended to hurt other inmates and workers. The movie was shot in the late 1960s or early 70s, in some hardened California prison, like Alcatraz. Black male inmates in the film wore long afro hair styles, and the film showed all kinds of plastic, bone, aluminum, and wood materials used to construct contraband weapons that wouldn't be picked up by metal detectors.

Toothbrushes can also be used as contraband, but inmates possessed plenty of those in the Wayne County Jail. Inmates can take off the bristles, take half of a double edge razor, melt one end of the toothbrush, and place the razor in the soft melted end until it drys and hardens. Metal shanks in the narrow part of a shoe sole are also used as weapons. A toilet plunger, watch, heel, toothpaste container, picture frame, and even tennis balls are all items used for hiding contraband. Other forms of contraband are ball point pens, wire from notebooks and teeth, pencils, metal parts from mops and buckets, rolled up magazines with rubber bands, springs from mattresses, and, of course, money and narcotics.

The class learned the terms for searches: frisk, field, and complete search. A frisk is the search of a person for concealed weapons: running the hands between the legs and under the arms while the inmate is spread eagle (legs spread apart). A field search means to look for more than weapons: things like narcotics, theft and waste, health hazards, and vermin. The clothes, hair, and pockets should be thoroughly filtered through and searched. A complete search requires a thorough search of the body, which means ordering the inmate to take off all clothing, opening his or her mouth, and bending over to search the keister (Yiddish slang for buttocks or anus) for contraband.

Two days before completing the class, trainees were given their first glimpse of what the jail really looked like. We were divided into two groups, leaving about 20 trainees apiece for each guide. As the class walked from under the new jail through the dismal underground tunnel that leads to the courts and old jail, fearful trainees huddled closer together, somewhat frightened at prospects of the unexpected. The tour guides were Officer Cerise Major, a Black female with a beautiful smile and personality, and Officer Chester Godley, a Black male. Both were very cordial and helpful. Godley was extensively involved in union affairs, and was later left out in the cold after involvement in a fatal traffic accident, in March 1989, that resulted in the death of a Black woman. The Department did not try to help him through that ordeal, even after he gave them almost twenty years of dedicated, loyal service. (Read Chapter 28, I'm MADD over Drunk Driving.)

"Don't say anything to the inmates because some of them can act very ignorant towards rookies," Officer Major informed each group before we neared the stairs leading up to the old jail. Walking up, we approached a long metal sliding gate. Officer Johnson, a Black female, was working in the turret, a fortified guard station situated in the old jail's garage.

This station controls all the old jail's garage doors for incoming vans and vehicles used for court and prisoner transfers. To our amazement, there were numerous buckshot holes in the glass and all around the turret's exterior. Apparently, the station was involved in a shootout or came under attack, presumably from someone involved in an attempted escape. Seeing that gave us every indication that this job could prove dangerous.

"Open up, we've got a class to take to the jail floors," yelled Major, who always seemed to be smiling. "So, now y'all wanna see a real jail, huh? Well, you've come to the right place," responded Johnson, as her unwelcomed presentation did nothing for the trainees' confidence. She buzzed the group through the sliding gate that sounded rusty, creaky: mystical and rather scary.

After everybody squeezed through, Godley's group went left through a first floor door to a room being readied for construction, eventually to hold the old jail's inmate clothing. Major's group, the one I was in, went straight ahead and got on an old decrepit elevator that slowly climbed past the floors, as if it had been maintained and oiled just once since the jail's inception. The old jail was built in 1929, and this elevator sounded and operated as if it had been in existence longer then that. After a terrifying climb that seemed like an eternity, the group arrived on the sixth floor.

Walking in the old jail for the first time, I felt a strange, unsettling feeling, as if ghosts from the past were beckoning me *not to* take this job. Everyone associated with the jail setting experiences that initial fear, but after mingling and dealing with it awhile, that fear subsides and eventually leaves.

My group was the first to test the waters of the old jail, which at that time seemed to house the more hardened criminals, perhaps because of its obvious structural difference and doomed ambiance, compared with the new jail. The old jail had paint peeling, acutely severe plumbing problems, bar cells only, a majority of doors and bars that opened only with keys, far less space for inmates, and appeared to be more of a *bread-n-water* type mental setting.

Officers working in the old jail preferred it to the new one because of the privacy factor: Inmates could not detect where the officer was all the time, and officers didn't have to look at the inmates all day long through windows, like in the new jail. There were no guard stations to sit in, and basically officers could become *police* officers, not pawns for superiors, and could station themselves strategically. Regularly, officers tired of the new jail and wanting to make a move, used their bidding power (seniority) to transfer to the old jail. After experiencing the system over at the old jail, many never wanted to come back to the bureaucracies of the new jail ever again. Though I only worked in the old jail once, I could feel the difference in mentality and morality: not a great, substantial difference but the privacy factor made a significant change in officers' confidence and morale.

We were taken to ward 614, which housed aggressive, sexually assaultive inmates. After going through three sets of bars and gates, the class was assisted by other officers working on the floor. We heard a little history about the kind of inmates the class was about to see, and Major asked for volunteers to walk down the catwalk of the ward, just to get a glimpse and actually see what the cells and being around the inmates felt like. The catwalk is a narrow pathway in front of the bars of the inmate ward. Hesitant but curious, I chose to be the first to test my nerves, and gingerly and slowly walked down the catwalk. There were several inmates sitting on the ward. One of them seemed to sense some fear: his name was Mack Brown, a big muscular Black man, about 45 years of age and 6-foot-3-inches tall, weighing about 260 pounds, with a long, braided afro of laniferous, ulotrichous hair. A vicious, razor-toting inmate, Mack had multiple charges of criminal sexual assault, and only preyed on and broke into the homes of elderly, divorced women. He held them at knife-point, and forced them into having anal and oral sex with him.

As I proceeded, Mack approached the bars to immediately test me: "Look at this damn fool! You think we're nothing but animals in a cage, don't you?" At first, I tried to ignore him by taking a few more steps towards the end of the catwalk. After further thought, I decided to step farther away from the bars and keep much closer to the wall. There were several other Black inmates watching TV, and two others were engaged in a serious chess game: I played chess a little. Still aware of Mack's presence, I decided to lean slightly closer to take a better look at the positions of the chess pieces, and finally broke my silence and suggested to one of the players that he should move his bishop for checkmate, which he did after weighing his options. "Don't be trying to ignore me, ya sissy-ass motherfucker," Mack yelled at me without provocation.

Everyone in the group heard the outburst and appeared to be

awed. The group had been previously informed by Officer Major not to say anything to the inmates, but I couldn't resist. I had to say something to this lost soul: "Why don't you just shut the hell up? That's why your dumb-ass is in here in the first place: nobody has said one word to you! I wonder, what-in-the-hell is your charge? What did you do to get here, rape a helpless little girl or an elderly women, or something? What's wrong with you? Can't you get with someone your own age? You're a very sorry excuse for a Black man. You're a very weak-minded person, yet, you *could* be strong. You need to get a life!"

For a moment, Mack looked flabbergasted, but that didn't stop him from continuing his barrage as the cadets and Officer Major looked on: "Ah man, fuck you! Who do you think you are? Wait till you start working around me, I'll set your damn ass straight," aggravated, Mack shouted, and momentarily grabbed his nut sac with one hand, a comb with the other, and started loosening up the braids and raking strands of his thick, nappy, unkempt hair. I shot back: "Ain't nobody scared of your funky ass, and whenever I do get a chance to work with you, my man, we'll have a long discussion because you're lost, you need some help. Otherwise, I've got nothing else to say to you until that day."

Slightly nervous, I finished my stroll. I had totally shocked myself when the words flowed from my mouth with such vigor. All the trainees and Major looked stunned. After Mack's ignorant outburst, some trainees thought twice about testing their nerves. The bars were very close to the catwalk, but I didn't flinch or buckle under pressure to Mack, or any other inmates who might have wanted to retaliate by trying to grab me. It was somewhat understandable that female trainees were afraid, but there were also several male trainees who refused to walk down the catwalk after that incident.

Some officers working in the jail, even after becoming state-certified, were terrified to walk among inmates. Before making a round of a ward, many officers had all inmates locked in their cells before entering. At one time, jail officials hashed a rule that all inmates must be locked down before making a round each hour. Braver officers *never* liked the idea and *never* did it, unless they had a notion that a momus superior would appear during making the round. In most officers' eyes, this procedure was nothing but a formality, and a systematic, institutionalized tactic for achieving conformity. Somewhere down the line, the officer was going to be in close proximity to the inmates while doing other duties anyway. All corrections officers working in Michigan had better get used to this close proximity because state and county jail correction officials plan for a more family approach to ease the stress of institutional incarceration.

When another new jail opened in Hamtramck, Michigan (a Polish community within Detroit's boundary), an unpopular, theorized method of putting officers on wards with over 50 to 60 inmates to socialize more with them, was implemented. This was the State of Michigan's mentality to gain the respect of its prisoners, implement social rehabilitation, and foster better relations between inmates and officers. Just think, once I received a reprimand and suspension for 30 days (going on an inmate ward without permission) for futuristic ideas that Michigan jail officials now deem proper and appropriate. In a way, some of my actions were way before my time, so to speak.

Even having a radio to alert for help doesn't make some officers brave enough to congregate closely with inmates. Never was a radio the ultimate solving alternative to some crazed fool who really wants to do harm, but without it an officer is totally helpless to alert anyone, and thus puts him or herself, other officers, and the institution in danger. I always made sure a freshly-charged battery was in my radio, but there was a time I took that aspect of jail corrections lightly and didn't care about carrying a radio all the time, not that I saw an incident or was involved in a possible altercation, because I never had one. One day I just saw the light and always had my radio supplied with a charged battery. Many officers were fearful of inmates because they had treated them inhumanely in the past. Grapevinely, inmates spread the word about certain officers, not cordial or respectful towards them.

Plenty of times officers had a dead battery, no battery, or a charged battery purposely turned the wrong way in their radio. Some officers turned a fresh battery around the wrong way when using the special, red-colored radios specifically worn by the rovers of each floor to alert Master Control by just a slight tilt: laying it down, or just bending over to tie one's shoelaces. Continuously, officers would forget about the sensitivity of those radios, lay them down, and trigger the alarm. Master Control announced the location of the radio alarm over the P.A. system and, if the officer with this special radio didn't alert the Master Control officer in time to tell him to announce a false alarm, it became hard to explain his or her actions to some petty superior. An officer could be in the rest room, get all relaxed, and forget about the radio's special feature. Though the radio's alarm mechanism buzzed for several seconds, if Master Control wasn't told in time of a false alarm, twenty officers could be on the floor ready for battle before that officer exited the rest room.

There were times when officers at lunch forgot about the radio's special sensitivity features and the alarm went off. Everyone, from Master Control to the command officers, knew it was just a mistake, but the officer had to write-up a report stating, why the radio's alarm went off. That report would read something like this: "*This writer* was at lunch and this stupid red radio that we carry around went off. *This writer* again forgot to *never* lay the radio down." Basically, that's what the report would say, but all the officer had to *do* was take the battery out or turn it around at lunch time. But some officers had the mentality of a worm.

This unique radio was usually carried by the rovers, who roamed both the north and south sides of each floor. After a very lengthy trial period, jail commanders stopped the idea of having rovers; they finally deemed it a waste of manpower because many officers abused the privilege by constantly staying off their designated floor. In general, the Department's perfunctory riddance of the rovers was good because some biased command officers enacted their favorite pastime: favoritism. With daily regularity, superiors scheduled their favorite officers or mandated wimps in rover positions and at prime assignments. This practice made many other officers quite frustrated and pissed.

There were always a couple of weeks in the schedule that displayed superiors' obvious and overwhelming partiality. When officers complained about it to the union, command officers modified their approach by writing up bias reports and reprimands. The higher superiors knew of these tactics of bias, and never intervened for the betterment of departmental morale. Never speaking up for Black officers, along with being inhumanely one-sided, jail officials tried to malign and belittle many Black officers, especially the males. Vehemently, jail union stewards were summoned by officers to argue the fact of unfairness and a total disregard of fair scheduling and assignments. Solutions were never remedial and the practice continued on.

In 1987, Lieutenant Harriet Hannan, a white female, and Lieutenant Tom Showlin, a white male, placed me in a station called First Floor Control for months because I so-called didn't receive *their* permission to go on an inmate ward. I was also given a 30-day suspension. This charge was coupled with the lies of **Robocop** Officer Lee Wallop, a hysterical, paranoid white male. The First Floor Control oversees and operates the doors entering and exiting male and female registries. It also had a camera-monitor that stayed focused on the front lobby entrance doors, the lobby desk and visitor's lobby area. If the officer stationed there had no company, or some social interaction, the day seemed like torture. I was frequently given this assignment because I was too outgoing and outspoken about my civil, constitutional, and workplace rights being violated. Jail superiors figured they could shut me up by putting me in the "*dog house*."

Jailers' training was helpful in some aspects, as far as giving the potential deputy/turnkey some real insights into what this forthcoming job entailed. Much of the information taught, however, was *never* pertinent or ever used. Basically, an officer has to have some common street sense when manning floors of habitual inmates. The most important aspect of jail corrections is being mentally fit, and physically fit to endure physical confrontations with an inmate(s); that's an absolute must. Also, for a Black person, it is necessary to have self-esteem and a strong will power to endure constant harassment and injustice. No matter what the Department conjured up or insinuated by using collusive efforts and other methods of deceit, I endured and fought back with more determination.

Tired of fighting "*The System*," many Black officers abandoned their rights for justice and were too eager to let matters be. This is the major reason why Blacks and other people of color are blocking their own continued success: giving up too easily and being stigmatized as the greatest criticizers and procrastinators on this earth. It was very difficult for me to just give up without a fight because the sheriff's department has a history of being unjust and cruel to people of color, whether officers or inmates. Many Black officers had completely lost their principals of pride, and had given up all hopes of accomplishing a generalized awareness involving the bias training, and treacherous manipulation of people of color by law enforcement.

6

Working the First Day,
The Beginning of the End

MY FIRST WORKING DAY IN THE NEW JAIL was Monday, January 21, 1985, and that winter was very severe: with one of the worst blizzards in years, coupled with extreme cold and subzero readings. Rising from a cumbersome, tossing and turning night's sleep of anticipation, I began the morning with intense prayer and meditation, hoping for the best in my new profession.

I could not erase from my memory that first jail experience: walking down the catwalk in the old jail and being riled by Mack, that ruffian. This was to be my first full day of direct contact, of working by myself as a rookie fresh on the block, and inmates have a knack of detecting rookies. Though I felt very proud of my new position of deputy sheriff, my confidence still needed a quick fix; I didn't know what to expect.

At Roll Call, Sergeant Milt Trombley, a white male with a squeaky, southern voice, welcomed the newly hired jailers. His presentation was met with a chorus of long sighs and yawns from some of the officers, who had heard Trombley's same ol' welcome many times before. Very excited, I hurried to get my station keys from Key Control, immediately after Roll Call, and got on the elevator headed to my assignment.

Working the afternoon shift was my first choice. I didn't want to deal with the traffic jams and get out of bed at five in the morning. My eyes were always full of crusty mucous and I had difficulty with equilibrium adjustments to the eastern standard time change. Everyone in America seems to have problems adjusting to the changes in the regional time frames; the changes feel like symptoms of jet lag. I had three choices: the morning, afternoon, or midnight shift. The occupations I had worked previously were morning shift jobs, so I wanted a change in my human timetable. For the first week or so, the annual change in daylight saving times in April and October made shift adjustments hectic. After the time was moved forward or backwards an hour, several officers were either too late or too early the following day. Officers had no excuses but to say they forgot.

My first assignment was the 7-Northwest station, and as soon as I relieved the morning shift officer, we both heard an inmate yell my first name from the ward: "Hey Krasne! What's happening?" Shocked and wide eyed with disbelief, I dropped my briefcase as the morning shift officer and I immediately began to look for the inmate who yelled out my first name. Calling out the first names of employees or officers is a *no-no* in the jail. Approaching, to lean up against the station window, a short, curly haired Black male inmate continued to address me as I furiously looked on: "Man, I didn't know you was working down here. When did you start working for the sheriff's department?" Looking more carefully, I noticed it was a guy from my old high school days, named Shine, who hung out with some of my old high school friends, who considered him *their* friend. But Shine and I were *never* friends in high school: I *never* associated with him or his kind.

In jail for burglary and grand larceny, Shine and several accomplices crashed a local furrier's front store window and stole furs and furniture. That takes a lot of gall. In the past, I had overheard some of his old high school buddies talking about Shine's skeptic personality and criminal reputation. Pensive, I finally acknowledged Shine and, after the relieved officer vacated the premises, summoned the more experienced officer down the hall to let Shine off the ward, informing him that I needed to talk with this inmate because he had called out my first name, and every other inmate heard it. Inmates should only know and call out the last names of officers, that's all.

Once Shine was off the ward, I motioned for him to come down to the end of the hallway, out of the eyesight of other inmates. "Look Shine," I told him, "*Never, ever* call out my first name again on these jail floors. We have never been that close, and don't ever call out my first name in this joint, again." Shine showed no respect. He insistently tried to interrupt me with on the contraries, buts, and innuendoes. His attempts of assertion were ignored and I wouldn't let him get in a word, edgewise: "I know, you know better than that; don't do it again, alright? Do we have an understanding?" "Ah, man I thought me and you was cool," Shine complained, trying to test my nerves and force the issue, while his irrelevance became obnoxious. Angrily, I shouted back: "We have never been that cool, and don't expect *that* to change just because you knew me from Mumford! You've never been a friend of mine and I'm gonna tell you once again, don't ever call out my first name in this jail. To you, my name is Officer Taylor, and I don't want to tell you that again!" "Man, you must think you're bad or something, just because you have some authority over people now," Shine continued his verbal backlash.

At that moment I really began to lose my cool, and I instructed Shine to return to the ward before I started to write-up my first reprimand on my very first day working in the jail. Later, Shine was moved from that floor, his classification changed. I was on the floor no more than twenty minutes, on my very first day of work, and was about to have it out with this Black male inmate, just because he thought we were friends from high school. Usually, when inmates see old friends from the streets who are officers in the jail, they immediately expect favors. This is a *no-no*. Other inmates will not appreciate the officer's favoritism and will began to disrespect his integrity. Inmates can be very trifling at times, and Shine was no exception. Once back on the ward, he went and sat in a corner and started mumbling obscenities, and venting detrimental things about me under his breath. I just sat calmly in my cushiony station chair without showing any remorse; I had controlled the situation. I had never bothered this man before, whether in the streets, or wherever. I never understood Shine's mentality or attitude, even when we both attended Mumford High School from 1969-1972.

After this unnecessary altercation, I signed my name into the logbook and proceeded to write down other appropriate information. There were many other Black male inmates I knew from the streets in jail, along with a few alumni from high school. Some had lived prosperous lives, but a weakening economy, lack of continuing education or training, difficulty securing viable employment, and the influx of drugs in Detroit, could change the strongest of men into criminals.

Three ex-Mumford High School students from the early 1970s were incarcerated in the new jail. One, Marcus Byrum, had been a promising baseball prospect for the Detroit Tigers. In high school his fast ball was consistently clocked at 92 miles an hour, and this southpaw was scouted, drafted, and finally pitched for the Tiger's minor league farm system in Montgomery, Alabama. In his first year of professional minor league baseball, he led the pitching staff in earned run average, strikeouts, innings pitched, games started, and complete games. That same year, Byrum was released by the club after team officials were alleged to have found heroin in his locker. He had lost a possible million dollar career over drug usage.

Coincidentally, one day in 1988, I worked the same ward Inmate Byrum was on. It was totally disgusting and sad to see that same gifted left arm that was destined for stardom, punctured and lined with numerous needle tracks. The boy messed up—he was such a competitor in high school and had a wicked, nasty fast ball. He was one bad dude and could hit real good, too. Another Mumfordite was accused and convicted of killing a car salesman while taking a test drive. This other one, nicknamed "Goody," played football. I never saw any of Mumford's female alumni in the jail—which seemed unbelievable, as scandalous as some were.

I also saw several young Black men, who roamed and resided in my neighborhood with no purpose but to commit B & E's (breaking and entering), and purse snatchings. For periods of time, no one in the 'hood would see them because they had been arrested and charged. After serving very short sentences, they were released back into the neighborhood to commit more crimes against their Afrikan-American community.

For the most part, being incarcerated can inadvertently become rehabilitating. It can spare some criminals from dying of drugs, getting death threats from rivals, intimidating drug lords or other pushers.

In 1985 and 1986, there were several Young Boys, Incorporated (Y.B.I.) gang members in jail, nearly all their charges involved murder, weapons and drugs. In the book, *Pipe Dream Blues: Racism & The War on Drugs*, author Clarence Lusane expounds on the history of this notorious, but organized, young Black male youth gang: "One Black youth gang in Detroit, Young Boys, Inc., grew from twenty-four members to 300 members, with estimated weekly sales of 7.5 million in heroin and cocaine. In 1982, they grossed close to $400 million. According to Michigan State University criminologist Carl Taylor, who has written an authoritative book on Detroit's youth gangs, *Dangerous Society,* the gang began with an investment of $80,000 that came from an insurance claim by two of the original members. By all accounts the group was extremely organized, highly disciplined, and unabashedly brutal. It imposed a 'no drug use' policy on its members, and the penalty for violation was death.

Young Boys, Inc., was able to exploit the financial crisis that Detroit's Black community found itself facing in the Seventies. The gang functioned as a bank for many Black Detroiters by giving loans at usury rates for house purchases and starting small businesses, since Detroit's financial institutions had been chastised by the banking industry for not making loans to Blacks in the city. Gang members themselves bought homes in the suburbs and houses and apartments in the city to process and sell drugs. Some members opened legitimate businesses such as video and record stores. Although some of the money derived from drug trafficking was reinvested into the community, the structural and entrenched economic crisis confronting Detroit's Black poor, particularly that of males, went unaddressed. The social and economic crisis of the community was exacerbated by Young Boys, Inc.'s care and feeding of Detroit's estimated 50,000 heroin addicts. Their activities accelerated the city's social deterioration and wrought uncalculated suffering."

In November of 1993, after he served years in a state penitentiary, a house of the Black founder of Young Boys Incorporated, was again raided by federal agents and he was caught red-handed in Southfield, Michigan. He was charged with the distribution of drugs.

There were also Columbian, Peruvian, Bolivian, and Arab inmates in jail mainly because of delivering, selling, or trafficking huge amounts of cocaine. Some of the police sting operations targeting them, busted truck loads filled with tons of cocaine. Officers needed an interpreter to understand their "da hockin' " lingo. Seemed like the Columbians had the most outrageous and costly bonds. There wasn't an Inca (Peruvian Prince) in the jail for drug smuggling charges with a bail set under $500,000. Sometimes the Department brought in a K-9 member from the drug brigade and had the dog sniff bail or confiscated money. Frenetic and deranged, the canine acted wild and berserk, jerking his head if there was any trace of narcotic residue saturated on the money. When exorbitant amounts of money were brought to the jail to bail out inmates with large bonds, and they were suspected of having drug connections, nine times out of ten the Department *would not assume* and *declare it* as drug money. Many inmates only thought of "building their futures on the rock" (cocaine and crack).

Enforcing *summary punishment* in the jail was always in effect, which means any punitive decision could be imposed by an officer without due process. It was *given* authority, unearned, and punishment was primarily left up to the discretion of the floor officer. (In that case, I, myself, was subjected to the Department's "summary punishment" many times.)

Before an inmate is reprimanded, an officer should always call a shift commander and let the superior impose the penalty, which is not always proper and in accordance with equal justice. Turnkeys are only noncertified officers, and most lack respectable sensitivity training in diplomatic tolerance. A 24-hour lock down was the most common penalty for a incorrigible inmate. More severe infractions usually resulted in a superior imposing additional time in the cell. Inmates could be confined for several days to the hole, which meant no telephone privileges, no recreation, and no visitors *if* they continued to cause problems for officers, superiors, coworkers, or other inmates. Many inmates were frequent visitors to the dreaded hole, and it didn't bother most of them to go there. Hell, inmates were already locked up; just taking away a few privileges didn't faze them one bit. Their attitude about going to the hole was mostly, that they could endure any penalties officers or jail authorities imposed. If an officer didn't care for a certain inmate(s), he or she easily instigated problems just to have a reason to send them to the hole.

To get away from the county jail's psychological confinement, many inmates vied for transfers to Jackson State Prison, like it was a change to some kind of plush resort. The food was better; they could get drugs, sex, more room to walk around, and there was a lot more privacy, according to those inmates who were mainstays in the penal system and had been in Jackson State Prison before.

I always called a superior when any speculation that could possibly lead to liability came in confronting an inmate problem. When a superior arrived, I gave them the deciding factor in evaluating what appropriate action to take. After thoroughly reading an officer's PJ-210 write-up, a superior should be able to make a just determination. A PJ-210 is an administrative form that should explain the incident clearly and entirely, with all the facts: time, inmate(s) name, person(s) involved, and what happened? Where it happened? What was the jail violation? And, very important, why it happened? The facts, accuracy, pliancy, and validity of the form were not always the truth. Superiors themselves, had specific wards where grudges were held against certain inmate(s). Sometimes when inmates cursed the superiors out, or threatened to beat their butts for imposing previous, unfair punishments, that particular ward caught hell. There were some gross, discriminatory injustices when evaluating inmate punishments. Common sense was not always the case, and usually shift commanders were misinformed about what occurred between the officer and inmate(s). With sheer regularity, officers lied about inmates, just because of conflicts of interest, personalities, and even racial motivation.

It was a different story, though, if a single inmate caused problems for the majority of inmates on the ward. Many officers handled that with a totally different set of rules. Inmates came to the guard station window all the time, complaining about a certain inmate's behavior or lack of hygiene. Officers were derelict in their duty if they didn't consider this a mounting problem, because complaining inmates may assault others for not adhering to the majority's wishes. Every ward had a *rock boss:* usually a strong-minded individual with spunk, somewhat well-liked, but mostly respected on the premise of an accord amongst the felonry. He usually was a gang leader on the outside, and most of all, wasn't afraid of anyone on the ward.

I always made sure all "rock bosses" and I were cool. If I had any semblance of a continuous problem with any inmate, instead of working out the problem myself, I'd sometimes consult with the rock boss and leave it up to him to find ways to solve the problem. Whatever judgement was enacted, I made sure the rock boss discussed the problem with the unruly, unpopular inmate first. If the rock boss failed to come to terms with a troublesome inmate, oh well, so be it! This kept me and many other officers from possible altercations with inmates, even though some officers could have handled such situations themselves. Officers often don't want to be bothered with and stressed out by worrisome, unnecessary quarrels with inmates.

One of the most valuable tools in the jail is the logbook. It provides valuable and needed information when the axe or *trick bag* tactics of jail officials or superiors fall on an officer's shoulders. But the logbook can also be used adversely when officers write down information that *never* occurred to cover their asses. Redundantly, many officers, lacking in creativity, wrote everything in the logbook that occurred within their peripheral vision. Some information logged wasn't necessary, and some officers wrote trivialities because they were bored and there just was nothing else to do. The first logbook entry should be the shift and the date. A few lines down, officers should enter their starting time, using military terms. After those two entries, the officer enters things like: presence of a first aid kit, fire blanket, jail rules manual, fire extinguisher (if it was charged or needs charging), a complete station AIDS kit, and the station's key numbers.

The AIDS kit was equipped with cleanup supplies: a small plastic dust pan and small whisk broom, a powdery solution to dry and absorb spilled blood for easier sweep up, a special liquid to clean the hands, and aerosol spray specifically for contaminated blood spills. The AIDS kits were randomly put on the jail floors, and at first each station did not have a kit. For months during Roll Call, concerned, informative officers, aware of the serious magnitude of the AIDS epidemic and the growing number of inmates infected with HIV and AIDS, complained about the lack of AIDS kits, and how to properly use them. We were later informed by jail officials that, "AIDS kits were being considered for all the guard stations," but officers never knew exactly when. Upon assignment, many of the blue containers were opened by officers, to discover and explore its containments themselves. One day a superior announced in Roll Call, "Wc've finally got all the stations equipped with the AIDS kits." In my tenure, jail officials never taught us how to properly use the equipment in those AIDS kit. It wasn't until the fall of 1987, almost three years into my tenure, that the AIDS kits were installed in all the new jail's guard stations: *seven years and far beyond* the time when the epidemic of AIDS became known to the general public as a worldwide threat.

The most important entry in the logbook is a thorough head count of the total number of inmates on the large and small wards. To be safe, this should be conducted several times a day. The number of inmate bodies must match the number of inmate cards in the station and, if they don't, the officer has a serious problem and must immediately locate the discrepancy before giving the correct ward count to the center station officer, who, in turn, gives the entire floor count to a officer working in Master Control. The Master Control officer tabulates the inmate count for the entire jail. Usually the count was taken so kitchen personnel could make enough food trays to feed inmates for dinner on the afternoon shift. The count must also match Master Control's floor counts for the entire jail population: if not, there's still a problem.

Many officers believed the inmate count was also for tabulating how much money the County would bill the state for the prisoners housed that day. The State, in turn, billed the Federal government. Other pertinent information to be logged: strange appearances, structural alterations, possible fights or fighters on the ward, and damages to county property. Things like broken windows, table or desk damage, plumbing or electrical problems, cell bar or doors not operating properly, damaged bunks, efficiency of toilet and shower operations, social and hygiene problems on the ward, shape of guard station, halls, and water fountain, and missing closet door knobs. Everything pertinent to security and health concerns should be thoroughly examined and inspected. Even the name of the officer in the station down the hall should be logged, in most cases, especially if that officer is considered a snitch!

Those superiors who had personality conflicts with targeted officers often scheduled them with the superior's favorites and would always side with the officer well-liked, *never* the one who was just.

Even if the officer down the hall was theoretically a partner, that wasn't always really the case. Having the name of the officer, collusive with superiors, written down in the logbook often constituted and solidified the reasoning behind the disillusionment when problems arose. No matter how efficient a targeted officer was on the job, superiors *always* played favorites. Officers had no idea who they were scheduled to work with until superiors had officers working together on the same floor daily. It got so bad sometimes that, officers, not in solidarity or disliking one another, would call their favorite superior and request a change in assignment.

Officers with few, if any, scruples wanted to see the pratfalls of others. I tried to work with every officer I was assigned with, even when I knew some were only stationed nearby to act as liaisons or communicative spies. Personality problems in the jail always existed amongst officers, or coworkers, more than any other job I had ever worked. This was mainly attributed to the many levels of ego immensity given impromptu, newfound authority. As my seniority grew, the trends of snitches consistently grew along with it. The majority of officer problems were the result of different opinions in the handling of jailed human beings. Surely, some Black officers were unfair, but *"The System"* was systematically structured to divide and conquer, and mainly the white officers' tactics were the ones that were just downright inhumane, scandalous, cowardly, and demoralizing. When collaborating officer-snitches wanted favors, or didn't like a particular situation, they called their favorite superior. Hastily, superiors went along with whatever *their* snitch entailed, and their roles were played out, accordingly.

From *Day One*, I never had many problems with inmates that I couldn't solve myself, like with inmate Shine. It was always the union, coworkers, officers, and superiors who caused pain, stress and unnecessary sorrows.

7

Mr. Briefcase,
Step Into My Office

ON MAY 29, 1985, WITH JUST A LITTLE OVER four months on the job, I received my first reprimand. The reason: carrying a briefcase on the jail floors. Coming to work, I'd see Detroit Police officers walking to and fro, carrying their briefcases, clipboards, notebooks and folders to their perspective scout cars. But here I was, an aspiring police officer, getting a reprimand for carrying a briefcase to keep my records and proper forms organized and in my immediate reach, which showed I had organizational skills and qualities. Not only are writing accurate reports and handling loads of paperwork the two most dreaded elements of being a cop, but they are major criteria. Police officers hate paperwork! The basic reason: in many instances, after risking their lives and carefully finalizing all the subtle details for a conviction, after the often manipulated misinformation of cases, the laws of the land lets criminals go free.

In many instances, criminals know all the loopholes to escape conviction (ala, slowly fading juvenile laws). On May 21, 1985, there was a hashed directive proposed by Jail Administrator Carlton Vance, a Black male, which stated: *"Effective immediately, Officers will report for duty in uniform only; carrying only authorized work implements. Absolutely no duffle bags, briefcases, bags etc. will be allowed. No radios, thermos bottles or any other items will be allowed. Any deviation from this order will be handled through the disciplinary process."* Later in 1987, Vance was promoted to undersheriff, but the directive would not go into effect until it was signed and endorsed by Inspector George McCarey, a white male.

These two jail officials hardly ever came to talk with their subordinates in the jail. Back in 1985, the undersheriff was Seth Wozniak, another white male administrator, who many considered insensitive to the problems of racial relations, which became clear as officers never saw him surface to address constituents. On June 3, 1985, Inspector McCarey sent me a departmental communication, explaining that my oral reprimand was for receiving the write-up about the briefcase. I never understood why jail overseers wrote oral reprimands. If it was oral, shouldn't the reprimand be an informal talk about the incident, face to face? McCarey's *Avoid Verbal Orders* report stated: *Be advised that this is a/an Oral reprimand. Copies of oral and written reprimands will be retained by the Divisional Inspector or Administrator. The original copy of oral and written reprimands will be directed to the Sheriff and will be placed in your central personnel file. On May 29, 1985 at approximately 1500 hours you did violate Order #85-1-20 dated May 21, 1985 relative to the carrying of non-work related implements into the jail facility. Failure to comply with the above mentioned order is in violation of Sec. D Para. 2.1 of the Wayne County Sheriff's Departmental Manual for Rules of Conduct, specifically "Obeying Orders."*

This directive was issued because some officers were suspected of bringing in drugs to inmates and filching items like telephones, toilet paper, inmate's soap, or whatever they could carry in a duffle bag (gym bag). The problem was not widespread enough to resort to implementing a rule that an officer, treated by the administration like an imbecilic moron, not carry his own policing files. That should tell you something about law agencies and administrative mentality. They will write a general rule to *hopefully* end the threat of contraband violations, rather than do some real investigative police work to get rid of the real culprits, those officers making it bad for others.

The expertise and character of an individual showed when such rules were implemented. These heedless attitudes on the part of administrators seemed to influence the darker sides of others' personalities, making joint and collusive propaganda a studious course in the bureaucratic sciences of manipulation and racial institutionalization. In all practicality, a briefcase should be considered a police officer's personal office, whereas a duffle bag looked unprofessional and, more noticeably, could consume many items of various sizes to be hidden and consequently stolen. The impasse had just begun. How could an old touch-tone telephone fit into a briefcase? Toilet paper, maybe, but a telephone? Come on, be for real. After a few weeks of harassing officers, the hashed and monotonous rule "of not carrying non-work related implements" on the jail floors, was considered perfectly normal and right.

The command officer who wrote my first reprimand was Sergeant Phyllis Harrington, a Black female who, my write-up aside, never gave me any other problems. Harrington later told me, after seeing how they use some of these jail rules, she wished she had never written me up for it, but jail officials were coming down on all the floor command officers to enforce every jail rule. What Harrington really meant was: coming down on Black command officers to keep the Black officers in check, but she always acted professional about sensitive, racial topics.

I could never figure out why anyone would risk his or her job to steal some toilet paper. Better yet, why would someone want to fire anyone over some toilet paper? But those minor essentials for the home can save an officer plenty of money over the years. Taking a roll of toilet paper per week, meant money saved; the same ideology for soap. Soap in the jail were those miniature versions mainly used in the bathrooms of inexpensive, or cheap, hotels. Inmates called it "state soap." Several times white male officers wasted plenty of the County's money by throwing soap at each other in the hallways, like kids throwing rocks or snowballs at each other. Many inmates refused to use the soap after the packages were opened and smudged with dirt. A floor full of white male officers chunkin' soap at each other in the hallway, meant everybody else had to be ready to duck at anytime. With a briefcase, I could at least protect myself by blocking flying soap.

8

Toilet Paper,
The One Great Necessity

EVERY INMATE FLOOR IN THE NEW JAIL had closets that stored cleaning supplies: mops, buckets, rags, brooms, soap, garbage bags, toilet bowl cleaner, plungers, bunk mattresses, and big cardboard boxes full of toilet tissue. There were other closet usages, including gambling, sleeping, hiding, making love, and a whole lot of other mischievous and suspenseful acts.

Surely, there are excusable delays in shipments of supplies in any organization or business, but the purchasing department left much to be desired. There were times when deputies went weeks without soap, toilet paper, and other necessary supplies for inmates. When this happened, responsibility and resourcefulness to keep the calm was left entirely to the deputy. In 1990, county commissioners only approved $155,000 for janitorial supplies, while the Department asked for $216,450, a reduction of $61,450, which showed a neglectfulness of responsibility for the jail's cleanliness. That figure clearly emphasized why many fed up officers brought in their own cleaning solutions, and how the unfiltered, recycled, dusty air became filthier, and contagious microorganisms multiplied.

Some of the most obvious, serious health issues seemed unimportant to jail officials and county commissioners. It was unnecessarily ridiculous and needlessly stressful for an officer to keep informing thirty-two inmates that *one roll* of toilet paper must be rationed and last an entire ward for a few days. That's 32 different personalities an officer has to keep satisfied. It was even worse to tell inmates that there was no toilet paper because of departmental laxity, or because the deputy and his partner down the hall had only a third of a roll for themselves.

The toilet paper issue brought to my mind those times when my family drove south for the summer to visit those very rural, country relatives of ours. Most of our southern kin folks lived miles deep in the dense wooded habitat of Arkansas and deserted rural byways of Louisiana. If it rained several days before our arrival, it was practically impossible to drive a car through the muddy, unpaved roads of rugged, slanted terrain. So, before making the trip, my mother, or one of my aunts, tried to get in touch with the relatives, so Uncle Gus could meet the family at the crossroads, where there was a church and cemetery.

Just down the road from the rendezvous spot was a popular Ku Klux Klan hangout: all the surrounding town's people and the local law enforcement officers knew about it; hell, some of the law officers were *in it!* My father and one of the other relatives carried pistols and a 12-gauge, double-barreled shotgun, in case there was ever any trouble. Though I was very young, I was *never* afraid, and carried my own weapons—Willie Horton and Rod Carew baseball bats, primed and ready to bash some "power-to-all-field" home runs on some white man's head. Suddenly peering down the road, we could see Uncle Gus coming from a distance. Gus, about 6 feet tall, weighing about 240 pounds, was a fair-skinned Black man, who always wore coveralls: I never saw him in a suit and tie. He guided a wooden buggy around town that was pulled by a mule named Sarah. "Unc" was a true muleteer to his heart.

After the family met at the church, we locked and left our cars, climbed in the buggy, and Gus carted us through the woods to see relatives on my dad's side, who were in the thick of it. Many times, as a child, I wondered how Uncle Gus got a mule and not his forty acres. "Get on up don yonda, girl," Uncle Gus quipped at Sarah, as he sought to control her by grabbing on and whipping the reins, while spitting out multiple successions of dark brown, glazed tobacco wads. His sunken cheeks, brown, tar-like saturated lips and fingers, forehead lines in crackling hardened skin; his missing, dull decaying yellow and brown teeth, all showed the damaging affects of nicotine and many years of chewing tobacco.

Sarah was very old, looked weary and worn out from being Uncle Gus' only mode of transportation for decades: he ***never*** took a test to get his drivers license. All over Sarah's hispid stomach hairs were little splattered balls of hard, dry mud. While Uncle Gus steered and commanded the squeaky, creepy buggy through the woods, it leaned several times, and almost tipped over from the overly slanted angles in the road. Several tree branches swung back, hitting family members in the face or head, just like in those "swinging tree branch" scenes in the Three Stooges.

While enroute, or before Uncle Gus and Sarah arrived, or while waiting at the house in the woods to see our relatives, somebody always had to use the rest room. In the woods, there was no modern convenience of rest rooms, but there was an overabundance of available outhouse facilities. Everybody always seemed to forget to bring toilet paper. After living in the more civilized, developed society of an urban metropolis, city dwellers tend to forget there are still people in other regions of the country, who experience uncivilized methods and lack current developments. "Hey, Aunt Sis, do we have some toilet paper," Cousin Neil asked my mother, while trying to fend off a pending bowel movement. "Uh shoot, I forgot it! Nobody else remembered to bring any?" Saying this, my mother then jokingly hollered, "You better just grab some of those tree branches and use some of those leaves. They work just as good." "Auntie, please, I might get some dodo on my hands," Cousin Neil wailed.

With all the oak and sycamore trees around, one didn't have to worry about ever running out of leaves. Neil, a real big fellow, about six feet tall, weighing 230 pounds, walked around awhile looking for a good spot, somewhere seemingly unnoticed, just like a dog sniffing for a place to squat. After settling on a location, Neil jumped twice to reach and snatch several long branches filled with hand sized, emarginate leaves, and commenced. Minutes later: "Aunt Sis, anybody, got a rag?" It all escalated somewhat when Cousin Neil, while trying to wipe, mistakenly used a crunchy dry leaf that crumpled up between his fingers. It was difficult to gather up leaves, especially dry ones, like toilet paper. Afraid of several prospects, I never used leaves because I didn't want to encounter a reptile, wild boar or hog, a KKK member, or especially a praying mantis on one of them. I always had the frightening thought of hidden microbes in the cleaves of a leaf infiltrating my body through my anal passage.

At the age of nine, I could never figure out why the scent of human defecation would attract hordes of insects and snakes. Once, I simultaneously encountered a 12-foot rattler and a 6-inch lizard while using the rest room in Arkansas woods. While still in the process of defecation, I jumped up from a squat position and ran, shouting frantically while pulling up my Levis, as relatives came to my rescue. I never had enough time to use the toilet paper! My father shot the snake with a shotgun; tore his ass to pieces! After running away from the snake, several roaming prairie dogs had no problem returning and sampling my treat. Those dogs slopped it up like Gravy Train. It was so gross. I eventually went back to the car and discovered an old used, partly-oiled rag in the trunk. After that incident, I discovered that using a Sears shopping catalog or a telephone directory worked just as well as toilet paper: the last resort being the leaves of trees.

Toilet paper: it's a necessity of life; it was the most requested commodity used by American troops in Operation Desert Storm. Sometimes it got so ridiculous, supplying inmates with toilet paper that deputies started putting entire rolls in the window slot of the station, so inmates could roll it out and get it for themselves. But this ingenious method also had its flaws, because inmates have nothing but spare time. Many of them spent hours rolling one entire roll onto another empty cardboard roll, while watching television, or while an opponent pondered the next gambit move in a chess game. Eventually, as the roll grew thinner, the inmate stuck his fingers up in the slot and pulled the remainder of the roll through, usually when the deputy wasn't looking. Most inmates had to feel like they were getting over on deputies, just as if they were still on the streets, committing crimes like shoplifting, larceny or burglary, and getting away with it. Thus the deputy was placed between a rock and a hard place: he or she had to supervise and possibly reprimand an inmate over some trite toilet paper issue. When supplies were overly abundant, inmates were sometimes given their own personal roll, which was expected to last them a week. This method didn't last very long either because, in most cases, inmates are wasteful.

Officers working the jail floors performed several imbecilic and critical functions. We acted the roles of mother, father, social worker, food handler, kitchen supervisor, locksmith, storekeeper, shoe distributor, psychiatrist, emergency medical personnel, janitor, economist, judge, artist, juror, financial advisor, baby sitter, recreational director, maintenance worker, postal inspector, counselor, legal adviser, secretary, duplication operator, publicist, clothes handler, computer operator, crisis manager, mover, medical adviser, dry cleaners, laundry handler, garbage handler, hotel manager, hooker, gigolo, bookkeeper, plumber, accountant, religious leader, waiter, waitress, banker . . . and sometimes even God!

But most of all, we played the role of the sheriff.

When supplies of toilet paper were below satisfactory levels, I always told inmates to share. Now, sharing is difficult for a lot of inmates because many are selfish. Hopefully, the inmate in need of toilet paper didn't have to use the toilet after lock down: "Hey Taylor, would you happen to have some incense? I've got to use the stool after lock down, and gotta have something to keep the smell down. Know-what-I-mean?" Many inmates expressed these sentiments, knowing that, at times, I carried incense to burn and lessen the effects of an imminent foul, odoriferous stench inside the inmate wards and jail floors. The gold packages of Gonesh incense, its scent identifiable only through even numbers of 2,4,6,8,10, and 12. Eight and ten are my favorite fragrances—were well accepted by inmates and officers. When certain floors in the jail weren't disinfected, many officers turned to burning incense: the fetor of the hallways and closets required it the most. But the worst area of the new jail to take a full whiff of air, was in Male Registry.

Many times inmates approached the station window and asked for incense to burn on the wards to reminisce about smoking weed: "What kind of incense is that? Man, that stuff smells so good! Hey dep, why don't you let me get one of 'dem' sticks, cause brother it sho' reminds me of those days when people was smoking that good red bud and Acapulco gold," intoned Malufo, a Black male Jamaican Rastafarian with long stringy braids. Malufo continued in wishful thinking: adding the complementary touches to complete a spoofed oasis. He spoke in a deep baritone voice, and inhaled through his nostrils Gonesh #8 incense smoke, slowly seeping from my station to the ward through the window slot.

Malufo was in jail for transporting a truck load of marijuana from Miami to Michigan. He was also facing possible life imprisonment as a major suspect in a triple homicide in New York, involving the notorious and ruthless Jamaican and Nigerian posse gangs, controllers of a major pipeline of heroin and cocaine in the Midwest region of the United States. Malufo was also a sorcerer: a cultist of voodoo and a manipulator of supernatural power over others through the assistance of witchcraft. Scared, none of the other inmates on the ward were particularly fond of him, and rightfully so. Jail officials decided it was best to keep him out of danger by putting him in a cell by himself. Sometimes when I worked overtime on Malufo's floor on midnights, I could overhear him praying and chanting rituals to curse all his enemies.

Officers also burned incense to kill odors coming from overflowing, uncollected ward garbage bags filled with food and milk spoilage. After inmates ate the jail's many, processed and contaminated foods, which lacked nutritional value, unbearable stenches of catabolic elimination in the closed confinement of a cell with a door, was torture with very little ventilation. Inmates using the toilet after lock down had better flush immediately or their cell mates would definitely have multiple disputes. Jail cells had loud disposal apparatuses that flushed thunderously, with a quick continuous swirling action, when activated. Malodors filled cells quickly, and diffused through the door gaps to overcome the ward. Bad smells had immediate effects on inmates and officers, sometimes inducing gagging, nausea, retching, and suffocation: "Come on dep, could you let us open the cell door, I can hardly breathe in here," begged an inmate, who literally was trying to survive a toxic, poisonous gas attack.

Institutionalized forms of processing and serving malnourished foods, was a main, created cause of bad elimination, bad health, and even deaths, and caused the life expectancies of incarcerated Black men to dwindle. Between the years of 1984 and 1994, the life span of Afrikan-American males fell below sixty-five years. Given this fact, why are Afrikan-American men paying social security, with their life expectancy being below 65 years? It's really lower than that, when you consider the deplorable living conditions many people of color are subjected to.

Remember to *never* trust statistical propaganda and, if any of the statistics prove worthy, listen to the newscast everyday because anyone with a righteous awareness-conscious mind can *see* that a total generation of upcoming Black youth has a life expectancy of less than sixty-five years. In the future, if this trend continues, Black men, will hardly ever work 20 to 30 years on a job, won't be able to support their families, retire and utilize their own life savings. It is becoming more unlikely that self-support is even possible to achieve with the high influx of illegal and legal immigrates, and the migration of dwindling job markets. In other words, Afrikan-Americans are working the majority of their life, only to leave accumulated money to Uncle Sam— who is Nobody's Uncle. Are Afrikan-American lives being thrown away through a government waste disposal system, just like toilet paper?

9

The Citrus Fiend

O N July 19, 1985, I RECEIVED MY SECOND WRITE-UP. It was not written by jail superiors, but by Raymond Gleason, the food service manager. He was a big, fat, burly and robust, white man, weighing over 300 pounds, who months later went on a liquid, vegetables, and fruit only, crash diet to lose some of it. Gleason reported me for getting some orange juice out of the refrigerator in the kitchen. Upon receiving the petty report, I immediately sent a response to Sergeant Phil Hopkins, a Black male, who I felt, at that juncture, was a confidant of mine.

My retort stated: "This reply is in reference to the Food Service Manager's write-up on Officer K. Taylor, for entering the kitchen to get some orange juice. *This writer* drinks orange juice, not milk, chocolate milk, and lots of pop. *This writer* asked several trustees to retrieve some orange juice for the deputies' consumption. The trustee replied, 'I can't cause I'll get written up.' Several trustees said the same thing.

This writer and officer then went and got some orange juice, which is customarily up front for officers' consumption. There were no food service personnel available to get it for me, so I retrieved it myself. It isn't fair to receive petty, unnecessary write-ups for some O.J. Especially when we are the backbone of this building's security and supposedly pay for our so-called cuisine. Orange juice isn't prepared: the food should be Mr. Gleason's main concern, not orange juice consumed by officers."

Many times, I, and other Black officers experienced very bad physical reactions to milk, and I never got accustomed to drinking a lot of dairy products. But this was what Gleason instructed kitchen trustees to serve all the afternoon shift officers.

Back in 1971, the milk producers' ad campaign, "Everybody Needs Milk," was just a lie. Cow milk is generally best for cows only. The enzyme necessary for digestion of milk is lactose, and over 80% of Black children have no lactose in their intestines. In 1993, an investigative report showed that many orange juice companies' claims of providing 100 percent natural orange juice, proved to be a farce. For years, one particular company in Michigan delivered millions of cases of adulterated orange juice, to inner city schools, and to jail institutions in Michigan and around the nation. This company's orange juice was made up primarily of chemicals, sugar, and only about 10% orange juice concentrate,

Undoubtedly, the morning and midnight shift officers always had orange juice, milk, pop, whatever choices of beverage, at their disposal. But the afternoon shift always seemed to have only choices of chocolate or homogenized milk, and more than often the milk was past the expiration date. Fed up with the continuous stupidity of this hastened, newfangled, reformed rule not letting officers on the afternoon shift have some orange juice, I retrieved some for us. To remedy the situation, Gleason started ordering more fruit, particularly boxes of fairly ripe oranges, pears, and apples. So I started bringing in a large plastic container, and filled several empty plastic bread bags with oranges to take to my jail floor. I started cutting up the oranges, and hand squeezed them into a half gallon of naturally fresh orange juice.

Also, it should be considered that when food service ordered lots of fruit, and it was not consumed readily, it would start a fruit fly epidemic, especially in the summer months. Fruit fly larvae fed on the ripening fermentation, and their rapid incubation swarmed the kitchen and dining areas. Indirectly, in retrospect, I was doing the kitchen a favor by making my own orange juice and getting rid of potential food spoilage. There were times when officers had to take time to make good agricultural choices because of bad fruit, hovered over by multitudes of *Drosophila melanogasters.*

The steel canisters that look like fire extinguishers, and held the syrup mixture for the pop machine, always needed proper readjustment by kitchen workers to get the right taste. Sometimes, even after they thought they had solved the problem, the pop tasted worse.

"What-in-the-hell is this? It taste like cream soda," said officers choosing selections of Pepsi or Coke, as other officers, who already knew the results, agreed. The Vernors didn't have that same gingery, bubbling, sparkling taste Detroiters were used to: it tasted like sweet molasses. Vernors is a tradition to many citizens around Detroit, so I knew something was wrong; growing up, I drank Pepsi and Vernors the most.

It was a shame jail trustees could drink all the orange juice they wanted, while officers were subjected to the unnecessary trivialities of propaganda, just to get a carton of orange juice. To stop the flow of officers getting orange juice, Commander McCarey hashed up an order to restrict officers from retrieving it from the kitchen. It stated: "*All officers are to stay from behind the food service counter and out of the kitchen area. Further violation of this rule will result in disciplinary action.*"

After about two weeks of adherence, officers ignored McCarey's rule, as the novelty wore off, and sergeants, corporals, lieutenants, and officers alike, once again went into the kitchen, straight to the fridge, and helped themselves to hundreds of cartons of O.J.

10

Columbian Coffee,
Mounting Groans

HERE WERE TIMES WHEN OFFICERS WERE harassed for simply bringing a cup of coffee onto the jail floors. I guess superiors felt that caffeine would agitate officers, get them high or jittery. Officers had an option to drink decaffeinated coffee, since a big deal was made out of coffee more than any other beverage by Command Officers. Why such a big commotion over coffee? An invigorating cup of steaming-hot coffee in the morning is considered a worldwide tradition. Some officers got smart, and started bringing in tea bags, hot chocolate, and instant coffee granules. These beverages *also* contain caffeine, but command officials did not bother officers about these drinks. Hot water was retrieved either from the janitor's closet or rest room sink on the jail floors. The sink water in the rest room was the preferred choice, because officers usually fought off gangs of roaches in the unsanitary, housekeeping closets.

Inmates would trade several of their goodies for just one cup of hot coffee, or a teaspoon of coffee granules. The inmates used empty pint milk cartons and plastic juice containers as a cup or mug. To sound intellectual around the jail about certain brands, I jokingly used advertising terms like "mountain grown" and "gourmet supreme," but these terms meant nothing. Ground beans of coffee have a more wholesome taste than instant granules any day. Like the commercials in which diners at "America's finest restaurants" are given instant coffee, only two of 18 coffee drinkers actually prefer the instant, according to Consumer Report.

Even when officers drank juice or pop on the jail floors, strict command officers still had something irrelevant to say about it. Command officers who cautioned other officers about having coffee on the jail floors were not concerned about health, but rather concerned about petty, insignificant power issues. Before getting on the elevators for duty, throngs of officers rushed to get snacks from the cafeteria to take to their floors.

Officers knew that one particular superior would most likely appear and preach to them like they were children. His name was Sergeant Frank Dawdy, a stringent autocrat and a Black man, who walked upon officers getting coffee or snacks from the vending machines in the cafeteria. "Officer, you know you aren't supposed to come in here before you go up to the floors. You can only come down here on your break or for lunch!" A real, antagonistic jerk, Sergeant Dawdy seemed to always harass Black male officers about having a cup of coffee.

When I worked the morning shift, a cup of coffee was sometimes necessary to perk up, and it was very helpful in stabilizing one's equilibrium waking up early in the morning. Nearly every officer who drank coffee tried to get some before going up to the *Jungle*, the jail floors. Some officers brought in a cup of coffee from the streets, and sat it on a table during Roll Call. Others hid theirs so command officers like Dawdy wouldn't be aware that they were attempting to carry it onto the floors. A spot frequented for breakfast and coffee by the Detroit Police and Wayne County Sheriff's Department was a Middle Eastern Coney Island restaurant named Zorba, located directly across the street from 1300 Beaubien, main headquarters of the Detroit Police Department.

Sergeant Dawdy was the biggest momus in the jail, and he remained a bothersome nuisance throughout my tenure. He was a stickler, and redundant about it, for petty issues—coffee was not an issue on other shifts. The real farce is that after getting harassed daily over a cup of coffee, working officers had to witness command officers brew pots of coffee for themselves day after day and year after year in their offices. Some of the loudest arguments, and apparently the greatest issues among command officers were about, "Who was going to make the next pot?"

Throughout the new jail there were several coffee makers. Two were in Male Registry, usually manned by loyal, hyperactive, wide-eyed white males. Another coffee maker was in the sergeants' office at the front lobby desk; one was in inmate clothing; two were in R.D.C., and the rest of the coffee makers were in other command offices. There was even a coffee pot in the confines of Master Control, which was also equipped with a small, compact refrigerator stocked with milk and cream, stirrers, plastics spoons, sugar, napkins, and Styrofoam cups taken from the kitchen. Each coffee location was independently financed. Officers could pay either two bucks a week for unlimited excess, or 25 cents a cup. Many officers never paid for their cup, or instead of a quarter slipped pennies or nickels through the plastic slit atop a coffee can converted into a cash register. Many officers were petty thieves by nature.

Quite frequently, white male command officers would assign only white male officers and maybe a token, *communist* Black on particular floors. There was a coffee maker locked in a locker on the tenth floor, which was always occupied by white males, and several white male commanders knew of its whereabouts. While making rounds some commanders regularly went to the tenth floor to get a cup of coffee when other coffee makers in the jail were empty or short on supplies.

The command structure was *pettiness personified* jail officials creating just havoc, chaos, and stress, among their constituents and subordinates. Shift commanders and jail officials wasted and destroyed many valuable minds, precious energy, and time as they concerned themselves with petty things, like a cup of coffee, that masked underlying and persistent, endorsed harassment. The Department never promoted harmony; theirs was always a *dog-eat-dog* mentality. What the *Department* and its superiors needed to do was to allow others and themselves to just chill, read a newspaper, eat some glazed donuts, and have a steaming hot cup of coffee.

Suicidal Tendencies:
Is Life Always Worth Living?

UICIDAL PREVENTION HAS ALWAYS BEEN A MAIN objective of many correctional institutions across America and
the world. Why? Because the family of a suicidal inmate
will surely file a lawsuit for the Department's negligence in
care. For this reason alone many officers are reluctant to work with
suicidal or sexually assaultive inmates. There are many intangibles,
and loopholes in the law whereby an officer can be put in a *"trick
bag"* and held in contempt. A poorly trained officer is always in
danger of being thrust between a rock and a hard place.

Though I never actually witnessed a suicide in progress, or the
results of one, many were attempted and committed in the county jail
without the public being informed. There is a *hush-hush* policy because of the ramifications from negative publicity, which would further cripple departmental morale and respectability.

There isn't much an officer or a prison can do for an inmate who
has lost all hope and tragically decides to end it all. Basically, the
only remedies to stop a suicidal person from hurting him or herself is
to: Give constant monitored surveillance; use reassuring quotes; make
sure there are no means for self-harm; listen attentively to all situations and feelings without giving advice or suggesting simple solutions; be honest! If an inmate's words or actions become frightening, express that concern. Being honest with a person is more helpful
than cheerfully discounting the importance of his or her emotions.
Share feelings of sadness, hurt or hopelessness, if you can, so the

individual doesn't feel alone. Get help. Do *not* maintain secrecy. Don't risk anyone else's life; go for help wherever you can find it.

Suicide is sometimes linked to the use of chemical substances. Nearly one-half of all suicidal youths were involved in drugs or alcohol shortly before their deaths. In 1990, suicide was the third leading cause of teen death. For every teen suicide, there are fifty or more unsuccessful attempts. Teens with suicidal tendencies use alcohol or drugs to escape their problems, or to dull emotional pain. In 1990, a federal survey of 11,631 high school students found that 27 percent *"thought seriously"* about killing themselves, and one in twelve said they had actually tried. The U.S. Centers for Disease Control survey also found that two percent said that they had sustained injuries serious enough to require medical attention after suicide attempts. Ninth through twelfth grade students were questioned in every state and United States Possession. Sixteen percent said they had made *"a specific plan,"* and eight percent said they had attempted suicide at least once.

The annual suicide rate for that age group (fifteen to eighteen year-olds) was 11 per 100,000, according to CDC statistics. The CDC found that thoughts of suicide, and actual attempts, were significantly more common for girls than for boys. Thirty-four percent of female students said they had seriously considered suicide compared with twenty-one percent of males. And while 10 percent of girls *said* they had attempted suicide, only 6 percent of boys admitted to an attempt. The margin of error for the entire sample was less than 1 percentage point

In 1991, Hispanic students consistently reported the highest rate of suicidal thoughts and attempts (30 percent and 12 percent, respectively). Whites reported 28 percent and 8 percent, followed by Blacks at 20 percent and 7 percent. One reason proposed for the marginal differences between Blacks and whites, is that whites seek and receive treatment for emotional problems sooner and more frequently than Blacks do, and their suicides, either attempted or completed successfully, are better reported. Here are some danger signals for youth at risk in or out of corrections:

- Suicide threats
- Statements revealing a desire to die

- Previous suicide attempts
- Sudden changes in behavior
- Depression, crying, sleeplessness, loss of appetite, hopelessness
- Final arrangements, such as giving away personal possessions
- Marked decrease in school performance
- An increase in drug or alcohol use
- Lack of communication
- Isolation
- Resentment toward authority
- School absenteeism without permission
- Running away from home

Since 1976, there are over 31,000 people who commit suicide annually. Between 1980 and 1992, the number of suicides among America children ages ten to fourteen increased 120 percent. According to a 1992 report from the Centers for Disease Control, 1.7 children per 100,000 in that age group killed themselves. Family problems, exposure to violence, substance abuse and severe stress in school play vital roles in the significant rise, and that the rise in completed suicides means that "*more lethal means*" are being used. Fifty-seven percent of younger children and sixty-eight percent of older teens used a gun to kill themselves in 1992, up from fifty-six and sixty-three percent, respectively in 1980. Hanging was the next most common method.

The problem of teenage suicide is worse in America's urban Public School System, where Black kids are seldom sent for counseling until their problems are out of hand. In marked contrast, white kids in suburban school systems are routinely sent for minor difficulties. Each year, according to authorities, a troubling number of children kill themselves in juvenile custody. The extent of the problem, however, is under-reported because of inadequate national reporting requirements and the stigma and legal liability that suicides entail.

The official death count is approximately ten annually; some experts say the true number may be many times that: up to 100. One youth was so desperate he swallowed a broken light bulb, according to an investigator who worked on a study released in the fall of 1994 by the Justice Department's Office of Juvenile Justice and Delinquency Prevention. It also noted that 63 percent of those in juvenile facilities are Afrikan-American or Hispanic. The national study found that only one-fourth of confined juveniles are in facilities that meet four basic suicide prevention guidelines. Crowding, insufficient training, and lapses in screening and monitoring of kids in custody allow for more than 17,000 acts of self-destructive behavior annually. Suicides in custody come at a time of growing public frustration about youth crime; some say this fuels a creeping indifference about the handling of delinquents.

I believe this problem persists because there is no love, no compassion. No one cares until it is their own kid in trouble. There are also many detention conditions that can aggravate suicidal tendencies: overcrowding, untrained staff, dirt, roaches, and rats. These conditions combined with public apathy, the desire for a quick fix, and racial disharmony, insure that jailed youths will continue to kill themselves at a troubling rate. Given the statistics of teenage suicide, building more jails has little reason and purpose. Firstly, building jails is ten times more costly than educating and rehabilitating young people.

Although encouraging mediations with an individual contemplating suicide doesn't always help, it couldn't hurt. Countless times in the jail, inmates in real doldrums talked to me for support in fighting off their depression. I tried my best to deflect any thought of even discussing suicide. My general method was to encourage troubled inmates to envision when times were better.

There are three classifications of suicidal inmates: non-suicidal, potentially suicidal, and suicidal acute. The last two are the most critical, and the inmate(s) must be watched carefully. A potentially suicidal inmate tends to be more depressed, usually has made previous attempts, and constantly talks of suicide. A potentially suicidal-acute inmate is reaching a crisis standpoint rapidly, and has made recent attempts. For instance, if an inmate says he wants to kill himself instead of being in jail, he should be considered potentially suicidal. Inmates with multiple social problems, such as convictions and sentences for rape or murder, may be suicidal. Problems like divorce, family health, intimate relationships, the death of someone close, and financial problems may result in suicidal tendencies.

I always looked for inmates who constantly hollered obsceni-ties, or was having hallucinations: illusions, abnormal behavior, or said they heard voices. Many suicidal inmates will start giving away their personal possessions—not just the ones they own in jail but outside as well. The doctor, officer, or social worker, should watch this carefully, because giving away possessions is a critical and cri-sis standpoint. Close attention should also be paid to eating habits, sleeping habits (too much or too little sleep), and interaction with other inmates. More than anything else, an *attempted* suicide is a cry for help, a last-ditch effort to reach out to humanity rather than reject it.

Because of the volatile mixture of job stress, a troubled relation-ship, and the inability to be in control, police officers are about twice as likely to kill themselves as those in other occupations, reported the National Association of Police Organizations in Washington, D.C. About 300 officers killed themselves in 1994.

After a bad day at work, many police officers let off their steam at home—which in many cases results in domestic abuse, and marital discord. With the mentality of building more prisons and the lack of employment opportunities, and the surety and prospects of a con-tinuing crime and drug problem, this trend will only get worse.

In the past, suicide prevention efforts began when inmates were first brought into the old jail. They were screened and if, through a wide variety of indicators, found to be suicide-prone, were housed in a special section called *Three Annex*. Back in 1970, four suicides and forty-seven attempted suicides took place in the old jail. In 1971, forty-one inmates attempted suicide; two succeeded. The next year jail administrators couldn't prove to the state or the public that sui-cide prevention was really working. No such special attention was given to women prisoners because they comprised only a small frac-tion of the jail's inmate population, and were in general more closely supervised.

In addition to receiving closer supervision than prisoners of any other section in the old jail, inmates in Three Annex also received closer scrutiny from the medical staff. Most important for the poten-tially suicidal, the inmates received help from each other. Three Annex primarily housed rapists and those designated mildly depressed.

The majority of suicides in the jail are by hanging. When an inmate hangs himself, he is usually close enough to the floor that all he has to do to save himself is put his feet on the ground. Because of that, jail administrators drew a line between successful suicides and suicide attempts. It was not uncommon for prisoners to cut their wrists or swallow razor blades just so they could leave the jail and go to the hospital. Inmates believed they had a better chance of escape there, and some considered the hospital a better environment than the jail.

So why suicide for some inmates? Studies have shown that prisoners are extremely suicide-prone during their first days in prison, when they are most pessimistic about their trial outcome and regaining their freedom. Inmate Cyrus Flint, a gray haired, middle-aged Black male, a mainstay who had gone through the revolving door of the jail system for twenty-three years said, "Sometimes it builds up, I start thinking about my family, I can't eat what I want to eat, and no one comes to see me. I get no mail and often no hope of getting off lightly for what I've done. It's bad enough I get no sex... so, suicide can look pretty good."

In the late 1960s and throughout the 70s, prisoner cooperation was essential to suicide prevention; not enough guards were available to provide the constant supervision that a suicidal inmate needed. Most suicide prevention came from cell mates. Two suicides in 1971 were not in Three Annex, and could have been prevented by a more efficient screening process. Inmates in the old jail were usually brought in with no record of their medical or psychiatric histories. Manpower has always been a problem and, as a result, inmates received minimal attention from the deputy and medical worker, who continued to screen while backlogged with incoming prisoners. Guards and social workers should always look for suicidal indicators. These might be a casual comment; information gained by censoring the prisoner's mail; or an unexpected call from a family member.

On July 29, 1972, a three-judge Wayne County Court panel ordered county officials to hire an additional eighty guards, attendants and paramedics to prevent general assaults, murders, suicides and homosexual attacks in the old jail. The order came in a fifty-one page decision about the county's request for a new trial regarding the 1971 lawsuit filed by inmates over the deplorable conditions at the old jail. The county's request for a new trial was denied.

In the early 1970s of Sheriff Barrett's era, no one on the jail's staff considered suicide prevention efforts as particularly innovative—just practical and extremely functional within the severe limitations of the corrections setting. Most people connected with medical supervision preferred to see a recreation program implemented. Back then prisoners had no exercise yard, and only participated in passive types of recreation like chess and checkers, exercising only on their cell block.

A lot of pressure can build up when there's nothing to do but sit in a cell all day and night, thinking without positive and creative outlets for that thought. Long-term psychiatric imprisonment, or even long periods in the general inmate population, often results in loss of a sense of control and responsibility for one's daily activities. Contradictory as it sounds, the problems of the suicidal inmate are less because the jail's medical staff and officers are uncaring or untrained, but more *because* of this suicidal inmate's responsibility for daily activities on the ward; they need closer supervision than they get. After discharge, however, former psychiatric inmates gain by being able to live and work together in a community setting that differs from more typical programs for ex-inmates: family care homes, boarding homes, group homes or halfway houses, established to operate under the supervision of paid staff.

In these more independent ex-inmate communities, group members themselves, rather than staff, are responsible for maintaining the integrity and proper functioning of the organization. Each group develops its own business, usually a service like lawn care or janitorial work. This business is owned and operated by the group members. Groups receive consultation and guidance from a home coordinator who is available forty hours a week. Coordinators serve under contract with a mental health agency, and are expected to phase out their involvement with the group as the group's decision-making skills, cohesiveness, and business aptitude develop.

The most necessary ingredient community survival of these independent ex-inmate groups is peer social support: sometimes the regulated norms of reference groups governing their behavior aren't structured to the best available scientific and psychiatric levels. Still, these types of programs create conditions for members to practice mutual respect and responsibility for their own welfare; similar to prison work release programs. The by-products of such a program are dramatic, not only in a greater sense of personal worth, but also in the reduced use of psychiatric hospitals and other similar facilities. In addition to the program's ability to restore human dignity and feelings of worth to persons with serious mental illness, it also saves taxpayers millions each year.

To break the monotony for myself as well as for the inmates, I created educational, thought-provoking games, and tests using addition, multiplication, division, and subtraction. Other games tested sports knowledge and Afrikan-American or European-American history for inmates who wanted to participate. Many inmates liked spelling tests, and the vocabulary test matching words with their proper meanings.

The difficult job of evaluating inmates was often put on the shoulders of incompetent or untrained officers thrust into the role of psychiatrist and social worker. Adding to this problem, many white officers just weren't accustomed to the cultural behavior and thinking of Black men, and lacked sympathy for our struggles. Given their lack of empathy, how could whites accurately or effectively interpret a Black man's actions or conduct? *They can't!*

On June 11, 1972, inmate Harold Cross died from a beating after a homosexual rape. A three-judge panel said his death could have been prevented had county commissioners acted promptly in complying with previous court orders to hire more jail personnel. Cross' death was the end result of the commissioners' defiant attitude toward court orders. To comply with the three-judge decision, some attendants were required to have psychiatric and paramedical training to learn to help disturbed patients already incarcerated, and to screen others for treatment by the jail's regular medical staff. The ruling by the court adopted a plan, submitted by the sheriff's department, to provide inmates with reasonable protection from assault and prevent suicides by tighter, monitored surveillance.

Whites continually experiment on Blacks through propaganda, much of it based on having successfully eliminated the positive contributions of Afrikan-Americans from American history. Having kept Blacks from a quality education and good jobs, whites have then hypocritically justified their own baseless and skewed scientific thesis of white superiority: See, they say, how poorly Blacks perform. Trying to figure out what makes Blacks tick has always been for the white man an intellectual exercise rather than a human goal. Many potentially suicidal Black inmates were therefore judged by this double standard, just as some officers of the white minions judged targeted, or minority officers as if they were a separate species, and not as they themselves would want to be judged. Some superiors regularly and automatically believed unstable-minded, white officers when they targeted and accused Black fellow-officers.

Inmate cursing, especially the hollering of obscenities, was a common, everyday occurrence in the jail. For these reasons I never judged inmates as suicidal for screaming and cursing loudly. If that were the case, a large majority of officers would also be considered crazy and suicidal. Inmates yelled at deputies, nurses and social workers about meal selections, the phones being cut off for disciplinary reasons, mail delays, medication, the type of music being played, lighting— just about everything imaginable.

Talk about suicidal—Saul Eastwood was one particular inmate who stood out more than the others. Very muscular, he was a real, in-the-flesh "Mandingo" and black as tar. Many officers had already labeled this monomaniac as psychotically insane and dangerously suicidal. After cursing at command officers, he would dip into the toilet and fill milk cartons with his own shit and urine, later throwing it at other inmates on the ward. He would take tubes of his shit and smear or draw lewd graphics with it on the cell walls. This was the grossest action I had ever seen in my life.

Because of this health hazard, Eastwood was given an entire ward all to himself. He was housed on the fourth floor of the new jail, which in 1985 was used as a psychiatric floor, as was the 7th floor Annex in the old jail. Locked in a bar cell, Eastwood walked around buck-naked, never putting on clothes, and would grab and shake his dick at officers and nurses alike. I felt lucky to never work that floor, and smell that obnoxious odor all day.

When there was nothing else to do, or even on lunch break,

officers came down to 4-Southeast just to see this spectacle of a man. "I am God," Eastwood sometimes told officers. When I heard that, I became curious and made light conversation with Eastwood, curious to know when was he going to end world suffering, wars, and prejudice. Eastwood seriously believed he had experienced a *"brush with the unknown."* One day, after several displays of wild exuberance, Eastwood stared intently at me with a very thoughtful expression. "Officer Taylor, did you know that the injustices of this world will not end until everyone believes in me. I am the saviour of all humans. Whether you are Black, white, Jewish, Arab, Mexican, Indian, Russian, or whatever, this world will continue to suffer until I decide it's getting better between humans."

"What-in-the-hell?" That was the general reaction, as officers looked at each other in disbelief. But Eastwood spoke intelligently when someone took time out to talk about things he could relate to. He then glared at the ceiling as if in some hypnotic trance, and started to recite biblical parables. The other officers appeared frightened, but I was not yet alarmed. "Look," I asked, "If you *are* God, why did you create diseases like AIDS?" "First of all," Eastwood answered, "No man on this earth will be free from wars and diseases until all men are respected as one, and all believe in me. My resurrection is coming soon."

In calmer tones, Eastwood continued to voice his solutions to worldly problems: "AIDS was created for all those freaks out there in the streets, who continue in mass perversion and lack sexual morals." Suddenly it actually sounded like Eastwood made a lot of sense, but some officers laughed at him, which made Eastwood ferociously angry. He vowed several times to "one day get those who disrespected him," and make them regret it. In a different environment, and with some social skills and psychological help, Eastwood could have been a scholar: his articulation was more precise and clearer than many officers working in the jail. If he had only been less antisocial, he might have been judged differently. About ten minutes after Eastwood would finish an intelligent conversation, however, he'd grab his genitalia and curse out the officers again.

Although Eastwood spoke intellectually with the intent to avow ethical societal behavior, he was a sight to behold: a psychotic, troubled individual, who needed constant surveillance. Eventually, Eastwood had to be removed because he alone took the space of twelve inmates. The sergeant supervising his removal summoned six hefty officers, including myself, to escort him from the ward. Before entering the ward, we all put on latex gloves and wore surgical masks. Eastwood was neutralized long enough for the nurse to inject sedatives, after we strapped him into a strait jacket. Totally uncontrollable, Eastwood seemed to gain strength and grow stronger while struggling with six officers forcibly trying to remove him. We actually began to believe that Eastwood was guided by some inner spiritual force. Whenever officers wanted some entertainment, all we had to do was go to 4-Southeast to see Eastwood; we were never disappointed.

Stone was another inmate who was very strong and bordered on the psychotic. He didn't have an ounce of body fat on his chiseled, 5-foot-4-inch frame, and weighed in at about 160 pounds. One day he swore at Sergeant Frank Dawdy about "not getting information concerning a transfer and out date" because Dawdy hadn't gotten back to him in several days. "Why don't you come in here and move me yourself, you big sissy-ass, punk motherfucker," Stone yelled to Dawdy, a mammoth Black man, about 6-foot-5-inches tall, and who outweighed Stone by about 100 pounds. Dawdy looked scared, and called up eight officers to help in Stone's removal to the hole.

I also happened to be one of those eight who rushed Stone, rendering him incapable of doing any harm to himself or others. Leather shackles and a strait jacket restrained Stone, who was really hyped-up, his adrenalin pumped with an accelerated heartbeat. Before he was removed, Stone realized he could no longer fight us, and he started banging his head repeatedly, up against the cell wall. Once again officers were forced to go back inside to stop him before he split his head wide open. But it didn't seem to hurt him at all. Stone was fire and energy put together. Exhausted, he eventually calmed down, the fixity in his long stares indicating he would like to kill us all.

"It took eight of y'all deps to control that one man... y'all ain't about shit," yelled Fish, a Black male inmate on the ward for multiple drug charges and years of failing to pay child support. "Why don't you just shut the hell up, before you get some of this too," said

Officer Seth Nadler, one of the more cowardly white males, who *never* made key rounds on the wards unless all the inmates were locked down. Nadler only got "bad" with an inmate in the company of other officers. But, still, Fish decided to shut up.

On the seventh floor in the old jail, inmates on the psychiatric ward wore fire retardant robes of indestructible synthetic material to prevent suicides by fire. The garments were also extremely difficult to tear or shred, making attempts at hanging or strangulation practically impossible. There seemed to be many inmates suffering from acute suicidal symptoms in the old jail. On ward 614 were the aggressive sexual predators who also stole from other inmates. Customarily, all inmates in all jails steal from one another the same way they did in the streets.

Each floor had inmates classified as to weight, height, race, and age. Inmates classified as suicidal preferred the confines of the new jail, because they could get away from the constant sexual and physical abuse that seemed to occur more often in the old jail. There was better surveillance of inmates in the new jail because of structural and strategical differences. When choosing which jail you wanted to work in, the freedom of the old jail appeared advantageous. An officer didn't have to supervise constantly or look at inmates through a station window all day. Also, superiors had to be admitted on the wards and into other sections of the old jail by officers on duty, who could thus be warned of their arrival. In both the new and old jails, some shift command officers were observed sneaking up on officers in order to catch them napping. Some actually crawled around corners of the floors to avoid detection.

Suicidal inmates aren't afforded many socially stimulating activities. As a result of that boredom, they constantly play tricks on officers to amuse themselves. Rehabilitating suicidal inmates is a insurmountable task, which takes a lot of courage and patience. It also requires constant care and attention. It's hard enough trying to transform the lives of inmates with common sense and education, making them realize their full potential, let alone one whose mentally ill and has given up on life. In the spring of 1991, the government of the State of Michigan was fined a *paltry* $10,000 a day by the federal government, for failing to supply adequate psychiatric services to inmates.

Eighty percent of Black male prisoners are habitual, recidivistic criminals, and many appear to be in progressive stages of psychosis. Because of this, Black neighborhoods are endangered, and face dire economic and social problems once psychologically impaired inmates, unprepared for society, are paroled or have served their time. This systemic condition in corrections exists because there is minimal, if any, progressive rehabilitation (trades, job training) in the *institutional incarceration* setting.

Typically and historically jails tend to breed an even more contemptuous scourge: recidivistic criminals released back out into the world without jobs, who are also untreated mental health risks. You can rest assured that there will be an increase in inmates developing psychiatric problems in prison, as "*The System*" continually neglects their self-esteem and health. The diseases of the 1990s and beyond, will not only be AIDS, cancer, diabetes, heart attacks, and the like, but also mental illness. Things usually get worse before getting better, when it pertains to the psychiatric mentality of suicidal individuals incarcerated for long periods of time.

Black men are in a system that not only doesn't care, but is actively racially biased against them. They live without hope, with little prospect of a viable livelihood in inner city neighborhoods or the rural South, where a Confederate mentality still lives. Building more jails is the fastest growing industry in America, and inmates' labor, which is mostly Black, is used by white industries that thrive on paying cheap Southern Confederacy slave wages that's reminiscent of the reconstruction era.

The late Dr. Bobby E. Wright, a renowned clinical psychologist, understood the minds of enslaved people. He discussed suicide in his book, *The Psychopathic Racial Personality and other Essays.* I quote: "In the not too distant past, suicide in the Black community was virtually nonexistent. In fact, in considering all possibilities of life and death, suicide for Blacks was not an option. Further, all the traditional reasons that have been projected as enhancing the suicide dynamic did not manifest themselves in the Black community.

On the contrary, the conditions that produced the feelings of helplessness, hopelessness, powerlessness, etc., which create havoc for European people, seemed to have strengthened the resolve of

Blacks who considered them as being part of our destiny.

It should be very clear that the problem of so-called Black suicide cannot be resolved at this time. To believe otherwise presupposes a sense of direction and level of power that does not exist in the Black community. Black suicide is a political dynamic. For political reasons, Blacks are being programmed for self-destruction and 'Black suicide' is one of the results. Lynching by any other name is still lynching. The method that has been developed and is now being implemented cannot be found in any of the literature or in any research data, but it is one of the greatest discoveries of psychology.

The author classified this process as 'mentacide,' (Wright, 1976) which is defined as the deliberate and systematic destruction of a group's minds with the ultimate objective being the extirpation of the group. The acceptance of Blacks and the concept of 'free will' absolves whites of any responsibility for their victims' condition. In fact, whites have developed an effective defense mechanism, namely, 'the guilt of the victim.' It is so effective that their victims accept their plight as being 'God's will.'

It should be noted that 'mentacide' is a worldwide phenomena which is being implemented against the entire Black race. Therefore, Blacks in Afrika will begin to manifest the behavior of Blacks in the United States. It's also clear that there is a direct correlation between the level of white involvement and control of Black institutions and Black self-destruction.

It should be clear that there cannot be an analysis of 'Black suicide' using traditional white techniques because to do so would assume an inherent equality between Blacks and whites. It ignores the prevention of opportunity, options, and control by Blacks over their own destiny.

To remove any element of doubt, I am proposing that what is termed Black suicide is really deliberate race murder which is being committed by whites in the United States. Whites in the United States have achieved their 'specified environment,' therefore, they must be held accountable for the behavior of its inhabitants.

There is little disagreement among behavioral scientists who attest to the fact that situations can be contrived in a manner which will influence people to engage in self-destructive behavior. Further, once it is determined that such a condition caused the behavior, the focus of attention shifts from the victim to the perpetrator, except where Blacks are involved. Political brainwashing is a violation of the Geneva Convention rules governing the treatment of prisoners of war; and there is little doubt that a psychotherapist would be charged with a criminal act if it were determined that a patient, even one who had consented, had been encouraged to commit a self-destructive act which led to injury and death.

Yet, the treatment of Blacks in the United States is unparalleled in history, and we are subjected to far more serious psychological attacks than those permitted with prisoners of war. To deliberately prevent a people from developing life-sustaining options and to promote conditions of self-destruction is an act of genocide. Therefore, Black suicide is a method of genocide which is being promoted and controlled worldwide by the white race. Paradoxically, there is no such phenomena as 'Black suicide' when suicide is defined as the willful and deliberate act of taking one's own life."

One of the biggest political graft scandals in Detroit and Wayne County history began with a suicide. One night in August 1939, Janet McDonald, 33, and her 11-year-old daughter, Pearl, sat in their car in a closed garage and turned on the engine. When police found the bodies, they also found packets of letters and notes addressed to Detroit's daily newspapers, the head of the FBI office in Detroit, the Detroit police commissioner and the governor of Michigan. McDonald, a typist for an illegal numbers house, said in the letters that the head of the police racket squad took bribes to leave the business alone. She took her life, she said in the letter, because of her unrequited love for a racketeer who was the payoff man to the cops.

The story dominated the newspaper locally for months and led to the appointment of a one-man grand juror for Wayne County and a special prosecutor to look into the charges. By the time it was over, convictions and prison terms were given to the mayor of Detroit, the Wayne County prosecutor, the Wayne County sheriff and 14 ranking Detroit police officers. Judge Homer Ferguson, the one-man grand juror, was later elected to the U.S. Senate.

Incidents of suicide continued despite continuous legal action against county jail conditions. On August 4, 1972, the suicide of inmate Arnold Fraser, in the old jail, might have been prevented if the jail was properly informed of his mentally ill status. Fraser, crawled up a jail cell bunk and used his own belt to strangle himself to death. Once Wayne County sheriff deputies had accepted custody of Fraser from the Detroit Police Department, they could only use the excuse that, "They had no way of knowing that he had been in institutions for the criminally insane for 11 years."

Why did Fraser have a belt in the first place? That alone is baffling. This is a clear violation of jail rules today, but in the early 1970s inmates often carried their clothing to their cells. At that time the old jail lacked the facilities to store inmates' clothing. Fraser had confessed in 1961 to brutally beating and killing a Detroit woman, but was judged incompetent to stand trial on grounds of insanity. He was committed to Ionia State Hospital and later transferred to Ypsilanti State Hospital.

He was released from Ypsilanti State Hospital on August 1, 1972 because the medical director judged him competent to stand trial. Fraser was turned over to the Detroit Police Department, which delivered him to the Wayne County jail. "The only document which accompanied Fraser when he arrived at the old jail, was a copy of the 1961 murder warrant. There was nothing to show he had been previously institutionalized," jail administrator, Frank Wilkerson said.

The lackluster attitude of county commissioners toward providing funding for a diagnostic admitting section for screening new inmates, and for storage space for inmates' clothing, contributed to Fraser's death. Providing storage and psychiatric screening would have afforded social workers an opportunity to research a new prisoner's present condition and past history, and corrections officers to insure that inmates only wore jail clothing.

Fraser's death was allowed through institutional blunder, but there are now methods of a respectable, less painful death, provided through a sedative machine facilitated by Dr. Jack Kevorkian in Michigan. His machine and the continuing litigation surrounding it, have been chronicled in newspapers around the nation, and are the targets of many comedy routines. Kevorkian provides a service to people who want to end their lives.

Personally, I favor Kevorkian's assisted-suicide services, although

his idea has continually been met with stiff resistance for state legislative approval. I believe, if a person is terminally ill but has some
mental faculties, knows what they face, and want to do away with
their life, then he or she should be permitted to do so in any way
form or fashion comfortable for them. If a person isn't harming others, it's his or her life, whether death is tragically painful or graceful.
Suicide like abortion is an issue where there are important concessions to consider.

If the patient is not of a clear mind, there should be counseling
available for both patient and family, including intensive and extensive ethical review by the appropriate agencies. A decision could
then be made by a specially appointed panel. However, if a person is
mentally stable, the decision should be theirs alone. Support groups
are great motivators to give the sufferer additional, needed information before a final decision is made on a pending death by state
lobbyist and regulators.

While Kevorkian was serving time in an Oakland County jail, on
a hunger strike, Detroit Recorder's Court Judge Bob Grossman, the
same judge who decided whether the position of "*Jail Dictator*" would
be Sheriff Carmeno or Wayne County Executive Sterling, ruled that,
"Assisted-suicide is a constitutional right for an individual to do
what they want with their bodies."

The assisted-suicide issue won't go away. It will be in debate for
many years to come. Everyone wants to be healthy, energetic, and
have the mental capacity to survive the troubles and evils of this
world, but for most of us the answer isn't to commit suicide. Give full
attention to increasing your spiritual energy: pray, meditate, eat right,
exercise an hour a day (if you can), believe in your own capabilities.

Get involved with a church or community group; go back to school
and learn something new, innovative, and unique for your self-confidence. Seek a skill or trade that will set you apart from the rest of the
pack; stop hanging around deadbeats who lack faith and fortitude.
Read books; increase your awareness. Come on! You have the ability; stop procrastinating! Remember, constantly remind yourself, *never
give up*; *always* make living a priority. You'll *never* know what you
can accomplish in God's eyes, if you don't try, but especially, if you
stop living, right?

12

Music Theory:
Music Calms the Savage Beast

FTER THE VEHEMENT COMPLAINTS OF SEVERAL female officers to departmental heads over the *no bags on the jail floor* rule, it again became permissible for female officers to carry their purses and tote bags up to the jail floors. Jail rules forbade wearing lipstick, makeup, and jewelry while on duty. When their complaints were heard and upheld, many female officers spent long periods of time in front of rest room and station mirrors. Seeing makeup, and smelling sensuous, sweet perfume on a *somewhat* attractive female officer excited and sexually aroused male inmates, and even some of the female ones too!

The no bags on the jail floor rule was strictly directed and selectively enforced against all male officers. At one particular juncture, officers were permitted to carry radios on the jail floors, but because of some who brought in big stereo Boomboxes with detachable speakers, inmates, and even coworkers complained. Many officers enjoyed the convenience of having their own music.

Bringing in Boomboxes wasn't necessary because each guard station was equipped with an intercom system that could be hooked-up to a radio-cassette or CD player, and an audio cord to get good music with the same results. I was first shown the advantages of this by Officer Seth Nadler, a goofy white male prima donna, who later in my tenure at the jail proved to be no friend. Many speaker cones on the jail floors were busted, causing the sound to be trapped and distorted in the deafening cemented corridors and hallways.

In the new jail, construction materials mainly consisting of metals, concrete and glass, and the acoustics proved excellent, with good equipment set at the proper volume level. To quickly shut off his music, Officer Harry Koon, a middle-aged white male, used a device called the *Clapper*. This gadget turns anything electrical on and off by simply clapping. When a trivial superior was making rounds, Koon just clapped to turn the radio off.

Officer Koon, however, (who made the mistake of being a bigot), couldn't keep from revealing his clap secret to Black male inmates. They all immediately came applauding, up to the guard station window at an inconvenient moment, and turned the blaring radio back on, busting Koon. All the inmates, Black and white, hated Koon with a passion.

When officers grew tired of radios, many brought in miniature, three-way powered, four-and-a-half inch televisions. The men would watch their favorite sports programs: Piston basketball, Tiger baseball or Red Wing hockey. Female officers never had to miss their favorite European-American styled soap operas or sitcoms. Officers concealed their televisions and radios, *of course*, in prohibited duffle bags.

Officer Mike Byrd, a cool, slick-talking Black male, who was a stocky, on-again-off-again weightlifter, brought to his jail floor assignment two oversized duffle bags filled with a miniature compact disc player and over one hundred, fifty compact discs of eclectic music. Byrd packed and transported the music for over a year before superiors stopped his good thing. Officers loved working with Byrd because he had all the music you wanted to hear, and it made the day just fly by. It was always an enjoyable day when you worked right down the hall from Officer Byrd.

Music has a profound, calming effect on the psyches of inmates (ala, scene in the movie *The Shawshank Redemption*), and all day they would make requests and listen to everything imaginable. Music was an effective bargaining tool, and could tame and pacify inmates, unless it was heavy metal rock-n-roll blasted by a white male officer into a ward of Black male inmates.

Listening to heavy metal "*Shock Rock*," and its depressive, satanic lyrics: Ozzie Osbourne, Black Sabbath, Mettalica, Motley Crue,

Megadeth, and the sadistic Marilyn Manson, and others, is exclusive to young white teens, male and female. These idolizers have been known to ritually drink blood, commit animal mutilation, also stab and cut themselves. These acts drove some white parents to appear and tell their stories of dealing with their children on a Jenny Jones segment: dubbed *"I Want My Child To Stop Listening to Marilyn Manson."* Many white teens also listen to the diabolical phrases of the hard-metal rock group, Judas Priest. This music was said to have provoked many white teenage devil worshipers to commit suicide. Reading in the book of St. Mark, Judas Iscariot betrayed Jesus for only thirty pieces of silver. After Judas found out Jesus *was* the son of God, he became remorseful and committed suicide by hanging himself. Could this explain the name of this rock group and the meaning of some of its songs?

If a more civilized music than heavy metal or gangster rap were routinely a part of *"The System,"* officers might have it easier, and inmates certainly would. It bears on the larger issues of reforming a *white elephant* bureaucracy. Pun intended. Music is also used as a sound-as-weapon technique to flush out culprits in addition to calming the tension in standoff situations.

The A.T.F. tried to drive cult leader David Koresh from his Waco, Texas compound with a war of nerves: loud, obnoxious music; the chants of Tibetan monks; Christmas carols by Mitch Miller; *"Reveille";* and Nancy Sinatra's *"These Boots Were Made For Walkin'."*

The United States Army used rap and rock-n-roll music to flush out Panamanian leader and purported drug kingpin Manuel Noriega, after the December 1989 invasion of his country. Even in Russia, where a parliament building was seized by old-time communists, music was used to get them out from behind their barricades. When white male officers played hard rock music all day, Black male inmates and officers complained. Overall, the majority of inmates appreciated jazz or contemporary music, which didn't bridge the gender or crossover gaps very much.

Younger, more immature, Black male inmates liked rap music, and begged Black officers to play Kurtis Blow, Run DMC, Houdini, Salt-n-Pepa, Grand Master Flash, or L.L. Cool J., back when they were the initial upstarting rap artists. Now there are so many, you can't keep up with all of them. The one acceptable thing about rap is that rap artists are finally speaking the truth about social, racial, and economical consciousness, instead of falling back on lyrics filled with dope-rhymes; racially motivating comments; carrying guns; selling drugs; mass murder; cursing; and negative, sexual exploitation of females.

The mature older Black inmates appreciated the nocturne sounds of Luther Vandross, Freddie Jackson, Anita Baker, Gladys Knight, Stephanie Mills, Chaka Khan, Peabo Bryson, Whitney Houston, and Sade. They requested slow and easy listening music at lock down. They also loved to hear oldies but goodies by the Dramatics, Lou Rawls, Temptations, Dells, Smokey Robinson and the Miracles, and the Stylistics. Occasionally I tried to relieve inmates' tension by creating laughter, and brought in comedy tapes of Richard Pryor, Eddie Murphy, Moms Mabley, "Pigmeat" Markham, Redd Foxx, and Cheech & Chong— temporarily evoking forgetfulness about court, a judge's ruling, and their sentencing.

When officers had their own music they didn't have to rely on the musical preference of the center station officer. Many radios in the center stations never worked properly, because there was always something mechanically wrong with them. The center station's consoles were equipped with cheap radios: Sparkomatic or Rhapsody, which at most cost $30 to $40 apiece—you know, the kinds you'd see in some old 1950s, 60s, or 70s jalopy. The Department was extremely cost conscious when it came to the welfare or assurance of its officers. Officers regularly folded up matchbooks or pieces of paper, to stick atop or under the cassette in order to make it play.

Because of the jail's building materials: concrete and steels, the radios had very poor reception, and only received a couple of FM stations, and getting any AM station was impossible. During my tenure, the Department *never* replaced any of these partly inoperative, malfunctioning pieces of junk. When command officers called out center station assignments during Roll Call, some unlucky officers moaned disapproval of their assignment, because *that* station had a "fucked-up" radio. With only nine inmate floors, replacing them would have cost no more than $400. Four hundred dollars was less than the value of *one* gun allowance for *one* state-certified officer.

On every inmate floor were two Multipurpose rooms, one each on the north and south sides. MP rooms were mainly used for G.E.D., sewing, self-awareness seminars, and for a few years, the MP room on the north side of the ninth floor was used exclusively for church services; it was also the only MP room with a piano and organ. Church services were also held on the fifth floor, and the inside gym on the 13th floor. MP rooms were also used for the interrogations of inmates; haircuts by a barber who came in about every two weeks; and the Department's version of the FBI—the ISB (Internal Service Bureau).

Aspiring pianists: Lieutenant Shoulders, Officers Zander, Sweatbox, and I, came on the floor hoping to emulate Joe Sample, Stevie Wonder, Rodney Franklin, or Ray Charles. In Zander's case it was inspiring gospel music: he desired to be Andre Crouch, James Cleveland, Milton Bronson, or Frank Williams of the Mississippi Mass Choir. Officer Cook, a pretty, Black female with an ebony complexion and a gorgeous physique, teamed up and sang along with Zander. Man, she could sing. Male officers loved to work with Cook, especially when it was time to make a round. We always lagged behind, staring at her nice butt, and stalled for time to stare longer.

For a few months after lock down at night, Sweatbox and I aired a thirty minute talk show, either through the intercoms of the center or guard stations before shift change. We sang, as inmates sang along and talked to us through their cell speaker about the world and social issues, and their life perplexities. One favorite tune was "Duke of Earl," and Otis Redding's "Sitting On The Dock Of The Bay," because everybody knew the words. Officer Sweatbox and I sang the Temptations: "My Girl" and "The Girl's Alright With Me," the Spinner's: "One of a Kind," "How Could I Let You Get Away" and "Could It Be I'm Falling In Love," the Four Tops: "Tonight I'm Gonna Love You All Over," "Bernadette," "Standing In The Shadows Of Love," and "Still Waters Run Deep."

The intercom system was also used for practicing and perfecting departmental espionage: bugging. The intercoms served as eavesdropping devices to overhear officer and inmate conversations. Officers working the center and Master Control stations could simply flip a switch to listen, and for no reason at all but to have something to do to break their monotony, invade other officers' privacy while they were in their stations, or while inmates were in their cells.

Inmates' conversations sometimes revealed calculating, predatory minds and impulses, and newly refined criminal technologies and psychological methods. While locked down on the midnight shift, inmates would continually escape from their cells by tying a knot at the end of a strip of shredded linen and, after positioning the knot under the door, slid the rag upwards, inside the cell's door hinge, and dislodge the locking mechanism. Thus inmates gained entry onto the ward.

Intrigued to find the culprits, officers set speaker intercom levers very high at specific locations on the floor, where the practice occurred frequently, and listened for inmates out on the ward or, more dangerous, possibly out in the adjoining corridors. Several times while making rounds, midnight officers found inmates peeking and sneaking around corners in the hallway.

Multipurpose rooms also had speakers that were operated from the intercom stations situated in the guard and center stations. It didn't take long to find out the advantages and disadvantages of the intercom system when it came to music satisfaction. For officers to play their own music, all that was needed was a personal cassette player or portable CD player with a coaxial cable plugged up in the back of the intercom. Inmates loved the music, and many bowed to an officer's every whim. Officers had a powerful tool in good music. The theory of, how music can calm the savage beast holds true, especially with locked-up human beings.

The only drawback was that to inmates, officers were their own personal disc-jockeys or radio personalities: "Hey Taylor, you got any Rare Earth, Earth Wind & Fire, some Sly & the Family Stone, or Luther Vandross. What about some old Jimi Hendrix, or anything with a good beat. Man, it's so good to hear some decent music. Whoever is in center station, ain't playing nothing but that damn 'honky tonk' shit! It's about to make me start banging my head up against the wall!" Black inmates said this all the time, referring to bred, Caucasian officers, who lacked diversity in listening pleasures. A good healthy diversity in one's diet, is also as good in one's music.

Some white male officers only listened to country music, never changing the radio station all day long. None of the inmates requested country music from me. It didn't matter because I *never* had any anyway. Could it have been because of the trend to teen suicide in its racial audience; the underlying racial barriers it exhibits; or the lack of enough Black country singers? The closest group to country I listened to was the Commodores, or Z.Z. Top, a group I saw in Little Rock, Arkansas in 1976, at Barton Coliseum.

I'd even listen to the big-band sounds, but the rock-n-roll era of the 1960s and 70s was the preference of many Black and white inmates. Inmates came to my window, requesting to hear vocalists and groups that I had never even considered listening to. Some requested Peter, Paul and Mary, Pia Zadora, Engelbert Humperdinck, Simon and Garfunkel, Paul Anka, Roger Whittaker, and even Liberace. I'm very versatile when it comes to music, but Pia Zadora or Engelbert, naw, I don't think so! I'd rather listen to Roseanne Barr's rendition of the "Star-Spangled Banner" (just kidding).

The only time I prefer classical music is while jogging, relaxing, or reading Bible material in bed. Classical music also had a calming effect on inmates, and put them in a reflective, nonviolent mood, and to sleep (again, see the movie *The Shawshank Redemption*). The improvisations of Beatle melodies, in the style of Johann Sebastian Bach, by pianist John Bayless, relaxed inmates' minds. I listened to classical as I approached the two to three mile range of a six mile jog. But before those first two miles, and after the third, I'd listen to some other music, usually something with an aerobic beat, with a little pop to it, to get me in the groove!

"Bring on some Led Zeppelin, Mick Jagger & the Stones, Aerosmith, Kiss, Alice Cooper, Humble Pie, Grand Funk Railroad, Who, BTO, Queen, Edgar Winter, Yes, David Bowie, and Deep Purple, with a little 'smoke on the water, and fire in the sky'," white inmates asked, always requesting those rock-n-roll groups. I especially liked that era. When officers first started playing Prince, young Black male inmates would imitate him. Because of my father and the majority of my older relatives in the South, I had to listen to the Blues, but never really bought any of the albums, except for Johnnie Taylor. My father played Blues too much for my taste, and had a collection of those big 78 r.p.m. records that looked like albums. The classic Blues singing of Billie Holiday is a favorite of mine.

When I was 14, I found out that my school buddy Joe's aunt was Florence Ballard, one of the original backup singers for the Supremes. They called her "Blondie," and one day while I was over Joe's house, Florence walked in. She was absolutely gorgeous, and for years I had a crush for her. After she was fired in 1967 by Motown founder Berry Gordy, Florence became depressed and overweight, and dependent on welfare. I could see the lines of stress in her forehead. Nine years later, at age thirty-two, she died of a heart attack.

All day inmates loved to listen to the vibrant, inspirational sounds of Earth Wind & Fire: to me, the greatest preforming group of all time. However, the inmates' main man was Marvin Gaye, the master of sensitivity. At times inmates suggested singing Marvin Gaye's many melodious songs. Even the white inmates loved to sing Marvin's songs. It was a more harmonious era of music, economic and racial tensions were somewhat less noticeable because of greater opportunities and plenty of jobs. Over eighty percent of inmates are incarcerated because of financial reasons. Whether they steal and rob to purchase drugs to get high; to supply a family with food and shelter; to pay utilities; the social and economical issues confronting confinement and incarceration will always be a prominent factor.

Marvin Gaye stayed on Appoline, three blocks from where I lived in the late 60s. He resided in a gold brick styled Tudor. I was his paperboy, as I was for an original Temptation, Paul Williams, who lived down the street from Marvin. Aretha Franklin stayed one street over on Steel. Williams drank a lot, and at one time owned $80,000 in back taxes. He died of a self-inflicted gunshot wound in 1973.

Marvin Gaye was very gracious around the holidays, and once tipped me $10 for Christmas (a lot of money to a teenager in 1969). Another time, Marvin autographed and gave me several personally-prized albums with Tammi Tarrell. Needless to say, someone stole them! Marvin was a genius, but even back then I could tell he had problems. A couple of times, while delivering the paper, I was caught off guard as the housekeeper opened the door, giving me a glimpse of Marvin in a purple satin robe, standing majestically atop the spiral staircase.

When I was fourteen, I thought I saw the strain of trouble in his face. Marvin had a very sensitive nature, and although we were not close, I had great admiration for him. Months later, Marvin recorded an album about his divorce, and about his trouble understanding global problems. Marvin will always be remembered for his occasional scat and Hollywood schmaltz, but mainly for his unique and widely acclaimed rendition of the "Star-Spangled Banner," which was performed in Los Angeles, at the 1984 NBA All-Star Game. It made even the most unpatriotic attentive and reflective.

Of all the artists requested, the early Motown artists were overwhelmingly loved, especially Stevie Morris (alias Stevie Wonder), thought by many to be the greatest musical genius of all time. In the early 60s, I use-to-see this little Black blind boy playing trash can covers with drumsticks, in the alley between 23rd and 24th streets, near Buchanan, on Detroit's southwest side. My aunt Annie Mae lived right behind Stevie Wonder's mother's house, and she helped in Stevie's rearing. One thing about Stevie, he has never forgotten his roots, and remembers his friends in the 'hood.

When Stevie comes back home to Detroit, he sometimes showed up at aunt Annie Mae's house unexpected, surprising them. He gave the family tickets to his concerts when performing in Detroit. Much to the family's surprise, Stevie Wonder attended my cousin Carlee's funeral in November, 1991. Carlee provided Stevie with his first harmonica and bongo drums before Stevie became known as Little Stevie Wonder. It was truly a blessing to see a person of Stevie's stature, remembering where he came from and being natural. Until the funeral, I had always missed out on seeing him when he came to town.

Growing up, I was crazy about Little Anthony and the Imperials, Archie Bell and the Drells, Wilson Pickett, Sam & Dave, and Otis Redding. Another inmates' favorite was Jackie Wilson, who in his prime was dubbed Mr. Excitement, because of his electrifying ability to capture and hold the attention of audience's with brisk, pulsating movements and great vocal range.

The funky, psychedelic, soulful beat of the group that "gives you more for what you're funkin' for, feet don't fail me now" the Funkadelics and Parliaments were favorites of many Black inmates.

The Funk Master, George Clinton kept inmates dancing on the ward with the classic "Flashlight," "(not just) Knee Deep," "Freak of the week—ants in my pants and I need to dance" (with the late Philippe Wynne of the Spinners), "One Nation Under a Groove," the album called America Eats Its Young with the song "Call my baby Pussy," some uncut "Pee-funk the bomb," and "Aqua-Boogie" baby. Their album's cartoon flavor always intrigues their followers. It was different from the traditional album cover artwork designs. Since the early 1960s, these guys from the *Mothership Connection* have been "getting down just for the 'funk' of it."

In 1972, while I attended college at Arkansas A.M.& N. (now University of Arkansas at Pine Bluff–UAPB), the Funkadelics and Parliaments performed at homecoming. Back then, most Black people in Arkansas weren't that hip, and were unfamiliar with these guys and their bizarre, erotic music. The crowd was rather dull and subdued, but once the spaced-out music started, and some of the group members came from out of their floor seats with Peter Pan outfits and diapers on, creeping towards the stage, the crowd warmed up. These were my home boys. I was so glad to see them, that I went directly to the front of the stage.

I hollered, "Hey, I'm from Detroit," up to keyboard wizard Bernie Worrel, who responded by pulling me up on stage, and offered me a toke off a long, fatly-rolled cigarette. I refused, and Bernie gave me a tambourine to pound along to the rhythmic, funky beat. Bernie wore wide, bell-bottom jeans, umpteen medallions, and smelled like he had splashed on two or three ounces of musk oil. Bernie was a true 60s flower child.

Always favorites in the cells were Anita Baker, Luther Vandross (Vandross and Barry White are the master of making-love music), and Lionel Richie and the Commodores. Bearded and tattooed white male inmates seemed to like the classic rock & pop of Jimmy Hendrix, Janis Joplin, Bob Dylan, Jimmy Morrison and the Doors, Fleetwood Mac, and the Who. Elton John's album, Goodbye Yellowbrick Road is an all-time classic many white male inmates loved to hear. Inmates in need of spiritual uplifting asked for the gospel sounds of the Rance Allen Group, Mighty Clouds of Joy, Clark Sisters, Shirley Caesar, Tramaine Hawkins, the Mississippi and New Jersey Mass Choirs, Bebe and Cece Winans and the rest of the Winan's family. Most of all, spiritual Black male inmates loved to hear the late Reverend James Cleveland, who inspired many gospel singers. Although born in Chicago, Reverend Cleveland had many Detroit connections. The composer of more than 400 gospel songs, Reverend Cleveland was mentor to The Queen of Soul, Aretha Franklin, and musician for many churches. He performed and recorded with several Detroit groups, including The Meditation Singers, The Donald Vails Choraleers, and The Harold Smith Majestics. On the Detroit-based HOB (House of Beauty) label, Reverend Cleveland recorded his first hit, "The Love of God," backed by Reverend Charles Craig II and The Voices of Tabernacle. And in 1968, Reverend Cleveland founded the Gospel Music Workshop of America, Incorporated. In 1991, this group had 20,000 members strong in the Motor City.

Black inmates had a liking for the genius of legendary music pioneer, Curtis Mayfield, who sang "Superfly," "Eddie you should know better," and "Freddie's Dead." To me, the Superfly album is a collector's item that will always be remembered. In 1996, Curtis Mayfield released his first album, *"New World Order,"* since an unfortunate accident in 1990 that left most of his body paralyzed. During an outdoor concert, overhead spotlights fell from their moorings and crashed on top of him. Despite his near fatal tragedy, Mayfield was determined that he would sing again. *"New World Order"* is a living testimony to overcoming adversity, and shows the spiritual strength of the legendary, Curtis Mayfield. One of the most precious, magnificent voices ever, came from Minnie Riperton; Stevie Wonder felt the same way. I cried and mourned for several weeks when she died, and in remembrance kept a red, silk rose and her picture on my apartment door, along with the corn-rolled, braided-hair picture on the front of Stevie Wonder's Talking Book album. Seemed like the only time white officers warmed up to Black officers and considered them cool, even acceptable, was when they listened to their kinds of music. But regardless of white or Black preference, there was a wide variety of music for inmates to listen to. Whether the inmate was Black, white, Oriental, Scandinavian, European, Arabic, Mexican, Afrikan, Italian, old, young, religious, suicidal, or even satanic, it didn't matter, because *any* kind of music would calm those *Savage Beast.*

Tell-lie-vision:
The World's Megastar

P ROVIDING MEANINGFUL SOCIAL SKILLS is no more a priority for jails than good music is. This is also true for many family homes. In my earlier days entertainment used to include all kinds of creative family and community centered cultural training and experiences. These help one to grow mentally, emotionally, physically, and spiritually. My mother and I were involved in fun things like hobbies and making useful items that added variety and income to our family. We were also involved in planning and organizing camping or fishing trips, and outings for family or anyone else who might be specially helped by it. Being active in mentally and physically stimulating entertainment expanded our minds into other areas like appreciating good music, including learning from other musical cultures. A lot can be learned from attending helpful lectures, seminars, theater, concerts or museums.

Here are other areas of entertainment to consider: • Sharing with others health—promoting sports and games. • Gaining that valuable knowledge you've always wanted but neglected to get. • Using, developing and sharing one's skills, talents and abilities for the enjoyment and benefit of others. • Renewing communications—writing a letter, making a phone call, or a personal visit—to strengthen neglected family and social ties. • Learning the beauty and grace of dancing. • Gardening; home oriented crafts such as woodwork, carving, embroidery, crochet, quilting, cooking, or candle making. • Taking special classes, or going on educational trips. • Helping one's children with some projects they will remember much longer than a television program that will, in most cases, be forgotten in a day or two. • Participating in service activities for school, church or community. • Helping elderly people or neighbors in need.

People once thought in these ways; they made conscious efforts and time for such things, and became better human beings for it. Tragically, in our increasingly technological sit-down electronic age, the art of entertaining as a function of the family has almost entirely disappeared. For many Afrikan-Americans, especially teenagers, they have lost these native and cultural enhancements. Many teens appear confused, out of place, and become totally bored if they aren't playing a video game, hearing rap, or constantly in front of a television. To many young people these are addictions.

Here are some suggestions from experts on television addiction:

- Make yourself turn off the TV except for your must-watch favorite TV shows.
- Refrain from using the TV as background noise. Switch on the radio or spin the CD player instead.
- Make a written list of reasonable goals each day and cross them off as you go. Once you have accomplished your goals, watch a TV program as a reward.
- Before tuning in, ask yourself if you really want to, and why.
- Visit the video store less often; rent one movie instead of three.
- Limit yourself to one movie channel on your cable system. Rent pay-per-view flicks only on special occasions.
- Plan activities such as exercising, visiting with neighbors, playing cards with your kids, having an intimate dinner with your significant other.
- If you have five TVs, get rid of three or four.
- Start a fun new hobby.
- Don't eat meals in front of the TV.
- Call a family meeting and talk about the TV-watching patterns in your household. Agree to watch certain programs together and refrain from solo watching.
- Get rid of the remote control. Some people get addicted to the channel-switching, which gives some a feeling of power.

- If you have young children, don't use the TV as a baby sitter. Limit the hours they sit in front of it and don't give in.
- If you have poor impulse control, remove the TV from your home until you can deal with it.

In the last couple of generations people have become hooked on certain forms of commercial entertainment. They have failed to realize, or care, that they are neglecting to develop both their personal abilities and entertaining personalities. For the most part, television has changed the entertainment habits and living patterns of whole nations. Used rightly, television can be a wonderful medium to inform, expand and broaden one's life—it can enlarge a child's understanding of the world; it can open up important knowledge about new events, different races' history, the arts, sciences and social graces. But at its worst, television entertainment is filled with distorted and improper ideals, morals, ethics, relationships and role models. Between the two extremes of beneficial and debased programming is a vast wasteland locking up much human time with little or nothing of value in return for the time spent.

Many adults spend more hours passively in front of a television than in any other activity except sleep. Many children spend more time with television than with teachers or parents. This medium has come to dominate free time, to supplant critical reading, playing, physical development, social interaction, and skills development. Long periods of television viewing adversely affects a young person's ability to concentrate, read, write, and think clearly. More than ever before, these critical skills are necessary to succeed in *this* modern society. There are more televisions, radios, record players, tape recorders, CD players, and video cassette recorders in the average Black home than books or computers. This has a great deal to do with where our information-gathering priorities are.

Watching television is an all-American pastime, and Blacks watch more of it than *any* other people. Black households watched an average of 74 hours of television a week, compared with 51 hours for other households *(American Demographics, 1/89)*.

When inmates became ignorant and trifling, officers had several options for punishment. They could either: 1) call Master Control to shut off the ward's telephone; 2) refuse to give out any extra food trays; 3) keep flicking their cell or ward lights on and off, giving a strobe light effect while inmates were asleep; 4) tell the center station officer to turn off their music; or 5) turn off officers' own personal music so inmates couldn't hear any at all. There were other ways, some not as congenial, but the most effective weapon for a ward of incorrigible inmates was to *take the television off the ward*.

It is now an established, accepted fact that the public school system, for the majority of Black people in urban areas, is a dismal failure and will continue to be so. Not only can a great number of young Black kids *not* read, write, compute or articulate their thoughts, but there also exists in many of them a severe dislike and fear of the written word, and language. And, since there are only a few places where large quantities of life giving and lifesaving information is available to the majority of Black people—it is now too evident that most Black people rely heavily, and almost exclusively, on the mass media—television, radio, newspapers, and magazines.

Other additional reading material should be: • Books that provide information, knowledge, skills and inspiration that enables people to effectively deal with the real world. • Information—that is, working knowledge that is current, accurate and functional can be found in computerized data banks, which are controlled by the federal government, the military, private corporations and large universities.

The other area, where quantities of information can be found, are written materials, mainly books, scholarly theoretical and professional journals. Therefore, libraries, schools, universities and book stores are a functional part of a community aware of its own intellectual needs. Reading good books is important to develop in-depth knowledge and to build vocabularies. Reading helps one learn relationships between abstract ideas, as well as, developing a flow of general logic and ideologic philosophies. Why do you think the white male slave masters didn't want his slaves to learn how to read? Many slaves were killed after their slave masters discovered they were learning to read, or found books hidden. Reading develops individual, *critical thinking* skills: *the most important* intellectual skills of all.

Restrictions on books, newspapers, and academic correspondence courses kept many inmates uninformed about very important, up-to-date trends and aspects of social life outside the jail. Most inmates liked to read books of a relevant nature—self-published Black books. And since the jail was 80 percent Black, *that* should have been a primary focus rather than frustrating inmates' efforts to learn by putting at their disposal only Westerns, love stories, or white ideologies and political, sacred-cow sciences of the old pagan, Western Gentile World. Working on the ward was pretty monotonous as inmates viewed television like it was life-supporting—many grew immune to white European soap operas depicting a world of nothing but misplaced lives, deceitful sex, greed, adultery, and murder scandals. To get away from that dreaded negativism: censored reporting by the daily newscast, inmates always made sure to check out the cartoons and sitcoms, which gave them something to laugh about.

Educational authorities have noted an ongoing diminishment in student ability to think clearly. Reasoning and logically putting ideas together are processes requiring some organized *linear thinking*, and a great deal of *critical thinking* followed by the ability to *think synthetically*. These skills are supported by the practice of regular reading and by having time to think about things.

Verbal communication helps one develop the ability to present ideas and clearly explain more ambiguous subtleties clearly. Verbal communication skills were something departmental jail officials perhaps lacked and certainly had little regard for. They relied heavily on hearsay, gossip, assumption, and premonition; and white officials ignored, in particular, Black officers' attempts to talk about problems informally. Many officials had ulterior motives as they administratively implemented shutdown tactics, systematically structured to persuade officers to conform by inflicting so-called politically correct punishments like suspension, demotion, reprimand, and ultimately termination.

Television is a one-way communicator, but good conversation skills, that's a two-way street. You talk; then you listen to another's point of view. You learn not only good conversation habits, but also tolerance and respect for others. More importantly, the time taken to share friendship, concern and experiences with others in conversation, can also lift human spirits enormously. The development of speech in children is retarded if parents, or stepparents don't take time out to read and talk to them. A noted British speech therapist, who earned international acclaim, said: "People think that children will just learn to talk without any input, but speech is a taught skill and the people best equipped to teach it are moms and dads."

Because of segregation, Jim Crow laws, and racism, there was a lack of opportunity and education in the South. To read and to be educated were against the law until after the Civil War. Many mothers were taken away from their children and sold into slavery as soon as their babies were weaned. At best, the children of house slaves were taught in secrecy, sometimes by sympathetic whites. Most Black children were left alone in the fields all day, while mothers worked, until they could walk and work themselves; most never learned to read, picking up language skills as they could. Teaching a Black child was against a law that was strictly enforced. Because of these early anti-literacy laws, academic skills did not develop as a priority in many southern Black families. That legacy is still with us today, and unfortunately television has stepped in as a modern communications killer to fill the gap.

Educators are increasingly concerned about the steady decline in children's motor skills. Early success in motor skills can increase a child's confidence in his or her intellectual abilities, thus improving academic performance. Informal play is important to the motor skill development of a young child, and in his or her ability to participate in a group, or with another. A physical education professor, who spent more than thirty years working with thousands of children and adolescents, studying their motor skills, said that the decline in motor skills went "violently on the skids 10 years ago" (1980). That period coincides with an increase of women in the work force and, in many cases, a reliance on day care centers, where children get little individual attention. Many of these working women are single parents: either divorced or widowed. Sometimes the husband and father is in jail.

When a television dominates a home, bonding between family members is avoided; many parents use television to retreat from active child rearing. Recapturing those lost intimacies; lessons and skills learned through games and daily work that once created our very full family lives, will take imagination, discipline and effort. Heavy doses of television kills the initiative to take an active and creative part in entertainment or serious study. It has been shown that television, since its meteoric rise in the 1950s, has effected us more than any other technological development of this century. It has changed the way many of us live, because we are no longer active participants in the getting of information.

Now, of course, the age of computer technology is the next revolution. Computers are fortunately more interactive than television. The challenge now is to see that Black children, whose inner city schools largely lack computers and computer training, are literate in essential computer skills as well as reading skills. For the first time ever, not parents, church or school, but a machine gives citizens most of their stories, information, values and entertainment. Television (and associated equipment such as the VCR) has restructured family life: eating patterns; how we think, feel, dress; the things we buy; the things we do with our free time.

One study in the United States found that 60 percent of families changed their sleeping patterns because of television; 55 percent altered their mealtime patterns (each family member eating alone in front of a favorite program); and 78 percent used television as an electronic baby sitter. A person can literally spend nine years of their life watching television.

These patterns are realistic. I sometimes excused myself from a dinner table, full of gossipy family members to watch basketball, football, a good movie, whatever. Every Thanksgiving, Christmas, or Easter, right after the food was blessed and served, the men usually headed to the television, in the living or bedroom, with a plate full of food. The women sat and gossiped in the kitchen or dining room. These days many families don't even pray over their food, to give thanks to their creator for blessings and bounty.

Television can also engender habits. My mother, for example, had a habit of going to sleep with the television on, thus wasting electricity. In those days TV stations signed off for the night, leaving the sleeper with an accompaniment of white noise and higher electric bills. Many of my friends left the television on to keep their kids amused, hoping to settle them down. The TV became their baby sitter, as they did chores around the house, or while we snuck off to another room to talk.

Another researcher found that more than half of all elementary school children questioned, watched television while eating their evening meal. An even larger percentage watched TV while doing homework. I could never concentrate on doing homework while watching TV, but listening to soft music is, for me, more conducive to learning.

In 1972, one noted researcher asked set owners and non-set owners in eleven countries (Belgium, Bulgaria, Czechoslovakia, East Germany, France, Hungary, Peru, Poland, the United States, West Germany, and Yugoslavia) to fill out diaries during a period of twenty hours. He found activities that most frequently decreased among set owners were sleep, social gatherings away from home, and leisure activities like correspondence and knitting, conversation, household care, and reading the newspaper. More tellingly, engineers in some large metropolitan areas have had to redesign city water systems to accommodate the drop in pressure caused by heavy lavatory use during prime-time commercials.

One study in Canada found that involvement in community activities was greatest in a Canadian town with no television reception. After television arrived there, young people's participation in community activities dropped markedly. Other Canadian studies compared reading fluency and creative abilities of second grade children from non-television towns with those that had television. Higher scores on both counts were found in non-television towns. Once television came the scores dropped to the levels found in television towns.

Entertainment doesn't have to be a time-waster or time-filler; it can be a way to enrich and improve life. One can become a better person from learning the skills that enhance life. Yes, television has its positives. Right now interactive TV is being developed as an education aid. One can call up video footage of a desired subject by computer, and play it on a TV screen in much the same way one would a movie. In this case one is accessing a video library for research and education. At present, however, the negatives of television watching clearly outweigh the positives, culturally and morally, for all ages and races of the world.

Television can be very detrimental on a jail ward. Every day I watched inmates religiously view the TV, play cards or chess, and walk the ward as if they were zombies. I couldn't help wondering what kind of rehabilitation was this?

When inmates attended G.E.D., sewing and self-awareness classes, many viewed it as just something to pass the time; they wanted to get away from the claustrophobia of the ward and cells. Sometimes the teachers' main concern seemed to focus on getting enough inmate participation to meet state requirements for funding, and justify their salaries and jobs. The inclination of many officers was not to view particular activities as to their potential to teach skills to inmates. Except for the computers and the sewing class, jail activities were not intended to train, rehabilitate, or educate. Instead, jail administrators instituted showing the inmates movies?

In 1987, Wayne County inmates won a court ruling. The court order and decision was made for inmates to have access to all of the recreational activities afforded to them in the Wayne County Jail. Again, the court ruling was made by Recorder's Court Judge Bob Grossman. So, county jail officials bought thirty-nine movies a year for the inmates and showed them biweekly.

In 1988, the Wayne County Sheriff's Department was ordered by the court to provide movies to inmates, as a result of the 1987 lawsuit challenging jail conditions (Recreational, entertainment, etc.)

So, every two weeks, Officer Cox, a short pudgy, chain-smoking, Black female, was put in charge of showing movies. She carried around a clipboard with forms, pushing a metal stand on casters, (complete with a VCR in a locked bottom cabinet and a 19-inch television on top), as if she were doing hard labor. She'd call out the choices and, after finding out what movie the inmates preferred to see, positioned the cart on the ward, put in a movie, and locked the bottom compartment. Inmates scurried about to get the best possible seat for viewing. For two or more hours, Cox, the entertainment officer, did whatever she wanted while the movie played.

Many of the movies shown were those Dirty Harry types: violent, racist, misogynistic. Although there were several choices, most of them depicted high-speed chases with police; criminals breaking into law abiding citizens' homes and torturing them; gang violence; degrading of females; and devious plots to commit murder or espionage. There were also movies like "Lethal Weapon," lauding the tough cop image. Being in law enforcement, most officers can't help but feel a certain affinity with tough cop TV programs, such as: California Highway Patrol, Cops, Top Cops, Real Stories of the Highway Patrol, LAPD: Life on the Beat, and America's Most Wanted. Showing them to inmates made me feel uneasy.

When being a cop, it's very important to remain unaffected by media hype. I'm sure the national public will agree that the crime and summary punishment on some of these cop shows is somewhat exaggerated because of television's need for dramatization and glorification. In many cases the cops have made hasty, bad decisions. Watching these shows defeats the whole purpose of rehabilitation. Here are jailed, habitual criminals, charged with murder, arson, drugs, criminal sexual conduct, breaking and entering, burglary, assault with intent to maim: all hideous felonies, watching sex and violence in the movies and on TV.

Movies like "Menace II Society," and "Boyz 'N the Hood" were shown in the Wayne County Jail with an eighty percent Black male inmate population. The Sheriff's Department believed and considered these types of movies *"suitable as popular culture."* After seven years of showing these bloody, violent flicks to the wrecked minds of troubled Black men behind bars, the controversy finally erupted in June 1995, when the Wayne County Commission refused to approve a $25,000 contract for the Wayne County Sheriff's Department for videos. It wasn't until a white male commissioner from Grosse Pointe Park (a predominantly white community), introduced an ordinance to ban the showing of the violent videos.

On July 24, 1995, the Wayne County Commission ordered the sheriff to cease and desist, and voted 14-0 not to buy the videotapes that have the effect in *"inducing or provoking violent and assaultive behavior"* and ones that glorify racial conflict, prison insurrections or violence against women.

In retrospect, because of that vote, some inmates are forced to pay to watch a movie. Now what happens, county jails become profitable movie theaters? This trend is happening in many county jail and state prisons, where inmates can pay for cable or for a movie. Some sheriff departments in Michigan can add their own programming, such as training films on personal hygiene, but mainly the jails allow inmates to watch news and sports on TV.

With national attention focused on only building new jails, due to the erroneous perception that crime statistics are spiraling upwards, showing violent movies to inmates certainly gives young prisoners the wrong ideas and ideals.

Sometimes, when I knew my station was scheduled to see a movie, I'd bring in a few videos from home to combat the violence and poor quality. One of them was "Gorillas in the Mist," a true story about Dian Fossey, a white woman, who went to the Congo slopes of the Virunga volcanic forest in 1966, to study and protect the mountain gorilla in one of its last natural habitats. Poachers were killing gorillas to make ashtrays from their hands. They also sold gorillas for clinical research, and to world traveling circuses. Gorillas were being murdered, tortured; babies were stolen from their mothers and sold. Eventually Fossey herself was murdered in bed. Shaken by such tragedy, my feelings became involved. I had hoped the inmates would appreciate the movie too, but they showed no signs of sympathy for the gorillas.

Laughter abounded, and the inmates acted like it was a comedy. They didn't want to, or couldn't see the tragedy: "Look at that big motherfuckin' ass ape! That ol' silly-ass white woman gonna get fucked by one of them big, wide dicks. She's a stupid ass bitch! Taylor, why don't you bring in a x-rated movie, brother, and forget that damn gorilla shit," inmates hollered insistently, while grabbing and squeezing their nut sacs. Inmates always tried psychological persuasion on officers, hoping to convince them to sneak in porno magazines or flicks, drugs or other contraband for them.

Later in my tenure it became apparent to me that most male inmates treasured intrigue and murder, so the next time I brought in the action-packed government espionage movie, "No Way Out." It involved subtle violence, but was an enlightening thriller. It starred Gene Hackman, who also played a wonderful role in "Mississippi Burning." Black inmates really enjoyed "Mississippi Burning," but afterwards displayed intense anger at the blatant racism. There were a few white inmates on the ward, and the movie instigated several near-fights.

A vast majority of people believe that movies have a definite affect on people's minds. One such case involved two white male

Detroit police officers, who brutality beat a Black male motorist to death just because he wouldn't *"open his hand."* The case was almost thrown out after months of deliberation, because jurors were shown portions of Rodney King's infamous beating by L.A. police officers in Spike Lee's movie, *"Malcolm X."*

I once brought in the movie *"Brother from another Planet,"* starring Joe Morton—inmates could relate to this one. It was about a Black alien who escaped from planetary slavery in another galaxy. After escaping in a stolen spaceship, and crashing at the historic U.S. Immigration center (1892-1943) at Ellis Island in Upper New York Bay, the Black alien tried to settle in America's most racially divided urban society. In hot pursuit were two predatory, white male, alien slave officials, who sought to recapture him and return him to slavery. This alien was looking for freedom, as he tried to elude officials by blending in with Black citizens and their establishments. He saw Black people, the same color as he, shooting up heroin. He watched young Black male teenagers get high, trying to cope with Black urban life (one actually died of drugs in the movie). This frustrated Black male inmates: this depiction of the possibilities of racial inequality among other species. Most inmates didn't want to see what many of them had already lived; they just didn't want to be reminded.

Another movie that showed compassion for Black space creatures was "Enemy Mine," starring Louis Gossett, Jr. He also played a Black alien named Jerida, a galactic slave. The movie dealt with the humanitarian values and morality of the creature. Sadly, inmates would rather see someone shot, murdered, plotted against, than succeeding on the psychological and spiritual high-ground. Perhaps it is safer and more comfortable to see one's own reflection than it is to confront a stranger face to face, and be required to struggle to understand what ignorance makes us inclined to fear.

After observing inmate reactions, I grew disgusted and never again brought in a movie for them to see. Either Officer Cox, or the Department, chose to show Black exploitation movies like Shaft, Blackula, Black Mama, and Cotton Comes to a Harlem. These are 1960s or 70s movies that show negative role models for Blacks, especially Black prisoners! There were plenty of movies the inmates never selected to watch, like white propaganda films about reaching the *American Dream*.

Inmates really didn't want to watch those, but when the choices were few, any movie was better than none. Inmates would rather watch a violent movie three or four times, and argue about what should have been done for the culprits to get away, than watch a new or less criminal film. Of course it seemed that these were the only choices inmates had. Whether the Department picked the movies or not, there should have been a thorough research of the quality of movies shown. Even if the sheriff, undersheriff, or other superiors had to take a movie home with them to evaluate its content, someone should have taken that responsibility. We never knew who made the choices. There certainly didn't seem to be any expert consideration, certainly no Siskel and Ebert.

Haki R. Madhubuti, editor of Third World Press and author of *Black Men: Obsolete, Single, Dangerous? The Afrikan American Family in Transition*, emphasized the problem of Black movies and the media on pages 78-79 of his book. Though the movie "New Jack City," starring Wesley Snipes, had a positive aspect to it, we can also include it in the category of Black stereotypes. Now, do you call that rehabilitation? Especially if the movie only tells you to, Just Say No.

Why was Wayne County taxpayers' money being spent so inmates could watch violent movies? Was the Sheriff's Department asleep on this one? The whole concept of such pursuits are a useless and pitiful waste of minds, and perpetuate the cycle of the Black male criminal, and the myth that it can ever be profitable. There is also a correlation between cartoons shown on television and antisocial behavior in children. The movie industry has continued to neglect responsibility, and have gotten around this issue with a very lenient film rating system. Again, the apathy of family members, and the greed of white institutions, are tolerated, although they are major reasons why negative behavioral patterns remain intact. The rehabilitation issue and historical focus of the prison system is thoroughly discussed on page 224 of the *Contemporary Black Thought: The Best From The Black Scholar*, by Dr. Nathan Hare and Robert Chrisman. Hare has tried to institute a plan to overhaul America's entire public school system, and educate every young Black man, woman, and child, accordingly, in his book, The Hare Plan. Dr. Hare and Madhubuti are two Black men with a devoted consciousness.

14

Who's Gonna Bail Me Out?

I N THE OLD SYSTEM OF JUSTICE, bail bonding for inmates was in a total shambles. Poor people accused of crimes waited for months in the old jail only to be found innocent, while defendants with untold sums of money waited for their trials in freedom. Putting a dollar price on freedom is a mockery of the true American principle of equal justice for all—rich and poor alike.

After a thorough review of the old system, judges from Detroit's Recorder's Court sent proposals to the Supreme Court to overhaul the old, outdated practices. Those proposals allowed all, except those charged with serious felonies, a chance to post ten percent of their bond with the court. In the old days inmates had to pay the entire amount, or seek a bail bondsman. If the defendant appeared on his court date, 90 percent of the amount was given back. If found innocent of the charge(s) he or she received a full refund. The proposals' inception, greatly reduced the jail population and significantly eliminated the scandalous bail bondsmen.

Bail bondsmen were the moneychangers in the judicial temple, who gorged on profits from the poor at no risk to themselves. Poor defendants paid hundreds of dollars, even pledging possessions such as cars and property to the bondsmen. Yet, the bondsmen kept the money whether the defendant was found guilty or innocent, and the bondsman wouldn't undertake a bond if they felt there was a significant risk factor involved. Persons kept in the county jail for more than 90 days on money bonds were entitled to be released on a personal bond: no money was required unless the defendant failed to show up in court.

Both proposals made for speedier trials for defendants and, ultimately, quicker justice for the people of Michigan. To guard against bail-jumping, and some felt this would be the obvious result if the bail bond system changed, stricter penalties for jumping bail were enacted. In their proposals to the State Supreme Court, the Detroit judges suggested three amendments to the Michigan General Court Rules that were to apply only to offenses in which the maximum penalty on conviction did not exceed 14 years.

The 14-year cutoff was selected to exclude more serious felonies such as homicides, robberies, rape and breaking and entering. The first proposal provided a fixed surety bond that the accused could satisfy the judge by paying a cash deposit of ten percent. If the conditions of the bond were fulfilled, and the defendant appeared in court as required, 90 percent of the amount deposited was returned and the balance was retained as a service charge. If the defendant was not convicted of the charge the entire deposit was returned. Fines imposed by the judge as a sentence were not refundable. Regardless of the judges' orders, all Wayne County police agencies had to accept ten percent of the bond involving traffic mittimuses or misdemeanors.

The second proposal provided that an accused person, who had been kept in jail for 90 days or more because of their inability to furnish a surety or other money bond, must be released on a non-money personal bond. The 1972 state law stated "that any person jailed six months or more because of the inability to post a money bond must be brought immediately to trial or freed on a non-money personal bond." The judges changed this law in a third proposal saying, "that for any person who has not been brought to trial within six months, through no fault attributed to them, the case against them must be dismissed."

There are five types of bonds: (1) the cash bond; (2) the ten percent bond; (3) the surety bond; (4) the interim bond; and (5) a personal bond that judges imposed with the confidence that this person is trusted to show up for their next court date. In the event that the accused defendant cannot be trusted and has repeatedly skipped court dates, a *capias* warrant is issued. A *mittimus* are court papers from the judge containing the bond and time of the next court date. In actuality, it's a warrant that commits the defendant to be held in jail until the next available court date. These are general court procedures in all Wayne County courts.

There are certain policies and procedures regarding the bonding of inmates. A lien is conducted when a prisoner is leaving the jail, to check for present or past outstanding warrants. There are times when researching past charges on a lien can establish a criminal pattern. Before releasing an inmate from jail, there should always be a thorough check with the lobby desk sergeant, so he can check the bond papers for errors or corrections. The officer should never leave the sergeant's presence until he signs the proper documents for release and counts all the bond money.

When the computers in the jail were down, the officer was obliged to always call Field Services, which was located near the airport, for a lien check. If the lien system was down state wide, the inmate ought never be released, under any circumstances, until the lien system was restored. Bonds were to be posted within 24 hours at the jail. Bonds are accepted to insure the appearance of a pretrial defendant on his or her court date. Money orders and personal checks are not to be accepted for posting bonds, and the bond officer was responsible for all money transactions and filing.

Bonding procedures, often irregular and inconsistent, sometimes result in the release of inmates too soon or not soon enough. In the past, an attorney might post bond, only to have some policing agencies claim they were unaware of it. It is considered a conflict of interest for an attorney to post bonds for his or her inmate clients. Police officers are also prohibited from this practice, but it was often done discretely anyway.

An officer would just give the money to the proper authorities, supposedly friends, to release the inmate, or cordially give it to the bond officer, who in most cases, wouldn't say anything about it. A rumor might focus attention on the officer who bailed out a prisoner, but the prohibition against it wasn't enforced, nor considered a big thing. Officers have even been known to try to bail out a friend, lover, relative, or even dope suppliers; and some have succeeded.

Recorder's Court, the trial court for felony offenses in Detroit and other parts of Wayne County, was at one time widely considered to be one of the best, and it figured prominently in two laudatory National Center for State Courts studies in 1990 and 1992. Judges and court administrators worldwide visited the court to see how this busy urban justice system managed to dispose of a large caseload efficiently, supposedly without trampling indigent defendants' constitutional rights to counsel and due process.

But before the Court's era of reform, the so-called model system had a tragic flaw: The court-appointed counsels were paid a set fee, based on the seriousness of the charge(s), regardless of how much time they spent on the case. First-degree murder cases, which carried a maximum sentence of life in prison, paid $1,400; any non-murder case for which the maximum possible sentence was life—such as armed robbery, paid $750. Few other courts in the country paid assigned counsels this way. Most paid either by the task performed (motion to suppress, etc.) or by the hour.

Does the fee arrangement drive a wedge into the attorney-client relationship by pitting the attorney's economic interests against the indigent client's Sixth Amendment rights? Yes, of course it does, and since court-appointed counsels represented roughly 87 percent of the defendants who appeared in Recorder's Court, the question of economic disincentive was hardly an academic one. Each of the 29 Recorder's Court judges spent about two weeks a year assigning lawyers to new cases throughout the courthouse. Judges could choose from a pool of more than 600 private lawyers who qualified for court assignments.

As a result of this situation, an independent Legal Aid and Defender Association was established and assigned 25 percent of all court-appointed cases. Alarmed by both the low pay and the constitutional questions raised by the mandatory, flat-fee system, the Recorder's Court Bar Association and other bar groups challenged the payment system in 1989, on the grounds that it violated clients' rights and constituted an unreasonable and "*improper taking*" from the lawyers.

The "Enumerated Powers" are Ex Post Facto Law: laws which made past conduct illegal, changing the old rules, and made it a new rule in the future. Bills of Attainer means no trial, no hearing, enacting swift punishment, and a conviction without a trial. With Procedural Due Process defendants usually get a chance to plead their case. If a person was found guilty without a reasonable doubt, the courts are required to tell the defendant the charge; where to show up; and their right to a defense and trial with a jury of peers.

Substantive Due Process means fairness, and the content of the laws themselves to give adequate notice to defendants. The information given must also be clear and concise. The other three Enumerated Powers are, political participation; joining the political process, running for office, and speaking up for candidates, privacy; the right to personal matters, and equal protection; the right for courts to not be arbitrarily biased against defendants.

Since all of county, state, federal, and city governments are all their own forms of federalism, the Tenth Amendment shows that states have a strong reluctance to create a strong national government. Because of this reluctance, states are preserved to have separate sources of authority and are organs of administrations. States are all given important powers in connection with the composition and selection of national government. As a result, the Judicial Branch powers are distributed between the national, federal, state, county, and city governments. There are also State Powers, called reserved and residual, in which reserved, belongs to the citizens, except that "residual powers," which are mainly rules governing police powers (health, safety, welfare, and morals), are only applicable after the state legislature rules. And some of you say that your vote doesn't count?

Also customs, the military, and Supreme courts, jurisprudentially have their own power and complete control over their own rules. This is a primary reason why congressional legislators and politicians don't get involved in political and personal matters concerning law enforcement agencies. They are their own separate governing bodies, and it's considered counterproductive by all those important entities.

With all of these separations of power, it becomes quite clear why the judicial system in America remains in total disarray and chaos. In 1986, there was an alleged speculation case at the sheriff's department, involving Corporal Schilling, a Black male, who was the bonding officer. Before *Procedural Due Process*, his embezzlement trial was broadcast all over the news, but few working in the jail knew the particulars or final outcome of his trial. Schilling was finally acquitted of the charges, and for almost a decade he fought cancer and pursued a counter suit at the same time. He won in the fall of 1994. Tragically, after getting his just due, Schilling died in January 1995.

The Department had a hidden history of trying to keep the internal problems of Black officers totally *hush-hush*. Many Black officers were blackballed collusively by political and judicial manipulation of the courts.

Another embezzlement case involved Officer Pete Torinski, a white male sheriff's deputy, who had 19 years with the Department. In 1990, he was accused of defalcating and pocketing $12,000 in fraudulent fees for inspecting salvaged vehicles. He had conducted 770 inspections of cars that had been wrecked and rebuilt, but only turned in 281 reports. Under Michigan law, used car dealers were required to have a state-certified police officer inspect rebuilt cars for road readiness. The law set an inspection fee of $25. Instead, *this* sheriff's deputy charged $50 per vehicle, according to four Metro Detroit salvaged car dealers who testified at a preliminary examination *in court*.

Torinski asked that one check for $25 be made out in his name, and another check for $25 be made out to Wayne County. The dealers also testified that they paid the extra $25 willingly, because Torinski came to their garages, saving them the trouble of driving to the Wayne County Sheriff's Department Field Services office, located at Metropolitan Airport. The judge ordered the deputy bound over on one count of embezzlement by agent and eight counts of embezzlement by a public officer, both 10-year felonies, and 13 counts of extortion by a public officer, a misdemeanor punishable by 90 days in jail.

Authorities claimed the investigation, conducted by the Detroit Police Department and the Wayne County Sheriff's Department, came about as the result of a larger auto theft probe, but they declined to be more specific. Torinski's attorney argued that the extortion charges should have been dismissed because the dealers paid the extra $25 willingly, if naively. In 1991, this 46-year old white male, was convicted and sentenced to one to 10 years in prison for embezzlement and a year in prison for extortion, for pocketing $12,000 in bogus fees connected with his inspections of salvaged vehicles.

The difference in those two cases is that Officer Schilling, the Black male, was judged prematurely and unfairly through the media, left to fight a blatant injustice for nearly a decade before winning an acquittal for his case. Whereas, Officer Torinski, the white male, was *never* judged a priority or subjected to inhumane media coverage. It wasn't until after a thorough police investigation by two departments, who claimed their discovery of embezzlement *"came about as the result of a larger auto theft probe,"* and after Torinski lost his case in court, that there was *any talk*, *publicity* or *print* in the newspaper.

15

Male Registry:
The Prevalence of Funk!

ROM THE FOURTH TO THE TWELVE FLOOR in the new jail, the large wards (bay area) had 10 cells, and were 70 feet long and 15 feet wide with the capacity for 20 inmates. The small wards had 6 cells, and were 40 feet long and 15 feet wide with the capacity for 12 inmates. Altogether, a ward held 32 inmates. Can you see why not having a chance to get daily cardiovascular exercise, and breathing the same air constantly throughout incarceration can be hazardous to anyone's health?

A stickler for cleanliness, I detested seeing cigarettes butts and ashes left in ashtrays, dirty, grimy windows; foul odors—just anything unsanitary left behind, especially by unconcerned officers. With all the diseases, the multitudes of germs traveling in the air, anyone should be able to see the importance of good sanitation. The number one area in the new jail requiring constant sanitizing was Male Registry. The second most unsanitary areas were the closets on the inmate floors that stored mops, buckets, and cleaning equipment. Continuously, over the years, those two areas were olfactory problems—the obnoxious odors were unbearable. Sometimes Male Registry stank so bad that officers were forced to wear surgical masks.

Male Registry is where all incoming inmates are fingerprinted, photographed, clothed, and their records filed, until their release or transfer to another jail or holding facility. The next step was a trip to the Reception Diagnostic Center (RDC), where inmates are evaluated by doctors and social workers before being housed. Every April and October, according to seniority, officers bid for vacant positions in

Male Registry. Officers working there had a mentality and philosophy different from that of the regular floor officers, even though both worked in direct contact with inmates. It seemed that the majority of floor officers had a better developed, more congenial relationship with housed inmates. However, after a stint in Male Registry, many officers *never* wanted to work on the jail floors again.

Historically, Male Registry has exclusively been a white male officers' domain, and because it is the first place a prisoner comes to, there's an intimidation factor involved. Male Registry sets the stage. To see a *white* officer, first thing, when you already believe that the white-controlled system encourages Black male incarceration, causes anger in many Black inmates.

It's interesting to observe Black reaction to moving up within racist institutions with the adoption of ideological extremes. I'm not quite sure *how* this happens, but it appears that Black officers take on the brutality of manipulative power. However, many Black male officers would claim that they *liked* working in Male Registry because they had more freedom to roam the jails and avoid the continuous negativity and constant hassles that floor officers got from temperamental floor command officers. Forced to look at grimy, naked inmates, and overseeing the changing of clothes for eight to sixteen hours a day, I would think one might find the job both mundane and ruthless.

There is nothing glamorous about asking grown men, all day, to open their mouths, bend over, spread their cheeks, grab their testicles and cough. Nor is it exciting to inspect mens' rectums for contraband. The job could be especially nasty when a deputy came upon a *"keister"* that needed wiping. Two Male Registry officers usually transported more than 20 inmates at a time to the jail floors on the inmate elevators. The elevator was regularly overloaded way past its standard weight capacity limit.

To break the monotony of the jail floors and breathe fresher air, the charming, fair-skinned Black Officer Cheryl Fleming, 5-foot-4-inches tall, with a very alluring smile and pretty black hair, twice assisted me in transporting an entire floor of 70 inmates up to the 13th floor's outside gym. By ourselves, we handled the entire transfer to the gym and back again to the inmate wards with no complications. The transition also required three or four trips.

Though not recommended, jail officials never considered this a dangerous transfer for us—twice there were fights involving several inmates, and by myself, was able to defuse the situation without pushing the emergency alarm. After observing the good will and respect I received from inmates, jealous officers and envious superiors, those who had personality conflicts with me, exaggerated the danger of my going onto an inmate ward of twenty men, when I had previously been alone handling and supervising seventy inmates everyday, as the recreation officer.

To some jail officials, supervising seventy inmates at a time was perhaps unwise, but in retrospect, it gallantly proved to me my own courage and fearlessness at being outnumbered. I never feared inmates; they were the least of my worries. It was always coworkers and the duties of the job that required constant attention. "If you guys ever kidnap me and hold me hostage, just remember I treated you like men. I will be the first to ask you to order pizzas and some Grand Marnier," I'd quip to inmates. "Taylor, you're one crazy motherfucker," would come the reply. The inmates just smiled and laughed.

When inmates were being transferred from Male Registry to other jail floor locations, there was always one who would holler, "Beam me up, Scotty," referring to the transporter on Star Trek that energized people from one location to another through transparent imagery.

I couldn't imagine how deputies working in Male Registry withstood those suffocating stenches: they would nauseate anyone. Many inmates came directly off the streets, unshaven and unclean, many of them hungry and homeless. There were inmates in Male Registry either going to or coming from court, and the rest were usually waiting for extradition to another jail facility in Michigan (mainly, Jackson State prison, Ionia, Saginaw Regional, Ryan and Huron Valley Correctional, to name a few).

The ventilation in Male Registry was not sufficient to disperse the hovering and lingering stench, despite several sanitation attempts. Officers working in M.R. acted as though there was no odor as they became immune to the dirty clothes, pretuberculous and atrocious "weeping lesions" of heroin addicts; the foul body odors of men who hadn't washed-up for days.

The protruding, gruesome, sources from the odor of pus coming from uncared for bodies were all too visible. There were inmates with bad breath, irreversible stages of gingivitis and dental diseases, venereal diseases; urine and feces in their underwear. All these produced putrid, unhealthy odors. A trustee was always present in Male Registry, at the beck and call of officers, to clean and disinfect the floors, and dungeon-like cells with incoming and outgoing inmates packed in like sardines. Even this routine seemed meaningless. A trustee is an inmate who has specific job duties within or outside the jail. The detail could either be supervised or non-supervised (depending upon the trust factor). Trustees are paid slave-era wages—about 25 cents to a dollar an hour and are granted certain privileges.

Female Registry was never fully occupied like Male Registry, so the air in that department wasn't as bad. It was cleaner, more organized too! Using both jail registries as a reference, the proposition that women are the cleaner gender holds truth.

The race-mentality of some certified officers was noticeable. In many respects, white male, state-certified officers disrespected Black male officers, whether noncertified or certified, belittled Black officers' decisions, and selfishly refused to share useful experience or knowledge acquired by tenure in "*The System.*" Because of this, many Black officers learned certain operations only through hands-on experience, and was ever mindful of the possibility to confront a white superior's exaggerated scrutiny and hypocrisy about trivial, meaningless mistakes.

Because of the ever present pandemonium in the sheriff's department, white male officers working in Male Registry had this illusion of the importance of having a tougher demeanor—more power. M.R. officers beat up incoming inmates, and it was regarded as the "manly" thing to do. If floor officers beat up an inmate, in most cases, the officer(s) would be severely reprimanded or terminated.

In the early years of my tenure *Within The Walls*, there was no one of command stature readily available on the jail floors to witness and assist officers with inmate altercations. However, white male officers, accused regularly of beating inmates on the jail floors, were never reprimanded immediately for their assaults; only after a long administrative process were some finally held accountable.

Black male officers accused of the same infractions were dealt with swiftly, and were ridiculed by command officers and jail officials, not present at the incident, and who were also given biased, unsubstantiated accounts of the infraction by white superiors. Sometimes white command officers even sided with an *inmate* against a Black officer, and the officer was held responsible.

In 1989, several white male officers were terminated for their assaults on Black male inmates, but not until after a long drawn-out, political, in-house procedural process unfolded. Some white male officers used their newfound authority over incarcerated Black people, who were totally powerless, in institutionally acceptable, cowardly ways. After countless incidents of officer-inmate fighting, and to get lethargic command officers to take some action, the Department put in shift command offices, one on every three jail floors.

At one time the Department believed that an inmate who had not been found guilty should have some kind of representation. What was established wasn't quite what you'd call an inmate union, but inmates were permitted to submit grievances against those officers whom they felt violated their constitutional rights. In the days after jail officials launched this policy, many inmates submitted grievances, especially against white male officers. I'd say that about *eighty* percent were justifiable and the others pure hogwash.

As Black inmates filed grievances against white officers, the Black officers began to feel the heat from the *Trickle Down Syndrome*: Black inmates came down on white officers; white command officers and officials came down on Black officers in retaliation. Black officers got the fallout because, unlike the inmates, they were not focusing their frustrations, through a class action suit, on a system that created racial bias. Most Black officers were afraid to show white officers their dissatisfaction and malcontent, because of possible reprisals and arbitrary disciplinary actions by white male upper echelons through token Black superiors. This was done in the same way and for the same reasons that white male Southern generals sent the Buffalo Soldiers in against the Indians after the Civil War.

Instead of sticking together and helping one another, many Black officers, buying into or victims of the *existing feudal system*, circulated salacious gossip, resorted to destroying each other by rumor, hearsay, and innuendo because of envy, jealousy, and fear of the white male officials' excogitative institutional revenge.

Why is it? that when most Black people become educated, or get promoted in a racist institution, they turn to European oriented ideologies and strategies? It's the weirdest thing: divide and conquer. Most intellectual Black people are very communistic in their approach to the movement and to justice for Afrikan-Americans. Communism and capitalism cannot and will not help Afrikan-Americans.

It should be quite obvious to the conscious observer that this society is bent on destroying Black people, specifically Black men, as quietly, efficiently, and in a businesslike way. What is *never* discussed is *not only* the ability of Black men to survive America's worst conditions, *but also* their potential for revolutionary and progressive organization, which remains the greatest threat to white male rule.

Because of this potential most European-American systems and subsystems are structured to systematically shut out conscious Black men and women. However, if Black people wish to become imitators of white men, there exists within the political-industrial-military complex significant token positions which are used to legitimize the system and to cloud its true relationship to Black people: a relationship of slavemaster to slave.

In fact, the "slave" position is the highest rank that Black men, regardless of their titles and income, are allowed to occupy. Once again, I suggest that you read Haki R. Madhubuti's book *Black Men: Obsolete, Single, Dangerous? The Afrikan-American Family in Transition. The Kerner report,* a study issued nearly thirty years ago, stated that America was moving towards two societies, one Black, one white— separate and unequal. A major investigation by *the New York Times* (Herbers, 1978) confirmed the accuracy of the report.

In reference to *the Kerner report,* Robert Blauner, in his book *Racial Oppression in America,* wrote about America's race relation problems. According to Blauner: "Despite the Kerner Report, it is still difficult for most whites to accept the unpleasant fact that America remains a racist society. Such an awareness is further obscured by the fact that more sophisticated, subtle, and indirect forms, which might better be termed neo-racism, tend to replace the traditional, open forms that were most highly elaborated in the old South.

The centrality of racism is manifest in two key characteristics of our social structure. First, the division based upon color is the single most important split within the society, the body politic, and the national psyche. Second, various processes and practices of exclusion, rejection, and subjection based on color are built into the major public institutions (labor market, banking, education, politics, and law enforcement), with the effects of maintaining special privileges, power, and values for the benefit of the white majority." To research more about this issue, read Carter G. Woodson's book titled *The Mis-Education Of The Negro*.

Within The Walls, white male sergeants and lieutenants cunningly collaborated to orchestrate *that lies* be told in many Black officers' records, thus permanently besmirching their reputations. The majority of the time they did this through the cooperation of Uncle-Tomish, Sambo, Black superiors. Such chaos naturally created tensions amongst conscious, strong-minded Black officers. Once again, divide and conquer, frustrate and delay.

Jail and union officials quibbled over officers rates of pay, promotions—basically commanding our careers and aspirations. Thus, did the sheriff's department actively and intentionally oppress its Black officers to "keep them in their place?" Somehow it just seems that Black economic and politic clout is negligible and not implemented on the world level. This must change if Black people are to seize control over their destinies, education, and survival needs.

16

Homosexuality:
Fannie, the Fruity Drag Queen

G ENERALLY, ONLY MEN WORKED IN MALE REGISTRY, but occasionally a female officer walked over from Female Registry to get a female inmate's paperwork checked by a male superior. It was this knowledge, naivete, and only a couple of months on the job as a rookie that made my story of Fannie possible.

Let me give you some background. On the fourth floor was an entire ward of androgynous males who wouldn't dare go to any other ward because of the fear they probably would be beaten. Most homosexuals in prison don't understand delayed gratification or develop the self control to keep their sexual erotomania discreet. Naturally, when heterosexual inmates saw that some fellow male inmates always had large bulges at their crotches, they would immediately acknowledged it as a likely homosexual tendency.

Let me continue to set the scene for my story. Towels and gray wooly, itchy quilts (bedrolls) were stacked in cage-like laundry wagons in Male Registry. Before the laundry wagon system was instituted in the jail, officers had to go down to Male Registry to get bedding for inmates. It was worse in the winter months because officers went often to get needed, extra blankets.

The last cell on the end of each ward had two windows instead of one. Now all windows developed thick frost because of the cold, but those two end cells were the coldest and commonly permitted to have extra blankets. The wards were generally very cold in the winter months, and it was common for inmates to come down with bad colds.

and influenza. Medication was prescribed and dispensed by the nurse on duty.

One day I went down to Male Registry to retrieve extra bedrolls for inmates on my ward. While walking past the dungeon cells, filled with throngs of inmates changing from their street clothes to jail fatigues, I saw what I first thought was a woman; that was my initial reaction. From the long distance and rear view, the curvaceous buttocks really threw me off because, in reality, it was a man, with the nice, round shape of a woman. There was no way in the world anyone could've told me that this was a man from the rear view I had.

As a result of setting myself up this way I became a perfect target for the white male registry officers' pranks. About to exit with my arms full of bedrolls, I was approached by Officer Patrick O'Brien, smoking one of his characteristic, long stinky cigars: "My man Taylor, before you leave do ya wanna meet Fannie?" "Fannie, who is that?" I queried, wondering who-in-the-hell O'Brien was talking about, all the time questioning why this Fannie was in Male Registry in the first place, where only male inmates are allowed to gather and undress.

While O'Brien "shot the shit," Officer Keith Flacken, an Irishman from Dublin, whose family was suspected of having close ties to the I.R.A., joined in the act to protest and thus heighten the inevitable hilarity. All other officers in earshot eagerly waited the outcome. Inmates in line to give up their street clothes were also delighted to anticipate the exploitation of my innocence. None of the inmate clothing personnel would dare give away O'Brien and Flacken; this joke was also going to make their day.

Such were the more traditional affects of being a rookie that, when they were bored, some of the more experienced officers played fiendish jokes on us. This was the mindset of many who worked at the Department, and hazing came in the form of old-fashioned pranks. Even in job related training it was customary that the older, more knowledgeable officers refused to help the less experienced officers—they wanted us to learn the hard way.

As if they knew what was about to happen, all inmates cleared out of the area after changing their clothes. O'Brien slowly walked me over to Fannie, who was undressing as if in preparation for a strip tease. When Fannie removed a tight red miniskirt, she turned around. "Taylor, meet Fannie," O'Brien announced with contempt. Stunned, I dropped the bedrolls and gaped as Fannie inquired rapturously in a deep baritone voice: "Officer Taylor, how are you doing today? You're kinda nice looking. Baby, you wanna see me take off some more of my clothes?"

Completely wide-eyed, my face expressionless, I tried to recapture my composure by sighing and taking several deep breaths as officers hid their cackling and giggling with hands over their face or by turning away. I was embarrassed to say the least, and denied the encounter with a cruel reply. "I know you ain't talking to me," I protested loudly, "because I'm not the one, and I don't like faggots."

Fannie turned, angry. "Look, baby, don't knock what you ain't never had," he scolded. "I got something that might just change your mind and put you in my world," Fannie invited hopefully, as enticing, I'm afraid, as is possible to a man who has never had any homosexual tendencies that he is aware of. As more clothes came off, Fannie exposed his unattractive chest, the ashiest knees I've ever seen, and a scarred stomach and arms. Fannie looked malnourished, but without a further look, or from a distance, a lot of males would have mistaken him for a woman.

"Man, you'd be lucky to have the services of a dog, the way you look," I snapped, intent on thoroughly humiliating him before I left Male Registry. Fannie, the king of the fairies blurted back, "Look lover-boy, fuck you! You don't have to talk to me like that!" I persisted cruelly: "I really, really thought you were a woman, but close up *you* look terrible, whatever you are?"

Fannie's face deflated, and he took a seat on the bench. "Honey, I ain't no fuckin' man, and why don't you just take your little 'Willy' and get the hell out of here. You're about to get on my damn nerves child," Fannie added, while sitting and massaging his feet to wipe away the "jam" between toes that ached from wearing high heeled, pump shoes.

O'Brien, who started it all, saw that Fannie was getting upset, and gave me a slight nod, indicating that the boys had had their fun and laughter for the day; enough was enough. But I wasn't finished—

my motto is, don't start nothing you can't finish. I proceeded to launch a verbally assaultive barrage against homosexuality. "What do you get out of sticking another man in the ass with a dick; motherfucker, do you realize that you're a potential walking epidemic of AIDS. What does your mother and father think of you?" Then I told Fannie how he had on too much makeup, fingernail polish, and that his hair looked like a tornado had went through it, and his clothes weren't appealing at all, "Ya freak ass bitch!" I yelled, about to exit the smelly department.

Fannie gave no response after my last outburst; the situation had turned sour. "Okay Taylor, that's enough please; it's time to leave," O'Brien, who had started the whole thing, pointed out, not without a trace of unctuous piety. As I walked out Fannie began to cry, and Flacken gave him some tissue. I didn't mean to hurt Fannie's feelings, but it was a deliberately cruel setup by the white O'Brien and Flacken of two Black men, one young and inexperienced, the other easy and pathetic.

Although homosexuals didn't invent AIDS any more than heterosexuals did, for either group to continue spreading it by careless or intentionally destructive sexual or social behavior, or through the media by advocating the right to risk infecting others by lack of disclosure, is irresponsible in the same way O'Brien and Flacken were irresponsible when they knew all the facts and used them to take advantage of Fannie and I, two people particularly vulnerable to this particular and sadistic joke. AIDS, like male hazing and institutional racism, needs to be treated as an infectious epidemic.

Some scientists even believe AIDS was deliberately deployed as an "*ethnic germ*" by diabolical white male scientists and the World Health Organization to destroy multitudes of people of color. A planned experiment of a small pox vaccine was concocted in the late 1960s from two viruses (Visna and Bovine), which causes leukemia cancers in the reticuloendothelial systems of cattle and sheep, and it was distributed in many Afrikan nations. Because of European experimentation and racial madness, and because not everyone stays within physical and behavioral racial boundaries, every race and country in the world is now in danger of annihilation.

After returning to my floor with an armful of bedrolls, I realized I felt bad about the situation; I even wondered for a few minutes if I should have just gone along with the joke. So one day, while walking past the homosexual ward, I stopped by and explained to Fannie how O'Brien and Flacken had set us both up. Fannie was furious, claimed he despised them both, and remained angry about the incident for quite some time.

I occasionally walked down to the homosexual ward to see Fannie. He always waved, but I never waved back, just said hello and smirked; I never smiled. I guess I was afraid I'd give Fannie the wrong impression. In the ensuing years, I stopped visiting that ward because the other homosexuals caught on to Fannie's act and I had to tell them off too. Soon after I stopped visiting there, the homosexual ward was moved to the old jail. Eventually it was moved back to the new jail to permanently occupy two floors. Homosexuals liked the old jail better because they had more privacy, and that was probably one of the reasons why their floor residence was moved back to the new jail.

Male and female homosexuality in prison has become a social institution because the fed and the state refuse to reform the system so male and female prisoners can have protected, heterosexual sex. There is a group of older homosexual inmates, fixed in the system, who are considered the hierarchy among prison inmates as regards to homosexuality. Just about every movie that concerns prison conditions, or has prison scenes, has some known prison homosexual going out of his way to intimidate or coerce new inmates into his world. Usually the homosexual in the movie is well-built and well-muscled, his secret isn't out, or he hides it well.

In their book *Contemporary Black Thought: The Best From The Black Scholar,* authors Nathan Hare and Robert Chrisman talk about the problem of homosexuality in jails, and its continuing correlation with prison inmates who have gone years without sex or family involvement. According to the authors: "The system purports to frown upon homosexuality. Yet its very insular rules breed what it allegedly seeks to stamp out. Every man should have the right to unity with his so-called common-law wife or any consenting female. (The same applies to female prisoners.) Sexual intercourse between man and woman is as essential as life itself. The separation of man from woman is one of the greatest inhumanities to man and woman because it denies man the very creature who makes him whole and complete, and no man should be subjected to this emasculation, regardless of his crime. Not only has the ban on sex broken up families on the outside, but it has created more problems inside prisons. Young prisoners are constantly harassed, attacked, raped and forced into homosexuality for merely the sexual gratification. Prisoners are also known to lie, cheat, steal and kill over homosexuals or potential bed partners. Prisoners should be allowed to maintain their responsibilities as providers and to continue their sex life. These are the two components essential for his manhood."

The sheriff's department had a few officers working there that were rumored to "go both ways." In particular, two Black women, Carletha Spencer and Altareva Nelson, seemed quite androgynous and caused a lot of controversy. They were always together and rumored to be lovers. Many male officers, both Black and white, had a crush on Nelson and wanted to date her. She was very attractive and a lot of fun. Spencer was considered "kind of cute," but was thought to "act more like the man," and had the nerve to get mad when male officers tried to date Nelson. I always felt that a little tomboyish nature was alright, but that Spencer had way too much.

After awhile Nelson lost the "respect" of many officers because of her close friendship with Spencer, who always talked about auto mechanics, working on engines and transmissions, and riding her motorcycle. Many times after work they'd ride away together, Nelson holding on behind Spencer like Appolonia behind Prince in the movie *Purple Rain.*

Spencer wore several tattoos on her arm, not the more acceptable heart with a lover's name, but eagles and skulls indicating a tougher persona. It wasn't hard to figure out which one acted the part of the man. Both seemed somewhat soft and feminine, but Spencer was definitely the more masculine of the two and, on the jail floors, all kinds of rumors circulated about their involvement.

Many inmates viewed their relationship as offensive. Inmate Squires, for example, a Black male being held for three counts of second degree, criminal sexual conduct, made this unconsciously ironic statement: "Man, those two 'chicks' need to quit... going that way. We all saw them both go into the closet together; they tried their best to hide it. Man, we've seen them hug each other, and I've even seen them kiss one another. Man, that's a damn shame I gotta sit up in here and see two nice looking Black women doing shit like that. Wish I could get with their ass. If I had the chance, I bet I can change one of 'em!"

Unfortunately for her, Spencer was caught bringing drugs into the old jail, allegedly to give to inmates. Departmental suspicions had led to the check of a couple of double-decker cheese hamburgers she brought in one day for lunch. Between the patties were packets of heroin. She was later convicted and spent time in jail.

Officer Nelson, after going on and completing the police academy, was terminated upon accusations of drug peddling. It seems, and this is pure speculation, that a house she frequented was raided and the Department hushed up the whole incident. One day, and I will never forget it, I was ordering food at a Taco Bell when I saw Nelson with her husband, a man who had a marked and striking resemblance to the character "J.J." on the sitcom *Good Times*. Somehow their chemistry just didn't seem right to me, and I couldn't imagine why were they married?

We Want Clean Air.
Don't You Feel a Draft?

T HE QUESTION OF SUFFICIENT, RELIABLE, AND GOOD ventilation was always a problem in the new jail. For years, a proportionate number of workers, inmates, and officers suffered from asthma, emphysema, sinus problems, respiratory failure, and bronchitis. Even pneumonia-like symptoms, angina, and diphtheria diseases were prevalent at certain times. Viruses and bacteria from unclean, filthy inmates, developed contagious stages while lingering in unfiltered air.

Symptoms of diphtheria, which is an acute contagious disease caused by infection with the bacillus Corynebacterium diphtheriae, and characterized by the formation of false membranes in the throat and other air passages, caused high fever, weakness, and breathing difficulties in many officers.

According to two studies published in the *Journal of the American Medical Association:* "Afrikan-Americans and other minorities experienced asthma hospitalization and mortality rates that were significantly higher than whites. One study examined asthma mortality rates among whites and nonwhites from 1968 to 1987, and the other studied asthma hospitalization rates for children from 1979 to 1987. Both studies showed that the asthma hospitalization rate per 1000 children, increased from 2.67 for whites and 5.76 for minorities in 1979 to 3.53 for whites and 10.17 for minorities in 1987. *JAMA* also revealed that in 1987 the asthma mortality rate for nonwhite males was nearly five times the rate for white males. Asthma, including acute chronic bronchitis and lower respiratory tract diseases, affects an estimated 9.9 million people in the United States each year.

Dr. Floyd Malveaux, chairman and professor of microbiology and medicine at Howard University School of Medicine in Washington, D.C., commented on the new statistics: 'The new findings are very significant because they point out that although therapy is improving, there is a disparity in the death and hospitalization rates among the Black and white populations.'

The coordinator of the National Asthma Education Program of the National Heart, Lung and Blood Institute in Bethesda, Maryland, believed the rates were disproportionate because 'most minority children live in urbanized areas and have problems with access to care because of their low socioeconomic status.' According to the coordinator, minority children received care only when they experienced severe asthma attacks. Follow-up care for these children is inadequate because their parents don't know how to use the health care system effectively. The coordinator also explained that many times, parents don't realize that 'pets can trigger an allergic response' in asthma sufferers."

On February 8, 1993, the American Academy of Allergic & Immunology, National Institute of Allergy and Infectious Diseases, and the National Heart, Lung and Blood Institute, released a memo warning that "Asthma-related deaths and hospitalizations were on the rise, particularly among young Afrikan-Americans and other minorities. A critical factor in solving this growing public health problem is the need to increase the number of physicians practicing in inner cities as well as basic and clinical researchers from the minority community."

In 1993, The National Institute of Allergy and Infectious Diseases (NIAID) and the National Heart, Lung and Blood Institute (NHLBI) joined the American Academy of Allergy and Immunology (AAAI) in a program to train minority individuals—high school, undergraduate, graduate, medical students, postdoctoral trainees and investigators to work in the field of asthma, allergy and immunologic diseases. NIAID, NHLBI, and AAAI gave their support to postdoctoral level scientist for two years. In addition, the institutes provided funding for research opportunities to minority high school, undergraduate and medical students, under the supervision of investigators at established laboratories.

On October 12-13, 1992, the first meeting was held for the National Conference on Asthma Management. It was sponsored by the National Asthma Education Program (NAEP) Coordinating Committee. The conference emphasized asthma's cost to society, its public health problem, reasons for the increase in asthma morbidity and mortality, and why asthma severely affects a disproportionate number of inner city minorities. The conference findings stated that:

"Asthma exacts a heavy toll on our health care system. In 1990, total health care costs for asthma reached $6.2 billion. Although asthma is often considered to be a mild chronic ambulatory illness, 43 percent of its economic impact is associated with emergency room use, hospitalization, and death. Hospitalizations for asthma have doubled in adults and increased five fold in children. Between 1979 and 1987, the percentage of Americans with asthma increased by about one third, from 3 to 4 percent of the population, and the number of reported deaths almost doubled from 1979 to 1988. The toll has reached over 4000 annually.

Between 1979 and 1987, the increase in the hospitalization rate due to asthma was 5 percent per year among children up to the age of 4 years. Black children in this age group had approximately 1.8 times the increase of the white population. In 1979 in the U.S., Blacks were twice as likely as whites to die from asthma, but by 1987, Blacks were 3 times as likely to die from this disease. The death rate due to asthma for Black males aged 5 to 45 is even higher, six times that of their white counterparts. Many theories have been proposed to explain the increasing trends. Some people feel that patients are underestimating the seriousness of the disease. Some still operate under the perception that asthma is an "emotional" condition that is a nuisance but not a potential threat to their lives. Uninformed health care providers may have this misperception as well. Some people feel that patients and their families are ignoring the role of allergies. Parents may avoid removing pets from the house or cleaning the house more often if an inhaler alleviates asthma symptoms.

There may also be a lack of adequate training for physicians and other health care providers. A large number of health professionals do not know the current techniques for monitoring the patient's condition, recognizing the severity of the asthma episode, and educating the patient on how to manage their disease. A number of asthma medications are available, and health care providers need to be thoroughly familiar with the characteristics of each medication.

In fact, there may be an overreliance on medications that treat symptoms but not the underlying problem, chronic inflammation. Overemphasis on the use of bronchodilators may mask the severity of a patient's symptoms until the condition becomes acute. An increase in asthma and asthma-like symptoms could be attributed to a variety of factors.

For example, indoor air pollution such as paint fumes, formaldehyde, and secondhand cigarette smoke. Moreover, allergies from cockroaches, dust mites and even saliva from cats may be causing the increase. "Tight building syndrome" and maternal smoking have also been implicated. Outdoor air pollution, especially in inner cities, may also be a factor. Suspended fine particulate that is so significant for lower respiratory tract disease has been also suggested as a possible culprit.

The answer to why inner city minorities are hardest hit involves many of the same reasons suggested for other chronic disease disparities in this population. Generally inner city residents have limited access to health care. The emergency room may be the only choice that a family has, even if it may not be the appropriate place to manage asthma. Poverty itself is a complication for a chronic disease such as asthma. Parents who are struggling to pay the rent and keep food on the table find it difficult to pay for and keep track of several different medications for their children as well as the home monitoring and frequent doctor or clinic visits necessary to maintain their child's health."

On August 4, 1992, Erin Marcus, a writer for the Washington Post Health Section, wrote an article on asthma: "Millions Gasp for Breath as Serious Attacks Soar and Deaths Nearly Double," it stated:

"During the past decade, the number of U.S. deaths attributed to asthma nearly doubled, reaching about 4,600 in 1990, according to the National Center for Health Statistics. At that same time, the number of Americans suffering from the disease reached unprecedented highs, rising from 6.8 million in 1980 to 10.3 million in 1990, center officials said. Children are hit especially hard. The disease is the top cause of hospital admissions among youngsters, and children under the age of 18 accounted for about 36 percent of the asthma cases in 1990, according to government figures. Asthma caused U.S. children to lose more than 10 million school days a year, making it the top health reason for absenteeism from school. What triggers the asthmatic reaction varies. In the most common type, the asthmatic patient also has allergies that cause a reaction when foreign materials or allergens, such as pollen, dust or animal dander enter the body. The immune systems of some asthmatics produce excess amounts of an antibody protein called immunoglobulin E, or IgE, to protect the body. IgE binds to cells called mast cells, which are frequently found under the skin and around the airways. The IgE can then make the mast cells release histamine and other substances."

For people with some allergies, the substances can trigger a hay fever attack, sneezing, watery eyes or a runny nose. For an asthmatic, the response is more dramatic. The histamines can cause muscles in the airway to constrict and can attract fluids and other cells to the site, clogging the airways. It leads to the wheezing and shortness of breath that, if unchecked, can threaten an asthmatic patient's life. This type of allergy-related asthma tends to be more common among younger people—many of whom may outgrow it—and often runs in families. It is frequently worst in late spring, early summer and fall, when trees and grasses spew their pollen in the air. Researchers at the National Institutes of Health estimate that about 90 percent of asthmatics under age 10 have this sort of asthma, compared with about half of asthmatics over age 30. People with asthma also may be at greater risk of having attacks during stressful times."

The National Heart, Lung and Blood Institute awarded grants totaling $9.376 million over the next five years (1992-1997) to five medical centers nationwide for the study of strategies and approaches to controlling asthma in Blacks and Hispanics. Because of the sheriff's department's failure to recognize the air problem in the new jail—that existed since my first day of work in 1985, officer absenteeism increased fivefold over the next few years. The air problem was obvious, especially when younger officers were chronically coughing, and older officers were experiencing difficulty in breathing; several collapsed on duty. Of course jail officials ignored the problem.

On June 5, 1992, a survey was released by Healthy Buildings International Incorporated, a Virginia-based consulting firm, that showed that 67 percent of office workers in Detroit, said they experienced symptoms at the office, commonly associated with sick building syndrome. That includes fatigue, headaches, itchy or watery eyes, or flu-like symptoms. More than one-third of the workers reported taking at least one day off because of such ills. Nationally, that adds up to tens of billions of dollars in lost time. The survey was conducted in April 1992, among 1,000 adults in downtown Detroit, Chicago, Cincinnati, Minneapolis and St. Louis. Sick building syndrome became a concern over the past 20 years (1972-1992) as modern technology created ever more climate-controlled buildings. As buildings became more tightly sealed, synthetic materials, plastics, machine-made fibers, and sophisticated copying and printing equipment became more common.

Ironically the problems persisted even though many offices banned smoking. There are many things besides smoking that create health problems in offices, among them: mold bacteria in ventilation ducts; temperature settings that are too high or too low, and artificial products such as insulation or carpeting that may give off fumes. More than 80 percent of the problems with contaminated air were due to inadequate maintenance of heating, ventilating or air conditioning equipment, and ignorance of correct operating methods. Those deficiencies can lead to the accumulation of indoor pollutants, especially fungi, bacteria, dust and diverse chemical compounds.

Unfiltered air problems in the new jail were generally worse in the summer months because of the increased heat and nearly suffocating humidity. It was generally moderate in the spring, winter, and fall. The Department showed little, if any, regard for cleaning the air control system. Breathing problems grew tenfold. Nonsmoking officers were also stressed out working with inmates and fellow officers who were chronic cigarette smokers. The jail, a state mandated institution, only had *no smoking* areas in the cafeteria, and the integrity of that area was rarely maintained.

In 1992, the governor of Michigan banned smoking in all public buildings, except cellblocks. In addition, the U.S. Supreme Court ruled in 1993 that prisoners have the right to live in a smoke-free environment. Under Michigan's plan, inmates still could smoke outside. While most prison employees believe that stubbing out smoking is a good idea, some fear it could cause behavior problems. When officials approved the move, Michigan joined Texas, California and a few other states with smoke-free prisons.

Michigan prisons are about to be set free of smoke. The state Department of Corrections wants to ban smoking inside all prison buildings by 1997. But not all bans have been met with success. Vermont, in 1992, prohibited smoking in and outside the prisons. But it backpedaled fast when inmates started smoking powdered Tang. Smuggling surged dramatically, in some cases pushing a black market cigarette to $3. Michigan officials believed they could sidestep problems by phasing in the program and by offering quit-smoking programs taught by prisoners.

In 1987, three years after the new jail began its operations, and two years into my tenure, I began to experience a breathing problem that was solely related to poor maintenance of the air duct system. Quite strangely, the entire air/climate control system in the new jail (Andrew C. Baird Detention Center) was operated and controlled by county maintenance workers on the third floor by computers. The ventilation system was rarely adjusted accordingly, at least not by MIOSHA specifications. Unfortunately, since most county maintenance workers were usually white males, Black officers froze because whites seem to prefer cooler climates. It's a proven fact that most Europeans don't like much heat.

From 1984 through 1988, the fourth floor in the new jail housed psychiatric and some homosexual inmates. Then they were moved to the old jail, and were moved back eventually to their own two floors in the new jail. It was necessary to keep the climate on the 4th floor stabilized because of the type of inmates it housed.

Many strategies to save energy are penny-wise, pound-foolish. Savings from tightly sealed buildings are more than offset by medical costs and lost productivity. Regular monitoring of air quality in office buildings should be conducted, just as there is monitoring for the safety of elevators, because it has a big effect on the health of the people working there. Many bosses assume that workers who complain about poor air quality are faking illness. There's no question there are malingerers on every job, but any manager that doesn't take air quality seriously will regret it in the long run.

A Detroit Free Press article on June 28, 1991, "Smoke in workplace targeted," emphasized how federal agencies considered air-quality rules for offices and factories: "The federal government is considering a rule banning or restricting smoking in the workplace, officials of two federal agencies said. The regulation, if enacted, would cover all aspects of indoor air quality in offices and factories, said Frank Kane, a spokesman for the Occupational Safety and Health Administration (OSHA). But the section of the rule most likely to draw immediate attention would be a regulation banning or restricting smoking in the workplace.

The National Institute of Occupational Safety and Health (NIOSH), part of the Atlanta-based Centers for Disease Control, issued a draft report recommending that employers eliminate tobacco smoke from the workplace or "take steps to reduce exposures to the lowest feasible concentration." It was the first time NIOSH has issued specific recommendations on smoking on the job, said a NIOSH epidemiologist.

Kane said, "OSHA is likely to take its first step toward enacting a rule within 30 days. The agency is planning to issue a call for information concerning indoor air quality. It would cover everything from the performance of ventilation systems, to the hazards of specific pollutants, dangers from radon, and environmental tobacco smoke. At some point, there would have to be public hearings. This is the kind of thing that would affect quite a few people. A rule is probably several months off."

The draft report concluded that when nonsmoking employees inhale tobacco smoke from their colleagues at work—so-called "environmental tobacco smoke"—the nonsmokers have increased chances for a number of smoking-related diseases, including lung cancer."

There was a time I actually had the gumption to mention to Sheriff Carmeno, as he toured the old jail with a Black male sergeant, about the poor air ventilation in the new jail and the neglect of the health of officers. It happened this way. Days before starting the police academy on September 12, 1988, I was given an assignment in the old jail. I had never worked in the old jail before, which made me believe this assignment was either a setup, or someone was trying to protect me from more harassment, so I could attend the academy without further ado: not very likely unfortunately. The sergeant in Roll Call told me I was "replacing an officer for one day."

Sheriff Carmeno just-so-happened to come up on my floor. Carmeno looked around, spotted me, and asked, "What can I do to improve jail conditions?" I was totally surprised, caught a little bit off guard by Carmeno's question. I thought about it for a few seconds, replying earnestly, "First, you can start with improving that filthy air in the new jail. I seem to have no problems breathing over here, but at the new jail many officers, including myself, are having breathing problems."

Carmeno, stunned at my bluntness, appeared to be unconcerned, and walked away without answering. After that encounter there was never any feedback addressing the continuous breathing ailments; repeated complaints about the filthy recycled air all went unheeded. I worried about my own health and the health of my fellow officers and coworkers as well. Many officers also believed the significant breathing problems were also caused by the building materials in the new jail. As the conditions and upkeep of the air vents grew worse, white male jail officials had to be aware of personnel health problems; after all, many officers carried their own fans to their stations to keep the air moving.

However, sometimes having a fan didn't solve breathing problems because officers still had to breath the same foul, recycled air. When the jail wasn't sanitized, on humid summery days vile conditions were even more infectious. Because of the Department's lackluster, periodic cleaning out of "lung damaging" dust in the air ducts, officers feared Legionnaire's disease. In the almost five years I worked at the Department there were no pneumatic tests conducted that I was aware of to find out if there were high levels of bacteria. Many times officers actually thought about secretly calling the Environmental Protection Agency (EPA) to come and inspect the air ducts to determine if there was any evidence of Legionnella bacteria.

The old jail didn't have the problem of dusty air ducts because open windows were accessible. Just before his death, Lieutenant Shoulders diligently pursued getting the drinking water and air tested in the new jail, but an investigation was never forthcoming. Occupational safety and a healthier environment for inmates, officers, and coworkers were not top priority, and several officers died mysteriously. Workers all around America are getting sick because of poor ventilation in the workplace.

On August 31, 1993, a mysterious pneumonia-like illness killed three Jackson State Prison inmates and hospitalized nine other people, including a corrections officer. The medical director for the Jackson region of the Michigan Department of Corrections commented, "It may take a week or more for laboratory tests to pinpoint the nature of the illness." Jackson State Prison officials also tested for Legionnaire's disease, but those tests came back negative. As many as seventy people became ill, and thirty-three sought medical treatment. All the dead and hospitalized had weakened immune systems.

When they became aware of the illnesses, prison guards were afraid to do searches and frisk inmates, thus the security of the prison was in jeopardy. Jackson State Prison staffers and inmates were advised to take normal precautions, however, including washing their hands frequently and covering the mouth and nose when sneezing. The U.S. Centers for Disease Control in Atlanta was notified of the investigation.

It has long been known that disease spreads quickly through prisons, because of the overcrowding and large numbers of inmates. Although many viruses don't even respond to antibiotics, patients are usually treated with the drug erythromycin, which attacks a broad range of infections.

Indoor air pollution robs the United States of $60 billion a year in health costs and lost worker productivity. In December 1993, labor and health groups urged the House of Representatives to join the Senate in passing legislation to address the problem. The Senate passed its version of the Indoor Air Act of 1993 on October 29th. EPA data had indicated levels of indoor air pollution may be markedly higher than outdoor pollution.

Subcommittee Chairman Henry Waxman, D-California, concluded: "Pollution of indoor air is one of our most serious environmental threats, causing tens of thousands of deaths and hundreds of thousands, if not millions, of illnesses each year.

The new bill:

- Authorized up to $48.5 million a year through 1998 to fund research grants, as well as aid to help states identify and correct problems in sick buildings where indoor pollution from carpets, chemicals or other substances can leave occupants incapacitated.

- Required the EPA to inventory contamination sources, viewed as important in recent years as energy-saving measures seal houses, offices and other buildings and trap fumes inside.

- Created certification programs to better control the mushrooming air-quality-improvement industry, while calling for a public information campaign, featuring a toll-free hotline to educate people of possible problems."

A toxicologist representing the National Association of Manufacturers, said most of the illnesses and other problems stemming from poor indoor air quality could be dealt with by improving ventilation. And a doctor testifying for the American Lung Association, agreed that poor ventilation is a big problem, but said the law is needed to gain a better understanding on other causes.

When the new jail was finished in 1984, the Michigan Department of Public Health (MDPH) which regulates industrial hygiene, construction division, general industry, department of labor, and air pollution control, was not informed of the many complaints concerning the ventilation problems. OSHA, which means Occupational, Safety, and Health Administration, is a federally run department that regulates, monitors, and keeps tabs on building safety and health hazards. OSHA is strict when gauging oxygen standards. When a building has a 21% breathing capacity, it is considered standard and generally safe. A 27% breathing capacity is considered oxygen enriched. But when a building does not even reach an intolerable low of 18%, it must be considered as unfit, unsafe, and unhealthy.

MIOSHA is a state run department, formed in 1970, and it writes Michigan regulations involving companies with 10 or more employees. MIOSHA can only adopt OSHA regulated standards, and can only add to federal regulation, not revoke or change them. In 1987, OSHA wrote the Hazards Communication Standard and the Michigan

Right To Know law (MRTK) requiring that employers provide employees with the following: 1. Written Hazard Communication Standard program. a. training. b. equipment. 2. Material safety data sheets for all chemicals that enter your work area. 3. Material safety data coordinator for your work site. 4. Labels on all chemicals. 5. Training of employers on the safe usage of chemicals. If an employer fails to provide its employees with any of this information, the employee has a right to refuse work around or with that chemical product.

Other MIOSHA requirements on the job are: MIOSHA form 101, which is a monthly form specifying injuries filed with the company for the previous year. This form should list all incident reports involving injuries. Also MIOSHA form 200, which is a yearly form stating the employee's name, the department where the injury occurred, occupation of the injured, a description and nature of the injury, and the length of time off. Both forms are sent to the state, which does a categorized analysis to acknowledge and establish key locations or trends of high incident rates.

In 1995, after coming under heavy attack from congressional Republicans, OSHA had to change its way of operation and stop rewarding inspectors for the number of citations issued. The White House attempted to lessen political pressure and pacify business people who were accusing OSHA of being overzealous in enforcing laws.

After many complaints about the bad air in the new jail, MIOSHA safety engineers inspected the situation. They discovered that the area on the first floor near Male Registry and the basement, where personnel store inmates' dirty clothing for several months up to a year in thin plastic, created a persistent and foul odor. To help ventilate the area, a basement wall was knocked out for better circulated, but still, not fresher air.

I always felt that had world renowned environmentalist Ralph Nader checked this situation out, he would have proclaimed it negligence, after observing the many symptoms of asthma, influenza, colds, and bronchitis. Another concern about the air was skin infections. If officers didn't wash their face and hands several times a day, the skin itched and developed bumps, rashes and infections.

Each inmate housed should be searched and frisked, so washing the hands and face throughout the day should be habitual for officers. Many eye, eyelid, nose, mouth, ear, lip, and general skin infections developed because officers neglected to thoroughly wash their hands and face regularly. The most common bacterial infection was caused by rubbing the eyelids with dirty fingers and hands.

The White House estimated in 1990 that businesses would eventually spend $25 billion a year complying with the new Clean Air law. These costs, the Bush administration speculated, would be passed on to buyers of everything from typewriters to toasters. Small businesses he warned would have to comply for the first time as government regulators told dry cleaners what kind of machines to use to keep chemical compounds from evaporating into the air.

Neighborhood auto body shops and wholesale bakeries, the Bush administration warned, would now be forced to change the way they operate. Under the new Clean Air Act, large wholesale bakeries would have to control the aromas and install fume-burning incinerators in their chimneys. Federal regulators could now direct what kind of paint auto body shops could use, and how to spray it. Pollution control equipment companies would gear up for new business, but more importantly, each state's environmental bureaucracy was projected to expand in order to read all the reports and keep track of all the new pollution devices.

Be as the Republicans Administration's predictions may, Michigan's air law definitely needed revision. To begin to comply with the federal Clean Air Act, Michigan had to establish permit terms and fees and set up stiffer punishments for violations. Facing stiff competition abroad for goods and services, many companies spent thousands to fix what had been called the worst air pollution problem in Wayne County. Like water pollution, air pollution by industries and companies and individuals is created by everyone, who drives, smokes, sprays chemicals, or burns things.

18

The Jail Floors;
The Jungle

UNTIL 1990 THE POPULATION IN THE NEW JAIL was 1,152 inmates. Each floor had the capacity for 128 inmates—multiply that by nine and that translates to 1,152 inmates. Inmates were housed from the fourth to the twelfth floor. Out of 13 floors, only nine housed inmates. In 1989 the Department of Corrections administration demolished the entire 13th floor and both the outside and inside gyms, and started construction of sorely-needed additional jail cells. The new edition was completed in November 1990.

Before construction, both gyms were used by inmates, officers and coworkers for basketball, Ping-Pong, pool, and weightlifting. Athletically-minded officers like myself, hated the new cell construction because it took away our only means of recreation—we also had no gun range or training facilities. Thus, the sheriff's department took away our only access to recreation. Every law enforcement agency needs their own gym facility because exercise should keep officers from becoming fat, getting out of shape, and from developing mental and physical medical problems.

The Department *never* instituted a mandatory, departmental rule for officers to maintain a decent weight, or a specific level of physical stamina and conditioning throughout their careers. Every six months a physical agility test should have been conducted to insure staying in some kind of shape, especially since most officers were overweight because of torpidity and complacency, and by eating the cafeteria's many non-nutritional foods. Penalties for noncompliance should be

weeks of conditioning by police academy coordinators or a registered physical trainer. Neglection of such a policy demonstrated short-
sightedness about officers' sick-time off, and in promoting a positive
and fit Departmental image.

Many overweight officers tried all kinds of weight loss programs,
like Dick Gregory's Bohemian Diet, and concoctions like Slim Fast,
instead of exercising naturally—always the best way. The Department left this vitally important health issue entirely up to the officer's
discretion, a mistake since most of the work was sedentary.

If officers were required to stay in mental and physical shape,
character would build and a emotional lift in camaraderie would prevail. A physically fit body and mind helps to encourages morale. I
would have instituted a mandatory two days a week exercise program
for at least two to four hours. This regimen would definitely include
those old-timers whose stomachs bulged over their belts from years
of smoking and unhealthy eating and drinking. After running up only
three or four flights of stairs to a medical emergency or inmate fight,
many older officers were gasping for breath and ready to fall out.
You can't tap into the real potential of a person without a sound,
physical health program.

All officers have certain time restraints because of both family
and moonlighting obligations, but we had to be physically fit when
we first hired in, so, why not all the time? During my first two sum-
mers with the sheriff's department, I'd come in two hours early and
jog down Lafayette Boulevard past Blue Cross and Blue Shield, the
apartment buildings, sometimes by the Detroit River, through downtown, Greektown, and ascend back to the jail. Drenching wet and
sweating, I'd then walk through the lobby and tackle the staircase,
running all the way up to the twelfth floor and back to the basement,
three times. I'd then shower and work twelve hours.

Every summer the Department would initiate twelve-hour shifts,
but before the change, officers limited their interest in keeping fit by
playing basketball with the fellas every Tuesday and Thursday night
after work. Afternoon shift officers played basketball from 11:30 p.m.
to 1 a.m. After the additional jail cells were built on the thirteenth
floor, officers had nowhere (departmental-wise) to go to stay in shape.

All we had was some two-bit, 12-foot-by-20-foot unventilated exercise room to work out in, that was it. A humorous interlude was initiated by the media in 1985. They rumored that the outdoor gym on the 13th floor was, in essence, a swimming pool. Their conclusion was gauged from an overhead aerial view in a helicopter as reflections from blue, supporting beams, to them appeared to be water. Even if there was a swimming pool at the county jail, who in their right mind would want the role of lifeguard or swimming teacher to felons? Could you imagine the legal implications if a deputy let an inmate drown? The county was already crying broke over its many already-pending lawsuits.

In the basement of the new jail were the male and female locker rooms, both equipped with showers. Also in the basement was Key Control; a cafeteria with vending machines; an "itty-bitty" small weight room with a few free weights and a couple of ancient exercise machines; the Roll Call room; and a kitchen. Near the dock and the entrance to the kitchen was a freight elevator for deliveries of food supplies and equipment that only operated from the third floor to the basement. Command officers had their own locker room, and some of the most conniving plots and secrets were hatched there. Superiors' fond desires to be perfect in thine officers sight were dashed once we discovered that they were on the same very-human level as we were.

Deputies were issued computerized security cards, resembling credit cards, to gain entry into the basement through the first floor lobby's sally port cubicle. Inputting the card through the scanner sometimes meant long delays when the computer wasn't working properly, and officers waited impatiently for minutes. Sometimes a computer delay caused officers to be late for Roll Call—having to push the intercom button to alert a Master Control officer to override the mechanism through the computer to open the door. The entry card was mainly used when there was a lack of security, or the paranoia of a possible retaliation from a visitor(s), inmate(s), coworker(s), or officer(s). Most of the time the entry door to the basement was propped open with a wooden door jam. Anyone could've snuck or rushed into the basement with ease, if they had persistence, desperate, kamikaze intentions.

Sometimes computer problems caused long delays, and officers off duty and on their way home lined up on the basement stairs, or in the sally port coming on duty, waiting for the computer mechanism to kick in. When the wait seemed endless, we would use the visitor's elevator to go to the basement for work, or after work, to the first floor to go home. By the time the computer mechanism had kicked in we were usually in Roll Call or on our way home.

The first floor of the new jail consisted of the male and female registries; lobby desk; inmate clothing; bond office; mail room; visitor elevators; First Floor Control; and lawyer visitation booths for trustees and incoming inmates just arriving to get booked. On the second floor was the most vitally important section of jail security: Master Control. This completely computerized area had surveillance cameras constantly scanning sensitive security areas of the jail. The computers kept timed tabulations of every opened and closed door that was hooked-up into the system. All radio transmissions coming from officers in the jail, and other police agency functions patrolling surrounding Wayne County communities, were heard here.

The second floor also had an infirmary for inmates with infectious diseases: AIDS, hepatitis, pneumonia, and flus. Also treated were broken bones or injuries sustained in fights, and chronic illnesses. The infirmary also had methadone detoxification cells to house heroin addicts for withdrawal: a gradual to rapid weaning from opiate use. In a filing section of this area were kept the complete dental and health history of every inmate.

The Reception Diagnostic Center (RDC), another vital part of jail corrections, is where inmates are evaluated by social workers, and classified by height, weight, race, age, and even by their charges, before being placed on a floor. Shift command offices, commanders' offices with an administrative secretary, and Internal Service Bureau (ISB) interrogation rooms were also a part of the non-inmate jail space on the second floor.

There were also capias cells on the second floor for officers or employees involved in internal problems. Officers were sometimes jailed for selling or smuggling drugs into the jail, and for any felony or misdemeanor committed off or on duty. Separate jail facilities were necessary to jail officers or coworkers because of the fear of inmate(s) retaliation. Many officers did not treat inmates under their care with dignity.

Reputed Defense lawyer, the late Fletcher Campbell was one luminary jailed in the capias cells on contempt of court charges. Campbell typically drummed up business by riding around in a van he used as his office. He would come periodically on the jail floors and distribute flyers with a collage of news clippings made from his former clients as advertisements to possibly gain new clients: his main clientele were inmates accused of murder. He had a reputation of getting clients accused of murder "off the hook," so many inmates called Campbell immediately after looking over the flyers advertising his services.

The Sheriff's Department was known to occasionally place policemen or other law agency officers undercover on inmate wards to entrap deputies into wrongdoing. Most hardened criminals will not tolerate the deployment of a peace officer on their "rock." If found out, he will be descended upon like flies on shit. Any such officer would have to stay incognito, unless an inmate on the ward had already negotiated a plea bargain to shorten his jail term, and agreed to work in tandem with the Department's so-called investigation. There is no difference in the treatment of spies and informants. Both compete and expect special treatment and privileges for their valued, biased information.

Entrapment is a common practice among police agencies, and it is particularly convenient for officers and jail officials to entrap or steal items from officers in the New Jail because all the floor, closet, and station keys are interchangeable. Thus in reality one had a master key for nine floors. Officers could, for example, plant something in another officer's station while they were away.

Inmates facing long sentences for serious crimes will work undercover for law agencies and will squeal and lie on others to get their sentences reduced, or a few charges dropped. Working the same floors for years, officers became well acquainted with inmates' motives, actions, attitudes, fears, wants, charges, emotions, lovers, lawyers, relatives, likes and dislikes, prejudices, future goals, and most of all, projected release date.

On the third floor were trustee services, where only certified officers were entrusted with the daily supervision of trustees for specific duties performed in or outside the jail. The trustees' jobs were garbage pickup; loading jail supplies or food for the kitchen; mopping and polishing floors; shoveling snow; preparing cafeteria food; cleaning up administrative offices; and other delegated work.

The commissary office was on the third floor, and this was where all the goodies, the zoom-zooms and wham-whams (cookies and cakes) were stored. This floor was the officers' favorite because when the cafeteria food was uneatable, this was where officers went to buy something to snack on. We all thought, better to snack than eat that garbage, usually cooked by trustees, and served in the cafeteria. The ladies in charge of the commissary had carts, resembling lion cages, they rolled around on the jail floors. These had enough storage space for all the essentials on sale: razor blades, underwear, tobacco and cigarettes, regular large bath-size soap, deodorant, toothbrushes and toothpaste, undershirts, and shaving cream, to name some toiletries.

Inmates used this horrible, stinking shaving cream called *Magic Shave*. Black male inmates saturated their heads with it, let it stay on for about half-an-hour, and scraped off all their hair using just the scoop-side of a plastic spoon. Such a head was actually free of nicks and cuts. I hated the smell; it was nauseating. Only Black male inmates who wanted to shave their heads used this shaving cream; other long-haired Blacks sat intently, getting their unkempt, tenderheaded scalps braided.

Candy bars, nuts, potato chips, Kool-Aid, snack cakes, Reese's cups (I bought many of those), mints, licorice, lifesavers, assorted flavors of Certs, gum, pastries, and other tasty confectioneries were also on the commissary wagon. It even had Tums, which sold out regularly, because of the constantly aching stomachs caused by food poisoning from unhealthy and spoiled food. Of all the items sold, cigarettes and loose tobacco were the commodities most treasured by inmates. Big stogies regularly stunk-up the inmate wards.

The scenario was this: Five or six inmates would be sitting at a table, two standing. They would empty up to ten packs or more of Bugler or Kite tobacco, and roll cigarettes for hours at a time. An inmate with plenty of cigarettes was considered the "Man," and had many friends. Inmates and officers alike, when supplied with cigarettes, had added power to manipulate poorer inmates who smoked.

"Hey Dep, let me do some work for ya... like wash the station windows, or mop the floors and ward for a couple of them cigarettes," inmate Craig Fuller, a short, pudgy white, forty-ish male with yellow decaying teeth, begged, while experiencing a chronic nicotine fit. Fuller was in jail for one count of arson and another for breaking and entering.

"You better get one of your friends on the ward to give you a Kite or Bugler cigarette. I'm tired of giving out my Newports to you guys," Officer St. Ignatius replied. He was a tightwad, stingy white male chain-smoker, who smoked like a chimney. Most of St. Ignatius' family stayed in Spain, and were historically involved in Christian salvation centers similar to the Salvation Army.

"But them cigarettes don't taste good at all. Ah, come on dep, I can't smoke them, they're too harsh on my throat," a fidgety Fuller entreated, hoping for a reprieve from the "*Saint*" that never came.

To keep a tab on how much money each inmate spent, the commissary ladies carried computer tabulated sheets with inmates' names and the money in their accounts. Those with money were the only inmates allowed to shop. The only way money could be forwarded to an inmate's account was by a money order brought to the bonding office in the jail—only written in increments of $20. As each inmate shopped and bought from the commissary wagon, the commissary lady tabulated the goods on a calculator and gave each inmate a receipt. That amount was deducted from his account.

Inmates who tried to steal items from the wagon, were the recipients of a fit. "What-in-the-hell do you think you're doing," Marcie the cart lady hollered to a thieving inmate caught in the act. Marcie was a Black woman in her late 40s, who wore a long, curly, "country-fied" jheri curl. "Oh, I'm sorry, I thought I could just get it," the inmate innocently answered, knowing full-well he was in the wrong!

I was approached twice in my tenure by inmates who had their own money and had missed the wagon: "Officer Taylor, will you please buy me some cigarettes from downstairs out of the vending machines, or from the store? Because the prices are too high on the wagon," several inmates claimed. "No drugs, just cigarettes guys," I'd always tell them. Though I could have written up a report on the inmate for having money in his possession (contraband), many of us regarded this as just helping an inmate get some cigarettes. The officers who searched these inmates in Male Registry obviously didn't do their job of searching thoroughly, because each inmate had a twenty dollar bill. When something like this occurs, a setup immediately comes to mind. Money is of no use to a inmate in jail, so it might as well be used to some extent.

The commissary ladies were very lenient about giving credit to officers, but some officers abused their generosity. Many officers actually went several weeks indebted for just two or three dollars. I never had any problems getting "goodies" from the cart. All the commissary ladies always gave me candy, gum, mints or licorice free of charge, just because I always paid my debt on time.

In 1987, another important detail was initiated—Laundry Detail. Situated on the third floor, its official duty was to schedule and deliver twice a week, clean inmate clothing and linen to the floors. Once inmate clothing was unloaded off the delivery truck at the dock, it was brought to the third floor to be sorted by size, and folded up by trustees. Between 1987 and 1990, the Sheriff's Department spent upwards of $200,000 a year for laundry services alone. (General Fund for County Jail, years 1987-1990, Report 87, 1990.)

There were always problems with cells that needed maintenance work. Several bottom-bunk inmate beds collapsed because of a lack of support beams. This was caused by concrete loosening around the bolts affixed in the wall. Instead of immediately fixing this problem, permission was granted for the inmate to use a milk crate for support to avoid further damage, or possible injury. That same milk crate, put in a cell for support, was also commonly used as a weapon in fights.

Plumbing was also a lingering problem in the jail. Showers in particular, worked erratically, and the drains became clogged with floating dirt, scores of dead roaches, wax paper, grease, and rotting food. Officers, fearing the petty reprimands of superiors, insistently reminded inmates to clean the showers. It didn't help, and the showers stayed clogged and filthy, a health concern as well as a plumbing problem.

Church Services: Worship, Is it a Key to Rehabilitation?

HOURS BEFORE THE START OF CHURCH SERVICES, a sign-in list was passed around the inmate wards for those to sign who wanted to attend. The officer in charge of transporting inmates to the ninth floor collected all attending inmates' cards. Once reaching the ninth floor's multipurpose room, he gave the cards to another officer working in a station on the north side. The officer in charge of the transfer was supposed to stay in the room with the inmates, but many didn't because of conflicting spiritual beliefs or a desire to spend that time in leisure. Overseeing the inmates was often left up to the officer in the north side station until church services were over.

All church services started with prayer: "Oh yes, God has been mighty good to us. No matter what your present predicament, fate, or life experiences are, remember that God is still in charge and HE is good to you and to me. We can't forget that this is a day that the Lord has made, and we might as well rejoice and be glad in it. We must glorify His name; let's sing His praises today. Everybody turn to page 500 of the Worship and Praise hymnal, and let's rejoice in the old spiritual 'Amazing Grace.' Let's all sing about God's many blessings," encouraged Father Glennery, a white male minister, about 55 years of age, to a room full of primarily Black male inmates.

There were enough hymnals for every inmate, and they were always locked up in a locker. A piano and organ were there for the church pianist to accompany the singing. Whew, thank God! "But before we lift up our voices to the heavenly father, let us bow our heads in another prayer," continued Father Glennery as some inmates drew closer to slumber and the yawning became contagious.

Father Glennery intoned: "Our father, which art in heaven, Hollowed be thy name. Thy kingdom come. Thy will be done in earth, as it is in heaven. Give us this day our daily bread. And forgive as our debts, as we forgive our debtors. Lord, lead us not into temptation, but deliver us from evil: For thine is the kingdom, and the power, and the glory, for ever. Amen."

The Lord's Prayer was prayed in solemn unison and, after two more prayers, the pianist played the introductory chords to *Amazing Grace*. Inmates started clearing their throats before singing: "Amazing Grace, how sweet the sound, that saved a wretch like me. I once was lost but now I'm found. Was blind, but now I see."

Inmates thus sang the first verse of the famous spiritual written by John Newton, a former white slave master when he wrote it. Then the second verse came: "Through many dangers toils and snares. I have already come. Twas grace that brought me safe thus far and grace will lead me on."

As I listened, I was reminded of Newton's guilty conscious about the enslavement of Blacks, which started in the English colony of Jamestown, Virginia, in 1619 with twenty Afrikans, just twelve years after the colony was established. As I returned to the present time and place, I realized the inmates sounded like out-of-tune migrating refugees, or cattle rustlers camped out under a full, luminous moon, rather than inspired men of faith.

But their purpose wasn't to sound like a finely tuned gospel choir; they were there to hear and sing God's praises for the remission of their sins. Still, as they sang, I anticipated hearing the howl of a late night coyote in the background. Somehow, I had to admit, it was already depressing enough hearing the cadence and flip-flop of the inmates' sandals, a sound I imagined worn-out, tired slaves had made as they trudged along after a long hard day in the cotton fields.

When architects designed the new jail, jail administration, county commissioners, and civic and religious leaders all neglected to consider a place for inmates to worship. A chancel, anything that provided a place to kneel and pray would have been better than just an multipurpose room and a jail cell that required upwards of $35,000 a

year to maintain. Instead of a half-gym located on every odd numbered floor, jail planners could have included a tabernacle with seats
and altar where prayers could be received by each individual's chosen deity. Inmates could have been ushers and trustees, and taught
principles of successful living to inmates or presented them sermons.

For those who needed it, the love of Christ, Yaweh, or Allah
(God) would have spread throughout the jail, and for some inmates,
and maybe for some officers, would have had a better chance to
change their lives. After release from jail, former inmates would have
something to talk positively about to the people they had previously
mistreated.

Father Love, an older white man in his late 70s, made appoint-
ments to talk with inmates in the bullpen adjacent to center station.
Most inmates in the bullpen were awaiting either trial or transfer to a
permanent facility after sentencing, and needed the assurances of
God's love. After ministering to inmates, Love would always top off
his visit with a hug and a kiss on the cheek: his spiritual consultations were always very emotional. It was appalling to me that Father
Love drew harsh criticism from some officers who distrusted him only
because of his close ties with inmates.

The strongest institution for Afrikan-Americans has historically
been the church. The United States government doesn't come close
in its attempts to emulate God's role. Having no regular church home,
as is true in prison, means that an individual has no commitment to
try and further the welfare of the church. This is true in all ethnic
families and communities. My own opinion is that some religious
concepts still enslave the minds of Black people. The many different
religious coalitions and denominations continue to splinter Afrikan-
American unity.

The Church is one of the few organizations in which many Black
people feel empowered and recognized. There are a lot of egos in
church. I think it is important that churches run by Afrikan-Americans and other people of color all over America need to unite and
buy land to grow crops, and breed cattle and poultry to feed both
their own parishioners and the ever growing number of poor people
in this nation.

It is necessary for people to eat, and the ethnic Arabs and Chaldeans know this and have shown the way and capitalized on selling basic commodities: food, oil and gas. Before these essential commodities can be controlled by Afrikan-American people, historically held down by the United States government, they and other peoples of color have first got to stick together and become a collective for their own economic good.

Carefully reading the words of some old church songs, one can clearly understand that slaves were not happy and carefree in their slavery. In most of the lyrics there is found a quiet, sometimes bitter resignation and resolve to be free. Slaves pretended to be happy to avoid a hassle or a beating, and deep sadness was clearly expressed in much of their own music and art.

Slave songs and poems are filled with hope and despair, and the melodies are often sad and mournful to our ears. The spiritual lives of Afrikan slaves went underground when they reached America and were forced by the white race to adopt a religious ceremony not their own. How they sublimated their love of freedom and their identity as a people within the dictates of a religion that exhorted one to look forward to a better life *only* after death and *only* in heaven, is a marvel of human ingenuity and intellectual dexterity.

Translating slavery to the twentieth century, we can use as an example, the famous dirge called "Trouble": "Trouble, trouble, trouble, Done had trouble all my days, Trouble, trouble, trouble, Done had trouble all my days. Seems, boys, like dese troubles Gwine to carry me to my grave." This song is autobiographical and recognizable to Black officers working for the sheriff's department. The fixed, institutional standards of slavery have always put Afrikan-Americans in chaos and separation. Thus did Black officers in the Sheriff's Department fear retribution if they spoke up about injustice.

As sad as it is, the scars of slavery remain visible towards the end of the twentieth century. The white-American myths of manifest destiny and racial superiority have kept the descendants of slaves free in name only. The Republican proposals to dismantle thirty years of affirmative action, civil rights amendments, and quotas originally established to broaden the rights of all people, insult the intelligence and ambitions of every American, who is not white and male. Equal opportunity in housing, jobs, and education is also a privilege of white-male America.

Black America is denied equal trash service, police patrols, fair insurance and taxation, fair employment, and well-maintained rental properties in our neighborhoods, let alone access to golf courses in exclusive white country clubs. Like James Brown said, "You don't have to give me nothing, but open up the door, I'll get it myself..." Black Americans are seeking respect, dignity, and our unalienable rights under the Bill of Rights in this so-called *"Land of the Free,"* even as you read this. Yes, we have come a long way, but we need to love one another more and stop fighting each other for power. We must stick together so our children can be empowered.

Whites have stigmatized Black men as criminals, but we definitely aren't any more criminal or violent than other men throughout the world. Why did few Americans *assume* the Oklahoma City bombing was co-engineered and carried out by a white, male veteran of the Gulf War? After driving her car in a lake and drowning her two sons, why was Susan Smith so confident that she *would avoid* suspicion by blaming a Black man in a watch cap for their kidnapping? What about those school shootings committed by young white teenagers in Pearl, Mississippi, West Paducah, Kentucky, Stamps and Jonesboro, Arkansas? After all, in Boston, years before *those* documented tragedies, many Black suspects were rounded up when a homicidal, white male shot and killed his pregnant wife, and blamed it on a Black man. Later, after the police focused their investigation on the white male, he buckled under pressure and committed suicide by jumping off of a bridge into a river.

White people must reflect upon the negative image of Black-Americans they have broadcast to countries all over the world. During the First World War, white American soldiers stationed in Europe warned European women that Black American soldiers had tails like monkeys. Today's immigrants from Asia and the British or French Islands *still* think Black-Americans are shiftless or lazy, even in the face of the Civil Rights record, and accept blindly that they "were freed" by Abraham Lincoln. Domestic racism festers in the American byewaters and in the hearts of the descendants of southern white sharecroppers, who still resent that the Negro got forty acres and a mule, and whites stole those from Negroes too, when Sherman went back North. Those all over the Old South, who managed to reclaim the family land left to Black descendants by altering Deeds and Wills in local courthouses after the Civil War, often regret their ancestors as too free with their "white" genes.

The white para-militaries, who train in rural and suburban communities, have already become a problem for minorities and lost multimillion dollar lawsuits and all their assets. They have since detonated bombs in a Federal building, and are now feeling the rumblings of an unwieldy government giant just waking up in time to swat them out of the air. So, from Allegheny County Pennsylvania to Dorchester County, Maryland; from the wide-open spaces of Utah, Montana, and the Dakotas to the Grand Canyon of Arizona, the racist are taking off their white hoods, and letting their hair grow in.

Food for thought. If you really look at it, you will see that just about every urban city in America is surrounded by white suburban communities. Also, nearly each urban inner city in America is locked in, blocked in by a waterway. In the city of Detroit, for example, we are locked in by a river *and* another country (Canada). Attack the urban centers of major cities, even smaller ones, and the Black population in America would decrease dramatically. Need I say more?

Racism is picked up by those Afrikan-American brothers and sisters who have become tired and weak, and have succumbed to the European plans of demoralization. They have joined the establishment, and they persecute their own people. This is happening in prisons all over the United States.

Church services in the new jail weren't full of joyous yipes, "*holy ghost*" dances, or "*saved*" celebrations, as they were in most Christian, Black-Baptist churches. The Black inmates at Reverend Glennery's services were grave: expected to be contrite and seek God's mercy and forgiveness for all their crimes and sins. To some extent, church services can be a moral rehabilitating force for some individuals. I will qualify this by suggesting that, with prayer, some inmates change their behavior when they have time to think about their inhumanity and their crimes against individuals.

Once in awhile I like to attend different churches just to see how other people worship. One Sunday I attended a church of the Pentecostal faith. I was invited there by Karen, a wonderfully kind, inspiring young Black woman, with enormous talent. Karen played violin for several jazz groups in night spots in and around Detroit. I met her at the health spa, in the steam and sauna rooms. We talked about God, church, life, but spent the bulk of our time together talking about my problems working for the sheriff's department: "Karen, I need a change of environment, need to worship with different races," I told her one day when I was tired, and growing immune to the same ol' church programs.

And when I finally attended Karen's church, I discovered that worshipping in a predominantly white congregation wasn't exactly something I was used to, or had ever had in mind. After all, I had visualized Jim Bakker and Jimmy Swaggart. But Karen's church was an enriching experience; it had missions all over the world. Visitors, signing up prior to services, were later sent an impressive brochure delineating all the affiliated departments: music ministry, Christian education, youth ministry, care ministry, and a worship schedule. The packet contained cards with scriptures in prophecy praising God, scriptural terminologies, and a map of the church's location. There was even a welcome card. So much given information told me, right there, that the organization was serious about serving God's people.

But the praises from the congregation were too well-mannered. There was never rhythmic hand clapping, or foot stomping to the music, as there would be in a Black Baptist congregation. It is expected in the Black church that someone will eventually get "*happy*," and catch the spirit of the "*holy ghost*": gyrating, or dancing up and down the aisles, shouting praises with arms raised. But all this was missing from this white church, and that took a lot of getting use to. White people haven't been through the trials and tribulations Afrikan-American people have. Perhaps joy isn't as valuable to them.

The church service was too laid back for me, but fulfilling anyway, and that's important. On the Sunday I attended the pastor gave a sermon about divorce. Boy, did he talk about divorce. His message, his very *flair*, was stern: "Divorce is deplorable, and it's not God's will to separate," proclaimed the pastor. A stark silence came over the parishioners; there were no Amens to that! I disagreed with him. Yes, God doesn't *want* married couples to break up, leaving broken families and their childrens' lives in disarray. But since we all come up short of the glory of God, I believe God forgives our imperfections, and desires the best for us.

We must admit that marriage isn't always undertaken for love; it's motives are sometimes greed, selfishness, and financial necessity. Such marriages usually end in divorce. Though some marriages survive bad times, many people stay together and just put up with it, going along with multiple, habitual problems like my parents did. Everyone does agree that divorce wrecks the family structure. At the time I attended Karen's church, I was suing the sheriff's department for violating my civil and constitutional rights from an "*illegal search of my person*" at a police academy graduation ceremony. All this went through my mind as I waited to go up front to the altar—that's when I took the legal court documents with me to pray over them. As I did so, I felt God's presence telling me to *never* stop writing this book to tell *my side of the story*. This comforted me because I was being railroaded by white folks in the courts and jails of Wayne County.

When we were all seated, the pastor introduced a newlywed white couple who were traveling to Nairobi, Kenya, later that day to assist an international church mission in feeding millions of hungry war-ravaged children and refugees. This was their last service before leaving on their long journey. "I want everybody in the church to stretch out their arms towards this couple, and lets all pray for their safety so their work will not be in vain, so they may see the fruits of their labor turn into positive results," the pastor proclaimed. We all lifted our arms upward, our palms stretched out towards the couple. Oh yes, we could feel the Holy Spirit.

Karen's sisters attended that service, both gorgeous, attractive women. Although prayer took complete concentration, I must admit I was a little distracted. However, I was totally aware of why I needed to be in that church: to praise God's name and receive His, or Her, blessings, which I so desperately needed.

Why do most inmates become involved in religion while incarcerated? First let me say that by no means are church services in jail conducive to sincere religious confession in contemplative seclusion: this was jail, where indignity and the loss of freedom are the everlasting norm. Some inmates are devoted atheists, with a disposition toward a vague deism. Many men were content to make life hard for others, and lacked any kind of faith. But I've never seen many very old atheist, have you, although some men would except religion fervently, only to deny it again as times kept hard and long jail sentences dragged on?

The subject of religion produced heated, sometimes puritanical, debates: "Those damn fools, believing in someone they haven't even seen or visioned is stupid. Man, I'm my own damn God," protested inmate Brogna, a 6-foot-3-inch tall, two-hundred, sixty pound white guy, who looked like a WWF wrestler. He was a full-bearded biker type, with multiple charges against him of armed robbery, federal weapons violations, and one count of conspiracy to deliver and distribute four kilos of cocaine. He wore a tattooed swastika on his left arm with enormous pride. Brogna's Nazi beliefs defied and awed many of the religious faithful. Many times disagreements about religion turned into vehement arguments, and sometimes into brutal fights.

Reverend Powers, a Black male, and Father Glennery, a white male, were the ecclesiastical directors of the jail's ministry. They weren't just flamens, preaching sermons to inmates with spotty attention spans, they were two concerned men, who cared about the welfare and fate of jailed human beings in need of a life change and a quick fix in faith.

When church services were boring, a chorus of yawns and groans rose. To spark more interest in the services, I helped out by singing, praying, and once gave an inspirational lecture on how to stay positive and wait for the grace and blessings of Jesus Christ. One day Father Glennery asked me to speak, believing an officer's revelations might have some impact on them. My first sermon was short and straight to the point:

"I know that there's someone very powerful and that almighty person is everlasting. Jesus loves you all and despite your crimes, and sins, He still has great plans for you all. You've got to have faith, without that, what is there? This jail is just your calling card, a phase in life where different trials and tribulations are set upon you, to see how much faith and determination you really have in yourself and The Man above. We all must learn from the experiences we had and the ones we are gonna have and build upon them for a better day. I know He's real, because I wouldn't have survived this job so long, if He wasn't. So remember... keep the faith, and never cease to pray, continue to walk up right, and when you get lonely, call Him noon, day, or night. Cause, He'll be there, He'll be there, and there's no need to worry, for God never fails. Remember that!"

It got good to me as I got going. I had picked a song and turned it into a sermon. Father Glennery clapped, and some of the more involved inmates got "*happy*," while others said, "Amen." I was glad Father Glennery gave me a chance to speak homilies because the inmates showed appreciation for my conscious divinity, and respected me for the realization of the message.

I'm not the most devoutly religious person, but I am observant and spiritual, and there's a difference. Reverend Powers was a skilled and soulful homilist, you know, how many Southern-style Black preachers make those whizzing noises, like they're experiencing a seizure, or a terrible flu or cold. The word of God was the only viable source of blessings in the jail for inmates. Of course, there were no offerings or tithes. Money is contraband in a jail, so passing around a collection basket was out of the question.

Could the church in jail accept contributions of candy and cigarettes? Question is, would the Lord still pour His blessings to an inmate who tithed 10 percent of all the candy and cigarettes they accumulated every week? It could have been arranged for money to be taken from inmates' accounts each week, but there were no deacons or trustees (only jail trustees) to count the money, or present to give second motions for inspired inmates wanting to join, or be baptized. Besides, there was no baptismal font and no blessed holy water to wash their sins away.

Religious demands by prisoners are increasing in penal systems all over the country. Michigan state officials have become sick and tired of knuckling under to what they call expensive, off-the-wall, or potentially dangerous religious demands by prison inmates. Some interesting examples are as follows: A group of Michigan inmates joined with the *Witches International Coven Church of America* and requested they be allowed to practice their mystic craft in state prisons.

Certain Muslim sects at Jackson and other Michigan prisons have sought exemption from grueling kitchen duties because they say their religion does not allow them to work around pork. The state of Michigan actually built a sweat lodge for worshipping Native American inmates at Kinross in the Upper Peninsula, and fears that requests for similar religious facilities can be expected at more secure lockups. My favorite, however, is that members of a group known as the Church of the New Song claimed they must be served filet mignon steak and a glass of Chardonnay for lunch while in prison in the western United States. In Michigan, a Corrections Director said he fully expects more such requests.

Inmates ask for private meeting rooms and other facilities, as well as religious supplies such as candles and incense. Some inmates demand special diets of kosher foods, or no pork. In addition to the tax money spent, a major concern is that prison gangs are setting up phony cults or infiltrating established groups like the Melanins, an Islam offshoot, at Southern Michigan Prison in Jackson, Michigan. The gangs have been known to use private meeting rooms, furnished by the state, to plot riots, escapes, and attacks on guards.

In March 1995, Michigan's governor lobbied to exempt inmates from the Religious Freedom Restoration Act passed by Congress in 1994. The number of inmate requests for special treatment has mushroomed since the act's passage. Court rulings upholding the act in prisons in some states leave the remaining states' prison officials little choice but to approve these requests. This, of course, could mean greater security risks and escalating prison management costs, which leads to *higher* taxes. Many state officials condemned the 1994 act for further complicating life for prison administrators and pushing state prisons' security measures to the limit.

A Director of the Criminal Justice Programs for American Friends Services Committee, an inmate advocacy group, acknowledged that the Religious Freedom Restoration Act causes management headaches at prisons. The Director also said the State Department is lax in documenting gang activities and other problems, and that neglect has hampered the group's ability to implement useful inmate advocacy. The Director also suggested there be a gang task force to assess the extent of the problem. The debate over inmates' religious rights must be thoroughly examined again by Congress, to ensure denial of requests that are totally unreasonable.

Black inmates in Wayne County wanted greater freedom of religion. This demand was fueled by the reality that many Black inmates are angry at a system that denies their manhood. The first thing a Black male prisoner sees when he first comes to Male Registry are many white male officers and guards. From that point on, he just wants to worship a Black Messiah, a Black God, a Black Jesus.

Before the benediction, Father Glennery had one last word, "Before we all go back to our homes let's remember that God is good. He truly lives today, please don't forget that! If you stick by His word, live right, treat people right, God will bless you forever. Let's turn to page 187, and sing 'Bless Be the Tie That Binds,' to the glory of God." After discussing the wisdom of God's word being righteous and being a mighty weapon, inmates formed a circle and held hands for the final prayer. The pianist played a soft, reflective tune to end the service, and I signaled to the officer in the Northeast station: it was time to go. The inmates once more struck up a tired, off-key white hymn, this time: "Bless be the tie that binds, our hearts in Christian love. The fellowship of kindred minds, is like... to that... above. Amen."

"Father, you know that we need you. Many of us, don't have no wheres to go. We are asking for your blessings, and for you to bless the people who will decide and judge our fates. Lord give them a change of heart and to grant some leniency in their final decision. These blessings we ask in Jesus name. Amen." This was the prayer from inmate Dave Simpson, a Black male, in jail for burglarizing several metropolitan churches in Detroit and its surrounding suburbs. When Detroit police responded to one church's alarm, they found several large burlap sacks full of church property between the pews, and Simpson on his knees at the altar, asking God for forgiveness.

After church service—if the transfer officer was not readily present to take inmates back to their respective wards, the officer(s) manning the north stations might call Master Control to page that officer. This went out over the entire jail, including the lobby. The officer paged was usually annoyed about the announcement because he might be labeled as "*goofing off*" somewhere. He would retaliate: "You didn't have to have me paged. I was just on the other side of the floor," said Officer Bradley, a Black male. "Well, I didn't know where you were," said Officer McKenske, a white male, who had no patience and no known godly love for anybody, especially Black male inmates who were Baptists, and comprised most of the congregation. McKenske didn't like any religion but his own, the Catholic religion. Subconsciously, I believe that McKenske was the kind of person who'd burn up a church.

It is estimated that there are more Catholics than Protestants, Jews, or Muslims in the United States. Christianity, however, is by far the world's largest religion, with two to three billion followers. Back in 1986, I caught a glimpse of the Catholic religion from Detroit's Catholic archdiocese, when I frequented Archbishop Edmund Szoka's mansion. Now I knew him, and called him Shaka Zulu when we saw each other, and he got a kick out of that. He was a man who jogged everyday around the spacious driveway and yard of his home: he was in better shape than much younger men.

His chef, Steve, a young Black male in his mid-20s, was my friend, and I visited the archbishop's mansion many times in the mid-80s. Steve and I had the time of our lives when the legate took a trip to Brazil, went away on missionary work, or traveled to the Vatican to see his best buddy, the Pope. One time, when the nuncio was away in Brazil on a two-week mission, Steve and I went out to a nightclub to party. We met Cerise and Tanya, a couple of foxy-looking young Black ladies, who rode up from Toledo. After leaving the nightclub, they followed us back to Szoka's mansion, a colossal house with three tiers of staircases, and lots of room to frolic about. Both women looked in wonderment at the remote controlled electronic gate, and became more eager for a night of fun. We ate, drank, and talked for hours, sitting on expensive, Victorian-styled lounge chairs at a long, mahogany conference table in the archbishop's house. His home had every compliment to a good time. We told the women we were recording producers and kin to Berry Gordy, the founder and president of Motown; we said something like that. Whatever it was, it worked. We did nothing out of the ordinary, we were totally conscious of the spirit in Szoka's home, but we still had fun. In the summer of 1990, Szoka left for the Vatican after his promotion to Cardinal by Pope John Paul.

During my tenure *Within The Walls*, I tried, as did many other Black officers, to get rid of our bitterness and anger, but the sheriff's department continued a policy of bigotry against us. Jail officials routinely rejected Black officers' grievances and resented our independence and strong minds, by using petty infractions to stall promotions. There was a poster on the Roll Call bulletin board, informing officers "where to call for help when having problems with alcohol, drugs, and family counseling."

Psychological help was offered to officers through an affiliated mental health organization, but I relied heavily on the pastorate of Pastor Powers, and Fathers Glennery and Love. We often talked about complex issues confronting our world: Our conversations dealt with racism, the Black economic dilemma, world hunger and homelessness, and unemployment. But for the most part we discussed the Department's two different standards for white and Black officers. All clergymen in the jail hoped for changes in departmental ideology. They all said the same thing, "Believe in God, wait for his blessings, and everything will be alright."

Thinking of the tribulations of those years, I knew that God had another plan for me and took the sheriff's job from me. I know it wasn't just by chance that put me in a position to write and inform, about an experience that made me a much stronger, more conscious, faithful human being. One hears of people proclaiming that God is responsible for all the good things in their life. There is much truth in this, and without my belief in *"The Creator,"* this book would not have been possible.

In essence, the Department created the means and the vehicle, because my **HIS**-story has its share of pain, turmoil, racism, despair, falsehood, and depression. There still is an element of hope. I still care and pray for those white jail officials who caused me such vexation and difficulty. After years of dealing with inmates and the jail system, white attitudes often reflected a mental state of suspicion, paranoia, and conspiracy. Also there are many different personalities and conflicting egos working in the jail, and this makes life hard in an institutional setting.

Yes, there is a certain attitude a deputy must have in a jail setting, but it is equally important to possess expertise in handling religious, racial and social differences, and to know how to build bridges and get through communication barriers. Many acts committed in jail are heinous, imbuing the physical place with a depressing and repressive atmosphere, making it sometimes difficult to work in.

The Department has been content historically to keep Black officers oppressed to marginalize and limit their power. The means has been to make it more difficult for them to advance. It took Black officers longer than it took whites to get promoted in rank, and that's one reason why Blacks, as a group, are perhaps able to be more exuberant, in their praise of the Divine for getting them through adversity, much of it caused by whites. *Only* The Lord knows for sure, but have mercy on them anyway. Amen.

20

Hunky-Dory Jail Rules.
No Exceptions to the Rule!

HE ENFORCEMENT OF JAIL RULES FOR INMATES and officers changed like Michigan weather: very unexpectedly. Rules were designed ostensibly to revamp "*The System*," and conformity was enforced to selectively harass and control certain officers. Whomever jail officials deemed threatening and outspoken, possessed of an independent conscience, was subjected to a backlash of propaganda in hopes of eliminating, discouraging, and containing any rebellious tendencies. Trendy precedents were secretly set by jail officials, who instituted specific codified procedures and plea bargains for certain officers only.

There were only two standards at the Department: white officers had *flexible guidelines* and Black officers had *fixed rules*. White male jail officials constantly repeated a litany of inflexible jail rules for the betterment of inmates, coworkers, officers, and the Department. In reality, jail rules were only enforced if an officer fought groundless charges and bucked an unfair system. What was astonishing was that officers working in the jail had more rules and regulations than did habitual inmates.

Shift command officers seemed to be evaluated and promoted if they faithfully adhered to tactics of harassment, and facilitated the dismissal of officers targeted for selective liquidation. A targeted officer was usually one with ambition, good math and verbal skills, administrative ability, and competence in handling a tough situation. This officer also had to be adaptable in handling the complex of intricate psychological inmate problems, especially those of *Black* inmates. When white superiors evaluated and perceived the potential, and expressed finer qualities of Black officers, many, with true racist sentiments, arbitrarily enforced petty jail rules to stigmatize and characterize that officer as one who *"disobeys orders"* and is *"incorrigible."*

If the truth is told, rules were also enforced and reprimands given because of differences of opinion and individual, personality styles. Allegations of misconduct against most targeted officers were prompted by rumor rather than pure truth. Some officers didn't care about what happened to some fellow officers as long as they were the ones still holding a job. Such officers never spoke out against injustices within the system, and were the Department's most often-mined source of rumor and innuendo. When I accused other officers or superiors of trumping up charges, I was ignored by jail officials, and the charges were never considered for further investigation or examination.

Practices of *"operational influencing"* were modeled on the domino principal, that one lie engenders others. Targeted officers' methods of procedure and job performance were always scrutinized and questioned, even when these officers flawlessly supervised inmates. Officers envious of another officer's ease in handling inmates caused internal havoc; they fostered misconceptions and created rumors about the unproven. Periodic polls of Black officers revealed astonishingly low morale and pessimism, a high degree of skepticism and stress, and racism. Deep down, no one really liked working in the jail, but it was a job that grew on most people as a "power trip," affording the opportunity to do the minimum while sitting down. Then one had the time to be complacent about it.

Polls also revealed overwhelming negativism among officers in general, and a perceived Departmental favoritism to white officers. This was ironically substantiated when Black officers, accused of infractions of jail rules, defended themselves in writing; many times these written statements never elicited even a response, never mind an explanation, from higher command. Much of the Department's stealthy racism remained a departmental secret, so that civil and moral violations of rights were kept from the public's awareness. The Department would lose all face if the public were to become aware of the intentional undercutting of Black ambition within the system. Many Black officers hoped for a federal investigation of "how their rights were being violated without remorse." The results would have revealed a government agency that denied racial equality.

There was a so-called race relations division, a farce consisting of one Black male in-charge, Officer Edwin DeWitt. When Black officers sought help from this so-called NAACP representative, and filed a complaint, the only response was *more* harassment from jail officials. I called the Detroit branch of the NAACP in 1989 to get information on how to file a civil rights complaint and to get an annual report of where contributions to that organization went. "We don't give out that information," said secretary Sheila Mason. "Why not, isn't that public information?" I persisted, quizzing her to find out if the organization was living up to its promise of "advancing colored people."

One irritating thing about authority is that those who perceive they have achieved it, lose the respect for others trying to achieve their equality under the Bill of Rights. On a supraliminal level, the Department played racial favorites in deciding fundamental issues that really required only fairness and intelligent discernment. White male jail officials rejected all notions of justice, and were reluctant to be ethical, first referring to their own experience—naturally selective apartheid—as a moral gauge. Infractions of civil and constitutional rights abounded because the above-mentioned race relations outfit, and the union, gave shameful representation to Black officers. It is a popular notion that in every controversy there are three sides: the *instigator's* side, the *victim's* side, and the *truth*. The Departmental hierarchy continued to harass Black officers, disregarding all but their own side of the argument.

Application of jail rules was a knotty issue because every command official had their own specific criteria for fair enforcement. Many jail rules involve the care of inmates, and in the 1971 class action lawsuit against the Sheriff's Department, the court required that any inmate who attempted suicide, was believed to be suicidal, or who was judged to be mentally ill, be given an opportunity for indoor recreation at least three times a week. The judge also decided that inmates must be allowed to meet with their family at least two times per week in an attorney visitation room, small rooms with a six-inch opening, instead of the regular general population visiting room which had no opening. Inmates are allowed to talk by phone with family members at least twice a week. At least forty-eight hours before an inmate is removed from the jail to another place of detention, the Department is required to inform the inmate's lawyer of the transfer, either by phone or writing.

Since the County jail is basically a holding facility for nonconvicted inmates awaiting trial, once the jury's verdict and the judge's sentence are handed down, the convicted inmate is supposed to be transferred to a state prison facility or halfway house. This was not always the case, as the Department violated officer, inmate, and civilians' civil and constitutional rights with equanimity. They got away with holding prisoners longer than required by law because the overloaded Wayne County's criminal and civil courts were backed-up in arranging a date for transfer or release. Because lawyers demand large fees, another example of injustice in the system, and bottom-line economic issues confronting Black people, many remained in the County jail longer than required.

The Department constantly used the Judicial system against outspoken people. Although Detroit's Judicial system was once proclaimed a role model for urban cities around the United States, it institutionalized bigotry and unfairness in court proceedings and trials. White male jail officials also tried to make Black officers feel that their claims of discrimination and injustices were unworthy, and that something was wrong with their cognitive skills. In so doing, the Department dehumanization schemes set Blacks against each other with divide and conquer tactics. In other words, any Black who refused to *conform* to *their* system needed only corrective measures of punishment, suspension without pay, or termination.

The reason why most jail rules of real importance concern inmates and their care, is that a dangerous situation could result in lawsuits from officers' negligence. Year after year, inmate, officer, and civilian lawsuits drain the County budget—there are always numerous lawsuits pending in court. The court logs were typically so backed-up that judges and prosecutors became a party to hurried lackluster plea bargaining and arbitrary decisions. To improve the judicial system in Wayne County, modern administrative principals, and procedures that categorized the crime and criminals track record, were implemented. The courts and parole boards periodically released the so-called *safer* inmates because of overcrowding. If the charge was not felonious or habitual, inmates were released to make room for more serious offenders. Nowadays, in most cases, severely habitual criminals are being released.

Decisions to transport an inmate requiring hospitalization should be made in five to ten minutes of assessing the situation. I can't count the many times when inmates, who were ill, or had been injured in fights, regularly sat in the bullpen for entire shifts before going to a medical facility for treatment. The bullpen is a waiting cell located next to the center station, and is used to hold inmates until they are transferred to an appropriate location. It was difficult for me to understand the lack of professionalism, not to mention humanity, in such neglect. When I was *Within The Walls*, there were several officers, Black and white, who didn't seem to care if an inmate suffered needlessly. Delaying medical treatment was usually the result of some officer not taking care of business: talking on the phone, listening to the radio, sick and tired, or plain just didn't give a damn!

There were, however, rules *on paper* for just about everything you could imagine. The Department's main purpose seemed to be Jim Crow by paper lynchings. Thus, weeding out those who didn't agree with their system of racial intimidation and favoritism. Common sense will tell you that every rule is not applicable in every given situation. Enforcement of rules against me and other Black officers was often intentionally arbitrary, and designed to keep us in our place.

Another problem *Within The Walls* was administrative chaos. Officers should possess a semblance of intelligence and confidence, of what appropriate actions should be taken to get the job done without doing harm to any individual, or the institution. This was not always the case with administrative officials who commanded the jail and courts. The jail was a revolving door of shift command officers. No one really liked working there, and it was hell for officers to constantly adapt to new faces and individual philosophies. Command officers were periodically demoted and transferred back to the jail because of disciplinary problems and lack of communication with peers.

Officers were basically locked up just like the criminals were in their cells, only we were in a claustrophobic glass cubicle. Surely jail rules must evolve to maintain a viable, secure, and respectable institution, but in the majority of cases, white male jail officials arbitrarily changed rules to plot strategies and weed out officers deemed threatening. As soon as floor officers would get used to jail rules, officials instituted changes that did not work to officers' or inmates' satisfaction.

Even though it was the floor officers who dealt everyday with the same inmates, their suggestions to improve operations were systematically ignored. Jail officials insisted upon implementing prehistoric ideas that lacked continuity. Why change something that works and replace it with something that doesn't, all for the sake of change? It seemed there were changes in jail policies and procedures every other week. The officers and even the floor command officers couldn't remember all the rules, and constantly went back to review their files to look up trivial and minor jail rule changes and violations.

For three days straight during my tenure, sergeants and lieutenants were required to read out loud during Roll Call, departmental memos and state changes in procedures and policies. For two days we were all bored, reading and hearing stuff we already knew wouldn't work. On the third day, instead of reading the memo in its entirety, the oft-commended Sergeant Sampson, a tall, light-skinned Black male from the Barrett era, got so fed up from reading the lengthy communications, he quipped, "Look, y'all done heard this shit over and over again. If you ain't got it now, you will never get it! I've got other information that needs to be addressed. So I'm gonna have Officer Dobbertin print up some copies to give out to all of you to read, when you all get to your assignments." Before leaving Roll Call, Sampson gave his reason for not reading the entire memo: "There are deputies that should be relieved from the midnight shift, because they can file for overtime." Fifteen minutes past relief time, officers just getting off duty can submit for the extra time spent on the jail floors. Getting paid for it—well, that's another story.

The procedures to feed inmates constantly changed. Day shift officers fed inmates twice: 7:30 a.m. for breakfast, and around noon for lunch; whereas the afternoon shift officer fed inmates only once: around 4:30 p.m., before officers had dinner. Midnight officers never fed inmates, unless there was a special situation involving an inmate on a special diet, or an inmate's need for a snack before taking medication. Many officers chose the afternoon and midnight shift just to receive a fifty cent shift premium; but they did less work, and were not subjected to the totalitarian top brass, who walked around in the jail mainly during the morning shift.

At one time inmates were fed in the hallways, but this was found to be a bad idea when several metal closet doorknobs turned-up missing. These were being screwed off their base and used by inmates as projectiles. Inmate fights in the hallway were also hard to control and, after several incidents, the Department decided to start feeding inmates on the wards, which was safer and more efficient for the officers. Inmates, however, argued vehemently against this: "We need to get off the ward sometimes," they complained. On the basis of these complaints the Department then issued a directive to feed inmates in the multipurpose rooms, where there were serving freezers for milk, fruit, and other perishables. Officers never welcomed this change because of the transfer from the ward to the MP room. Instead of a fifteen-minute operation on the ward, breakfast, lunch, or dinner became a thirty to forty minute detail. While transporting inmates from the ward to the MP room, there were several incidents endangering officers' safety. Once again the order came down that inmates were to be fed only on their ward.

The decision to feed inmates on the wards presented its own problems for the officer on duty. To get a simulation of freedom inmates naturally wanted to feel like they were "dining out." But this was the jail, and there were even a few officers who wouldn't feed inmates until all had made up their bunk beds to the officer's satisfaction. To cope with the extra food trays for my ward I invented a game I called "*Lotto*"; participating inmates chose a number from 1 through 100 (the winning number was picked by me). The numbers closest to the number I chose won those inmates extra food. Sometimes I'd spin all the inmate cards in a milk crate and pick as many numbers as there were food trays left.

But even these fair methods caused trouble: "Damn dep! Man, I can never win the lottery and you never seem to pick my card! How long have you been doing this, now? I never win," said a dejected loser, expressing his consistent lack of luck inside the jail and out-side as well. I replied sarcastically, "Seems like you can't help it, brother; you just have some real bad luck anyway. Just look at some of your crimes and charges." I said all this just to get him off my case as diplomatically as possible. Some inmates, it seemed, were never satisfied, no matter what. Officers didn't have to give out any extra food trays; we could've been stingy and strict, and loaded them back into the cage. My method of distributing leftover food trays anticipated charges of favoritism that would rise up in the minds of inmates.

My penchant for feeding hungry inmates is purely hereditary. I hate to see people starve, or beg for food. I can't stand to see Sally Struthers on those late night, world relief commercials showing cry-ing, starving Afrikan babies with flies on their faces, or hovering around them. Regardless of any financial predicament my family was in, we would never let anyone go hungry. Maybe that's why so many Afrikan-Americans are so fat. Especially those from the South, who believe feeding folks well. I couldn't stand to watch tons of food being thrown away because "it may spoil." The Department could've generated good will towards its employees and officers by giving this food to needy people.

Many white officers, and sadly some Sambo-ish Black officers, acted like they would rather see the extra food thrown away, then to give some of it to a starving inmate. Sometimes there were as many as fifteen trays of leftover food, and officers would load them back into the serving cage to go back down to the kitchen, where they were discarded by trustees into enormously large garbage disposals. When a white officer loaded the extra trays back into the cart, in-mates got angry and congregated at the station window in throngs: "Dep, why can't we get some of those extra food trays; they ain't gonna do nothing but throw it away. There's a whole bunch of good food left, dep," would be the understandable complaint from inmates.

"The jail rules say you're only allowed *one* tray, *one* milk, *one* juice, *one* piece of fruit, and that's all you're gonna get. Now get the fuck away from my window," snarled Officer Sperma, a racist white male. It seemed that whites did only what jail rules required, while Black officers were more considerate. Some even took up playing

"Lotto."

When inmates saw me grab a milk crate and start spinning the inmate cards, they automatically knew it was "Lotto" time, and came to the window to participate. "Lotto" made the day go by, and inadvertently produced good humor. Giving away extra food also showed the humane side of any officer who wasn't concerned about some petty jail-rule issue. It demonstrated that monotonous duties weren't the only things an officer could do, and that some officers didn't have ego problems.

Inmates' towels, clothing and bedding were never a severe problem. If there was a shortage of these necessities, I told inmates to do their own washing until the laundry wagon came with a clean load. There was a Laundry Detail that delivered clean clothes, towels and linen to the inmates twice a week. This practice was instituted in 1987, two years into my tenure. From 1984 to 1986, officers were in charge of retrieving and providing inmate clothing and bed linen. Keeping a stock of clean towels and linen, however, posed some difficulties. It was like the jail was becoming a hotel, where guests steal towels to wash their car, or clean up around the house. One towel a week was issued to each inmate, which was sufficient if kept clean. Inmates, however, also used towels and linen as head rags, some to resemble Middle Eastern Muslims, others because their greasy styles required something to hold their hair in place.

Head rags were, of course, against jail rules. Head rags can conceal contraband, which is always a problem, and they can also be used tragically to strangle someone. A rag, or strip of bed linen, knotted at the end, could also be slid up inside the cell door hinge to dislodge the bolt, disabling the locking mechanism. This gave inmates access to the ward, even the hallways, when they were supposed to be locked-up for the night. Such a situation was dangerous for the two officers working on the midnight shift, who by state mandate are required to make a round every hour.

Clean linen and clothing are essential for decent-smelling wards and cells. Proper clothing sizes were not always stocked, and many inmates had to wear the next nearest size, or whatever was available. Bunk mattresses were stored in a jail floor closet. Before an inmate was even housed on the floor, the deputy would take him to the storage closet to carry his own mattress(es) to the cell. Tired and downtrodden some inmates looked like Jesus carrying His own cross to His crucifixion.

After a thorough examination from the doctor or nurse, inmates with back or chronic sleeping problems were given permission to have two mattresses. The inmate's permission slip was customarily placed in the station desk drawer, and this was the document proving the inmate's right to an extra mattress. The officer was also required to write the information in the logbook, although sometimes it was not. Lack of logging-in the information meant the inmate would have to go through reevaluation by the doctor or nurse, or the officer would have to call the medical department for verification of the inmate's right to an extra mattress. This slip was essential when there was a shakedown on the ward. Doctor slips were often torn, lost or misplaced, usually by an officer who did not like that particular inmate.

Plumbing maintenance is essential for conserving hot water and eliminating leaks. This was a recurring problem not eliminated by plumbers. Either poor quality materials, or poor workmanship caused hazardous conditions. Inmates sometimes aggravated the problem by swinging on overhead tubing above the cells, causing broken water mains to flood the wards and jail floors. Inmates caught swinging on the overhead pipes received a mandatory, 48-hour lock down.

Inmates often took cold showers because of a shortage of hot water. This problem may have started when inmates affixed little slits of plastic in the thin crevice of the shower button, causing the shower water to run continuously. If the piece of plastic was not removed, water sprinkled for hours. Inmate showers were powered by a mechanism that allowed water to spray for about 15 seconds at a time. In order for the inmate to get a continuous spray he had to keep pushing the button, over and over. Thus some genius discovered the plastic slits. The showers in the officers' locker rooms didn't have these timers, but if they had, there's no question in my mind that we would have done the same thing the inmates did.

When the water was extremely hot, the whole ward looked and felt like a steam room; even the glass of the guard station became fogged-up. When I came upon a station where the windows were full of steam, I automatically knew that the hot showers had been on for quite some time. Puddles of water were often found on the jail floors and in the corridors between the two stations. Officers had to be cautious and walk gingerly, so as not to slip and fall. Can you imagine running to breakup an inmate fight, only to see officers slipping and falling in puddles of water? It has happened, and injuries were sustained in the process.

Officers have even slipped purposefully, injuring themselves to get off work for awhile and get paid sick leave. This wasn't my style, but I've witnessed a couple of officers successfully complete the tactic and get away with it. By and large it's true, however, that officers dodged puddles of water when walking on the wards, and anyone risked slipping on the grime, grease, paper, and food that sometimes turned the ward floors into a slippery glaze.

The county didn't want to pay plumbers for exorbitant overtime, but it was necessary in some cases. When plumbers were not available on the weekend, officers tied towels around leaky pipes to keep their floor from flooding. The rag procedure would be repeated for several weeks to a month or so, before the pipe was finally repaired, despite officers logging the damaged pipe everyday to "cover their ass." A maintenance closet between the two guard stations controlled the showers for both wards. Weeks before a plumbing problem was officially diagnosed and taken care of, officers trudged down to the shift command office to retrieve the maintenance closet keys, and day after day, week after week, month after month, turned the showers on and off to conserve water, often scheduling inmate showers on another ward.

When my ward's shower was out of order, I was deluged with impatient inmates who came to the station window requesting a shower. How could I refuse anyone who wanted to smell clean and maintain good hygiene? When such a situation occurred, the rule of "not letting inmates on other wards but theirs" was willingly violated. I would give each inmate three minutes apiece on another ward with a workable shower. Some inmates became infested with parasites when they didn't shower regularly, or had unclean linen and bedding. Besides, it is essential for inmates to maintain good hygiene for the health of officers.

One morning as I entered my station to start my shift, turning on all the ward and cell lights and opening up the cells, inmate Herb Thaxton, a middle-aged Black male, with multiple charges of criminal sexual conduct (rape), crept up to the station window with a note that read: *"Dep, when I woke up this morning I was checking around my penis and found what I think is a crab. I put it in a piece of paper if you would like to see it. Dep, could you please contact a nurse and keep this a secret from the other inmates."* Of course I didn't want to see it! I definitely had to handle this situation discreetly and keep this a secret, so the other inmates wouldn't have a warranted gripe to *join the bandwagon*.

I called Nurse Brad, a Black male, Dick Gregory look-a-like, and explained: "Brad, I've got an inmate up here who just gave me a note that says 'he thinks he has caught the crabs.' Could you come up to take care of this situation, please, before it gets out of hand?" I was careful that Brad knew the sensitivity of the situation, so that he would pretend he was there because of some other medical problem. Brad gave Thaxton a medical ointment that turned a darkish color and killed crab infestation while taking a shower. The other inmates grew more suspicious of Brad's visit, and when Thaxton grabbed his clothing, towels, and linen—all the things that crabs breed in and infest—and put them in a garbage bag, the inmates then knew what was going on.

Of course other inmates started to claim they had crabs too. When another set of clothing, towels, and linen were brought up to the ward for Thaxton, a group of inmates approached the window: "Hey Dep, that dude over there got crabs don't he?" The few remaining inmates, unaware of what was happening, turned down the television to listen carefully. Then they all turned and looked straight at me. "Hell, I don't know. He just wants to make sure he doesn't get them from anyone else," I blurted out, hoping to throw them off guard.

There was a brief silence: "Hey Dep, we need some ointment too. Get the buckets, mop and disinfectant so we can clean up this whole ward. We don't want to catch it if someone's got the crabs in here." As they spoke I could feel a tingling sensation, like ants were running all over me. I consented readily, as much for my own health as so the inmates wouldn't bug me to death for ointment and cleaning equipment. Then I went unhesitantly to get disinfectant so there would be some peace of mind on the ward.

When Thaxton returned from his shower, he was treated like he had contracted AIDS, or some plague of biblical proportions. The other inmates kept their distance from him for days. Thaxton's cell mate Paul Jones requested a transfer to another cell, but after the cell and ward were washed down several times with disinfectant, he eventually forgot the idea of moving and settled down. Not only did inmates stay away from potential parasite carriers; officers did too, and refrained from searching or coming in close contact with infected inmates. I surely didn't want to catch no crabs, having experienced them while attending college from being with one Helen Hughes, a Black female star basketball jock who averaged over 30 points a game. Such were the liabilities of life *Within The Walls.*

21

Contraband:
The Big Shakedown

SHAKEDOWN IS A THOROUGH SEARCH of inmate cells and wards, usually looking for contraband. When shakedowns were conducted, white male officers exhibited sheer delight, getting a kick out of destroying Black male inmates' treasured photos of family, girlfriends and personal memorabilia, by throwing them all over the ward or cell floor. They would then stomp and trample piles of scattered possessions, the inmates' only real contact with outside civilization.

Planning for a shakedown, superiors first called up their choice of officers, and rendezvoused with them below or above the targeted floor. Once officers gathered, the superior would tell them "what specific contraband items to look for." More often than not, the presence of contraband was a rumor rather than a *specific* "item," which resolved into a search by officers and superiors holding grudges against particular inmates on that ward.

Some officers smashed and stole candy bars, juice, and milk that inmates had kept cool in their cell sinks. To stop the use of sinks as refrigerators, jail officials made a rule forbidding deliberately running sink water. The Department justified this by explaining, "The plumbing and water pressure was hampered." While making rounds, officers constantly demanded that inmates "take out this little thin slit of torn plastic," which, of course, inmates had jammed in the thin crevice of the sink button to keep the water running. This same method was also used to run the shower.

Shakedowns were also used to periodically and systematically brainwash inmates about the omniscience of authority. In reality this was nothing short of mental cruelty. Once officers entered the ward they would separate inmates into groups and instruct them to "stand and face the wall; put your hands up against the wall and spread your legs apart." Next, an officer would check the hair and mouth of each inmate and, depending on what officers were looking for, told inmates to take off their clothes and "spread their cheeks." It was queer to see grown men bend over and use their hands to separate their buttocks so officers could inspect a dark rectum.

While wearing thin latex gloves, some white male officers looked like surgeons about to perform surgery. While this was going on, other officers searched the cells and ward, or suspiciously scrutinized inmates' movements. I always made it a point to be categorized as a "searcher of cells," not a searcher of anuses. Most shakedowns were conducted by clusters of white male officers. I once observed officers confiscate drug paraphernalia rather than drugs, as the inmates were getting high regularly. The inmates had punched a hole in 11-Southwest, Cell 7's window, and were getting drugs from the street, more than one hundred feet below. That's a long way to haul up drugs without getting caught.

It was sometimes noticed that while officers fed inmates in the hallways, steel closet doorknobs would disappear. It was suspected, of course, that an inmate had unscrewed the knobs from the base. This was a legitimate and serious threat, especially when the doorknob was put in a sock, or other piece of clothing, and used as a projectile. When contraband sweeps were conducted on the wards, officers sometimes found hard clubs made from newspapers, which had been saturated continuously with water, and then dried out for weeks. These clubs were as hard as baseball bats. For that very reason officers were specifically prohibited from bringing a newspaper onto the jail floors. The inmates would, of course, gather at the station window to beg for one.

Officers were permitted to carry a book on the jail floor; it was a difficult moral dilemma for a command officer to restrict an officer from reading a Bible, for example. The only difference I can ascertain between a newspaper and a book as reading material in the jail setting is that the gazette takes up a lot of space; but in reality, both occupy the officers' attention. As a matter of fact, reading a book takes up more attention than reading a newspaper, because more than not, there are more pages and the reader gets drawn into a story. As for the paper problem, all that was required to insure that officers can see over the paper is to instruct them to fold it and lay it on the station desk while reading. But jail officials are petty in nature: not wanting officers to stay informed; and officers eventually resorted to sneaking newspapers onto the jail floors in their pants. To keep the newspapers from being found we hid them in file cabinets and desk drawers in the guard stations.

On several occasions officers confiscated fruit being fermented into homemade wine. The fermenting tank was a toilet or box containing a plastic bag filled with oranges, pears, apples, sometimes grapes, and sugar. It was mandatory on a shakedown to strip the linen from the mattresses in order to search around the bunk beds, but some acts were inexcusable and unnecessary. Many Black male inmates tore out the centerfold pictures of Black female models from the library's copies of Jet magazine. These they hung on the cell walls, or on the inside of the cell doors. White male officers usually went out of their way to tear them up. Inmates would save juice, that white officers would confiscate and drink themselves.

Officers entering cells encountered all kinds of pencil, magic markers, and chalk drawings on the cell walls: skulls, hearts inscribed with a lover's name and pierced by an arrow; German swastikas; renditions of sleazy characters selling drugs; and money signs. One could also frequently find sketches of car emblems from expensive cars: Jaguar, Cadillac, Mercedes-Benz, Maserati, BMW and long, stretch limousines, all drawn with pencils, chalk, and magic markers.

Young Black male inmates often had problems adapting to the jail system and leaving behind the negative elements of the drug culture on the outside. Some were creative and skilled in crafts, turning empty cigarette boxes into simulated pagers and fastening them to the string belt of their jail pants. Even in the so-called rehabilitating confines of jail they *still thought* they were dope pushers.

Within The Walls there were always sickening racial slurs written on the cell walls: "Fuck all Niggers," "Niggers ain't shit," "Honkies kiss my ass," "A white boy sucks good dick." Some inmates drew calendars on the cell walls, crossing out each day spent in jail with a colored marker, and a big circle drawn around their "out" or release date. Inmates took a particular interest in drawing Detroit's downtown skyline, mainly the Renaissance Center, Detroit's most recognizable landmark to many local people and world citizens alike.

Many inmates drew cartoon characters: Mickey Mouse, Goofy, and Road Runner were favorites. Though it was very creative, I remember one drawing as particularly sexually exploitative. It showed a sexually inviting female Smurf, holding her skirt up high to flash her *"money maker,"* while a male Smurf ogled at her lustfully with wild excited eyes, his tongue hanging out, all the while masturbating and ejaculating. So sad, really, that so much potential and expressed talent should be confined *Within The Walls* of a cartoon world of sexual voyeurism. Somehow there must be a better way than building more prisons.

22

The Union, The Confederacy, 502 Blues

ZEALOUS JAIL OFFICIALS ATTEMPTED TO THWART the admission of Black officers into the police academy. After nearly five years *Within The Walls*, I had to let go of my childhood dream—to be a police officer. One good thing about failing the academy was that officers were permitted to continue working in the jail at the same rate of pay as officers who had passed. State-certified officers, commissioned to carry a gun and badge, received about the same wages as noncertified officers with the same seniority, who didn't pass the academy. This gave officers no incentive, and was psychologically and morally defeating; clearly it encouraged greed rather than ambition.

Before sessions of collective bargaining, the union and the Sheriff's Department gave *all* noncertified officers a fictitious label of "**Police Officer I**," an initial position of turnkey. This designated euphemism was geared to pacify those noncertified officers who felt unwanted, underpaid, unappreciated, and unimportant. The union and Department would then elevate those officers *one* status higher to "**Police Officer II**," hoping those fatuous and vain officers would appreciate the title, instead of the money. This, however, wasn't the case.

Newly hired sheriff's deputies waited an average of three years or more before ever attending the police academy because of contract squabbles and undercutting between the Department and the union. Because of earlier negotiations, deputies hired prior to October 1984 didn't have to wait that long. However, those officers hired before October 1984 were also getting paid nearly double that of officers hired only two or three months later, as was in my case. It was demoralizing that officers with only two or three more months seniority were getting substantially larger paychecks for the same work I was doing.

Because of this, a conflict of interest also surfaced internally within union ranks. At a union meeting in 1986, a contract agreement was suspected of being rigged. Jim Morely, the union president, had given one of his long, drawn-out, "trying to influence" speeches about "...the ramifications of both sides of the vote, and what it entailed." After speaking, Morely instructed officers to cast their vote by standing on one, or the other, side of the room. Those officers who preferred state-certified training, with a chance to carry a weapon and have the ability to arrest, stood on one side of the room; officers willing to believe the rumor of a substantial raise of three to four thousand dollars over the next two to three years stood on the opposite side. Officers waved for the opposing officers to come over to their side, trying to sway the vote. It was truly a farce.

Officers who felt that certification was more valuable than extra money in their pockets won overwhelmingly; it was a landslide victory. By giving the Department and union total control over present and incoming officers' futures and careers, the vote also allowed the Department to determine when a noncertified officer could attend the police academy (MLEOTC). The winning side of the room swelled with enthusiasm as some stood on chairs and hollered their support for waiting over three years to tote a gun. Most officers on the losing side had a family to support. All this was done by a stand up vote, and no ballots were issued to absent union members. As a result of this vote every noncertified officer hired after October 1984 experienced a career setback. Family or not, I knew what was best for me: a substantial raise. You would think that would have been the attitude of most officers with a family to care for, but it wasn't.

This particular union meeting was held way out near Metropolitan Airport in Romulus, Michigan, where a majority of white officers lived. For the majority of Black officers, who lived in Detroit, it was a long drive out to the suburban communities of Wayne County. It was also unfamiliar territory, and many never attended union meetings because of the cultural distance as well. Heated discussions erupted at this meeting, one in particular involving noncertified Officer Pride Johnson, a cocky Black male, and state-certified Officer Greg Kennelly, a white male.

While the meeting was still in progress, Pride started to discuss the decision with one of his friends. Kennelly turned angrily towards Pride and demanded, "Why don't you just shut your fuckin' mouth up!" Pride, not one to back down from a challenge, especially from a white man, recalled his military years, and without hesitation blurted back, "Who-in-the-fuck do you think you're talking to? Look bitch, why don't you come over here and shut me up, ya punk-ass, red neck son-of-a-bitch!" Everyone turned around to see what was going on. Turning beet red in the face, Kennelly jumped up from his seat to approach Pride, but was restrained by the white male officers sitting near him. When they finally got Kennelly seated, he resorted to giving Pride the "F--- you" sign, you know, the sign given with your middle finger to some crazed driver about to cut you off, in the days before drive-by shootings, of course.

Pride turned around in time to witness Kennelly's "finger barrage" of racism. That did it!: "Bitch, you don't scare me. Why don't you just come on up here, or better yet, when this is all over we can take it outside if you want to get with me? We can settle this in another fashion," Pride added. After two years of Departmental, racist ideology, Officer Pride Johnson eventually transferred to the Detroit Police. Many officers, Black and white, left the Department to seek better opportunities with other law enforcement agencies. Although I disagreed with Pride's vote for certification instead of a substantial raise, he was still, after all, one of the fellas.

Many times officers contemplated striking, but state law prohibits police officers to demonstrate their opinions about negotiated contract squabbles on a picket line. At the drop of a dime, many officers would have walked the line and put the burden of manpower in the hands of the Department. Every three or four years there were numerous job openings, either from transfers to the Detroit, Michigan State, or Oakland Police Departments, or from heavy attrition. One way or another, hiring campaigns seemed to come right on the heels of Departmental elimination of those who stood up to the inequality of institutional racism.

Even after union and Sheriff's Department contract negotiators prolonged bargaining for almost a year past the initial deadline, officers still had a problem receiving prorated wages from the first agreed date. Cozening within the Department, union, and County, historically siphoned workers pay by creating payless paydays, payless pay months, and even, during the Kenneth Barrett Era **Year of Our Lord** 1969, 1970, and 1983, *payless years*. Could you imagine the stress on officers and their families? Many of them experienced difficulties recovering from that yearlong era of financial instability. Officers worked without pay through all of this, showing loyalty, and still were not given fair equity for the financial inconvenience suffered. This was a notorious disregard of human dignity.

Many Black officers participated in a 1973 class action suit against the Department, citing lack of promotions. Supposedly their records were purged (refer to the case, Reed vs Wayne County Sheriff's Department). More recently, in 1990, it was rumored that officers in the old jail had some of their records purged, while officers working in the new jail were not granted that same privilege. In 1991, noncertified officers finally started to receive uniform allowances. Few officers, however, used their clothing allowance on uniforms, most of them spent it to pay bills, go on vacation, or spent it on themselves. State-certified officers received their gun and clothing allowances around tax time in April, a perfect time for it. Gun allowance was $450 for keeping their weapon in order, and clothing allowance was $350 for new uniforms and dry cleaning. Add that $800 to a substantial income tax refund, and officers were really living. Working lots of overtime at this time of the year was grand.

The Department's reluctance to issue nine millimeter semiautomatic handguns, puzzled its officers. The Department juggled the idea for many years because these handguns carry more bullets, load quicker and, with additional cartridges, an officer should be able to withstand multiple fire. Officers wanted sixteen in the clip and one in the chamber. The only reason given by the Department for not buying them was that 9-MM semiautomatic handguns often jammed. The truth is that criminals, especially violent habitual ones, have dangerous high-powered weapons that could outblast and outlast the Departmentally issued six-shot 357 Weston. A Sheriff's deputy would have additional firepower only by reloading with two, six-shot speedloaders. The seconds taken to reload are critical, and surely would give the criminal a few uncontested shots.

There was also the question of how to get rid of existing firearms. A meltdown or auction was suggested; but that would only put more guns in the hands of criminals, who were already stocked in all sorts of more powerful weaponry. In 1991, the Detroit Police Department sold their old guns to an arms dealer for almost $700,000. In the spring of 1991, the Detroit Police Department decided to convert to 9-MM handguns.

Back in my tenure, it puzzled me that the Sheriff's Department didn't have full jurisdiction to patrol Detroit's highways and streets. Was it political bureaucracy, or was it a grudge held from a historic shooting in 1972, involving the Detroit Police and the Wayne County Sheriff's Department? Three Black male Detroit Police officers, working on a unit called STRESS, raided a blind pig, where Sheriff's deputies congregated: gambling and drinking.

The Detroit officers told the story that a man with a gun walked into the apartment building, so they followed him in and fired shots, killing the man and wounding three others. The problem was the victims turned out to be Wayne County sheriffs. Kenneth Barrett was the Sheriff of Wayne County back then, and Police Chief John Nichols was the Detroit Police Department's head man. That incident effectively started the decline of Barrett's career.

For years Wayne County Sheriff's deputies in the jail were considered weaponless baby sitters, without even the right to make an arrest. Detroit Police officers were doing the street work—real police work. Sheriff's deputies do patrol the outlying communities of Wayne County, and handled some critical situations, but most officers in the jail will never experience a drug bust, a hostage situation, apprehension of an escaped criminal, a domestic quarrel, or even a traffic stop. It seemed that sheriff deputies were not respected, in or out of uniform, when they identified themselves as police officers.

One incident illustrates this point, and involved several Black male officers and Officer Dobbertin, a white male. This group was drunk, and drove down the wrong way of a major street. When they were stopped by the Detroit Police, and identified themselves as Wayne

County Sheriff's deputies, Detroit police officers subjected them to harassment. Read their Miranda rights, the deputies finally phoned Sergeant Sampson, a fair-skinned, forever talking Black male, who vouched for their release, and the situation was covered up.

Considered a code of honor—in most cases, officers are treated leniently when caught driving under the influence of alcohol, drugs, or stopped for a traffic violation. Such an incident occurred when I left work in the company of several other Black male officers. I was riding with Baldwin, who had multiple marriage problems. We were driving ahead of a car in need of bodywork to meet highway driving standards, and it was full of Black male officers, who were drinking.

I was the first to see the flashing blue and red emergency lights of a Michigan State Police car in the passenger-side rear view mirror, and told Baldwin to slow down and pull over on the median. The State Trooper surely thought he had just stopped a car full of Black males. Idling several hundred feet ahead, Baldwin and I waited fifteen minutes to see what would happen. The trooper immediately saw the two fifths of liquor and partially filled cups in the car, but the noncertified officers were eventually released after showing their I.D.s. Hey, they were cops!

Those same Black male officers always went after work to see Shalah, an Arab store owner, to buy liquor, or other items, on credit. Shalah was very friendly to us, as he put the items on each officer's tab, and anticipated payment of those debts on payday, every other Thursday night. When those officers didn't pay up on time, Shalah lost some respect for, and felt some animosity toward, Black male officers at the Sheriff's Department. These particular Black officers were always in debt, aided and abetted by Shalah's generosity, but, hey, they were cops!

The union sold adhesive Sheriff's stickers for the back window or bumper of your car: the back window being preferable. There are hundreds of cars and trucks with these stickers in Wayne County, most never even associated with the union or Sheriff's Department. The stickers give credibility to traffic violators, often police officers, and make people believe that possibly the driver of the car is a police officer. The stickers cost union members only fifty cents. After completing the police academy, and completing nearly five years of psychological torment, I decided it was time to scrape the union sticker off my rear car window. After doing so, the Department's past and current history came to mind. I *never*, *ever again*, wanted anyone to know of my affiliation with unfair policies, institutional racism, weak union representation, and too much toil and strain.

23

The House Party:
BEST Disc Jockey in the Country!

IN AUGUST 1985, WITH SEVEN MONTHS OF SENIORITY and taking only a single day off work, I decided to have a back yard party. It was time to do a little celebrating... all work and no play makes me a dull boy. I invited personal friends and a few weeks prior to the party I handed out invites to certain officers in the jail. At this particular time, I was highly regarded in stature because of good attendance, virtue, and dedication to jail principles. To not show bias or favoritism, details about the party were also posted on the bulletin board in the Roll Call room. Though in reality, I didn't want some of those ignoramus, white male officers to come, they were at least given the opportunity to attend.

Several friends came and a few officers attended, the mixture was enhancing and "fresh": it was a success. Everyone claimed they had a good time... that was the general consensus. The only white officers that came were Dobbertin and Daschle, two males. Accompanying them were four jumbo 6 packs of beer (twenty-four, 16 ounce cans). Throughout the party, they just sat, laughed, talked and drank themselves into "submitted oblivion." Their style of drinking was similar and catered after those white fraternity house parties like in the movie "Animal House," starring the late John Belushi. But this was not a college frat house party, this was my home! After seeing them both stack their beer cans into a pyramid, like they were building blocks and then tossing them aside on my well manicured lawn, made me wonder "was this a good idea to invite white guys?" When Officers Dobbertin and Daschle decided to dance at my back yard party, all eyes were on them. Everyone started laughing, it was hilarious and a sight to behold. Still, despite their trashy ways, I was glad they had a good time.

Many Blacks are programmed to understand and accept, that this type of party rowdyism is the way whites typically have their fun, so I let Dobbertin and Daschle get loose and have their way—even despite the fact that I didn't appreciate it! What-the-hell, the cans were worth ten cents each (State of Michigan can and bottle deposit). Why do white guys act so rowdy, when they drink excessively? Especially at sporting events, like at Tiger Stadium, the Pontiac Silverdome, or Joe Louis Arena, where intimidating gladiators of hockey promote violence through multiple fisticuffs. Yes, of course, many people act ignorant when they drink too much, but white people have a different mentality after consuming lots of alcohol: beer, wine, liquor, etc.

While attending a Detroit Tiger's game with my stepfather, our seats were in front of a group of young, loud, ignorant, rowdy white males. Every inning they went to the concessions stand to buy beer.

Working for a security firm in 1976, one of my assignments was at Rynearson Stadium, on the campus of Eastern Michigan University. I was assigned to crowd control at a rock-n-roll concert with several rock groups: Yes, REO Speedwagon, and Peter Frampton. Whites drank and doped themselves up so much that overdoses occurred. Medical authorities anticipated such and had erected a tent, specifically for people who became sick or were on the verge of dying from an overindulgence of drugs and alcohol. What a shame that the necessity of an "O.D." tent had to be built. The atmosphere was like Woodstock of the 60s; a "flower power" event.

Topless white females walked around getting golden, bronze sun tans, and because the wait at the rest room lines were so long, concert goers pissed anywhere they could, not caring who was watching. I parked my car inside the stadium's fence, to watch a long line developing outside of it. While I was sitting in the back seat of my Buick, four door, deuce-and-a-quarter, taking a lunch break, to my amazement, two beautiful, topless, impatient white blond females in tight cut up jean shorts, approached my car and spoke.

"Hey baby, do ya mind if we open up all four of your car doors and take a quick piss between them?"

Hesitantly, with a confused stare, I smiled and replied, "Sure, go right ahead, as long as you don't piss on my car I don't care. Hey, when you-gotta-go, you-gotta-go." What was I suppose to say... No? I just looked at them as they squatted between the car doors to piss—they were so high that they didn't care who was watching.

Susan, about 5-foot-7-inches tall, weighed about 125 pounds, was definitely a "Brickhouse" at 36-24-36, and a beautiful specimen. She was so gorgeous that I thought I was dreaming—I had gotten a contact high from all the marijuana being smoked around the rest rooms and from people playing Frisbee nearby.

Tiffany was just as beautiful, but slimmer, with a couple of bad scars on her stomach, and she had a black eye. She was the girlfriend of Pete, a white male biker, who got mad at me when he found out that I had let Tiffany and Sue piss between my car doors. Pete was the typical sunglasses wearing, deep bearded, Harley-Davison, skull tattoo, white male macho racist, jealous type. Men, what would you do? if two fine white females with their breasts hanging out, approached you with a bladder problem?

I also encountered a bizarre incident at the concert, when Tom Seifert, a hallucinating, wild-eyed, nineteen year old white boy, was squirting ketchup and mustard on concert goers sitting in the middle of the football field. Saturated with the condiments, two white couples came to complain to guard Chris Armstrong and I about Tom's antics. We went to check out the complaints, whereupon the fifty yard line, we witnessed this fool running through multitudes of seated fans and splashing them.

When Armstrong and I finally stopped him, I asked: "Man, what is your damn problem? You better stop this shit right now!" While telling Tom to stop, without saying a word, Adam Zielinski, a big guy in a pair of studded jeans, and Tom's main friend, tried to sucker punch me from the blind side. Just barely missing my nose with a right hook, Adam slightly lost his balance. Armstrong and I pounced on Adam's back, picked him up and body slammed him to the astroturf, like we were both in on a vicious, aggressive gang tackle in football. Adam was handcuffed, and while dragging him to the security tent, Tom, the actual perpetrator of the petty crime, and two of his other partners pleaded for his release, and offered us money to let Adam go. As we whisked our prisoner away, a loud yell of approval came from the crowd of 60,000 plus. After all that, we still didn't have the real culprit who squirted people with ketchup and mustard, but we did have ourselves an attempted assaulter.

At that time whites were also *streaking* and one streaker decided he'd climb up a tall, 30-foot light pole. Seeing the potential danger, rocker Peter Frampton suddenly stopped his band in the middle of playing "Oh Baby, I Love Your Way," and told the crowd: "I must stop playing the song to inform you, that if that fool doesn't come down from that pole, I won't play another note!" The entire crowd booed loudly, and some threw half-full beer cans and rocks at the naked climber. When the streaker finally decided to come down and reached the bottom, he was arrested, hauled away, and charged with indecent exposure and disorderly conduct. Frampton proceeded.

Officer Eddie Wright (Boo-gay was his nickname) was the disc jockey for my party. The music could be heard for blocks—the pumpin' of Boo-gay, the Master Blaster, attracted attention from uninvited people nearby. There were plenty of women and men to choose from. While I stood by Boo-gay as he kicked-out the jams, mixing in his deep baritone voice which hyped the dancers, along with a mixer's feverish pitch on a loud but clear stereo sound system, I, semi-jokingly, hollered over to Officer Dobbertin as he tossed another beer can over his shoulder onto my lawn.

"Hey man, what-in-the-hell do you think this is, your basic garbage dump?" Looking up with drunken eyes, Dobbertin spoke with a slight befuddling slur: "Hey... Look! We came over here to party... we're here... so, what-the-fuck! This is a fucking party and this ain't my damn back yard!"

Quite perplexed, I looked at him sternly, and subconsciously, said to myself, "this silly white fucker!" After carefully analyzing what Dobbertin had said, I could only laugh. I continued to wonder what would have been Dobbertin's answer, if he had not drank umpteen beers? After the party, Dobbertin and I were friends, supposedly. Officer Daschle was also drunk, staggering while dancing, and throwing beer cans over his shoulders too, as if it was commonplace. After that I always hoped that one of them would invite me to a party over their house, so I could repay them and emulate their way of partying, just to see their reaction when someone trashes their premises.

While I barbecued ribs and chicken, grilled hot dogs and hamburgers, the scrumptiously delectable, hickory smoke filtered through the air. I waited until everybody was good and full of strawberry daiquiris and had the "munchies" before any food was served.

Later, a big surprise came that gave me this dubious reputation of always having many women available at my parties. One of my moonlighting jobs while working at the Department was being a chauffeur driving limousines. Butch Pepperidge, the owner of the company, and I were cool. Butch was a big time pimp that ran a high class, call girl ring, and he came over to the party in two long white stretch limousines, and parked both of them in my driveway. Butch, and another chauffeur got out, opened the doors of both limos, and low and behold, one by one, twelve gorgeous females stepped out... six in each car. This stirred up a lot of attention, you should have seen the facial changes and expressions of the crowd, especially the guys!

"Damn! Damn! Damn! Ooooo-wee! Oooooo-wee!" All the men reacted, as each cutie stepped out of the car and into the back yard. After their pompous arrival, Boo-gay elevated the party music to a higher intensity level, with a heavy mixture of rhythmical sounds... the celebration was on! This was the first party I had given while working for the Department. My next door neighbor and I together gave a party at the end of every summer—the Friday or Saturday before the Labor Day holiday.

Officer Wright also had his share of harassment from shift commanders, particularly Sergeant Frank Dawdy. Though Dawdy was a big, supposedly proud-acting Black man, he always caused havoc, particularly for Black male officers. We could never figure out why he refrained from bothering white male or female officers with his pettiness. Seemed like the Department only used Dawdy for his redundantly treacherous and petty ways, of keeping Black male officers in their place. Hundreds of complaints from numerous officers submitted to the union against him, but nothing was achieved to alleviate his harassment.

A month before Wright's departure from the Department, he confided with Corporal Schilling, a Black male, who worked in the bond office, about Dawdy's harassment tactics. Wright regarded Schilling as a close relative because he had watched Wright grow up. In 1986, Schilling was accused of embezzling money from bond office coffers. The indictments were printed in the newspaper and televised for a few days. Many officers never heard the outcome of that case, which was an acquittal of the charges brought up against him by the Department. Schilling, while in pursuit of his lawsuit that lagged on for nearly a decade, later became ill with cancer, and died after winning the lawsuit (Read Chapter 14: Who's Gonna Bail Me Out?).

"The corporal lied to me about the necessary papers, to be filed when officers are being harassed in the jail," Wright indicated, and also added: "Sergeant Dawdy harassed me about wearing a t-shirt, having a goatee, white socks, my shoes, and my hair. He would then pass another officer with similar infractions and say nothing to that officer, especially if they were white. Even when white officers were in clear violations of jail rules and uniform codes."

Male officers were not allowed to wear beards, unless they got a doctor's excuse advising the officer not to shave because of skin irritation. Goatees or any type of earrings were strictly prohibited, but narcotic officers' restrictions were different, and more lenient to entrap civilian's or potential law breakers into wrongdoings because it gave them the element of being an ordinary person. The historical stigma programmed to the public, about male officers being clean shaven is a stereotyped mentality. Police officers come in many shapes and sizes, and an abundance of disguises and appearances. However, male officers permitted to wear diamond or gold earrings in their ear... well, you can have your own opinion on that.

It was of no surprise to us to see Sergeant Frank Dawdy taking up for the inmate, instead of siding with officers. He agreed and succumbed to departmental philosophy, instead of looking at situations objectively with professional integrity. He commanded very little respect from his peers, and the only reason he had survived working at the Department was because of his intimidating size, longevity, and dedication to carrying out departmental cronyism. He would have been more useful being stationed near Inkster, Michigan, where most of his relatives stayed and friends frequented. But many of Dawdy's peers ran him away from there. A small neighborhood called "*Little Saigon*," an area known for its dope trade, should have been his main patrolling area, since he wanted to harass Black males.

Dawdy was always trying to be such a tough cop. But tough cops don't stand atop a bridge using a speed gun to catch speeding boaters on the waterways, or harass jaywalkers or sidewalk spitters. Tough cops patrol crime ridden areas, infiltrate big business fraud schemes, bust dope pads, save lives while risking their own, and deter possible disastrous situations by using their brains, not their brawn all the time! There was plenty of necessary police work out there for Dawdy to harass and apprehend habitual criminals, instead of using the jail's hidden clauses of underlying administrative bigotry, as his protective shield.

Most police officers were only in the career of law enforcement for the "*power trip*." Many have never been in a position to boss anyone around, and especially to exhort state commissioned authority. Everywhere Sergeant Dawdy was assigned to work, after a short stint, his peers wanted him transferred because of what he portrayed. Always causing havoc, he was constantly a negatively seduced pest in the jail system.

Eventually Dawdy's persistence of harassing Officer Wright paid off, because he was terminated. One day, Officer Wright was called to the command office, to receive one of Dawdy's many trivial, perpetrated conduct incident reports. Quite furious, Wright balled-up the report and threw it at Dawdy, the paper landing on his desk. Wright then looked directly into Dawdy's face, saying: "Since this is all you got to do with your time, writing-up little silly-ass shit like this on me, then I think you should sit here and write-up another one!"

The reprimand was written because Officer Wright was off his floor, a rule equivalent of a traffic cop, issuing a ticket for jaywalking across a street; a trivial, meaningless violation. After a heated exchange of words, Dawdy ordered Wright back to his floor. Officers in the jail left their floors constantly, and back in 1985-1986, the rovers did it in abundance. Rovers were additional officers on the floors to assist in work related duties. They mainly acted as extra security, relieved two or three station officers for a 30 minute lunch break, and two 15 minute breaks (Michigan law requirements for eight hour shifts). In 1987, jail officials eliminated rovers, because some abused the given privilege, and in addition to superiors playing immense favoritism by assigning their favorite departmental minions to rovers, regularly.

In many cases, officers looked out for one another, at least that was the way it should have been. As long as an officer informed his partners that they were leaving the floor for a few minutes, there was nothing wrong with the practice. Superiors wrote-up anything trivial on officers, whom they thought were taking advantage of others, appeared threatening, or didn't respect their superiority and intelligence (however, slight). That's why it's vital to "let your hair down," enjoy yourself sometimes by going to a party, or give a party and be a good host, to relieve some of that unnecessary stress.

24

Trial Board Hearings and Panels: Kangaroo Courts

A S MANY REPRIMANDS AS I HAD ACCUMULATED, it was surprising that I never resorted to expressing myself as did Boo-gay. Unless I honestly felt deserving of a reprimand, I *would not* put my signature on it. I had no problem being honest about my convictions. Most of the time a reprimand was just a piece of paper full of written perplexities because of personality conflicts with superiors. I often expressed my disapproval by sending written rebuttals to every high echelon in the Department about the bias injustices of shift command officers. This only incited those same shift commanders to write additional reprimands. The shift command office's general strategy was to get me on anything, because I just wouldn't stop pointing out their ineptness.

Black male officers knew that numerous reprimands were detrimental, and did not look good when seeking future employment. But what could we do when targeted by racist autocrats? Whether we signed the reprimand or not, it remained in our personnel files throughout our tenures. The records for Trial Board hearings were continuously circulated for collaboration, and reviewed by command officers selected for Trial Board panels. Despite cancellations of Trial Board hearings, write-ups and trivial in-jail charges remained in my archives, and were stored accessibly for review and constant scrutiny.

I, along with many other Black officers were poorly represented by the union and, throughout my tenure, Pete Jovello, a white male was my only union representative. Department shift commanders collaborated as witnesses against me, lying at Trial Board hearings. For decades the very people who participated in Trial Boards bargained away officers' careers at clandestine lunch meetings. The Commanders worked in secrecy to accumulate jail violations against certain officers they disliked.

Identical groups of all-white and one-Black high-ranking male officials, familiar with my circulated history of reprimands, appeared on each of my Trial Board panels. These Trial Board Command Officers acted like court magistrates. The trouble was that Command Officers on the Board were loyal, aging Departmental flunkies, vested in "*The System*," and accustomed to rendering intemperate verdicts to Black officers. Instead of being magisterial, their attitudes were egotistical: the perplexities of a Trial Board decision were reduced to conflicting propaganda tales.

Trial Board panels grilled officers relentlessly, trying to confuse them instead of getting to the real issues at hand, the real source of the problem: ol' boy-ism and racism. This parody of a Trial Board was a mockery of justice, and a demonstration of sheer deceit. Some interrogation techniques had been honed by years of inflicting psychological harassment on inmates and officers. It was during such Trial Board Hearings that I sometimes felt like standing and applauding a performance; many Black officers literally waved a white handkerchief and gave up in the face of relentless and well-orchestrated despotism. Such tyranny was perceived only as Divine Right by the white males participating; they defined their collusiveness as *male bonding*. The Department created legions of these administrative puppets, who never thoroughly or fairly analyzed the performance records of its Black officers.

Those officers who abased themselves were shown mercy: "Yes, Mass-sa. I'se dos whatever ya say, y'all want me to kiss y'alls' ass some moe?" However, officers indifferent or hostile to the proceedings entered this courtroom as guilty until proven innocent, according to Delbert Chambers, the so-called Black male prosecutor (labor relations). How is it that people who have historically experienced the horrors of being poor can so easily embrace capitalism, and righteously exploit their fellow humans? For several Trial Boards and office visits, I was not afforded union representation, while white male superiors at the jail ignored previously agreed upon union and county bargaining bylaws.

In pursuit of the paper-lynchings of Black officers, white jail officials labeled us as sly, crafty, full of devilment, deceitful: it was a resurrection of the rhetoric of *not-dead-long-enough* slave masters. Trial Board hearings were legal hangings in effigy, staged only to discredit Black officers. Though not quite **public** hangings, Trial Board hearings made me recall a scene in the movie "Roots," in which Kunta Kinta is whipped by another "nigger" in front of other Blacks and sympathetic whites, who were forced to watch. Intimidation is everything and one beating is worth a thousand words. Trial Board hearings are the slave beatings and Ku Klux Klan lynchings of the 1990s; Black brothers and sisters feel powerless to do anything but watch in the face of such evidence of the white man's institutional bigotry. To be forced to be a silent witness to the persecution or your race, even to **join in** that very persecution **just to survive**, was to the Department **the epitome of loyalty**.

Citizens abiding all over America have to deal with police brutality: are actually expected to believe what their brutalizers say. Since white institutional actions at the Department were duplicious, cowardly, racist, why would anybody believe what whites within that institution said? White male jail officials, really the Department troublemakers, tried endlessly to short-circuit the drive of Black officers to control their own lives. Their write-ups insinuated problems with character, patterns of disobedience, or an incorrigibility that closed the case on many a Black officer.

The Afrikan-American Delbert Chambers was one of the County's persistent, institutional antagonists to labor relations. He was a crony of the Kenneth Barrett era, whose strategy at my own Hearings was to insinuate a "**too-friendly**" relationship with inmates, characterized by "**overfamiliarity**." All I did was treat all inmates like human beings, showing encouragement for their educational aspirations and their creativity. I was actually doing the Department's job by attempting to **rehabilitate**, of all things. Remember, officers do a variety of jobs **Within The Walls** (To see some of those job junctions see page 103 of Chapter 8). Some inmates of course don't want to learn anything, but I was biased not because of race, but by the nature of the crimes an inmate was charged with, or his willingness to change.

Black superiors were not gratified by the cooperation of white male officials in the persecution of Black inmates or officers, many of them believed that as long as it didn't happen to them it was just part of the job. There was no official analysis of patterns of harassment by superiors; accusations of such were ignored. Racist lore and unproved data were the basis of accusations by envious, or racist, officers to mislead shift commanders, who *relied heavily* on *intuitional race identity* and *assumption*. Black officers were in bondage to the singular punishments of suspension and reprimand. No real remedies were in sight. The Trial Board panel, really officers *turned judges*, were unqualified; burned out from keeping Black males behind bars in the criminal justice system; loyalty to the Department; and their "*over the border*" judgements. They had no other purpose and Justice *did not* prevail.

25

Vermin Control.
Where's The Exterminator?

IN LIFE NEARLY EVERYONE OCCASIONALLY EXPERIENCES a vermin problem. In the early 1960s, my family lived on Vancouver street on Detroit's west side. It was a fairly clean neighborhood, but some of the homes and adjacent alleys were roach or rat infested. Our home didn't have that problem: we had ants. When I think about those days, I have to remind myself that sharing quarters with pesky critters is taken for granted by some folks. When I worked in the jail with other officers, I soon encountered varying opinions about cleanliness.

Officer Dobbertin had taken up the nasty habit of chewing tobacco, as did other white male officers. They thought it was necessary to present a tough demeanor and gain a reputation among inmates. Dobbertin, with little respect for anyone else, had the audacity to spit tobacco juice on the floors of the jail halls and stations like he was out on the street. One day during Roll Call several female officers complained about it: not only about the grossness of spitting, but also Dobbertin's need to carry around a Styrofoam cup to spit in. Visiting Dobbertin's station was certainly unpleasant. It seemed that only white male officers chewed tobacco. It seems that securing a wad from the plant of genus Nicotiana in their cheeks gave them a sense of ruggedness; it certainly couldn't have been for the taste.

Trying to encourage some cleanliness among fellow officers, I would ask how could they work in the jail eight to sixteen hours a day and not want it clean, knowing all the while that their houses were probably no cleaner than the jail. The usual answer was: "It's not my job to do any cleaning around here." Many officers brought in their own cleaning solutions of Pine Sol, Mr. Clean, Janitor In A

Drum, Lestoil, Spic & Span, and bleach, so that at least the floors, wards and stations were free from germs and unhealthy bacteria floating in the unfiltered air. Officers were forced to bring in their own disinfectants because the Department's shipments of janitorial supplies were sometimes delayed for weeks. When supplies were unavailable, my everyday ritual was to get a rag, inmate soap, and hot water to clean the desk, counters, doorknobs, station windows, and the buttons that control the cells and lights. Using regular hand soap for cleaning floors and wards was unfruitful, even counterproductive because germs and odors remained. Officer Fred Steadman, a Black male, always brought in cleaning solution to keep ashtrays and his station clean. In my tenure, he and I simultaneously dated Officer Keisha Flowers (Read Chapter 35; Dating At Work: They Only Come Out At Night).

All keys for all jail floor stations, doors, closets, and stairwells were interchangeable. As a result deputies would sneak to other floors and rob closets of needed janitorial supplies. Let me give you an example: If a particular officer worked the seventh floor exclusively, he could still open every other floor's station doors, and closets. He could even gain entry through the stairwell, and steal whatever he wanted. This master key philosophy was held only to save money; in actuality it encouraged stealing, and created distrust among those officers whose valuables turned up missing while they were away from their station.

One day I was called to come down to the sergeant's office. After a fifteen minute argument with a white male sergeant, I returned to my station to find what looked like a piece of soap, packaged and sealed in plastic. As I stared at it, it looked more and more like crack cocaine, and it wasn't there when I left the station for the office. I immediately called Sergeant Tim Hardison: "Sergeant, could you please come to my station lickety-split?" Hardison arrived in about a minute: he was one of only two Black male command officers I had faith in. After inspecting and smelling the package, Hardison gave me his opinion: "Taylor, it's nothing but soap." I countered: "Sarge, it wasn't there when I left for the office; no way am I going to touch it. There's no telling what kind of game your boys downstairs are playing."

"Hey man, I don't know what it is," Hardison continued, "but they are really after you, brother. They're just after you for nothing, really. I don't know why but they just don't like you, Taylor: the Lieutenant; Dawdy; Ryan; Hopkins; and now even Leonard. I'm trying to stick up for you but I'm kinda outnumbered," Hardison, always up front and honest, admitted. Before he left the station, Hardison warned, "Taylor, if you *are* doing anything, you better stop it right now; they may request a urine sample from you." After Hardison had gone, I noticed that the inmates looked like they knew something, so I asked Hurst, the rock boss, if there was anyone in my station while I was gone. Hurst and I were real cool, so he answered me carefully:

"What's that funny looking white boys name, you know, the one that wrote the whole ward up two weeks ago for a 48-hour lock down because someone took an extra milk? I sho' wanted to kick his ass for that. The whole ward couldn't see their visitors those two days. I couldn't even see my baby, Brenda; everybody wanted to kick his ass. He opened up *your* door and looked in the station file drawers while you was gone." I thought of the all-white manned floors below and above my floor. I always noticed trends in racial bias through schedule changes among shift command officers.

Shipments of supplies arrived weeks late, and in the haste of scrambling for supplies, some greedy officers would steal supplies from other floors. The thieves could've been scheduled to work on any shifts, so it was difficult pinpointing the real culprit(s). Because it was a problem keeping disinfectant in the jail, superiors stored barrels of it on the third floor. When floors ran out of disinfectant, officers had to bring and fill up their own empty buckets. Some officers wasted disinfectant by not knowing how to gauge the proper water amount necessary, or applied it straight. Sometimes barrels of disinfectant were kept in the sergeant's office to keep an eye on its use, to curtail abuse. It was *never* top priority to be considerate of officers' or inmates' needs. Each officer had their own discretion about cleanliness on the ward or station.

Disinfectant was always a necessity because some inmates rarely showered, and food like milk, meat and fruit spoiled while in the garbage bags. When garbage was collected daily the smell was tolerable; before there was such a thing as daily pickup garbage sometimes it remained uncollected on the floors for a day or two, and the smell was suffocating. It was even worse when all the jail's garbage bags were collected and piled up by the dock elevator for hours. The dock elevator was adjacent to the kitchen, and lingering offensive odors wafted through the kitchen and dining areas with the slightest breeze. Even after the garbage bags were removed, its odors lingered for days.

Closets where mops, buckets, brooms, and brushes were kept became a breeding area for roaches. Inmate wards were home to critters ganging up on crumbs from Hostess Twinkies, or other snacks they could feast on. Inmates always complained about roaches in their cells, nibbling on goodies in the dark. When I worked overtime and made rounds on the midnight shift, roaches would scatter like wildfire as the flashlight illuminated tables and dark corners of the wards and cells. They would run into little cracks in the cinder block walls. Who knows where they went from there.

Two Black male inmates, Gregory and Martin, caught roaches for entertainment purposes, and actually trained them to race. On race day inmates wagered food, valuables, and torn-up pieces of playing cards were used as money and collateral for commissary items. The race course was constructed from two cardboard shoe boxes taped together. The starting line was in the exact middle of both boxes so no matter which direction the roach ran, it was considered a race until one roach reached either end of the race course. Roaches, like ants, seem to scurry around with no sense of direction. I have no idea what constitutes a thoroughbred roach; I never asked, however, the races were quite exhilarating and fun to watch.

One roach was named Dasher. Gregory raced this roach for at least a month straight, and fed and trained it every other day. Dasher was considered a world class sprinter because it had won all the races but one. The roaches' housing stables were empty, plastic juice containers, covered with paper, tape or aluminum foil perforated for air. "How's Dasher today, is he ready for the big race?" I asked Gregory, while making a visual, security round of the ward. "Oh, yea, he's ready today, baby! He had some extra food last night, some of those 'wham-whams and zoom-zooms'; that will do him just fine. I can feel it: I know he's ready today." Gregory said it as a joke, but underneath he was definitely serious.

After Dasher had lost its only race in a month, Gregory thought about stomping the roach and recruiting another. "I guess I didn't give Dasher enough Hostess Twinkie crumbs last night before the race; that must be why he lost today. Maybe it's time for a new champ." While the race was in progress, I wondered how Gregory could tell when a roach was ready to race. I also wondered how anyone could tell if the perennial champion was female or male? Why are some roaches called cockroaches; surely a <u>*cock*</u>roach couldn't be a female roach?

Inmates took the races too seriously. Race day was held every other Friday and Saturday—that's if the roaches didn't defect. Inmates constantly scouted newer, faster roaches, but they had to be fed for a few days before qualifying as race material. I've seen frogs, turtles, pigs, rabbits, homing pigeons, dogs, and horses bred for racing, but never roaches. These pesky critters are insects in my book. I wouldn't even think about touching a roach, except to kill it. You had to see it to believe it. There were so many roaches that the wards acted as ant hills. There was an axiom about working in the old jail: *Never* leave a briefcase or bag on the floor, or near a wall, or you risk taking some roaches home with you. This didn't at first apply to the new jail's early years (1984-1987), but after several years the new jail was as pest-ridden as the old. In this the obnoxious Sergeant Dawdy was in his righteous mind.

I never had a problem complying with rules of sanitation when Dawdy ordered the wards to be cleaned and scrubbed. It was his belittling of officers, his abrupt way of blurting out instructions, that made us eventually indifferent to what he said. Commanders should have put Dawdy solely in-charge of cleaning details for both jails, instead of letting this *Sambo* loose among other Black male officers. Dawdy's only claims to fame were cleanliness and a tendency to bow and scrape. Officers whose wards were always dirty were hounded by Sergeant Dawdy. Deputies tried to understand him on the grounds that he was old, uneducated, and negative, but he knew disinfectant was hard to come by, and still always managed to get on officers' nerves. An officer working days selected an inmate to retrieve and put out ward mops and buckets every morning. It was general practice that an officer call other floors asking for cleaning supplies and disinfectant to sanitize the halls and wards. Locating disinfectant was sometimes impossible: either there wasn't any, or officers on other floors would *say* there wasn't any. Officers asking for disinfectant were often the very ones who had ripped some off.

We also had exterminators spray suffocating chemicals every two weeks, making it hard for officers and inmates to breath freely on the jail floors. Although officers were required to tell inmates, before the exterminators sprayed, that all food had to be at least twelve inches off the floor, many never did. Exterminators also skipped scheduled spraying, probably because the Department was late paying suppliers. Besides, the roaches drank up that poison and laughed out loud. The pest spray was biologically more damaging to us than the roaches. Possessed of bad ventilation and unfiltered recycled air, the jail should have been sprayed while most deputies and coworkers were off work. A better time to fumigate was on the midnight shift, while inmates slept with their cell doors closed, their blankets stuffed into the small opening under the door. This would have at least blocked some of the fumes. By the time the morning shift arrived, the odor would have dissipated and the spray evaporated.

The midnight deputy had flexibility and didn't have to stay in the same station and smell the roach poison like other shift officers did; yet this was never seriously considered by jail officials. Although roaches and dust mites can spread allergies, officers could experience more serious, future medical problems because of poisonous spray. The administrators who implemented jail rules had difficulty foreseeing this crucial issue, despite receiving several written and oral complaints from officers and coworkers. As officials sat behind their desks, thinking up damaging lies and shuffling papers, they failed to realize officers' insight about health concerns in the Department.

Female officers hated to go into the janitor's closets because of its smell and filth, and the frightening possibility that roaches might jump or crawl on them. Such officers always appreciated male officers who'd *suck-up* and collect cleaning equipment for them. Upon opening the janitorial closet, it was common to see roaches protruding from filthy drains. Roaches would jump on an officer from the tubed plumbing overhead. Roaches appeared from soiled mop heads and buckets, and came out of dirty, straw brooms. They bred in filthy drainage systems, the floor's strainer clogged up with other dead roaches and mop strands. Besieged, overcrowded roaches literally jumped on the necks and arms of officers and inmates.

To combat the infestation while retrieving cleaning equipment, I'd hose down the pipes and walls with scalding hot water, creating pressurization by using my fingertip. The temperature was often so hot that the top portion of my finger turned red. This was the only sure way of killing these riotous, man-eating roaches. A nozzle for the hose was never stored or available: it was considered contraband because of the metal or hard plastic. I sprayed those roaches down just like those white firemen did those children in Selma, Alabama. I stomped them just like those white policemen did in the 1960s, when they stomped Afrikan-Americans, or anyone who marched or rioted against injustice and civil rights violations. One time the roaches got so bad they had the *nerve* to invade the guard stations. An officer would be minding his own business, when all of the sudden, three or four roaches would parade across the desk.

The records for 1988 shows that the Department spent only $148.00 for pest control, a ridiculously low figure, and clearly an obvious reason for the increase of roach accumulation. I consider that pure negligence on the part of Department Officials.

26

Jim Brown's Clone: Excluded from the Dirty Dozen

SOMETIMES WHEN TROUBLE WAS "A-BREWIN'," Sergeant Tim Hardison came up to my floor to consult with me. At this juncture I considered Hardison my only friend and confidant in a position of authority. He was one cool cat. Hardison once allowed and gave permission to several Black officers to attend the wake for fellow Black female Officer Blakely's son. He was another young Black male statistic of a worldwide drug epidemic: death by using, enterprising, or association with the drug trade. It's genocide, intentional or not, and makes the survival of Black communities dubious, especially with city, county, state, and federal government budget cuts aimed at the working poor.

To attend the wake officers signed up before Roll Call. I hadn't known about the wake until after Roll Call, and hadn't submitted my name. There were about twenty officers granted permission to attend by the time I reached my floor assignment and signed my name in the logbook. I called Hardison on the phone: "Sarge, I didn't know about Officer Blakely's son until after Roll Call. Please, can I get out of here? I need a break. Come on sarge," I pleaded. At first Hardison acted like he didn't want me to go, citing "insufficient manpower" as an excuse. After a little more coaxing, Hardison conceded, "Yeah, you can go, get out of here for awhile, before they start messing with you tonight."

"You're alright sarge," I agreed. "I need to get out of this damn place, quick." We both laughed, and hung up. Hardison knew I wanted to avoid the harassment of his colleagues. I hurried to the locker room and exited the jail with other Black officers. After the exequies, several officers and I left the wake—on our way back we stopped at the liquor store. A few officers, who went to the funeral home, returned to work, but the rest of us decided we'd stay longer with Blakely. We went over to her house, where we ate, drank, and listened to oldies but goodies from the 1960s and 70s. Some officers sang stirring renditions from the Supremes, Temptations, Dramatics, Spinners, Smokey Robinson and the Miracles, and the Stylistics.

When it was finally time to leave, I exited singing Michael Jackson's *"I Wonder Who's Loving You?"*: "I-I-I, IIIIIII, should have never, never made you cry. But since, since you've been away. Don't you know I, hang around with my head hanging down, and I wonder who's loving you?" Everybody tripped out when I hit some of Michael Jackson's highest notes, but I was smooth because my throat was coated with Crown Royal and Grand Marnier.

Gone since six that evening, we didn't return to work until ten o'clock, one hour before shift change. It was a refreshing break, even if it took a funeral's wake to get it. The Black officers were set on having some fun that night; and we tried to make Blakely forget the pain of losing her second son in this tragic way. We were supposed to be back at 8 p.m., but Sergeant Hardison didn't say anything: he understood exactly what we were trying to do for Blakely. We felt like comrades, helping another through grief when she needed us the most.

I always respected Sergeant Hardison, who in 1990 was promoted to lieutenant. The humanitarian side of an officer is not always taken into account; more often than not, it is taken for granted. Not on the list, not at the wake, not later at Blakely's house, were there any white officers. Officers spent years together in time on the jail floors. That time together gave officers a semblance of family, and a desire for occupational sincerity. Maintaining loyalty tells a lot about an officer. If there are problems keeping officers interested in the betterment of society and respectful of members within their organization, then how can law enforcement expect citizens to have faith in its ability to keep neighborhoods safe and crime rates low? To me, Sergeant Hardison was the most respected Black man in the Department. He was a true human being, with a compassionate heart and a down-to-earth perspective. Officers didn't dare cross him, however, because he physically resembled Jim Brown, the legendary, Football Hall of Famer. What Hardison did for Blakely and the officers who wanted to support her, most command officers would have avoided doing. You could understand why. When inmates weren't locked down, it could become somewhat stressful on jail floors manned by only three or four officers. Burn out accelerated rapidly in officers, and produced uncaring "*Robocops*." If you believe that the good guys win at all, which they do once in a while, then you will be glad to hear that in January, 1993, Lieutenant Hardison was promoted to Commander, and on December 31, 1998, was promoted to Undersheriff—one of the best moves the Department ever made.

27

Attending Roll Call:
The Rigors of Roll Call

ATTENDING ROLL CALL COULD BE CRAZY, and often set the tone for the day. It could also be a time of great humor and a source of information and enlightenment. Roll Call was especially hilarious on payday, when everyone felt somewhat blithe, even jovial. Then there were those days when Roll Call was very trying, and made officers wish for a new profession. Before floor assignments were given, lengthy memos from jail officials were read, supposedly for three consecutive days. Some of the proposed changes were of little interest to us. Near the peroration of a typical speech, a chorus of dry coughs and throat clearings erupted from uninterested officers.

Sergeant Joe Ryan, a short, large boned white man, always carried a case filled with several pipes and choices of tobacco. He called out the names of officers and their assignments grandiloquently. Everything Ryan did was slow. Ryan always called my name out bombastically. Without hesitation, I mimicked Ryan and, instead of responding, "Here," or "Yes, sir," I called out, "RHINO" to the accompaniment of laughter from fellow officers. Ryan was built like a rhinocerous, and hated this name. He'd then blame me for anything he could think up. Ryan hollered at me, belittled me, and embarrassed me during Roll Call. I responded with a puzzled expression, and told myself I was just breaking up the monotony of Roll Call.

Sergeant Ryan typically relaxed with his feet propped up on the desk, blowing O's made of pipe smoke, and watching them float away and disappear. He did this while writing out the officers' schedule for the week. Officers knew when he was near by the familiar tobacco aroma. Ryan had a contrary disposition, but a good sense of humor. Walking by Ryan, I'd say, "Hello Sergeant Ryan, how are you doing today?" Ryan's only reply would be: "Uhhh-uh," with a deep "hum-hum." He never replied, "How are you?" Like many superiors, his response to codes was usually slow and methodical, and he arrived on the jail floor last, way after the situation was under control.

On Friday, January 17, 1986, two days after the nation observed Dr. Martin Luther King's birthday, Sergeant Ryan wrote-up a conduct incident report on me and sent it to Inspector McCarey. I never had any direct problems with Ryan, but he would go along with others' desires to discredit me. My reprimand was for "...not calling in and not reporting for duty." It went as follows: *Officer K. Taylor was scheduled to work on 1-17-86. He/She did not report for duty and did not call in. This behavior is contrary to Sheriff Department Rules and Regulation.*

I had previously arranged this day off with Lieutenant Shoulders, and this wasn't the first time I was accused of being A.W.O.L. because of a superior's oversight. Precise and keen communication between Command Officers occurred only when they deemed it fit, or when they were completely sure to be acknowledged, or praised.

On January 28, 1986, I wrote a departmental communication to Inspector McCarey, stating the subject (A.W.O.L. write-up on 1-17-86 by Sergeant Ryan), the problem, and the misinformed source. It went as follows: "I was given an A.W.O.L. notice for January 17th, 1986. Lt. Shoulders and I had previously arranged for me to attend a wedding on the dates of 1-17 through 1-21. I had explained to Lt. Shoulders that I might not be able to call in on 1-17-86 (Friday) because of the constant running while in Florida in preparation for the wedding. The lieutenant knew of my departure and apparently forgot about the arrangement we initiated. I was to have a sick day on 1-17-86, & my leave days were 1-18, 1-19, so I decided to take a sick day on Martin Luther King Day, as we both had agreed. The lieutenant obviously had a lapse of memory, which caused me to be marked A.W.O.L."

The second time occurred on Sunday, February 9, 1986, when I wrote Lt. Shoulders about a personal business leave day for February 22, two weeks ahead of time. This time it was necessary to inform

Shoulders that he had forgotten about my arranged leave day on January 17, 1986, which was written up as A.W.O.L., by Sergeant Ryan. My request for a leave day stated: "Dear Sir, I am requesting a personal business leave day on Saturday, February 22, 1986. I have an appointment on Monday, February 24, for a possible job connection. I need the extra day to prepare myself. Please notify me of the decision, if denied. I would also like to know what has happened about the A.W.O.L. that was unfairly written on me 1-17-1986."

If not paid for my time, I should at least have the A.W.O.L. taken off my record. I had let Lieutenant Shoulders know far in advance, and Shoulders later sent me a letter of apology for forgetting about my leave days. But the infraction stayed in my personnel records, and this was the second time I was so-called mistakenly written up as A.W.O.L. by so-called superiors. The first false report was on August 27, 1985, when I called-in sick; that report was also sent to Inspector McCarey and the payroll department. Lieutenant Shoulder's report was labeled "AWOL status of PO I K. Taylor." It stated: *"On 27 Aug 85, PO I K. Taylor was marked 'AWOL' in error. He should have been marked 'sick.' Due to the hurried nature of lobby desk, Ofcr Taylor's sick-call **was not logged**, however the L/D Sgt. recalled talking with Ofcr Taylor."*

Whoever the master of ceremonies was for Roll Call on a particular day was a sybil about lateness. Officers liked by the command officers got away with being late: one in particular being Officer Millie Frances, a short, moody, somewhat sexy, but also weird, **Betty Boop**-type. She often came in late, and would stand near one of two Roll Call room doors in her summery, hot shorts until her name was called. Several officers, who were still in street clothes like Frances, stood and waited by the door. "Here," they shouted, when the superior called out their name and assignment, then they'd rush to the locker room to get dressed into their uniform.

Some Command Officers played favorites and never looked up to see where the voice of a friend or protege came from. Female officers regularly avoided harsh discipline for lateness, even after five or six times in a month, *just* for being female. Personal biases were also overwhelmingly obvious and any officer who spoke out against them was harassed for it. A few Command Officers even wrote reprimands for, or put red marks next to, the names of officers they didn't like. In some cases red marks were posted on the schedule if the officer was only seconds or a minute late. The officer would hear about it when called to the office, before or after lunch, to receive a sixty-second late slip. When officers complained, Command Officers would respond, "We have to round it off to the nearest minute." The late slip really indicated two or three minutes in order to hide their pettiness of docking the officer's pay. Payroll would then deduct the minutes indicated on the schedule from the officer's paycheck. Three late notices within a month constituted disciplinary action, which was *never* enforced regularly or fairly.

If Command Officers did not like you personally, or if you were Black, they would arbitrarily switch your days off. Even if Black officers had more seniority, many had their schedules changed to accommodate the initiation of new white recruits. The week that new deputies came to work in the new jail, my upcoming off days always seemed to be Saturday, Sunday and Monday. New deputies had to be fitted in somewhere on the new schedule, but the schedule was changed at random to the unilateral disadvantage of many Black officers. It seemed that when I expected a weekend off, an unyielding superior would start me back at the beginning of the week and give me a Tuesday and Wednesday off.

The random days-off schedule once engendered a reprimand when I actually forgot which days I was off. It was bad enough trying to deal with the daylight savings time changes, but in this case I also had to deal with being made an example of. Frustrated by the reprimand, I wrote to one Inspector McCarey and told it like it really was: I had simply forgotten. It was my fault. I didn't deserve a reprimand for making a mistake. I was furious about the racial bias in scheduling. It had happened to me five or six times, and the union did little or nothing to correct the problem.

Most unfair scheduling was done by superiors who held grudges, or were envious. On March 16, 1987, another late report was written because I had a flat tire on the way to work. My reply to the Inspector stated as much.

"Previously, on October 20, 1985, I had written to Command Officers stating that on October 18, 1985, while on my way to work, I had an automobile accident that resulted in damage to a rear axle. To assure there would be no further damage a tow truck had to be called. At approximately 1510 hours, I told Lt. Shoulders about the incident. I arrived at work at 1545 hours." When I walked into the jail lobby, I immediately headed towards the Command Office amid catcalls from white male officers of, "Damn Taylor, where ya been, swimming?" "Nobody told you to use an umbrella?"

On October 22, 1986, another conduct incident report was written by Sergeant Paul Leonard to Inspector McCarey, stating that I had "*not reported to work.*" I had no problem signing late slips or reprimands, hey, it happens. My honesty was forthright, but after the flat tire incident I received another more serious conduct incident report. It was dated the day of the flat tire incident, and it, too, was written up by Sergeant Leonard, a light-skinned Black male with a thick mustache and slicked-down hair, who sent it to Inspector McCarey. His report cited me for having been late for either Roll Call or work three times within a twenty-eight day period, and thereby in violation of Section D, paragraph 3.6.5 of the Sheriff's Policy Manual.

Sergeant Leonard's report listed five late dates, the last two violations had a red line drawn through them. These two were termed *excusable* by jail officials, but remained in my personnel file rather than being erased from the report, or the entire report typed over. With all the needless paperwork jail officials generated, surely they could have found time to witeout the *two* dismissed infractions and make another copy of that one page. The other three tardy slips remained as official reasons for disciplinary action. Two of the three remaining violations could have been excused too, but were not. It seemed that no matter how hard I tried to do right, superiors were determined to execute a paper lynching.

Dissatisfaction with "*The System*" caused time-card fraud during Roll Call. The time-card notebook was placed on a table next to a door, so officers could sign-in and sign-out before heading to their floors. Officer Orealia Smart, a Black female, was actually fired for forging sergeants' and lieutenants' signatures for time not worked. Deputies grew discontented that the Department did not pay us for the ten extra minutes spent in Roll Call. All Roll Calls were held ten minutes before the actual, paid starting time. Day shift was held at

6:50 a.m., 2:50 p.m. for the afternoon shift, and 10:50 p.m. for the midnight shift. All officers should have been paid for those extra ten minutes. It wasn't until the spring of 1988 that the Department and County decided to pay officers for the extra ten minutes spent in Roll Call. Since I had started working for the Department in January 1985, I was owed a significant sum of money.

A six-day work week amounted to one extra hour of pay a week, which in 1985, was about $8.52, $1.42 for a sixth of a minute. The monthly amount each sheriff's deputy gave up was $34.08. Multiplying $34.08 by twelve months, I realized that the County owed me $408.96 a year for three years; a total that comes to $1,226.88. Officers with perfect attendance gave the Department/County an hour a week, 52 hours a year, and one hundred, fifty-six hours of their own time over a three year period. Officers were also getting taxed for that unpaid ten minutes for years. What about those officers who faithfully worked twenty years and didn't get paid for those ten minutes in Roll Call until 1988? Paid retroactively, the Department owed them upwards of $8,200-$10,000 dollars *or more*. Wouldn't you say that was a rip-off? To top that, officers paid $24 a month in union dues.

Harassment of officers was common *Within The Walls*. Some Command Officers really hated to see officers enjoying themselves in Roll Call, and turned belligerent over trivial incidents. I was quite aware of the psychological warfare, and I also experienced it in the Police Academy. Superiors set out to determine how much a targeted officer could endure. Some targeted officers took their frustrations back to the jail floors and gave inmates a hard time. Inmates, however, were the least of our worries; I never had any problems with them. My problems were definitely with employees; they were the ones who required the most attention.

There was a jail rule about officers' dress. If officers were state-certified, they had an option of wearing their uniform to work, but noncertified officers were supposed to change from street clothes into their uniform in the locker room before Roll Call, and undress before leaving the jail. This rule was *never* strictly enforced, except to harass those targeted officers who preferred wearing their uniform to work. Sergeant Dawdy always harassed noncertified officers about wearing their uniforms to the jail. He would stroll into Roll Call, his chest stuck out to keep his tightly buckled-up pants from falling down beneath his big belly. "All you officers that are wearing your uniform to work, well, if I continue to see y'all wearing it to work, expect to get a write-up from me," Dawdy announced in a deep voice.

There were two clear-cut advantages to wearing the uniform to work: it allowed five to ten extra minutes for leisure; it was convenient when time was short to make Roll Call in time. Leisure time was always essential when working in the jail: every minute counted. Some prima donnas thought they were the Lord Almighty once they achieved state certification. Some officers were wimps, afraid of inmates and the real intricacies of police work. The Department instituted the uniform rule because some state-certified officers in uniform were shot and wounded while off duty. The underlying reason why officers weren't to wear their uniforms to and from work was that citizens might think an off-duty officer was still on duty and ask for their help.

The noncertified officer, in uniform without arrest power or a gun, is at risk if he or she stumbles upon a crime in progress and felt obliged to assist. I preferred wearing my noncertified uniform to work in spite of all this. The uniform pants were a dark brown khaki with two big snap-button pockets on the upper-front thighs. The shirt had a big yellow, six-pointed star sewn on the left side. In my tenure, I've helped a few citizens off duty, who thought I was a sworn-in State-certified officer.

One incident happened in July 1986, at a party store in my old childhood neighborhood. In the early 1960s, I had played cowboy and Indians, cops and robbers here. I had been the "Sheriff in town." On my way to work, I double-parked my car directly in front of a beer delivery truck, whose driver was stacking beer on a dolly, to cart inside the store. I ran inside for a jar of papaya juice to take to work. About a minute-and-a-half later, a Black man burst into the store, shouting:

"Whoever's driving the beer truck, you better go see what's shaking, because some Black dude just went into your cab and took out a red gym bag." The delivery man saw my sheriff's uniform, and asked, "Can you come help me recover my bag?" My first reaction was that

I didn't have much time before Roll Call, but I felt his sense of urgency. "Yeah, lets go get him," I answered.

We both rushed out of the store and would-you-know-it—saw the thief at the same time. He was walking swiftly between apartment houses across the street, carrying the red gym bag. At that moment, Zarka, an Arab male and owner of the store, decided to come outside from behind the counter with a 9-MM Colt.

"You guys sure you don't need my help?" he confidently inquired. "I think we can handle it ourselves," I answered, not wanting the situation to get out of hand. I wasn't a state-certified officer yet, and technically, couldn't be of much help, even though my uniform said "*Wayne County Sheriff.*" The beer driver retrieved a baseball bat from his cab, I had nothing. We jumped into my 1981 Seville to apprehend a thief, who had traveled several blocks before we caught up with him. I had on an oversized sheriff jacket which made it look as if I might have a weapon. After traveling three blocks with the thief in sight, I sped up, slamming the brakes and came to a screeching halt at the curb, catching the thief off guard.

The delivery driver and I jumped out of the car together: "Get down, my man, get down, or you are dead meat," I directed, so loudly that nearby drivers stopped and residents came out of their houses to inspect the commotion. I didn't have a weapon, so I had to insinuate I had armored protection, by keeping my right hand tucked inside the left side of my jacket, as if I had a gun inside a shoulder holster. While the culprit was face down on the pavement, I frisk searched him for weapons, forcefully pushing my knee between his back and neck. The beer driver, still hopping mad, wanted to hit the thief with the bat. I emphatically restrained him from doing so.

"I told you not don't move, or I'll have to use my weapon," I told the thief repeatedly as he squirmed around on the pavement. My only weapon was my index finger pointed at the back of his head; but the thief couldn't tell what I had with his face pressed into the concrete. If he had tried anything, the beer driver would have scattered his brains with a size 34, narrow-barreled handle "Al Kaline Louisville Slugger." After recovering the gym bag, the beer driver looked through it for any missing items while I still secured the thief face down. The contents of the bag: a small propane torch, some tools, no money or any real material possessions.

After a more thorough second frisk, I let the thief up. He didn't skip a beat: "Man, I'm sorry, but can one of you guys let me have a dollar: I'm very hungry and have nothing to eat." I stood there, steadily shaking my head, and said nothing for a few seconds.

"Fool, you should have asked someone that before you went out stealing. Here's 75 cents and I hope you have learned a lesson."

"Thank you, sir, for *that*. God bless you," the thief blubbered, as a stream of tears fell down his face, and he then went on his merry way. The beer truck driver, with his Louisville Slugger still poised, commented.

"Damn man, I wanted to bash that son-of-a-bitch. The hell with all these crackheads. Every time I come in this area something always happens. Fuck them motherfuckers." I sympathized with him, but no one was hurt, and none of this probably wouldn't have happened had he locked his truck cab doors. I felt I had done something good, but it could have been disastrous.

"Who can I contact, brother, to tell them about what you did to help me?" The beer driver asked.

"You can call the Wayne County Sheriff's Department, at 224-2222, and ask for Sergeant Phil Hopkins. Tell him about the incident," I replied. I chose Hopkins because at the time I considered him a trusted friend. I never expected commendations for this deed, but I did hope for some kind of commendatory gesture, and I was willing to even accept a pat on the back from any superior.

After it was all over, I could only think about what would have happened if the thief had possessed a weapon. We both would have been sitting ducks for a propane torch and some tools. The news headlines the next day might have read, **"*Noncertified Sheriff Deputy killed off duty recovering stolen tools.*"**

The uniform rule was changed many times, and noncertified and state-certified officers continued to come to work dressed and ready for Roll Call. However, wearing a uniform to and from work *can* put an officer in a precarious situation; as a result many officers *never* wear their uniforms unless they are on the clock. Sadly, most officers don't want to get involved in anything that won't pay them, or is considered risky. Officers also tend to stick to the **letter of laws** drawn up by legislators with little, *if any*, law enforcement experience. Instead of reducing crime, laws that do not consider recidivism or rehabilitation issues keep habitual criminals on the streets and crime rates high.

It seemed the only time top brass came to Roll Call was to address the constituency when election time was near. They also came on the heels of a rumor that an officer was possibly bringing drugs into the jail. Jail officials were always eager to bust officers; and sometimes their paranoid hysteria to label was premature. Command officers searched briefcases and duffle bags of male officers, who were often treated like criminals. The purses of female officers were searched only when a female superior was available.

Internal Affairs sometimes brought in Nero and Bronzee, two elderly drug and bomb-sniffing, red retrievers. One day Nero was sent in to sniff around the Roll Call room at will. Though on a leash, Nero was held loosely by Detective Ron Mallard, a big white male mountain man with a beard to match.

"Whatcha smell, boy? You wanna go over there? Okay. Whatcha smell, boy? Whatcha smell? Ya got something?" Mallard's encouraging statements urged Nero on. While we stood at parade rest, Nero sniffed the groins of various male officers, the crotches of some female officers, and quickly focused on a table loaded with purses, lunches, and guess what else? *briefcases and gym bags*. Nero jumped up to lean his front paws on the table, sniffed, and slobbered all over the lunch bags, purses, and several books.

"Ugh," Officer Blakely, a Black female, moaned, "Get that damn dog off my Gucci purse." "Get that mutt off my chicken sandwiches," demanded Officer Jeff Sperma, a white male.

When officers brought their lunches, they usually sat them on this table near the door. Nero, still sniffing for contraband, grabbed one bag as if about to have some lunch for himself. Nero put the bag down only when Mallard asked, "Is that it?" I would think that if Nero grabbed a bag for any reason, this four-legged copper's choice *would at least* be checked. But Detective Mallard didn't check the lunch bag because Officer Sperma who complained that "the dog was about to eat his lunch" was white. Racial bias was common *Within The Walls*.

One day white male officers were tipped-off to another surprise search in Roll Call, and scattered pepper taken from the kitchen, on the floors in the locker and Roll Call rooms. White officers always seemed to know ahead of time when things were about to happen. When detectives brought in Bronzee to search, she started sneezing of course. It was cruel and unusual punishment, not to mention cruelty to animals. "I want a full inquiry and I'm gonna find out who did this," a high-ranking official yelled into the male locker room as Bronzee was hurried away from the over-seasoned floors. Officers could still hear the Bronzee sneezing by the basement stairway during Roll Call. Officials never found out who did it because white boys at the Department stuck together, and Blacks dared not tell on them.

On one of my days off, an officer nicknamed "Ice" called me at home to tell me, "The Department broke into your other locker. They said there was a bomb threat." For as long as I could remember, the locker next to mine had the word "bomb" written on it. It had previously belonged to Officer "*Pacman*," a Black male, who quit the Department in 1986 to work for the Detroit Fire Department. The Sheriff's Department had once again violated my rights. They, instead of "Ice," should have called my house. Officials knew that I, like many officers, were using an optional locker.

On hot steamy summer days I would sometimes bring in a six-pack of frozen Dole, 100-percent, natural strawberry popsicles, and take them into Roll Call to defrost a little. If I didn't feel like eating all six, I'd put the rest in a freezer in the kitchen. I could have eaten the whole box with ease, but officers came begging.

"Hey, Taylor, let me get a popsicle." "You got a dollar? "That's what you'd pay the popsicle truck outside," I'd reply.

I don't mind sharing, and I gave up a few popsicles, but the point was still ***Where's your dollar?*** because officers ***never*** offered. That alone told me a lot about some of the people I worked with. Some were cheap, but because we were paid bi-weekly, most officers occasionally asked for a loan between pay days when things were tight. Officers ***never*** had to worry about getting their money back from me. Knowing how to save money and balance a budget is another story, especially when you aren't being paid for years to attend Roll Call.

28

I'm MADD About Drunk Driving

O N FRIDAY, DECEMBER 16, 1988, the last day of enduring
fourteen weeks at the Police Academy, I was told, as
were five other Black cadets (four females and one male)
that we didn't pass the state test. A month later we were
all given a second chance to pass it. At the Michigan State Police
post in Lansing, *all* the Black cadets passed the second time around
and successfully completed Police Academy requirements; but I was
intentionally put through five weeks of bureaucracy, red-tape injustice. To my recollection, since 1985 through 1990, *only Black cadets
were told* "they had unsuccessfully met academy requirements." Finally, on Monday, February 27, 1989, I was personally sworn-in by
Sheriff Carmeno, in his office as a State-Certified Officer.

Three weeks later, an incident that required I be a Good Samari-
tan made me an unlikely target of departmental harassment. A car
accident resulted in the death of a woman and involved one of the
department's best-liked officers. On a dark, rainy, fog bound night,
my girlfriend Brenda and I had just completed grocery shopping and
were heading home. On the way we saw a stranded vehicle, with its
entire rear end smashed in. The trunk was demolished, and several
passersby and patrons from a nearby bowling alley were helping the
injured at the scene. One, an elderly Black man, was using a flashlight to direct traffic around the wreck. He alerted and rerouted drivers who had difficulty perceiving the accident through the fog, thun-
der and pouring rain.

I pulled over to stop and got out to see if Brenda and I could be of any assistance. A woman then identified herself as a nurse and aided an injured Black woman through the rolled-down passenger side window. When I saw the damage, my first reaction was, "Wow, how did the cars get turned around like this?" I found out later, from a Detroit Police traffic investigator, that speed and force of impact caused one car to spin around several times. Since most of our groceries were perishables, and I felt I should stay to assist at the accident scene, I suggested that Brenda go home and come back in thirty minutes.

While showing my badge and identifying myself to the crowd as a police officer, I noticed that one of the injured victims being helped by the nurse through the passenger window never opened her eyes:

"Ma'am are you alright? Ma'am, are you alright? If you can hear me, please just move your arm or moan," I called out to her.

Getting no response, I then reached through the driver's side window and placed my fingers against her neck to feel for a pulse; it was faint. It was clear that she was in shock, or worse, from the tremendous impact.

"Momma, momma are you alright? Momma are you alright? Please speak to me! Are you gonna be alright?"

A young Black woman cried out over and over. Her mother *never* answered and the young woman wept herself into exhaustion, buckled up with grief. I tried to reassure her, even while something kept telling me that her mother was slowly dying. As I looked at the mother's face she seemed to be slowly fading away.

Medical technicians, police officers, fire fighters, and rescuers are taught to make the best of any situation, to help keep the faith and confidence of relatives and friends intact. At least that was what we were taught at the Police Academy. To reach the injured woman, a passerby and I pried the driver's door backward with a jack. Then we bent the hatchback door upward and completely over, backwards against the roof of the car. I tried desperately to reach the victim from the rear of the vehicle, but lack of room and jagged metal prevented it. In the attempt I tore my pants and cut my inner right thigh. We also couldn't position the victim to assist with CPR because of the bucket seats.

As soon as the nurse created a breathing passage for the injured woman, emergency medical personnel arrived and took over: within ten minutes she was out of the car. At that point I went over to check on the occupant of the other car. A Black male was kneeling in the street as if in prayer, his upper torso draped over the driver's side front seat. Both hands covered his face, and there was blood all over the street and car, thick on the front seat and a trench coat. The driver's side windshield was roundly shattered from the impact of his face and forehead.

Though the Eighth Precinct was only a mile and a half away, it took Detroit Police better than fifteen minutes to arrive at the accident scene. One of the people aiding the Black male victim was an old college alumnus named Kippy. He held a white towel saturated with blood he had wiped from the Black male's face. I talked with Kippy briefly about our old college days, and turned to brief a Black female Detroit police officer about the situation. As we observed the Black male victim, his sports coat fell open, revealing a 9-MM handgun and a pair of handcuffs on his belt. Any one of the civilians at the scene could've easily lifted the weapon, so I took the gun and handcuffs off his belt, and the Black female cop seized his wallet. I watched her as she flipped through the wallet, looking for identification. To our dismay the ID revealed him as Chester Godley, a Wayne County Sheriff's officer, heavily involved in union business. Years back, in January 1985, when I attended the jailers' training class, Godley was one of the tour guides on our first sight-seeing tour of the jails.

Emergency Medical Technicians had already extricated the injured Black woman from the car and put her in the ambulance. The Fire Department was hosing down a dangerous gas spill in the street. I opened the door of Godley's car, and sat on the passenger side front seat, and leaned over to let Godley know that he had help and a Sheriff's Officer was there with him. He was in great pain, moaning loudly the whole time I was there. I smelled alcohol in the car and searched for liquor bottles or beer cans, to hide or discard them before they proved incriminating. But there wasn't any liquor to be found, although the Fire and Police personnel gathered nearby kept saying they smelled the alcohol too.

"Please, don't nobody light a cigarette, or a match. All that damn alcohol on his breath we might all get blown up," quipped a white male cop.

It was obvious to *all of us* that Godley had been drinking heavily. Rescuers carefully placed a neck brace on him, and I helped lift him onto a backboard stretcher. Godley and the injured woman were rushed to a local hospital in the same ambulance. As the ambulance pulled away, I went across the street to a pay phone and called the New Jail's lobby Desk Sergeant. Sergeant Gregory Morelly, a white male, answered. I was hyperventilating as I told him.

"Sir, Officer Godley has just been involved in a terrible car accident at Seven Mile Road and Lahser. There's a possible fatality. Will you please call over to the old jail to tell the command personnel over there?"

"Who is this?" Morelly demanded, adding, "I don't even *know* an Officer Godley." He conscientiously ignored the urgency in my voice.

"This is Officer Taylor; what difference does it make, who I am? An officer is hurt and in trouble. Will you please call over to the Old Jail," I hollered. I was angry and feeling frustrated because Godley was popular with everyone, and had worked primarily in the old jail for nearly twenty years.

Before leaving the accident scene, the Detroit Police knew I had informed the Sheriff's Department. When Brenda and I finally arrived home, I wondered if Morelly had passed the message on to the Old Jail. So, fifty minutes after my first call, I called again, but this time through the Department's telecommunications officer at the switchboard to transfer me to the Old Jail. This time, Sergeant Dunlap, a Black male, answered. I filled him in:

"Sir, about an hour ago I informed Morelly, the lobby desk sergeant in the new jail about a car accident. Sir, don't tell me he didn't call to tell you what happened to Officer Godley?" So I told Dunlap about the tragedy, and which hospital the injured were taken to. Dunlap was shocked and concerned.

"That damn Morelly never told me or anyone in the Old Jail about Godley being in a accident. I'll get somebody on this right away."

On March 20, 1989, three days after the accident, Sergeant Joel Schwarze, a white male from Internal Affairs, met with me in the Command Office to discuss the accident. He ordered me to write-up a report. I didn't want to write the report, but as a police officer it was my duty: I was the first officer on the scene. I had to state that I smelled alcohol in the car as I talked with Mr. Godley, and that I did not see any evidence of beer cans or liquor bottles in the car. I also stated that the report was written as factually as I could remember.

However, before I wrote-up the report, Sergeant Schwarze informed me that Godley's blood alcohol content level was near .24 percent. Such a high level meant he must have had at least 11 to 14 drinks of 86 proof alcohol. Under the law, persons registering at .10 percent or more are considered "*under the influence*" and liable for arrest. According to Schwarze, Godley was 2.5 to 3 times the legal limit. Drivers with a count of only .08 percent are considered impaired. Later I discovered that Godley had attended a union function that night, where alcoholic beverages are customarily served free-of-charge.

Many officers often drove home drunk from union parties. If Breathalizer tests were routinely given to officers after union parties, it's certain that many of them would register over the state's legal limit. As I thought about Godley, I recalled those union party days, and realized I could've been in that same predicament at any time because of free alcohol served at union bashes. In short, the union was partially, if not solely responsible, and should have taken some of the blame for the tragedy. Union officials and other officers knew Godley was *too* drunk to drive, and someone should have put him in a cab or driven him home. And speaking of Godley's union pals, *friends should know when to say when.*

There is a law that prohibits bar owners from letting intoxicated patrons drive. This law also tickets the bar owner for doing so. The woman injured in the accident I happened to stumble upon died the next day, and Godley's face required years of extensive bone reconstruction surgery and therapy. Several months after the accident I had to testify in court about what I had witnessed. I never knew what the charge, or sentence, was, but the Department gave Godley a lengthy suspension and would not permit him to return to work until after all court proceedings. The Detroit Police traffic scene investigator concluded that: "The positioning of the cars after impact showed a high rate of speed, and the rear impact pushed the cars into their peculiar positions."

Many police agencies believe that sobriety check lanes will curb the incidence of drunk driving accidents. One example of a city government's defiance of the courts was Sheriff Jacob Carmeno's decision to use sobriety check lanes on County highways. Before the matter was even heard in court, Carmeno ordered its implementation on several Wayne County roadways. The U.S. Supreme Court, in a 6-3 ruling, concluded that Michigan's sobriety check lanes did not violate the U.S. Constitution's Fourth Amendment ban on unreasonable searches and seizures. The Court further stated that the magnitude of the problems caused by drunk drivers outweighed any privacy rights of drivers pulled over in the check lanes.

Police set up a roadblock when implementing sobriety check lanes and check everyone passing through to screen out intoxicated or drugged motorists. A former Michigan high office holder, who supported the check lanes, once said in effect that "they were no more intrusive than metal detectors at the airport." Drunk drivers are a significant problem, but the idea that constitutional protections can be thrown out whenever problems become significant is somewhat troubling. To add to the dilemma, the word "*unreasonable*" in the Fourth Amendment leaves a lot of room for interpretation.

A better argument against check lanes is that the checkpoints are elaborate publicity stunts, disquieting to the public and ineffective in catching drunk drivers before they cause an accident. Michigan's sobriety check lanes were based on a Maryland program. Of the Maryland drivers examined in check lanes in the carly 1980s, less than half of one percent were found to have been drinking when they were stopped. Michigan State Troopers, following the Maryland program, had time to set up only one sobriety check lane before the procedure was taken to court. At that one check lane, set up for only fifty-three minutes on a highway near Saginaw, Michigan, State Police stopped one hundred, twenty-six drivers, and only two were detained for sobriety tests and one arrested for drunken driving: an arrest rate of only eight-tenths of one percent.

The real value of sobriety check lanes is that they have a deterrent effect; but this is difficult to prove. If sobriety lanes survive lawsuits that charge them with violating the Michigan, if not the U.S.

Constitution, they may be appropriate during events, or in places, *where alcohol consumption is expected*. If you base their existence on catching drunk drivers, then police agencies must take a closer look before expending manpower and resources on sobriety lanes. Check lanes are not the best way to rid our highways of drunk drivers. Police departments *know* where most drunk drivers can be found, but setting up sobriety check lanes on the highways is not the answer.

It is a known fact that most car accidents occur within eight to ten miles of home. Most people, who drink and drive, frequent neighborhood bars and taverns. Any real effort to deter drinking and driving should start near neighborhood watering holes rather than on the highways. Programs such as Mothers against Drunk Driving (MADD) provide free taxi rides, and many Police Departments provide free rides home for anyone too drunk to drive on New Years Eve and the early hours of New Years Day. If Police Departments really want to stop drunk drivers, let them hang out where these drivers drink.

As a responsible officer, I stopped to assist injured victims along the road. Some officers had mixed feelings about my involvement in this negligent homicide case. The case was dirty, and it was rumored that Godley had a passenger in the car at the time of the accident. The deceased woman's daughter, the driver, who came out of the accident uninjured, claimed "there was someone else in the car, who got out and ran." That person was *never* identified, however, it was another unsubstantial rumor started among some officers who said that I had attended the same union function Godley had that night. That, of course, was a lie—the intent of this rumor was purposely intended to harm, but it was just like other hearsay and innuendo created *Within The Walls*, with no facts or evidence.

Godley's injuries resulted in severe amnesia. Theoretically, the union had promoted drinking alcohol at the function he attended. We all know that every responsible adult should never exceed their limit, but when liquor is served at parties, people are encouraged to accept the freebie without realizing how quickly alcohol enters the blood stream. After five or six drinks of 86 proof liquor, many persons are legally drunk. *Alcohol is the most commonly used depressant*, and affects the central nervous system by slowing down brain function and depressing pulse rate, blood pressure, respiration and other body functions. Though legal, *Alcohol is the most abused drug in the world*. If citizens assume big, tough police officers can hold their liquor better than anyone else, they need to reevaluate their thinking. Stress factors in police work can often contribute to a tolerance lower than the average drinking citizen's.

On Monday, April 19, 1993, more than four years after his accident and numerous court battles and departmental red-tape, Godley was reinstated as a sheriff's deputy. He continued to be a pillar of his community, and served as a role model for young kids in Detroit by working as a manager and coach with various athletic and Little League baseball teams. I have come to see that my experiences with Departmental harassment and racial discrimination are nothing compared to involvement resulting in the loss of a life. I continue to pray for Godley, the woman killed in the car accident, and both families. I extend this to all the families whose loved one's lives have been shattered and stolen because drunk or drugged drivers operate potentially dangerous vehicles while stoned. My sympathy and prayers go out to you. May God bless and keep you all.

Suggestions and Ideas:
Try it, You'll Like it

EVERY HUMAN INVENTION OR SYSTEM has deficiencies and kinks that need to be worked out through trial and error. In the jail, there were suggestions by officers to improve the jail system: feeding inmates, upgrading the computer and rover system, inmate classifications, response for jail emergencies, peer group counseling, and pat down procedures, to name a few. Jail officials typically ignored these suggestions, if they came from Black officers. The official would listen and, after a lengthy nonresponsive pause, dismiss the officer. The suggestion appeared to have been forgotten, but would later often be implemented by those same white jail officials, who then claimed all the credit for themselves, or gave it to their flunkies.

The Department periodically had Shift Commanders schedule all officers to attend a brainstorming session. It was mandatory that officers attend these, in my mind, dishonest assemblies. While superiors listened and recorded other people's ideas, the enthusiastic inventor or theorist spoke on, not always aware that he or she would never receive credit because the Department itself would steal and implement the suggestions. Shift Commanders wrote down the ideas and complaints of officers. The ideas were co-opted and the complaints used against the complaining officer by some higher-up.

One particularly interesting idea came from Officer Tom Hughes, a Black male, who later quit the Department for the Inkster Police. He bid for and attempted to vend a tinted, smoke-screened adhesive sheet with a mirrored surface. This device, like a two-way mirror, permitted officers to watch inmates on the ward without being seen themselves. This way, inmates could not follow officers' every movement from the ward.

On the very day Officer Hughes suggested the adhesive sheets, Sergeant Ralph Pomeroy, a white male, announced in Roll Call that jail officials were thinking about putting reflective sheets on each station window. At first it was announced that the Department had decided to install the sheets on just three floors. Pomeroy requested that the officers on floors 10, 11, and 12, give some feedback about the new product. Pomeroy then looked around the room to select the first judges. The sheets were first installed on a floor manned with white male officers, who knew that Officer Hughes stood to make both money and a name, from this venture because all officers hated inmates to be able to see them in the station. Though not totally effective, the sheets made it difficult for inmates to see officers clearly.

If an inmate needed privacy *Within The Walls*, he or she only had to go into their cell, vie for law library time, or sign-up for G.E.D., or some other class. But officers had no privacy, whatsoever. Most of the white officers were in favor of the sheets from the start; only a few resented an opportunity for a Black man to succeed. At the end of the first day of testing, the degree of success or failure of the reflective sheets was explored and discussed extensively by white male officers in the locker room; the majority said the material was effective. There were a few critics of the product, but overall most approved the sheets, commenting that the sheets enabled the officer to watch the inmates rather than being seen.

The next day in Roll Call another select group of white officers were assigned to evaluate Hughes' adhesive sheets. Finally, on the third and last day of the experiment, the floor chosen was manned by Black officers; I was one of them. We were finally given the privilege of evaluating the material. My initial criticism was that these adhesive, reflective sheets should have been on all station glass when the new jail was built in 1984. I assumed from my experience in "*The System*" that the commissioners of Wayne County and the Sheriff's Department, didn't see any need to pay extra money to protect the privacy of its officers.

The other Black Officers on the floor also thought the sheets were effective. No officer likes the inmates staring at him, especially without a real reason, but after awhile you get tired of complaining to your superiors, grow complacent, and grow accustomed to little privacy. The station windows were constructed of wired, tempered glass that shattered into little irregular puzzle pieces of glass.

On the surface it appeared that Hughes' product had succeeded with everyone, but later in the week, to the dismay of Black officers, the sheets were taken off the windows. Wondering why, some of us complained, but nothing was done. After three straight days of argument back and forth in Roll Call, a consensus emerged: Officer Hughes had not gotten the contract. His product was sufficient and worked, but white officers' *"quality control"* overruled whatever Black officers had said about its effectiveness. Once again it was a racial issue.

Three weeks later, the County contracted the job out to another company, white of course, whose product was no better than Hughes' had been. The material was slapped onto the station windows, and nothing more was ever heard about the rejection of Officer Hughes' bid. It's logical to assume that someone else had a lower bid, or that Hughes' material just wasn't as good as the chosen bidder's. Many officers, however, evaluated both products and saw no difference. Officers continued to wonder out loud who the chosen bidder was, and how much lower their bid had *really* been. No one really believed price was a factor. We even speculated that the Sheriff's Department had purchased and installed the material themselves, using Wayne County workers. Whatever the case, Officer Hughes' idea was co-opted and his product rejected. Officers had the hands-on experience on the floors and knew exactly what it was like to have no privacy.

In 1987, the Department decided to frost all cell and ward windows and block any hope of the sun's rays shining in, or inmates looking out. They also frosted the windows because inmates, who tried to smuggle drugs and weapons into the jail, could eyeball the distance from the street below to their floor with ease. They would then punch a hole in the window to lower twine or shredded linen to the street below. Once the string reached street level, drugs and other contraband were tied to it and hoisted up.

Coming to work one day in the pouring rain, I noticed a long string being lowered slowly from a northwest cell window. Every floor had four stations, named nautically by geographical location. The string was coming from a small ward, which housed twelve young Black males charged with their first felony offense: Murders, rapes, criminal sexual misconduct, drug possession, weapons. Two inmates had knocked out a 2-inch hole in a cell window, and Polly, an attractive young Black "*Redbone*" female of twenty or so, waited on the sidewalk to attach drugs to be hauled up. Polly pretended she was waiting for a ride home, or for a cab, as she stood there, impatiently holding a big golf umbrella to shield her from the rain. I was suspicious of Polly, who constantly looked around as if guilty of something. The shifts were changing, and Polly couldn't put the goods on the string while people rushed by her through the downpour.

Watching patiently and partially hidden in shrubbery across the street, I let the crime proceed as Polly tied what I presumed to be drugs onto the string. At that point I rushed inside and alerted Ralph Pomeroy, the very white male lobby desk sergeant. Pomeroy balked until Officer Larry Russell, another white male, came to my defense: "Yeah sarge, I saw the string too, and feel the same thing is happening." Pomeroy and another command officer ran outside to search Polly, confiscating three small packages of crack cocaine and two plastic sandwich bags full of marijuana.

After Polly's on-the-spot arrest, Pomeroy emptied the marijuana into a brown paper bag as evidence, and stuffed the plastic bag with a note that declared, ***You are all busted***. He tied the note to the string and tugged. As the line was hoisted upward, jail officials burst onto the ward and into a cell where the inmates were still in the process of carefully pulling up the string. You can imagine the looks on their faces as they read the announcement. The inmates also had to pay for the damaged window, an act considered "***destruction of county property***."

Commendations were often given to white officers for deeds like my own, but officials considered the Polly-incident only my duty. The lack of recognition didn't bother me because I was only doing my job. After all, the inmates and Polly were easy to spot coconspirators. After a thorough investigation, it was discovered that the window had been punched out with a round metal doorknob, stolen from the hallway as inmates lined up to be fed. Inmates often un-screwed doorknobs and used them us projectiles, putting them in a sock to ward off an enemy's attack.

A cell window is structurally sound, with steel and cement around the base of its foundation. It takes a lot of pounding to break one. An inmate would have the time of his life trying to escape through a cell window only six inches wide, and descend several stories to ground level. To my recollection, there was *never* an escape through a cell window while I worked in the jail. An officer had to be deaf, or deliberately ignoring the ward goings-on, for an inmate to get away with the noise it takes to break a cell window. I noticed that when officers kept personal radios in their stations, the volume was often turned up too loud to hear a window being broken. Constant knock-ing and banging should, of course, alert an attentive officer, but the excuse used was that the broken windows all occurred on the mid-night shift. On the midnight shift there was only one officer assigned per side. When rounds were made every hour (a State of Michigan Corrections requirement) on the midnight shift, officers from both sides conducted them together. One officer operated the station con-trols and logged the round, while the other keyed in rounds and checked the cells and wards for strange occurrences.

When the midnight officers were on the other side of the floor, or at lunch, inmates customarily dismantled the locking mechanism on their cell doors by sliding up the door hinge a rag knotted at the end, and escaped into the ward. Inmates could then enter the sally port area if its sliding door was inoperative, or slightly ajar, then another door could be opened with the same rag technique, to gain access to the hallways.

Before the cell and ward windows were frosted, bored inmates familiarized themselves with coworkers and officers' cars by watch-ing the nearby parking lots during shift changes. I think there was a direct connection between this activity and the theft or vandalizing of several officers' cars. Sometimes an inmate approached me: "That's a nice Cadillac you got. What year is that?" I became edgy and re-plied, "It's a four door 1983 Sedan DeVille. Why do you want to know?" I made it a point to write down the names of those inmates who paid close attention to officers' cars and jewelry, just in case a car was tampered with, or something came up missing.

In my years with the Department my car was never stolen, but it was tampered with twice. I found long deep scratches on the door and trunk, as did other officers on their cars. I remember that acid was once poured on the car of a white female officer. I never considered this incident inmate reprisal, and I still believe the vandalism was the result of personality conflicts with coworkers, or malice from disgruntled citizens, who saw the sheriff's department union stickers in their car's rear window.

When parking spaces became available later in the evening, I usually went out to move my car closer to the jail. If that nosey inmate stayed on the phone most of the night, I wrote the length of time down next to his name. Usually inmates were just passing time, but curiosity about my car made me suspicious and I didn't like so much attention centered on my "*ride*."

Before all cell and ward windows were frosted, officers could also keep an eye on their cars from certain strategic windows. Inmates observed this and came to the station window: "Dep, we'll watch your car for you." Later, the same inmate would request extra food. Those officers who were regularly disrespectful to inmates, using vulgar and racist language, were the victims of car theft and repeated vandalism. As a result, it was common for both employees and officers to leave their newer, or better, cars at home.

The Department also frosted all cell and ward windows because inmates on the south, or Greektown side of the jail, stripteased for the patrons below. During the hot summer weekends, there were long and slow traffic jams in, and surrounding Greektown. To ease traffic overflow, Detroit Police officers set up roadblocks and cordoned off a four block area. Sexually inactive and bored young Black male inmates actually performed in the windows before lock down each night. If inmate cells had bars, officers could see in and stop the show, but cells with doors required the officer to listen in on the intercom, or look through a small square window from the ward. Inmates would usually migrate to cells at the extreme end of the ward and congregated to stage a lewd freak show, as the people below went to or came from dinner.

Supervising inmate behavior is tedious and frustrating for officers. It is extremely stressful ushering inmates in and out of their "houses." On several occasions I observed inmates streaking in the windows. They danced on the metal tables bolted into the cell wall to the music piped-in from center station, or the officer's personal music. Patrons would gather on the northeast corner of the Sheriff's Department's Administration Building, some with binoculars.

For months the "*Freak Show*" was a popular weekend entertainment value. Finally, after many complaints from Greektown businesses, a few officers and superiors were prompted by the number of complaints to go outside with binoculars and view the show firsthand. Police radios in hand, officials and officers out on the pavement immediately reported the location of the disturbance to officers inside the jail. The offending inmates couldn't put on their clothes fast enough, and the Department charged them all with "*indecent exposure*" and added more time to their jail terms.

Europeans have historically analyzed and synthesized the actions of the Black race, especially the males, into facile intellectual theories. However, European-Americans and Afrikans-Americans live in very separate and unequal worlds. Their experiences of the larger society are rarely the same. Principles, family life, and values are altogether different. This translates into a major problem when more affluent and hidebound European-American males disproportionately incarcerate Black males, who lack the white males' opportunities for education, career choice and fast-tracking, and a positive societal image.

But many of these Black male inmates aren't crazy, or evil, as they have been portrayed, just immature, bored, ignorant, and in need of direction, other than the attention of women who came to the jail on weekends just to enjoy the spectacles of Black nudity. Dancing, young erotic Black male inmates were always looking for female attention to see if their egos and manhood were still intact after the "*no sex*" horrors *Within The Walls*. Because heterosexual sex wasn't permitted in jail, some chose homosexuality as an alternative. Some time with wives and lovers would probably have done more to moderate antisocial inmate behavior, than all the jail rules written out and enforced, never mind those suggested and ignored.

30

The Medical Staff: Inside General Hospital

THE NURSES WITHIN THE WALLS WERE STRESSED OUT just as much as the officers. They had to contend with inmate bullcrap everyday, and then listen to umpteen complaints and lots of requests for medication and medical treatment. Nurses were required to make at least two rounds a shift, but one round was common because of the personpower shortage. Each nurse worked three floors. The morning nurse made rounds at 10 a.m. and 3 p.m., about an hour before getting off duty. The afternoon nurse usually made the first round before 4:30 p.m. and the second between 7 and 9 p.m. The midnight nurse came by around midnight, and then only on request.

We always knew when nurses were behind schedule by the way they approached the station window: "You guys had better hurry to this window because I'm in a hurry today. I'm not ready for y'alls jive ass games right now, so ya better c'mon quick. Ya better hurry up and bring yo asses to this window 'ratt' now. You better stop taking your damn time, cause I'm gonna leave if y'all don't hurry up," Nurse Shirley Rose hollered urgently. Nurse Rose was an elderly Black female with a southern, country drawl, who migrated up north from the deep dense woods of Mississippi. As she served medications to my ward, I could see she was already frustrated by the mischief of a previous ward. Rose's dialect wasn't basic, English articulation (it was more like Ebonics), but some nurses and officers spoke the ethnic language of many Black generations.

Sometimes nurses instructed deputies to announce their arrival over the intercom. They were always in a hurry. If an inmate didn't come for his medication in a minute or two, was asleep, or taking a shower, the nurse would vacate the station and leave them all gaping in amazement. In Rose's case, her quick departure that day left officers joking as to whether she had a bladder problem, or had just won the lottery. Leaving the window without dispensing all medication, meant deputies would most likely wind-up on the receiving end of the *Trickle Down Syndrome.*

If inmates missed their medications, they became argumentative, or suddenly sick, and requested to see a doctor or nurse. When this situation transpired, deputies knew they needed to protect themselves by logging the incident, or writing-up a report, explaining why inmates missed their needed medicine? and why the nurse left the station without giving it to them? Looking back on it now I can see that we deputies got flak from disgruntled inmates, misinformed superiors, and impatient nurses.

It was customary among inmates to hoard medication, especially Tylenol. Two pills, were given out to anybody requesting them on each nurse's round, were maximum! What was really astonishing was that some inmates accumulated Tylenol, crushed them and snorted the powder. No one I ever spoke to could even imagine what that sensation would be like. Standard operating procedure also required nurses to watch inmates while they swallowed their medications with water. Many an inmate put his hand to his mouth and, when the nurse or deputy made the slightest turn or looked away, palmed the pills and walked away. Another device inmates used was to put the pill(s) in a dry mouth, and carry it undissolved to the cell and spit them out. The inmate would then set the pills somewhere to stay dry. The majority of inmates wanted to save their medication for emergencies and bedtime.

When an inmate got caught palming medications, nurses either cursed the inmate out, or wrote-up a reprimand. All the nurses were wise to the inmates' thieving ways, and registered their frustration and disapproval with puffed-up cheeks and explosive sighs. Weary, overworked, sluggish, sometimes a nurse accused an inmate unfairly of pill games: "Look sir, I'm tired of you taking me like a fool. I know you haven't swallowed those pills and I wish you'd stop playing games with me," Nurse Rose articulated slowly in an exhausted voice.

On the day in question, because of staff shortage, she had damn near worked the entire jail alone, even updating inmate medical records.

A middle-aged Black male inmate named Peanut, the object of her ire, played dumb as Rose belittled him. He had built himself a reputation by always giving the nurses a hard time. Peanut was about five feet, two inches tall, with long, deep, old darkened scars, crisscrossing his stomach. He faced numerous charges of arson and breaking-and-entering. Peanut had multiple illnesses, the worst being acute asthma, and severe, progressive Type 2 diabetes. Peanut finally turned his attention towards Rose, who was staring intently at him, making sure he took his medication. "Who-in-the-fuck you looking at? You dumb-ass bitch," he commented.

"Hey, wait a minute, my man, you don't have to use that kind of language, you're disrespectful. You must want to be locked down for forty-eight hours," I shouted as Peanut grumbled discontent under his breath. Nurses appreciated officers that backed them up. The majority of nurses weren't afraid to challenge persistent, or *hard-headed*, inmates, when a war of words or nerves erupts. However, certain inmates had to be given their medication no matter what the circumstances, or personality conflicts, were, even if the inmate cursed out the nurse, doctor, officer, or a superior. He better get it, or officers would get a severe reprimand, or even worse, face a possible suspension, termination, or lawsuit.

No nurse handled difficult patients better than Nurse Denise Gentry. She was about forty years old, slightly above average height, weighing in at about one hundred, forty pounds, and possessed of a sensuous walk and radiant smile. She styled her long shiny black hair in a sometimes-drippy jheri curl, and wore a favorite ambrosial body oil from the sweet attar of flowers.

Gentry always let inmates know if they steered her in the wrong way. She required no back-up from officers or superiors. When Nurse Gentry appeared at the station window, inmates rushed up and acted out in anticipation of getting a whiff of the unique, exotic fragrance created by the oil and her body chemistry. She also wore musk oil. The jail's unpredictable ventilation system, and my oscillating fan, pushed the scent through the window slot, directly towards the inmates' nostrils.

"Da-da-da-da-damn, nurse, u-u-u-u-you sho' is smelling good today. Wha-wha-wha-wha-what is that good smelling fra-fra-fra-fra-fragrance you got on? It reminds me of one of my women out there in the world. Th-th-th-th-that medicine you gave me the other day is too strong for me. It makes me sleep a lot. I th-th-th-th-think I should take some-th-th-th-th-thing else. Do you th-th-th-th-think I should," Inmate Aguirre inquired. He always stuttered in fours before getting it right. Aguirre was a middle-aged Black male, who also spoke in a snaggle-puss dialect. His slow speech caused him to trip over words starting with "Th," or those requiring tongue and lip usage.

Trying to avoid being outright disrespectful, Nurse Gentry and I snickered under our breaths. Aguirre always had something to say to Gentry as she dispensed medication. We both were quite accustomed to Aguirre's speech defect, and his hilarious behavior kept everybody laughing. "Thank you for the compliment, but I ain't your woman," Gentry joked, "If you could stay your butt out of jail, you just might get one. I've got something else you can take. Just come on and get this medication, so I can get the hell out of here; its been a long day," and Nurse Gentry gave Aguirre medication for his many ailments.

Nurse Gentry was a proud, beaming, down-to-earth Black woman, and inmates found out how sharp she was when they played pill games on her. She was well-liked by coworkers and inmates alike, but you caught hell if you played mind games with her. Nurses like Gentry never hesitated to reprimand an inmate for his shenanigans. It was easy for male inmates and officers alike to develop mild crushes on nurses like Gentry. The nurses' medical evaluations and diagnosis were often critical to Departmental responsibility, court orders, and commitment to the institutional health of the inmate population. In many cases, the psychological well-being and physical health of inmates deteriorates in jail, because incarceration doesn't encourage inmates to seek medical treatment or advice for continuing ailments.

In the 1960s and 70s, no decent medical treatment was available to inmates in the old jail. The medical facilities improved dramatically, however, after a 1971 class action suit against the County and the Sheriff's Department. The suit occurred in the Kenneth Barrett era. Barrett, a well educated, middle-aged Black man, always had difficulty getting funding from the all-white male county commissioners and state legislators to improve conditions in the old jail.

Nurse Alice Cayruth, was a short, pudgy middle-aged white lady. She was a sweetie pie, but often looked sad, so we'd talk about life and her problems in dating relationships. Just like the prisoners, she also needed the rehabilitating effects of attention and affection. One day, right out-of-the-blue, Cayruth started weeping. "Cayruth, are you alright?" I asked gently. She wiped the tears from her face with both hands. "Oh these men, they just get on my damn nerves, Taylor. Why are you guys so insensitive?" Unable to say a word, I gulped. She was right and I couldn't argue the fact. The way the present system works, most men lack sensitivity because society portrays them as the upwardly mobile breadwinners in a man's world, and since many men have fallen short of that, their fragile egos can't take the pressure or a bad word. Women buy into this too.

A few days later, and much to my surprise, Cayruth's outlook on relationships appeared to be one of nostalgia for wine and roses. Trouble was, when Nurse Cayruth came to administer medicines at my station, and if I had my Walkman hooked-up to the intercom, she always asked for me to play her favorite male vocalist, Freddie Jackson, singing the vintage Nat King Cole and Billie Holiday classic, "Good Morning Heartache." I didn't want to play it because when I did, Cayruth got emotional every time Freddie Jackson sang: "I guess I'll start each day out, just by saying to you. Good morning heartache, what's new?" Then Freddie's voice swelled with passion:

"Stop hurting me now, can't shake you, no how. Why don't you just leave me alone? I've got those Sunday blues, straight to my honey blues," and Cayruth really melted away. The lyrics preceded a sexy saxophone solo, and Cayruth wouldn't leave my station until she had heard the song several times. Afterwards, it would take about thirty minutes to console Cayruth, before she could finish giving out medication and complete her round. Tears and emotions flowed easily when Freddie Jackson sang for Nurse Cayruth.

On the other hand, Nurse Brad, a Dick Gregory look-a-like, was a lanky Black male, five feet, five inches tall, and weighed about a hundred, thirty pounds dripping wet. He had been a nurse in the Wayne County jail for over twenty years, and he once bailed me out of a potentially catastrophic situation. It happened one day in the spring of 1988, as I worked the 7-NE station. I had worked this particular floor and station several times in my tenure, and I knew the personal characteristics, temperaments, and profiles of each inmate very well.

Late one evening before lock down, two Black male inmates cursed each other indignantly from one end of the ward (cell 16), to the other (cell 7). Their loud commotion was giving me a severe migraine, and riling up the other inmates as well. Experiencing my brain cells being torn to pieces, I asked both fearless gladiators.

"Look, I'm tired of all this damn noise. You two are disruptive and disturbing the other inmates. Would you two like to settle your problem with a boxing match?"

"Hell yeah, dep! I'll fight that big punk. I'll kick his ass," the smaller, 5-foot-9-inch, one hundred, forty-five pound inmate yelled. The 6-foot-2-inch, two hundred pounder yelled back: "Man, I'll kick your little faggot-ass. Come on dep let us out, lets do it."

Their weight and height differential made it seem like a total mismatch, but I ordered the other inmates to lock down (which they did gladly), so the boxing match could take place without interference. In the heat of disputed battles, real men *should* sometimes settle their differences in hand-to-hand combat, rather than *engage* themselves with dangerous weapons or propaganda.

When all the inmates were finally locked in their cells, I summoned one of my *boys*, Officer Steve Shepherd, a Black male, from the station down the hall. Shepherd stayed in my station to man the controls, while I entered the ward to referee. Ofc. Shepherd let the fighters out of their cells, to gather in the middle of the ward, and I began to announce the combatants.

"Greetings boxing fans. Coming from the historic Wayne County jails' boxing stable, twelve two-minute rounds of boxing. Let's get ready to Rummmmm... ble! In this corner, wearing green-stripped, Fruit of the Loom shorts; weighing in at about 145 pounds, with a record of eight knockouts and no defeats. Hailing from the Motor City of Detroit, Michigan. Let's hear it for the Black Stallion."

The other eighteen inmates rocked the ward with a roaring, thunderous ovation. Their overwhelming enthusiasm for the Black Stallion was so apparent, that I began to wonder if the whole thing was a good idea. The volume of their applause was frightening, so much so that I turned to Officer Shepherd and gave him one of those "Ah shit" looks! Those locked-up surely welcomed the opportunity to watch someone finally get a chance to kick the bigger inmate's ass. Everyone considered him a total nuisance on the ward. Many inmates told me later they "wished it could've been them fighting him." I announced the other combatant with some hesitation.

"In the other corner, wearing blue boxer shorts, weighing in at about 200 pounds, with a record of 17 knockouts and two defeats. He hails from the peach state of Georgia, and resides in Macon. Let's hear it for Mister Prooooo-lific."

This time there was a lifeless, sporadic applause, almost mockery. Mr. Prolific had secured a reputation for his constant querulousness—even the officers didn't like him. The Black Stallion was definitely the crowd favorite.

"Before we start this fight... Look damn-mit, stop pushing me; now just wait a minute, you're gonna get your chance," I demanded as both fighters kept nudging up against me too much, eager to get at each other.

"Like I was saying, before we start this fight, if I see any indication of an injury, bruise, intent to maim, and especially blood, I must stop the fight immediately, no questions asked. Okay? May the best man win."

The fight was on: *no* gloves, *no* mouth piece, *no* ropes or boxing ring, just bare fists. After three rounds and almost five minutes of boxing, or whatever you would call no solid punches landing, Mister Prolific, the oldest of the two, started to lose steam and zest. And I was wrong about the mismatch: the smaller man was hungrier. Suddenly, at the 56-second mark of the third round, the Black Stallion landed a solid left hook, that caught Mister Prolific flush on the right cheek and mouth, causing him to retreat two steps backwards. Initially, there was no indication of any injury, but soon after, blood started to trickle from the inside of his mouth, and I immediately stopped the fight.

After inspection, Mr. Prolific, to my utter amazement, had a piece of metal sticking through his lower lip. The fool had fought with braces on his teeth and never told me. "They're there to correct my teeth and gums," Mister Prolific explained to me after I looked in his mouth.

"You stupid-ass fool," I yelled, "Why didn't you tell me? You knuckle-head motherfucka!"

"I didn't think he would hit me that hard!" Mister Prolific complained, holding his mouth, while the other 18 inmates laughed at him. Embarrassed because he lost to the smaller inmate, Mister Prolific contemplated snitching on me for letting them fight. But all the other eighteen inmates on the ward stood-up for me, especially the **rock boss**.

"Taylor, don't worry about shit! If he tries to fuck-you-up by squealing, he better not come back to this jail. He was the one who wanted to fight so damn bad. You just let the punk be a man... he better not say a damn thang! You got nothing to worry about brother," said John Spears; big, Black, and balding; mid-forties; about two hundred, ninety pounds. Spears was known to head several big drug operations in Detroit, and its surrounding suburbs.

But Officer Shepherd and I were *really* worried. We both wondered how were we going to handle this? The gash on Mr. Prolific's lower lip looked really bad, especially with a thin piece of silver metal protruding. It seemed obvious it would require stitches. Prolific needed immediate medical attention of a hospital to get sewed up. I immediately called Nurse Brad.

"Man, I've got a very serious situation up here on the seventh floor and desperately need you to come up right away. Please, don't bring anybody else... come by yourself, okay."

Nurse Brad arrived lickety-split. I met him at the elevator to tell him the whole story, so he would know how to handle the situation before approaching my station. After carefully pondering the situation, Brad took Mr. Prolific off the ward to a secluded section of the hallway and talked with him privately for several minutes. Brad came back and told me everything would be all right. What Nurse Brad did was write-up a medical report indicating that Mr. Prolific had slipped on some water on the ward, while he was on medication, and cut his lip on one of the steel tables. Mr. Prolific was sent to the hospital and stitched up, and I never heard any more about the incident, so I assumed it was taken care of.

In reality, there were many puddles of water on that ward because of multiple plumbing problems, so I was covered. I was really annoyed that Mister Prolific did not tell me about his braces. Thomas Hearns, Mike Tyson, Boom-Boom Mancini, Joe Frazier, Joe Louis, George Foreman, Riddick Bowe, Evander Holyfield, Roberto Duran, Sugar Ray Leonard, or Muhammad Ali, never went into the ring with braces on their teeth.

Other nurses in the medical department were Ashley, Shorter (who worked midnights), Shirley, and nursing administrator Maxwell. All were cooperative with the inmates and served their basic needs. Nurses Ashley, Gentry, and Shorter were nice-looking, charming Black women. There weren't many deputies who didn't welcome their presence, and their good natured, socializing relieved many-a-day's boredom.

Nurse Anita Ashley, in particular, seemed tempted to mingle more, but she still had that high school affection for matrimony, even though she really wanted to venture out. Nurse Gentry on the other hand, was a sensuous woman when dealing with men. She later married Officer James Driscoll, who was later promoted to sergeant, then to lieutenant. I wasn't the only one shocked at this marriage. Driscoll, a 20-year veteran, while one day working in Master Control, twice, *deliberately* pronounced my first name as "Crackney" over the public-address system, instead of just using the customary "K. Taylor."

After twenty years of service, Nurse Patricia Shorter retired from the county. If it hadn't been for Shorter's kindness and conversation during those lonely midnights, I wouldn't have made it through those eight hours of overtime and the harassment of the very white, Sergeant Joseph Marek. Just like many other coworkers, Shorter and I often discussed the Department's historic racial biases and its mistreatment of Black officers and inmates.

In the early years of my tenure, inmates were taken to Westland Medical, a long way from the downtown jail area of Detroit. Inmates from the Wayne County jail were also taken to Detroit Receiving and Southwest Detroit Hospital. But because of contractual squabbles and tax problems, the County stopped doing business with Southwest. In 1990, Southwest Detroit Hospital was an important source of health care for inmates and the city's poor, but it owed $1.2 million in back taxes and planned to layoff workers as it struggled to survive. The Internal Revenue Service filed liens against the institution's assets for millions of unpaid payroll taxes—that gave the IRS power to seize the hospital's cash flow and assets if it failed to pay their debts.

Despite their financial problems, officials at the hospital, one of nine Black-owned hospitals in the country at that time, told the County they would keep the hospital's doors open despite the large tax bill and debts owed to creditors. Community leaders considered the hospital a badly needed medical resource for people who couldn't afford to go elsewhere. In 1990, nearly half the hospital's patients received Medicaid or General Assistance welfare benefits. All General Assistance was cut off in 1992 by the governor, and Southwest Detroit provided $3.5 million in free medical care. Like many hospitals, Southwest Detroit experienced lean financial times because Medicaid and Medicare aren't as lucrative as private health insurance, particularly managed care.

Inmates with diabetes, asthma, or injuries usually sustained in fights, were permitted to exit the ward and enter the hallway to see a nurse. The facilities and personnel of the Medical Department were adequate for the proper care of inmates. There were special rooms in the infirmary for inmates with infectious diseases like AIDS and hepatitis, and rooms for drug addicts. Heroin users need methadone hydrochloride, used as an analgesic and to treat heroin addiction. When an inmate was diagnosed as a heroin abuser, they were immediately put into a special cell with no bed, and a slanted, cement floor with a drain for incontinence and infected sores, effluvia by-products of heroin addiction.

In the class action lawsuit of 1971, inmates petitioned that an individual just doing jail time shouldn't have to be housed with or next to an inmate with infected sores on his hands, arms, face, feet, thighs, legs—literally from abused veins all over the body. Heroin users even shoot-up in the groin. After prolonged heroin usage, areas of constant injection swell, bruise, and scar. Most heroin addicts look and act lethargic, their responsive time slowed by the drug's effects on the nervous systems. Back in the early 1970s, I saw a close friend and his buddies shoot heroin. As I watched the needle injection process, and the blood squirting and flowing from their arms, I couldn't help but wonder why someone would want to do such a thing.

In December 1993, the Nursing Administrator of the new jail, announced that "*an inmate with a bad cocaine or crack cocaine psychosis would be sent to the psych wards on the fourth floor and station five southeast to be examined thoroughly by a psychiatrist. The Medical Department in the jail had a program for cocaine and crack cocaine withdrawal. The only exception was pregnant women, who were taken to Hutzel Hospital and jailed there until they delivered.*" Male inmates were entered in a methadone detoxification program underwritten by the city of Detroit.

To my knowledge, I've never searched an inmate infected with AIDS, or any other infectious diseases. If an inmate had a contagious disease, his inmate card was to **clearly indicate that** in red ink—any precautions officers should take, and any medical symptoms to be aware of. Latex gloves and a surgical mask weren't considered sufficient by officers to search or handle an inmate with an infectious disease. Most officers would have felt more comfortable with long sleeves, a face mask, and a protective, plastic suit (ala, the 1995 movie *Outbreak)*. There was no way I would endanger my health and life for a Department that didn't care about properly training its officers to search inmates, who were a danger to public health.

When officers confessed they didn't want to search an inmate with AIDS, that statement often resulted in disciplinary action against the officer, excluding them from being employed by other law enforcement agencies. But I didn't apply to work in law enforcement to deal with criminals, who had contracted incurable, infectious diseases; that job I left-up entirely to the medical personnel. The only kindness I could dispense was to feed them pancakes or pizza, the only food flat enough to slide under the infirmary door. I signed-up to stop crime, deter violence, keep inmates locked-up, and pursue justice.

Whenever there was a CODE-2 medical emergency in the jail, nurses responded with utmost professionalism, carrying a breathing apparatus, and medical supplies. Most of the time medical staff arrived way before a superior, even though both offices were on the second floor. In my tenure, only the cadets training in the police academy to become state-certified officers were taught to give CPR and first aid to inmates. These two necessary lifesaving measures weren't taught to incoming deputies in jailers' training. I never saw an officer administer CPR or first aid to an inmate with a deadly, infectious disease, but I assume it has happened. That deputy would certainly receive the highest commendation for bravery: putting his life on the line by giving mouth-to-mouth to an inmate with full-blown AIDS. But that's what law enforcement is all about; it requires risking one's life for the good of the larger society, even those citizens who, some would argue, have given up their full rights by infringing on the rights of others.

As far as diet is concerned, nurses and doctors controlled what inmates ate. It was a farce that inmates on diets often got more food than inmates eating regular fare. This led many inmates to request to see a doctor in order to receive authorized recommendation for additional food supplements. When the food trays came up on the floor, deputies had to personally hand out the special trays. It was like operating a catering service, even though many times the diet trays ironically contained the same food as the regular trays. Pasted on the front of each diet tray was the ward location and the inmate's name. Deputies had to make sure the right inmate got the correct tray. When diet trays were given to the wrong inmate, or ward, the inmate, who received another's tray, insisted on getting his proper food. Many acted ignorant, if they didn't. Some inmates on low sodium diets received only cottage cheese and a piece of fruit. Vegetarians, many because of religious principles, would eat no meat.

Processed food like codfish patties, made up of 75-percent batter, was a familiar feast for inmates. After they scraped off the moistened batter, inmates sometimes found a discolored, dried out, nutritionally bland, piece of fish. I know because we sometimes ate what was on the inmate food trays too. Eighty-five percent of the time the cafeteria (except for Chef Smitty on midnights), served officers the same meals it served inmates. It didn't make much sense to me worrying everyday about whether an inmate got two boiled eggs, wheat or white bread, homogenized, skim or chocolate milk, orange juice, rice instead of corn, cheese, and satisfaction guaranteed.

Trustees in the kitchen knew in advance where the diet trays were going, and often gave personal friends extra food by writing-up extra stickers for their trays. One deputy I observed serving dinner, saw a lot of extra food on a diet tray and questioned the inmate about what kind of diet he was on.

"To gain weight, dep," answered Rodney, a beggar and perpetually hungry white male. He was healthy and already big as a house: stood only 5-foot-10-inches tall but weighed nearly 230 pounds.

"Man, you ain't on no weight gain diet; you must think I'm stupid or something," the deputy challenged, but decided to give Rodney the food anyway because his name, "Rodney Osgood" was written on the food tray's name tag. When the proper food supplements were absent, inmates fretted and complained.

"Hey dep, they didn't gimme what I'm 'pose to get. I'm supposed to get another piece of fish and two more slices of wheat bread." Other inmates would put in their two cents: "Yeah, dep, I'm supposed to get cottage cheese, more fruit, three boiled eggs not two, and two slices of toasted wheat bread."

"They didn't put the right food in mine neither, dep. I'm supposed to have nothing but leafy green vegetables, I'm a strict vegetarian. And my faith doesn't permit me to eat any of this swine or the white man's devil food," said a Muslim inmate.

"Fuck it dep, if they don't want the food, give it to me, I'll eat it," volunteered a particularly hungry inmate, who didn't care what he ate as long as he got fed.

"You can have it, 'cause I'm not throwing it away," I answered, *never* known to throw food away unless it was spoiled. Then, after all that, of course, the deputy had to call food service to get the inmates' orders correct.

A Detroit News article entitled, "Ouch! Headaches cost billions," clearly emphasized for me that employee headaches cost American businesses more than $17 billion a year in lost productivity. The Michigan Head Pain and Neurological Institute says half of the headache sufferers miss at least two days of work each month. The pain is so bad that 20 percent of the people seek emergency medical treatment twice a month. "Headaches are a major public health problem and very much misunderstood and underestimated," said the head of the

Ann Arbor institute. "We're seeing people being disabled for weeks and months at a time."

About 40 million Americans suffer from headaches regularly, resulting in 150 million lost workdays a year. A study by the Centers for Disease Control in Atlanta found that the number of people suffering from migraine headaches jumped 60 percent in the last decade (1983-1993). A psychologist, and author of *How to Stay Cool, Calm and Collected When the Pressure's On*, agrees. The psychologist said more of his patients are complaining of migraines and missing work as a result. "Stress is at an all-time high in most work places because of downsizing and reorganization and constant organizational changes," he said. "Companies are trying to do more work with less people. That definitely is making people sick."

While layoffs, downsizings, increased job demands and bad bosses don't help, heredity and pollutants are bigger culprits. A study in 1992 called *American Workers Under Pressure* found workers who had poor relationships with colleagues tend to have more headaches than people who work in a teamwork environment. This study clearly explains my position, because I was *surely* having poor relationships with colleagues, my so-called peers.

At one particular time my consumption of Tylenols was fueled by chronic headaches, and raised unwarranted concerns from officers. My migraines were mainly caused by *on-the-job* stress created by harassment from jail officials, officers, bad air and poor ventilation. Everyday for a period of about two or three weeks, I consumed four to six Tylenols a day. I even tried some old-fashioned headache folk remedies, such as sleeping with a pair of scissors under my pillow, running around the house several times, standing on my head for about 30 minutes, and even applying a bag of hot oatmeal to my head. None worked. Nor did hot teas from peppermint, catnip, chamomile, or spearmint, work.

When I worked overtime on the midnight shift, I had no problem getting Tylenol from Nurse Patricia Shorter. Other nurses were just as understanding and obliging, when officers required or requested medicine, medical attention or treatment. One day, while working the afternoon shift, I called to ask Nursing Administrator Maxwell, Shorter's boss, if it was alright to come down to get a couple of Tylenols for my aching head.

"Now Taylor, you know we aren't supposed to give medicine to the officers; you know better than that," Maxwell blurted out. But I didn't know that; I was totally unaware. Her statement confused and troubled me.

"But Nurse Shorter has given me some before, on the midnight shift," I protested.

"What? Shorter gave you some Tylenols? Well, I'll definitely have to discuss that with her, like tomorrow, when she comes in to work," Maxwell added angrily. The very next day Nurse Shorter called me:

"I can't give you or anyone else any more medicines." I immediately knew why. Feeling like a fool, I explained, "I'm very sorry Shorts, I didn't know about the policy." "Taylor, don't even worry about it. You didn't know," Shorter assured me.

After the incident, rumors were started that I was always taking Tylenols, and getting addicted to them. The rumors were started by officers who received medicines from nurses, too. I was their scapegoat because I harmed Shorter's good reputation by asking Maxwell (the boss) for some Tylenol. The sheriff's department would rather an officer bring in their own medications, but when targeted officers brought prescribed, or over-the-counter drugs into the jail, they were setting themselves up for a possible plant or setup.

The reason why officers griped was because they wouldn't be able to get any more Tylenols or other medicines. Nurse Shorter was completely in control and understood the situation I, accidently caused. Some officers, but mainly inmates *were* really hooked on those compounds of acetylsalicylic acid. As soon as inmates were served medications, officers got served up too. Why not? It saved us money.

I once burned my upper right thigh, and Nurse Cheryl Sims, a mid-aged, flirtatious, Black woman, took me into the rest room to examine it. I was embarrassed, but she reassured me, "Remember Taylor, I am a nurse. Why are you acting so nervous?"

After pulling down my pants, Sims diagnosed and treated my thigh with antibiotic ointments, medicated washing fluids, and supplied me with tape and gauzes for two weeks. Despite the pain, I came to work, limping around the jail without missing a day. I saved the Department money by not taking sick leave. Without Nurse Sims' treatment, I would have been risking further infection. Within a week my thigh was in better shape, the pain tolerable. Nurse Sims' diagnosis was correct, and the burn healed within ten days. I tried to hide my pain, lest I be an easy target for inmates. The Department *never* really appreciated officers who worked their regular hours and overtime despite overcoming injuries, pregnancy, sicknesses or nagging symptoms of colds and flus. Once again, life *Within The Walls* was a problem only with racist, or power-hungry fellow officers, superiors, coworkers, and jail officials, hardly ever coming from inmates, or nurses.

Overcrowding:
Take Off Them Shackles

VERY ONCE IN AWHILE IN MY TENURE the news and media reported that the jail was overcrowded; this was not always true. Sometimes the wards with the capacity for thirty-two inmates housed only twenty-five. It was common knowledge that inmates were either being transferred to or from another facility, or were out for their day in court. There were times, however, when wards were below capacity for days, weeks, and months, despite the jail population being largely recidivist. Nearly eighty percent were rearrests, returned to a safer haven after three years released or bonded out of jail. Many of the crimes increased in viciousness at the end of each cycle out through the revolving prison door, and inmates with extensive criminal records were receiving light sentences, many prematurely released by incompetent state parole boards and jail officials.

When the issue of overcrowding surfaces, state and county prison officials usually release hundreds of the so-called less dangerous inmates from jail. I believe there is too much money spent to house repeat offenders. I also believe in the three-strikes-you're-out law. In the case of deliberate murder, capital punishment is actually a less expensive alternative than spending upwards of $35,000 a year to house each prisoner for "life." If prison officials say there's no one to pull the switch, that's a damn political lie: many officers would gladly pull it to get some of these crazy fools off this earth. The U.S. economy (jobs, and job training) remains stagnant. New jobs are mainly in the "service" industries and pay minimum wage: *McDonald's, Burger*

King, Taco Bell, Kmart. So, as a result, the jail actually *breeds* recidivism. For the most part, this is why there are only two choices for most Black males in America: education or incarceration.

There is a technique used primarily in rural communities of the South for protecting the public from criminals, who spend their lives in and out of prison. This is to inform neighborhoods, relatives, and friends of a perpetrator's activities, so they will become aware and get involved. This information could illuminate for the general public the patterns of crime in any neighborhood. This has already come to pass through the controversial Megan's Law, requiring the police to inform local citizens if a convicted child molester is released from prison into their towns or cities.

Police Departments should publish crime(s) and their scenes in a gazette to show what happened? and when? If the criminal continues to offend, he or she deserves no plea bargain, a harsher sentence, and no early release for good behavior. In other words, if your name is published and the whole city reads your name and your crime(s) and you still have the nerve to go out and re-offend, then you need a harsher sentence and the category of intransigent. Such a program should include white collar crimes too. Sometimes public shame can make someone think twice about breaking the law.

"Hey Taylor, I'm back," said inmate Clem Johnson, a Black male, about twenty years old. Clem still had a baby face, and was caught-up with selling drugs and breaking into occupied dwellings. Clem's greeting to me preceded his third stint in jail. I could only turn around and shake my head in disgust. "You sound happy about it, you silly-ass. You think this is a hotel? Will you ever learn? Don't you get tired of this place? Don't you have anything else better to do with your life?" As I said this my blood pressure rose. Clem had a record as long as the Constitution and its Amendments. It was so frustrating to watch strong, able-bodied, intelligent Black men in jail again because they couldn't create financial resources within the law.

Jail overcrowding has always been a political issue. This was brought to light in an interview with Vernice Davis-Anthony, former Assistant Wayne County Executive, in-charge of Wayne County's health facilities in 1984. She was interviewed in the *Native Detroiter* magazine, and asked what the major health care problems in Wayne

County, aside from health care for the poor and infant mortality are:

"Another significant problem area is violence and the impact that violence is having on our young people in Wayne County. Specifically, in the City of Detroit as well as nationally, homicide is the leading cause of death for Black males between the ages of 15 and 24. But the rate for Wayne County is over 300 per 100,000 which is higher than any other urban area in the country.

We were also recently informed by a study that was done by Dr. Leland Ropp at Henry Ford Hospital, that the leading cause of death for young Afrikan-Americans in Detroit, age 9 through 14 is homicide. That's a startling statistic to consider. We have just completed a task force report looking at the issue of violence as a public health program, which can be prevented if we focus on the risk factors contributing to violent behavior and begin to make changes there.

We're also very concerned about the high percentage of our young people from Wayne County that are incarcerated. We looked at some recent state-wide data and discovered that while Wayne County represents 23% of the arrest state-wide, Wayne County youths represent almost 75% of state wards. So our young people are being incarcerated at a much higher rate than other counties and we have to ask ourselves why is that happening?

In fact, one in four Black males are in jail and there are more Black men in jails than in college. So, one of the major areas that we're concerned about in Wayne County is how do we deliver effective juvenile crime reduction programs that really do make a difference. This will be a priority area as we look toward 1991 and into the 90s.

We will be establishing what we call community based alternatives to work with young juvenile offenders here in Wayne County focusing on our young drug dealers. Young males selling drugs and other drug related crimes is a major cause of incarceration of young people from Wayne County. We know that it cost $50,000 per person, per year to send them out-state.

While there, we provide a lot of support, treatment, education and group counseling. Then they are sent right back to the streets of Detroit and they can't cope since we have not worked with the community or the family and we have little support systems. As a result, they end up getting right back into a life of crime. Our proposal is to keep them in Wayne County. Those who have committed nonviolent crimes, provide that support and those dollars to those in our community that are willing and committed to working with these young people."

In Wayne County, as in many other urban metropolises, statistics show a dramatic increase in the number of young people charged with crimes: rape, armed robbery and murder—that can carry life sentences in adult prisons. According to the Wayne County Prosecutor's Office, the number of 15- and 16-year-olds charged with "life offenses" increased more than 2-and-a-half times, from 170 in 1993 to 453 in 1994. While many of those youths were charged as adults, most were sentenced as juveniles and committed to Department of Social Services for treatment.

Meantime, in 1995, the overall number of juveniles arrested in Wayne County dropped. To combat the high rate, Detroit's police chief made a special effort to control youth gang activities and replace them with more productive outlets for young people. There were two possible explanations for the increase: the unusual wave of juvenile crime in 1994, or police doing a better job of making arrests, especially in Detroit. In 1994, DSS officials agreed to remove from Wayne County's overcrowded youth home all delinquents committed by judges to the state.

Wayne County's Juvenile Detention Facility also began refusing to admit state wards, who were arrested for committing new crimes or for being AWOL from a state program. This resulted in Wayne County officials being forced into lowering the population of the detention center under the threat of a Federal Lawsuit over conditions there. That was the last thing Wayne County needed (historical lawsuit of inmates in 1971). With an official capacity of 215, the 35-year old facility held more than 300 juveniles at times. In the past, the population was as low as 160, but as of May 3, 1995, it was 213.

Because of Wayne County's spiraling surge in teenage convictions for murder, rape, and robbery, filling Detroit's juvenile centers and causing a space crisis, the Department of Social Services phoned around the country weekly in search of vacant beds. From May to July of 1995, DSS arranged to send three dozen of Michigan's worst offenders to the medium-security Glen Mills Schools in suburban Philadelphia and to the high-security High Plains Rebound program in Brush, Colorado, 90 miles northeast of Denver. DSS officials had a waiting list of 125 children and simply not enough beds in public or private programs to handle the huge influx of juvenile delinquents.

It is projected that out-of-state programs may actually give Michigan taxpayers a break on juvenile treatment costs. To house a juvenile in the well-known, local W. J. Maxey Training School cost $207 a day in May of 1995. At the High Plains Rebound program in Colorado the cost was $179.50 a day, and at Glen Mills in Pennsylvania the cost was $98 a day. Juveniles sent out of the state are screened: those with the least family support at home are chosen. Not only is there a need for better education for these young people, but also a stronger family support system early enough in life to keep them out of correction centers that often set the stage for the next step, prison.

In 1991, the United States had the world's highest per capita imprisonment rate, far worse than the Soviet Union and South Afrika. For every 100,000 U.S. residents, 426 were behind bars awaiting trial or serving time for crimes committed. This is the highest incarceration rate in the world, ahead of South Afrika's rate of 33 people per 100,000 residents and the Soviet Union's rate of 268 per 100,000. Incarceration rates in Europe generally ranged from 35 to 120 per 100,000 residents, and in Asia from 21 to 140 per 100,000. For Afrikan-American males, the rate was **3,109 per 100,000**, compared to South Afrika's 729 per 100,000. The U.S. incarceration rate more than doubled over the past decade (1980-1990), according to a private group, *Sentencing Project*, which favors alternative punishments.

In 1991, the percentage of Black inmates in jails across America represented a whopping 45 percent, and in 1992, The United States imprisoned Afrikan-American men *four times more* often than Black men were jailed under South Afrika's apartheid system. And with 1.33 million people behind bars, the United States ranked second to Russia in the number of its people in jail, according to *America Behind Bars: The International Use of Incarceration.* Findings also showed that the U.S. incarceration rate for Blacks, who made up 13 percent of the population, is six times that of whites—**1,947 per 100,000** Blacks, compared to **306 per 100,000** for whites.

Across the nation, 6,725 people held in jail in 1993 were under age eighteen, including 5,100 who either had been convicted as adults or were being held for trial in criminal courts as adults. Local jail costs throughout the country cost a whopping 9.6 BILLION dollars during just one twelve month year ending June 30, 1993. Can you imagine what that amount could do to wipe out the National Debt? Early childhood intervention, education, job training, couldn't possibly cost nine billion dollars a year to implement, but these programs might well save the U.S. economy nine billion if teens were ever given a chance. Excluding capital spending, it costs an average $14,667 to keep an inmate in jail for just one year, a salary an individual outside the walls could live on (maybe not comfortably) for a year.

The number of arrests rose from 11.7 million in 1983 to 14 million citizens in 1993. In addition to increased drug violations, the study found higher than average increases in arrests for assault and weapons violations. In June, 1994, white non-Hispanics, the largest, wealthiest, and most powerful population in the United States, made up 39 percent of the jail population. Black non-Hispanics, about 12 percent of the U.S. population, were 44 percent of the jail population. Hispanics, Black and white, were 15 percent, and all other races were only 2 percent. Women comprised 10 percent of the total jail population.

United States Representative John Conyers, D-Michigan, Chairman of the House Committee on Government Operations, said these reports are evidence that the U.S. criminal justice system is flawed. He also added that "Having a higher rate of Black imprisonment than South Afrika, a nation with the horrors of apartheid, is not acceptable in the United States of America."

The higher crime rate is reason usually given for the largest number of prison inmates in the world. The nation's murder rate is at least seven times higher than in most European countries. There are six times as many robberies and three times as many rapes reported per 100,000 population in the United States, as in West Germany prior to unification with East Germany. *America is the most violent nation on the face of this earth*.

But the report also blamed "harsher criminal justice policies" during the 1980s, when more states adopted mandatory minimum sentences, tightened their parole eligibility criteria, and otherwise relied more on imprisonment than any other alternatives. The United States Sentencing Commission said, "New sentencing guidelines and tougher penalties for drug law violations may result in a 119 percent increase in the federal prison population between 1987 and 1997."

In 1994 the federal Bureau of Justice Statistics put the nation's local jail population at double in ten years (1984-1994). These inmates numbered almost half a million (490,442). The largest of this group, drug offenders, numbered about 106,000 individuals. This study also looked at the 3,304 jails operated by counties and municipalities across the country. Local jails house about a third of the almost 1.5 million people incarcerated in the nation; the rest were in state slammers or federal pens. Five states housed *half* of all local jail inmates: California, Texas, Florida, New York, and Georgia. Louisiana had the highest incarceration rate in the country at 377 people in jail per every 100,000 of the population. The population of all the local jails in the United States was so high as of June 30, 1994, that we had jailed 188 people out of every 100,000 citizens in the U.S.A.

Also in 1994, the nation's state and federal prison population topped one million for the first time in history, while figures revealed the number of Black prisoners far outdistanced the number of whites. According to the federal Bureau of Justice Statistics, the incarceration rate among Blacks was **1,432 per 100,000** compared to **203 per 100,000** among whites. Of the total, 913,143 were in state prisons and 93,708 in federal prisons. The total was more than double the 462,002 prison population of December 31, 1984. At the end of 1994, 2,962,000 adults were on probation and another 690,000 were on parole. Parole is a conditional release from custody by special parole officials of prisoners who have served part of their sentence; they remain subject to being locked-up again if they violate certain rules. Probation is imposed by judges and may or may not follow incarceration. Probation may have a variety of reporting requirements and rules, such as restrictions on travel or use of alcohol or drugs. The August 1995 Justice Department's report also found:

- Half of all offenders on probation in 1994 had been convicted of a felony; the rest of lesser crimes.
- One in seven probationers had been convicted of driving while intoxicated or under the influence of alcohol.

- Of the parolees, 95 percent had served time behind bars for felonies; the rest had been incarcerated for lesser crimes.
- About 21 percent of the nation's probationers were women; as were 10 percent of the parolees.
- About 58 percent of the adults on probation were white, and 32 percent were Afrikan-American. Fifty-one percent of adults on parole were white and 32 percent Afrikan-American.

The number of men and women in the nation's prisons and jails climbed to a staggering 1.6 million in 1995, culminating a decade in which the U.S. rate of incarceration nearly doubled, the Justice Department reported in August 1995. The Bureau of Justice Statistics said that as of December 31, 1995, one out of every 167 Americans was in prison or jail, compared to 1 out of every 320 a decade ago (1985-1995). The bureau also said, there were 1,078,357 men and women in federal and state prisons, which usually house sentenced prisoners serving more than one year.

Because many societal ills have dictated its grown—in 1995, the overcrowding issue for women escalated to epidemic proportions. Of the nation's 50,000 women in prison, forty-nine percent of them were Black, but more alarming is that eighty percent of incarcerated women were mothers, sixty-four percent of women in prison have other family members who were also behind bars, and 43 percent of incarcerated women were sexually abused. Eight to ten percent of women are pregnant at the time of incarceration. When women go to prison, their children are usually left in the care of relatives; half of the time it is the grandparents. The incarceration of these mothers has a profound impact on their children and families. Significant numbers of incarcerated women without relatives to care for their children are in foster care for a year, and the state has the right to initiate the termination of parental rights.

Between 1980 and 1989, the rate of increase of the female prison population was nearly twice that of men. Sixty-eight percent of incarcerated women have been convicted of nonviolent crimes such as drug-related offenses, fraud and larceny, and the remaining 32 percent for violent crimes. Fewer than half of these women had jobs at the time of arrest.

A startling statistic of gender injustice—the average prison sentence for men who kill their partners is two to six years, while women who commit the same crime—often in self-defense—receive an average of 15 years. And because most states have only one or two prisons for women, women convicted of crimes are shipped farther from home, making it more difficult to have family visits. According to the Bureau of Justice statistics, 43 percent of all incarcerated women are survivors of sexual and physical abuse. Many incarcerated women began abusing substances between the ages of 10 and 14.

In August of 1995, the Justice Department reported that a record 5.1 million Americans were either behind bars or on probation or parole at the end of 1994. The total number under some kind of correctional supervision amounted to almost 2.7 percent of the nation's adult population. Nearly three out of four were being supervised in the community on probation or parole rather than in cells. Since 1980, the number of people in prison, jail, on probation, or parole has tripled, growing at an average rate of 7.6 percent a year and at an actual rate of 3.9 percent in 1994. The resulting pressure on already overcrowded prisons and jails has pushed up the use of probation and parole. Overall, the state and federal probation population rose 2 percent in 1994 and the overall parole population grew by 2.1 percent.

In Michigan, where the state prison population jumped from 13,162 in 1984 to almost 40,000 in April 1995, there were 1,134 prisoners between the ages of 55 and 75, and 37 over age 75. If this trend continues into the next decade, the need for geriatric care will double, if not triple, or quadruple for the number of prisoners in the system age 60 and over. An older inmate, needing the extra care, will cost the state an additional $7,000 a year. Most states have avoided building separate geriatric sections in the belief that older inmates tend to exert a calming influence on younger ones. True as this may be, as the number of inmates rises, and sentences become longer, prisons will be forced to institute different exercise hours for older inmates, and programs such as gardening. New prisons are being built near university hospitals to make medical care more accessible. Prison design now includes wheelchair ramps and railings. For the most part, older inmates pose no threat and are no longer a danger to society. They can be dealt with at less expense outside the prison system.

But in Colorado, where there is no parole on life sentences, the

prison population tripled from 1985-1995. Here, building geriatric facilities is inevitable. According to a Bureau of Justice Statistics report in 1995, it costs an estimated average of $15,586 per person to
house state prison inmates each year. Because prison inmates don't
qualify for Social Security or Medicare, state governments receive
no federal dollars to offset rising costs. As of August 12, 1994, there
were 37,280 inmates in Michigan prisons and camps—more than double
the number than in 1984 when the state embarked on a prison building spree. Between 1973 and 1992, the American prison population
grew from 210,000 to 884,000. More prisons were constructed—cost-
ing taxpayers $37 billion—the most spent during any other period in
American history. In 1970, the federal government spent about 44
percent of its antidrug law enforcement budget. By 1987, that number
grew to 76 percent. In 1988, more than 750,000 people were arrested
on drug-related charges, mainly possession. Despite a focus on cocaine and crack, most arrests for possession involved marijuana. In
1988, close to 400,000 were arrested on marijuana charges.

In March 1993, Michigan's governor unveiled a budget plan that
increased prison spending in 1994 by 14 percent, the largest hike in
state history. The proposal called for an increase of $139.4 million in
Department of Corrections spending. On August 31, 1993, Michigan
lawmakers passed most of a $7.9 billion state general fund, including
a huge 13 percent increase in 1994 for prisons, but little or no spending boost for public schools and colleges. Part of that was an ap-
peasement plan to redistribute an additional $90 million taken from
rich districts to poor school districts (Robin Hood amendment). For
the first time the Corrections budget in Michigan was over the $1
billion mark.

Prison spending in Michigan soared when the state opened up
two new lockups in Saginaw and Detroit in 1994. The state of Michigan spent an average of $26,000 on each of its 33,200 inmates in
1993. But that cost could go as high as $60,000 dollars a year for
some inmates with special needs. At one time in my tenure, Sheriff
Carmeno and department officials thought seriously about housing
three inmates to a cell in order to cut costs. Such a decision would
have proved disastrous because of small cell space, lack of manpower, and the human need to breathe some circulated oxygen. Order

#10 of the judges court order, involving the inmates class action lawsuit of 1971, specifically addressed the placement of inmates on wards: "The Sheriff and Jail Administrator shall not lodge, house, or keep in any ward any inmate or inmates in excess of said ward's lawful inmate capacity."

Desperate jail officials considered penning inmates up like cattle for the sake of money, a situation reminiscent of the stinking, crowded conditions in slave ships, where humans were shackled by their arms and legs, packed like sardines in the orlops, and shipped first to Cuba and then to the United States to be slaves. Such actions are genocidal, and only the strongest and healthiest captives survived, their self-confidence shaken, their morale intentionally undermined. The slave ships were owned and operated by white Europeans, Jewish and Christian alike. The shipment of slaves from West Afrika did not end until the Black Americans in Liberia, who had founded that country during the *Back to Afrika* movement, stopped it by force.

By 1990 labor costs had dropped in northern Michigan. The state paid about $45 a day per prisoner—versus the $68 a day in Wayne County—not counting transportation and deputy overtime. The initiative stemmed from a 1984 state law which allowed for such outrageous charges. That law stated: "A county may seek reimbursement from an inmate for up to $30 per day, or the cost of maintaining the inmate, whichever is the lesser amount." With about 20 counties across the state building or planning new jail construction, some law enforcement officials fear the competition for inmates will increase.

In the fall of 1990, the Andrew C. Baird Detention Center (A.C.B.D.C.), named after a former Wayne County sheriff, completed a 13th floor expansion to the existing jail. Now the Department and Sheriff Carmeno were counting on revenue generated by renting out bed space to other counties or the state. Everything was set but the inmates didn't come, nor did the state prisoners. Sheriff Carmeno was faced with temporary layoffs of deputies, and the vacancies at the new jail cut into the county budget in other areas.

Is there still overcrowding? Why weren't counties cautious when planning for expansion? Part of the answer can be found in the amendments of the State and Local Partnership. As the bills made their way through the legislature, many counties were impatient to see what would hap-

pen once they passed. The problem was that it had not been determined how money would be handed out: by the number of beds, or
by the number of inmates?

County facilities weren't the only ones with the problem. In the
summer of 1990 a Michigan Sheriff's Association director received a
letter from the Michigan Department of Corrections requesting assistance in determining the reasons for the sudden drop in admissions
to the state system. It was speculated that there was a leveling off of
jail crowding—in not just a few counties, as expansion increased the
demand for spare beds decreased. It may pay to rethink expansion of
jail facilities without first determining the need for beds over the
long haul. It would certainly make all taxpayers and county commissioners happy.

In November 1997, the governor of the State of Michigan, repeat-
ing a familiar call he made in 1995 and 1996, told lawmakers that "the
state needs five new prisons immediately if the state is to avoid an
overcrowding crisis." He also ordered "the Department of Corrections to add more than 700 beds to existing facilities and seek prison
accommodations in other states." Estimates compiled by state agencies reviewing prison space needs suggested that 5,000 new beds
would add at least $150 million in annual operating and debt costs to
the budget. The corrections budget was about $1.3 billion for the
1997-1998 fiscal year, and most of that money went to house inmates
in about 43,000 beds at state prisons, camps and halfway houses.

In his report to the Legislature, the governor argued that "the
state had made great progress in reserving prison bed space for violent criminals." The state also added more than 13,000 prison beds
by double-bunking cells in the 1990s. If the Sheriff's Department would
have had its way by implementing *triple-bunking* in the Wayne County
Jails, imagine how many prison beds and how much in "*budgetary
costs*" that would have been?

Inmate overcrowding has many states thinking of innovative alternatives—one being "boot camps," or rather Special Alternative
Incarceration. This program features a 90-day, military-type boot camp,
followed by a long period of supervision from a probation officer in
the community. The average cost for each participant in a boot camp
program varies from $6,300 for the one time 90-day program com-

pared with $14,000 for a year in a minimum-security prison. Boot camp programs involves both probationers and prisoners. Participants cannot be a risk for escape or assault, cannot be convicted of violent crimes, must be serving for the first time, without any pending felony charges and be approved for the program by the sentencing judge. Since 1913, probation has been an alternative to prison for most individuals convicted of a felony in Michigan. In 1997, there were more than 50,000 adult felony probationers in Michigan, according to the Michigan Department of Corrections. In general, probation may last five years for felons and two years for misdemeanors. Probation terms may include up to one-year county jail time and home confinement, with a tether (electronic monitoring). A probationer is fitted with an electronic bracelet that is monitored to give the location of the wearer. Many times a probationer wearing a tether, must be in their home at a specific time. Halfway houses, supervised probation, electronic tethering and probation are all designed to help return an offender into the community.

Parole is a cost effective way to relieve the problem of overcrowding in prisons and jails. Paroled probation costs taxpayers about $3.50 a day, compared to $65 a day for housing a prisoner. As of October 1, 1997, the state budget for the corrections program cost $1.4 billion, which makes corrections the highest general fund in Michigan.

The overcrowding issue has always been a debatable one. I have seen many empty cells, and seen the crime rate high. I have also watched habitual criminals be let out on bail, or serve just a few months or years for vicious, heinous crimes. Is all the expansion really necessary? One thing's for sure: the jail system will always be a money making venture. Cities and towns with a predominantly Afrikan-American population will continue to be under-policed because it relies on incarceration to pay the entire law enforcement system. Officers, judges, lawyers, maintenance, prosecutors, secretaries, commissioners—all these salaries depend on high taxed neighborhoods with high crime ridden neighborhoods, to supply more bodies to fill the newly-built, very expensive jails.

CRIME DOES PAY, but it pays only those who work in and profit by "*The System*" itself. It doesn't help the people in the neighborhoods, pay for housing, job opportunities, health care, or hope. A system that feeds off others' failure, off others' poverty, and the violation of law that poverty encourages cannot be for a society's highest good. A national study (1985-1989) revealed that one Michigan child in five lived in poverty. That's a sharp increase from a one-in-eight in 1979. Children's Rights usually get more lip service from government than action. The study found that the percentage of Michigan children living in poverty averaged 20.3—up substantially from the 1979 rate of 13.3 percent. Michigan has twice as many poor children as the nation's average, which rose from 16 to 20.1 percent, a 26 percent jump.

In conducting the study, *The Center for the Study of Social Policy* found that the welfare of children had worsened state-wide. The number of Michigan juveniles behind bars rose from 119 per 100,000 in 1979, to 150 per 100,000 in 1987. Violent deaths claimed 73 of every 100,000 teenagers aged 15-19 in 1988, an 18 percent increase from the 1984 rate of 62 per 100,000. Unmarried teenagers were mothers to 7.8 percent of the babies born in Michigan in 1988, compared to 6.9 percent in 1980. The high school graduation rate fell 4 percent between 1982 and 1988, from 76.4 percent to 73.6 percent, and has not improved in the 1990s. In 1990, Michigan ranked 37th among states and the District of Columbia in eight categories of child care. Young families were found to be much poorer than they were in the 1970s and 80s.

The state of Michigan fared better in two of the study's eight categories. The infant mortality rates in the state fell 13 percent between 1980 and 1988 from 12.8 deaths per 1,000 live births to 11.1 deaths per 1,000. Even so, the state's ranking was 37th nationally in 1991. The overall child death rate went from 36.5 deaths per 100,000 children under age 14 in 1980 to 33.1 deaths per 100,000 in 1988. The national rate was 33.2 deaths in 1988.

In 1991, to ease the problem of overcrowding, the Michigan Sheriff's Association lobbied for a Senate bill allowing judges to sentence criminals for up to two years in a county jail, a year longer than formerly permitted. County jails are used mainly as holding tanks for criminals awaiting trial and sentencing. Taxpayers of Michigan and other states in the nation are burdened to keep criminals housed in jails, and will continue to encounter additional millage or tax increases

One potential plan requires the inmate to be accountable for his crime and pay for his jail stay. In 1991, Michigan's Attorney General expressed his opinion that prisoners who can afford it should pay for their prison stay, so the tax burden is lifted from the shoulders of the law abiding citizens of the state. He indicated that in these days of budget deficits and tight money, the state must generate revenues from every possible resource. He also suggested that banks and employers notify the state of accounts, pensions, or other assets held by inmates. Under state law, inmates can be forced to put up to 90 percent of their assets toward prison costs, which in most cases averaged $44 a day. Exempt from state seizure were social security and veterans benefits, money owed to crime victims as restitution, and money for alimony and child support. Earnings from prison jobs also were exempt.

Apart from the state program, about 40 counties in Michigan enacted individual programs to bill jailed inmates for the cost of incarceration. Unlike state prisoners, jailed county inmates serve only short terms and may be put on work-release status, which allows them to keep outside jobs. In 1991, the state of Michigan brought suit against those inmates with large bank accounts and other assets. Some inmates sued were getting pension benefits. The action represented an acceleration of efforts that recouped an average $250,000 to $300,000 a year from inmates. In the lawsuits, the state asked for independent receivers appointed to handle the inmates' assets until their cases were decided.

I can tell you firsthand that in both the old and the new Wayne County jails there was always unused and outdated machinery, cooking equipment, freezers, and office equipment, taking up needed space. The space was an eyesore of junk that invited spider webs and dust. Why didn't state jail officials utilize that space? Do you have any idea why? Who needs to build another new jail? Certainly not you, the taxpayer.

32

The Town Hall Meeting:
After the Refreshments

THE ONLY TIME OFFICERS, OR THE PUBLIC, saw the sheriff, undersheriff, or other bigwigs of the Department was when the Department commanded a drug raid; addressed drug awareness or concerns about airport security; offered safety procedures for citizens to avoid criminals; walked in an ethnic parade like St. Patrick's Day; spoke on talk shows, or ran ads on TV and radio near election time; or promoted themselves at an organization's fund raiser, such as the Cancer Foundation or Multiple Sclerosis. They paid more attention to media hype rather than pay attention to their constituents.

Only when a jail official had a topic of concern did officers see them. Sheriff Jacob Carmeno and Wayne County Executive James Sterling posed together in a jail cell on February 19, 1990, to promote a national foundation. The *Great American Lockup* raised money for charitable organizations by jailing, donating civilians for a couple of hours. The county budget and jail directorship clashes were just a few examples of several rifts between the two. After numerous squabbles, Sterling finally assumed control of the jail budget, and Carmeno had control of jail administration.

Carmeno had to alert Sterling of any decisions or changes in plans about jail operations. For nearly a decade the sheriff's administration and county government spent a bundle in county taxpayers money funding countless and fruitless court proceedings over power plays. The judge arbitrating critical decisions involving jail operations was always Bob Grossman. In January 1994, Judge Grossman was *accused* of smoking marijuana, after two white male Plymouth,

Michigan police officers on a routine traffic stop smelled the odor in the judge's car, but never searched it.

Over the years, struggle between the sheriff's department and County government for control, reminded me of the Levi Strauss trademark, which depicts two horses, headed in opposite directions, being bullwhipped to tear a pair of blue jeans apart—the jeans in this case being the jail. After experiencing four years of Carmeno's administration and Sterling's rule, I concluded that the lot of Black officers careers had not been bettered. Cronyism among white officials and officers persisted, and the white males in-charge generally saw themselves as conquistadors (with all the condescension inherent in that epithet) within the jail. Whenever it was threatened that Wayne County Executive Sterling was taking over jail operations, some officers expressed the opinion that the change would hinder department operations. But I felt differently, as did the majority of officers, and welcomed any change. "*The System*" couldn't be any worse than it was.

The administration did not increase citizen respect for law enforcement, and Carmeno, considered by many a publicity hound, paid little attention to enforcing equal justice within his own department. Too much of Carmeno's attention was centered on promoting his political platform and public image through the media (TV and radio), drug prevention programs funded by the government, however, *in the jail*, there was *no* rehabilitation, *no* job or educational training for inmates. This came to a head when the union accused Carmeno of squandering more than $500,000 on political jobs. The union threatened to support Lawrence Dornan, a young white male County commissioner, who himself was inexperienced in law enforcement. Dornan challenged Sheriff Carmeno's reelection bid in November 1992, and the union president, Jim Morely, made this statement: "The sheriff spends taxpayer dollars on political appointments to further his own agenda. That money should be used on locking-up violent criminals and departmental training to enhance law enforcement."

Jim Morely also maintained that Carmeno's promotion of his press secretary to chief of staff, was another form of mismanagement because she also had no law enforcement experience. The secretary had worked with the Department for nine years in a position primarily considered administrative. Once Carmeno was appointed Sheriff of Wayne County, the debate over promotions, fraudulent usage of county funds, and work conditions in the jail heated-up. County Executive Sterling tried to eliminate the chief of staff position by veto, when commissioners included it in the 1992 sheriff's department budget. A majority of the commissioners overrode Sterling's veto.

For a time in my tenure I thought Carmeno was a thoughtful, compassionate man who cared about all people. Three days before Christmas, 1985, my mother's cousin, Stella Barfield was killed in a head-on collision near Flint, Michigan. With just over a year in office, Carmeno personally sent me a sympathy card, expressing his condolences. It was a kind gesture indeed, but its legacy was short-lived. I was paid for attending the funeral held five days later, and I took three days off for bereavement leave without pay.

The Department had specific stipulations regarding bereavement leave. If the deceased was not an immediate family member the county refused to pay the officer for bereavement days. This rule was insensitive, when you consider that many officers spend up to sixteen hours a day substituting in the undermanned jail. When jail officials refused to grant days off with pay for my second cousin's funeral, I retorted, "Forget the pay, I'm taking the days off to *pay* my last respects."

On March 27, 1990, Sterling and Carmeno, along with a host of Black Wayne County administrators, and Wayne County Commissioner Michael Mitchell, held a town hall meeting at one of Detroit's largest and most respected Black Afrikan-American houses of worship (the late, Detroit Mayor Coleman A. Young's funeral was held there). Commissioner Mitchell's 7th district was one of the largest, serving approximately 156,000 people.

Let me backtrack. On June 22, 1989, I wrote a letter to *this* church's bishop, who had once served on the Detroit Police Commission, protesting the Sheriff's Department's racial biases. Four months later he wrote me back: "Thank you for your letter. I am in sympathy with your cause but I am not in a position to do anything at this time. The copies sent to the legislative body should be sufficient for them to look into this matter for you. In the meantime, I will be keeping you in my prayers." The "copies" the bishop referred to were the twenty or more letters I had written to congressional and civil rights organizations about the Department's ill treatment of Black officers and inmates. None of them offered to help, and only *one* gave a reply.

You can imagine my interest when, taking a friend home just minutes before the town meeting, I happened to pass the church and saw Carmeno get out of his car and try the locked doors of the main sanctuary. He obviously didn't realize the meeting was being held across the street. I was surprised he came by himself. It didn't seem logical for the sheriff of Wayne County to attend a meeting unaccompanied by additional officers. On the way home after I dropped my friend off, I stopped off at the annex used for the town meeting.

Some of Commissioner Mitchell's staff sat at the reception table writing-up name tags for the people in line. After signing a petition, I looked down the center aisle of the conference room. I observed Carmeno and Sterling, sitting at a table with the other Black Wayne County supervisors, ready to start. I searched for a seat, only to observe Carmeno scanning my every movement, because at the time, I had a lawsuit pending against the Department for an illegal search of my person at an academy graduation ceremony. I sat down, and Carmeno looked my way and whispered something into Sterling's ear. Sterling's eyes immediately followed Carmeno's gaze to my general area.

Commissioner Mitchell, an old high school alumnus of mine, brought the meeting to order and discussed the scheduled completion of repairs to County roads, airport expansion and rail transit. He talked about future renovations, the necessity of the county to keep corporations within the county, a world trade center task force, exported goods to countries who had gained their democracy, and "how necessary and important it was for the community to have these town meetings on a regular basis."

The audience, patient, if disinterested, was given the opportunity to ask questions: "Every time we have one of these meetings, it only seems to come around when it's near election time. Then after the election we never see you people again for years," an elderly Black woman commented, who stood up first to address the crowd. Although Commissioner Mitchell was quick to reassure the citizens that there would be two or three more meetings that year, we all somehow suspected that would *never* happen.

The town hall meeting started at six o'clock, and Carmeno left unceremoniously forty minutes later, after his usual rhetorical, boring speech about busting crack houses, drug raids, prevention, and guns—creating a paranoid feeling for fearful seniors. Then Sterling spoke, displaying a politician's best banquet material. He even said something like, "the only time we'd ever get a crowd out like this is when...," and he received a hearty chuckle from the gathering of mostly Black, senior citizens.

In the back of the room was a table of literature about various government departments of Wayne County. The county articulated goals of efficient government, balanced budget and a lower deficit. The one brochure about the new jail was totally misleading. It featured an old picture of a former Black male judge and a group of people on a jail tour. Also in the jail's brochure was a censored, unrealistic depiction of Master Control. White male officers were depicted on their feet, no chairs were around at all, and appeared to be studiously looking up at the monitors scanning the prisoner areas. In this picture I could find no compact refrigerator or coffee maker in the station, but I did see a photo of empty, open and closed front cell wards. The pictures in the brochure must have been taken near the *Grand Opening* of the jail, because everything looked clean, and operational.

The new jail's brochure showed the reader multipurpose rooms on the jail floor, once used as dining rooms for inmates, but now closed because of mishandling of appropriations and contradictory "new" ideas. The Department then thought seriously of tearing up the multipurpose rooms on the jail floors to make additional cells. The former dining rooms were during my tenure used for classes in G.E.D., sewing, church services, informal visits from celebrities and dignitaries, training in janitorial services, haircuts, and internal affair interrogations of inmates, coworkers, and officers. Also in the brochure one found the photo of a Black male, former Detroit school superintendent standing with Carmeno, photos of high school students, a security control panel in a center station, and a sketch of the jail, detailing that it had been built by architects Giffels Associates, Inc. and the Construction Management team of Barton Malow. The brochure also highlighted a speech by Carmeno, called *"Mes-*

sage to the Citizens of Wayne County," telling us how humane and secure the new jail was, and how willing the citizens were to pay for it. He indicated that the citizens already approved and supported the jail and his tenure there, and hoped they would continue to do so. Overall, there were some very informative resources at the public's disposal. After an hour of listening with one ear, I realized that the meeting's conference topic had switched to airport expansion, of little interest to a crowd that wanted to know what could be done for their neighborhoods, not the airport. By the time the crowd was served refreshments: coffee, tea, donuts, and butter cookies, Carmeno and Sterling had already gone, depriving *citizens* of the chance to mingle with, or question them, in a social setting. People were given 3 X 5 index cards and told to write their questions down. The cards were then given to the Black officials on the panel. Before they left, I had hoped to ask both men about several jail operations, and the Department's historical racism. Carmeno's and Sterling's pass on the questions indicated to the crowd, that either they had a very important date that night, or they didn't want to be bothered by the concerns of a Black neighborhood. They left the answering of questions to the Black Wayne County department heads left behind.

Well, there hasn't been another town meeting with Wayne County governmental officials at that church in nine years (1990 and 1999), although Commissioner Mitchell promised citizens three or four in 1990 alone. These days our politicians sing a different song: their oft-protested honesty and integrity, their very belief, shifts according to the audience they address. To the VFW one must, of course, protest a strong military and veteran's benefits. The average politician then walks around the corner or goes across town and tells the Quaker Meeting that our energies must be focused on peaceful negotiations and statesmanship. One believes in a woman's right to choose in front of that branch of the party, and that all abortions are wrong when addressing people with anti-abortion views. To the gay rights movement, a politician will address their approval of gays and lesbians enlisting in the military. To the Black Caucus contingents, it's equal rights afforded under the Constitution and the Bill of Rights for minorities (I hate that word: minority.) I believe *all this honesty and integrity is something we all need to worry about.*

33

Other Opportunities:
I Can't Tell a Lie

NUMEROUS OPPORTUNITIES WERE PRESENTED TO ME and other officers during 1986, to work at other law enforcement agencies in Michigan and across the country. Recruiters came from police departments in Fairfax, Virginia; Dallas and Houston, Texas; Memphis, Tennessee; Phoenix, Arizona; Atlanta, Georgia; Saginaw, Michigan, and even Detroit itself, looking for experienced and non-experienced applicants alike. I chose to stay because I admired the city, felt close to my family and friends, and had a vision and hope that the city of Detroit would once more return to greatness.

With Chrysler's commitment to build a new engine plant, the possibility of casino gambling, a new agenda and city administration, and the government's creation of a zone in the city of Detroit to encourage jobs and revenue through empowerment, staying in Detroit appeared to be the right thing to do. Although I had doubts about Detroit's and Wayne County's corrupt government and administration, I vowed to be an asset as employee and citizen, learning all I could about my new profession.

Working a year in the jail and doing the same ol' routine everyday was taking its toll on me. I observed that Black officers at the Department were going nowhere, looked upon as inferior by white officials, who controlled the jail. Officers working in the jail usually did their jobs flawlessly and handled inmates competently and with little fuss. Still these same Black officers faced institutional racism as supervisors wrote them up and reprimanded them for petty infractions, mainly because of personality indifferences with superiors.

Many older white male jail officials needed intensive and extensive training in race relations. Although the heyday of *if you're white, you're right* was slowly and painfully drawing to a close, the old white, twenty years plus seniority men, spent a lot of energy holding on to the pre-1970s attitude that civil and constitutional rights were *for whites only*. At the Sheriff's Department, *if you're Black, get back* was the order of the day.

So, in 1986, I applied to the Detroit Police Department, and was rejected at the oral interview (the first stage) by a panel of *guess who?* two old, balding white men, and a young Black woman, who sat through the entire interview with a legal pad and pencil writing down my responses, and kept her mouth shut through the whole thing (Does that sound familiar?). Their third question was if I had ever tried cocaine. I answered, "Yes, I've tried cocaine a couple of times, but that was all, I just wanted to see what it was like." In *this* case, with *this* panel, my honesty generated hysteria. Some oral police panels were more liberal; some Departments will send officers who use or abuse marijuana, alcohol, prescription or illegal drugs, to alcoholic and narcotic treatment centers while still employed.

Thinking back on it now, I should have lied about ever trying drugs. To be honest, there aren't many officers who haven't tried some drug (legal or illegal) at some time or another. I estimate that 70 percent of all officers in law enforcement have either used drugs (legal or illegal) or alcohol at least once in their lives. Eighty percent of all inmates in the nation's prisons have been incarcerated on drug charges, or their crimes were committed trying to obtain drugs, while "*under the influence*" of drugs or alcohol.

Institutional racism in both the Sheriff's Department and the Detroit Police turned my honesty into a crime, and the Black female just sat there quietly. She did lift up her head once, to stare into my eyes when I said "I had experimented briefly with drugs," and I think she knew from past experience that these two white males were going to reject me for such a tacit statement.

Both white men had told me before the interview that "telling the truth would not exclude me from consideration for the job," but of course, that was a lie because neither meant it. I was rejected for my honesty. Obviously, they lied—I told the truth and was penalized for it. In truth, *that* panel was quite naive. There aren't many people in Detroit or in America, for that matter, who hasn't tried some kind of drug, whether cocaine, marijuana, LSD, alcohol, sleep, or diet pills. White males and their medical approvals of regulatory regulations (Food and Drug Administration), however, have made many people make mistakes and wrong choices, in changing social attitudes and stereotypes about drug addiction as well.

The Department gave certain officers experiencing alcohol and drug problems the option to attend Alcoholic Anonymous and Narcotic Anonymous meetings regularly. To keep their jobs, many addicted officers went along with the plan, thus exposing themselves to a scrutiny probably impossible to live down. In 1985, the initial drug screening for a sheriff's deputy was a urine sample taken at the clinic. It wasn't until October 1988, however, that noncertified officers were tested for drugs *__before__* attending the police academy (M.L.E.O.T.C.).

The two-white-male Detroit Police panel put "VCSA" on my oral evaluation. This acronym spelled out that I was in *Violation of Controlled Substance Abuse*. So I was branded and labeled an abuser because I had admitted trying cocaine in the past. When I was first employed by the Sheriff's Department, I had taken a medical test, and gave a urine sample, which both came up negative for everything, including drug abuse. This was *never* taken into consideration after my interview with the Detroit Police Department.

One reason I may not have gotten a break was that the Detroit Police Department had very little historical respect for the Wayne County Sheriff's Department. As a matter of fact, sparks of anger had been struck between the two more than once. The fire had originally been kindled by a bust Detroit Police officers made of an illegal blind pig operation, frequented by Wayne County Sheriff's deputies. The bust was initiated by a Detroit Police unit called STRESS in the early 1970s. STRESS was very controversial and it was involved in several fatal shootings in March 1972.

Coming from the Sheriff's Department did not help me become a member of Detroit's finest, and one reason may have been that a Black male sergeant, a thirty year veteran of the Detroit Police Department, and several other officers had been in a shoot-out with sheriff's deputies that left one deputy dead. The sergeant testified he emptied his gun because he thought the deputy was a criminal. He was subsequently cleared of the charges and later assigned to the Homicide Section where he worked on many of the city's highest-profile murder cases.

I had the opportunity to apply for the Dallas Police Department, when Cerise, my fiancee, moved from Pine Bluff, Arkansas to Dallas to teach and live. She refused to relocate in Detroit because of the higher crime rate and cold weather, but I had my doubts about going to Dallas and we *never* worked it out. For the relationship to have worked, one of us would have had to make a serious adjustment. Remember, people always find it hard to change. The whole state of Texas (Houston and Dallas especially), with a very high Hispanic population, was forever recruiting police officers from other cities, trying to stem the influx of illegal aliens and drugs from Mexico. Their police academy curriculum was a more intense, strenuous discipline than the "*deputy dog*" routines, and biases of the Sheriff's Department's version of a police academy (M.L.E.O.T.C.)

After working nearly four years in the jails as noncertified officers, deputies were allowed to attend a police academy. Because of the institutional racism endemic throughout the prison system and the overabundance of white, upper echelon officials, Black deputies received more trivial reprimands and reports than white deputies did, giving those who *harbored* racial prejudices a reason to draw the conclusion, that Black officers were out of control more often than white officers were. One could as easily deduce that predominantly white administrators were consistently biased in favor of white officers and against Black (or other minority) officers.

Police departments from around the country come to Detroit every year to recruit prospective applicants. I believe recruiters knew that Detroit had experienced people, who were tired of layoffs and a base rate of $21,000 a year, after *five* years of service for officers hired after November 1984. *__That ain't no money!__* All this in a dangerous job—in a very dangerous city.

34

Center Stage:
Working in Center Station

THE CENTER STATION IS THE MAIN FOCAL POINT on the inmate floors, because the officer assigned there sees everyone that comes upon the floor, and should log all meaningful activities. I say *"meaningful"* because, many of the duties in jail are mundanely meticulous and simple (similar to working in a service industry job). The only time when an officer in center station does not see someone in their immediate sight, was when they came from back stairwells, near the visitors' booths and the bullpen.

At times, dealing with inmates' problems was rather tedious and worrisome, but overall the job was very easy. For some officers, boredom was a daily occurrence, and in light of that, many deputies developed severe eating habits, and became excessively overweight. Although we had two gyms (13th floor's outside and inside gyms), and a small weight room, very few officers used them to remain in shape.

Boredom can be one of the most crushing, grinding stresses which humans experience, and is a uncomfortable, quite unpleasant feeling that something is not right with our lives. It's a request for stimulation of a particular kind, a signal that our needs are not being met, a feeling of being trapped. Stress can lead to a variety of problems—depression, drug use, psychosomatic illness, or something as simple as sleeping a lot to escape the boredom. Boredom can initiate a vicious circle, and can engender great stress in a person. Stress, in turn, can cause boredom that then creates even more internal stress. Many divorces result from a husband or wife being bored with a job, bored now that the kids are gone, bored with a dull social life, but who can't or won't face the fact that the problem is basically *per-*

sonal. The human mind is hungry for change, challenge, learning, and new experiences. Variety isn't the spice of life. It's the stuff of life. This is one reason why rich people have special problems with boredom. They can have almost anything they want, but for something to be truly satisfying, it has to be worked for, worked up to. When nothing is really challenging, even the most glamourous, privileged existence is boring—one reason why so many people in this situation turn to drug use.

Despite all that, however, there were ways to cure boredom in center station—speaking over the intercom like "talk radio," or a D.J. kicking out the "jams" were a few of them. One day, a Black female officer, who was one of the many revolving union stewards called Master Control, as I, and Officer Sweatbox talked to the inmates on our floor. The inmates enjoyed our show, always looking forward to break that monotony. All of the sudden, a command officer came over the console's speaker: "Officer Taylor, please stop the radio show," and I had to end the show by saying, "Well guys, someone has stopped our fun for the night." Later, that same squealing Black female officer's son (a naval officer) was apprehended nationally, for the murder of a white female in North Carolina.

However, the most notable way to cure the boredom in center station for male officers, was to gather on specific floors and check out the female visitors. Sometimes there were very attractive ones coming to see the ugliest men. Situated between the back stairwell and center station was the visitors' elevator, and that entire area was in partial view of the officer working in center station. There was a buzzer switch by the elevator to alert the center station officer of the visitors' arrival. After the officer was alerted by the ringing, and woke up from slobbering all over the logbook, they would then let the visitor through by activating a metal sliding door.

The buttons to activate the metal sliding door were built on the opposite side of the center station. It was a daily occurrence for officers to take care of business on one side of the station, and had to go to the other side constantly to let visitors in. Officers literally went back and forth like a yo-yo, and this simple, architectural blunder produced stress and fatigue in many officers, especially on a very busy day that seemed like everybody in the world came to visit.

Whoever devised the plan with the buttons situated on opposite ends of the station had only one thing in mind—keep officers busy. Yet, they should've considered or thought to make it more convenient for officers to take care of business more efficiently, and thoroughly. Going from one side to another, pushing buttons for doors all day was really ridiculous, when officers had to update the computer, log in inmates and all occurrences, open up the bullpen's sliding door, answer a continually ringing phone, watch a thieving trustee cleaning the station and hallway, and push buttons for the north and south sides of the floor, when the officers in the southwest and northwest stations weren't in their stations, for whatever reasons. Center station officers had to push buttons to activate and open doors for the nurses, social workers, superiors making rounds, and many other reasons that essentially and literally, could make the center station officer a human pinball.

Once the visitor gained entry and reached center station, they handed over their visitor's slip through a rectangular, steel fortified receptacle, that opened and closed up. It served the same purpose as the circular device at a fast food chain, where the money and food is placed inside the stainless steel turntable. Fed up with this incriminatory, insensitive affect of a procedural act and jail rule, many officers opened their station door and personally took the slip from the visitor, to appear more civil and congenial. After receiving the slip, pertinent information was logged: name of inmate visited and their ward, inmate's number, whether the visit was a personal or professional visit (attorney or parole officer), visitor booth's number, and the time the visit started and was to expire. Then the officer calls that inmate's station and gives the station officer the inmate's name, and shortly afterwards, that inmate should arrive at center station for their visit.

I usually waited for the inmate to arrive at center station before logging in their starting time. But there were some officers who logged in the time immediately after receiving the visitor's slip, even though it wasn't conversation time and cheated inmates out of a precious two to five minutes. Inmates were not always readily prepared for their visit. Some were usually asleep in their cell, taking a shit or shower.

To get a waiting crowd in the lobby from their sight and to cover their asses, sometimes the desk lobby officers called specific floors that had an overabundance of visitors. "I'm afraid you're gonna have to shorten the visits to 15 or 20 minutes, I've got a whole lot of visitors waiting for that floor."

Understandably, shortened visits always made inmates argumentative, and instead they blamed and took their gripe out on the center station officer. This usually causes a problem, because the officer is labeled as "*unfair*," or even worse, a "*racist*," if the inmate was Black and the officer white. In many cases, to shorten visits wasn't fair to the inmates, and the hours should have been extended to accommodate the state's allotted 30 minutes. Inmates were permitted three visitors a week for 30 minutes each, so, essentially, inmates had an hour-and-a-half total. You may wonder, if **all** their visitors didn't come, would an inmate get an hour-and-a-half? if only one visitor came that week? No, they'd only get the 30 minutes and that was it, period!

Purposely, desk lobby officers would send up visitors just to get them off their backs and out of the lobby. When this happened, many times the center station area became flooded with visitors hanging out in the back hallway, and chairs were sought to put there, while the officer was literally forced to shorten inmates' visit time. Again, when **this** happens the **Trickle Down Syndrome** takes immediate effect, because the center station officer gets a bunch of flak and backlash from inmates. Boy, were some of them pissed.

There was one incident when Officer William Shark, a Black male, forgot to call an inmate for his visit, before I relieved him for lunch. Working as a rover this day, I took over center station, and to my surprise, Charlotte Miller, a short, but well built middle-aged Black female, approached the center station from the back hallway, and started hammering on the window with her fist. It was strange because I had just arrived to the station, and had not yet let anyone through the sliding gate from the visitor's elevator. Somewhat startled, I got up out of my chair to approach her.

"How did you get in here?" "Hell, I've been waiting back there for almost 20 minutes for my boyfriend, Sylvester Gainey, to come to the booth for his visit. Where is he?"

"You mean the officer that was in here before me didn't call the station officer? I'll be damn! Excuse me for a second, let me look in the visitor's logbook and see when that visit was supposed to start." I checked the logbook and sure enough, Officer Shark had entered the time of 7:05 p.m. (Charlotte was the first visitor that night), and it was almost 7:30. Shark had forgotten to call the station to summon Inmate Gainey for his visit. How could he be so forgetful? I called the station officer where Inmate Gainey was housed, so he could get started on his allotted thirty minutes. The station officer told me that "Inmate Gainey was wondering why he hadn't gotten a call for a visit?"

Gainey, a 6-foot-5 inch, muscular Black male, was in jail awaiting trial for murdering three people in a crack house. He left his ward to approach the center station, I activated the sliding gate to give him access, and once he reached the booth, Charlotte explained to him she had been waiting for over twenty minutes. Gainey left the booth and immediately approached the center station glass, starting banging, and complained, vehemently.

"Hey man, why-in-the-fuck? has my woman been waiting up in here damn near 25 minutes? What-in-the-hell? have you deputies been doing? I know I'm going to get all my time! Should get some more time for y'all fucking up."

"Yes, you will get all your time. Unfortunately, the officer I relieved for lunch forgot to call your station. So stop all your hollering, I'm gonna give you an extra five minutes for that officer's mistake, okay."

"Shit, y'all need to do something for that bullshit... got my woman waiting on me all that damn time," Gainey continued in verbal anguish.

"Look, I said I'd give you an extra five minutes, okay. Don't push your luck because it wasn't my fault."

"I don't give a fuck whose fault it is! Don't have my woman out here waiting on me so damn long!"

"Brother, you better just go have your visit, or have no time at all. I'm trying my best to accommodate you."

After minutes of debate, Inmate Sylvester Gainey finally went back into the booth. Soon after, lobby desk officers sent up an abundance of visitors, but I was still determined to give Gainey his fully allotted 30 minutes. But after there were three visitors waiting in the hallway for a booth, I had to stop Gainey's visit at thirty minutes. I got on the intercom: "Inmate Gainey your thirty minutes are up."

Gainey came out and immediately looked at the clock in the center station, which showed he had at least five more minutes, which was what I had promised him, but the back hallway was getting too crowded. I didn't have any more chairs, and more importantly, I didn't want some petty superior harassing me about "why it's so dangerous when there are too many visitors waiting in the back hallway."

"Hey man, the clock shows that I still got five minutes to go. You promised me five extra minutes."

"Brother, I'd like to give you those five extra minutes, but I have several visitors waiting in the back hallway and you at least got your allotted thirty." "Fuck that! I want those five extra minutes you promised me." Gainey's total rudeness, and my getting tired of arguing with him, drove me to call-in additional officers to escort him from the booth and back to his ward. Exiting the area Gainey continued to curse at me.

"You jive-ass motherfucka, I'm gonna get your punk-ass one day. I'm gonna take that five minutes out on your ass."

"I'll be down to your station when this officer comes back from lunch, because we need to talk, brother."

When Officer Shark came back from lunch, I explained to him that he "forgot to call Inmate Gainey for his visit."

"Damn Taylor, I'm sorry, I forgot. Guess I was really hungry."

I left the center station and went to the southwest station to talk with Inmate Gainey, who was pacing the ward, mad as hell. Cautiously, I approached the station window. "Gainey, come to the window, I need to talk with you."

Still enraged, Gainey came to the window very argumentative.

"Man, what-the-fuck you want? Why don't you bring your punk-ass on the ward for five minutes so I can kick your ass, you punk-ass motherfucka!"

Possibly facing an embarrassing dilemma, because the other inmates on the ward viewed me as "*brave*," I told Officer Cecil, a Black male, who was the station officer, to let me onto the ward. If I hadn't,

I would've been labeled by the inmates of being lesser than a man. Before being let on the ward, Officer Cecil had some concerns.

"Taylor, that's one big dude, I don't think you should go in there by yourself. He's already killed three people, so you know he don't give a fuck about life, or you."

"You might be right, but fuck that! I tried to be honest with him, so I've got to let him know something."

As soon as I stepped on the ward, Gainey tried intimidation by affronting me off. The other inmates were anticipating that something might happen, but I didn't budge, as Gainey itched closer.

"My man, like I said before, I was relieving an officer for lunch and he forgot to call the station for your visit. It wasn't my fault that your woman waited so long. Can't you see that I was faced with a problem because of that other officer's mistake? I tried to give you some extra time. But your attitude is fucked-up, and I'll never give you any extra time because you didn't try to understand. So don't look for any other favors from me, okay."

Gainey itched a little closer—pointing his finger all up in my face. "Man, you better get off this ward, you ain't big enough to talk all that shit. I'll kick your ass right here."

"But I am big enough to tell you what's right and what's wrong. And if you do decide to do something, there will be ten to fifteen officers kicking your big ass in fifteen seconds, and I *know* I can hang with you at least that long... so go for it."

A stark silence came over the ward, as Gainey continued to curse me out and did nothing. While slowly exiting the ward, I watched my back. After that exchange with Gainey, I never had any more problems out of him. Non-fearing inmates always talked unkindly, trying to reduce and intimidate officers, to check out their courageousness, and marginalize their manhood.

I even caught a few female visitors in the act of showing their pussy to their husbands, boyfriends, or lovers while in a visitors' booth. Judicially speaking, the officer can't do anything to the inmate, but can expedite a charge to take away that female visitor's visiting privileges. There were incidents when officers could've written-up female visitors and charged them with *indecent exposure*. One day while making a visual round of the visitors' booths, I caught red-handed Melody Buchanan, a stunningly beautiful, blond, white female bombshell, in the act of showing her vagina to her husband, Leon Worthy, a Black male, jailed for numerous charges of fraudulent telemarketing and credit card schemes. While licking his lips, Worthy saw my face appear in the booth door's small square window, and tried to play it off. Immediately, I opened the door, catching Melody completely by surprise.

"Ma'am, now, you know better than to come up in here with this kind of behavior. This excites this man and it isn't good for him to go back to his cell, to dream and masturbate after seeing this."

Melody grabbed the end of her floral dress, which was already tucked-up to her chest, and pulled it down. The girl didn't have no pubic hair and no panties on! Sarcastically, I continued, "But I must admit, you do have some gorgeous legs, a nice body, and a nice-looking-you-know-what, and surely any man would get excited, especially in a place like this. But please, I advise you not to come in here doing this again because, if you were caught by the wrong person, you'd be in some real big trouble for this. I'm sorry, but I have to ask you to leave now... your visit has ended."

Before leaving the booth, Melody started maneuvering in the chair very sexy and alluringly.

"Ah baby, I was just showing my husband what he was missing, and trying to make sure he doesn't do such stupid things no more. I'm expecting to have his baby in seven months."

"I'm sorry but you're gonna have to leave now."

I handled about seven women like that, and out of those, six were very attractive with no stretch marks, or any cellulose looking features. The one who was not that good looking was a fat, ugly, nasty looking white girl, Margaret Folgers, who weighed about 260 pounds. I told her the same thing. Whenever I mentioned, "I could take their visiting privileges away," female visitors promised to *never* do it again. Some officers wrote down the names of *flashers* and whenever they came back to the jail for another visit, those officers stalked and snuck up to the booth window, and peeked for a similar infraction, or for some, just to take another look.

Some visitors, especially inmates' girlfriends or wives with their children would became very emotional when their visit was over. Pathetically, some came back to the center station, and used their kids' sad faces to plead for "just a little more time."

One day, visitor Camille Norton, an attractive, very light-skinned Black woman, wearing a thick, wooly, turtleneck sweater, became overwhelmed with grief and fainted from the warm, inconsistently, uncontrolled climate in the new jail. She didn't want to leave her husband, a habitual bank robber, who that day was sentenced to 15-20 years, and in a few days was being transferred to Jackson State Prison.

Officer Cox, a short, pudgy Black female, who carted around a TV and VCR to show movies to the inmates, was the first officer to go back to the Visitors' Booth #2 to check on Mrs. Norton.

"Taylor, I think you'd better come back here to help me. She doesn't want to leave the booth, and I think she has fainted."

I summoned a rover to relieve me at center station, and I personally went to check on Mrs. Norton. When I reached her she was sweating profusely, and was visibly upset because she didn't want to see her hubby go back to his cell. She continually cried out, "I love you baby... I'm gonna miss you baby... I love you baby," over and over again.

"Are you gonna be alright lady?" I asked Mrs. Norton as she sat on the floor. Suddenly, she didn't say a word and her head slumped, she had lost consciousness. Because of that (in my tenure officers *never* assumed the role of medical personnel), I felt she needed immediate, professional medical attention. I whisked her up in my arms and carried her down on the visitors' elevator, to the medical department on the second floor. Once I exited the elevator, several superiors and officers working in Master Control and nearby command offices looked in awe, as I whisked by them with Mrs. Norton in my arms, trying to help the lady. When I reached the medical department, I laid her on a bed. Two nurses immediately came over to assist, one taking her blood pressure.

"What happened?" "I don't know, she was in a visit and just collapsed. Her husband is scheduled for transfer to Jackson Prison, and I guess she was overcome by that thought," I told the nurse.

Out of nowhere, Officer Keith Flacken, a perpetrating Irishman, who worked in Male Registry, with twenty years seniority, came in to scold me about "why did I bring the lady down to medical?"

"Taylor, you're not supposed to bring civilians down here on the second floor under *any* circumstances. That's a clear violation of Departmental jail rules."

"Look man, why don't you just go sit your ass down somewhere, the lady has just fainted from heat exhaustion, so I decided to bring her down here for immediate medical attention. Is that asking too much?"

Not saying another word, Flacken walked away with some bonding papers in his hand, and murmured some racial, negative innuendoes. With no rank, Flacken wasn't even a corporal, and had no right to come hollering at me, as the two Black female nurses looked at him like he was crazy.

Once, around the 4th of July, I was offered twenty dollars for just five more minutes of visiting time. That was hard not to take, because twenty dollars was three hours of pay at the sheriff's department. Another time, I did take $20 from a wealthy visitor, who asked me to please get some cigarettes for his son, and buy him a good meal. That Hispanic inmate had to eat that barbecue rib dinner, while fighting off the roaches in a unsanitized broom closet in the hallway. And if he hadn't the other inmates would've beat him up and taken it. I kept fifteen dollars from that deal because I got the free barbecue dinner from my aunt's house, and I bought three packs of cheap, generic cigarettes from the store.

Many times visitors brought cigarettes to the jail hoping to give them to inmates. If the package had no signs of tampering sometimes I would give them to the inmate. But only if the officers or personnel working with me that day were sensible and cool. Officers should always open cigarette packages and inspect them. Occasionally, I smoked, but never around people, but might smoke a cigarette while using the rest room to make a funky odor more bearable for the next person (Many officers bought their own Glade). In the jail, that was the only time officers could get any relaxation. Eating the cafeteria food made the rest room a familiar place for officers and inmates. Regularly, on a weekly basis, officers became sick with cases of food poisoning, diarrhea, headaches, and stomach ailments.

Male officers always had a difficult time convincing male superiors that they were sick, but female officers had full consideration,

after simply complaining. There were times when I called white superiors and they'd **never** flinched, after hearing my qualm of "being ill."
They'd just say "they couldn't send me home because they were
short of manpower," which in many cases was a lie.

Everyday, before and after visiting hours, officers are required to
inspect the civilian side of the visiting booths. The day of Tuesday,
February 11, 1986, I got a call from a white male sergeant to inspect
the visitors' booths for contraband, because at that period, it had
become a common practice for trustees, appointed to specific floors
for cleaning detail, to know visitors who were his friends, to leave
drugs somewhere in the booths. Later, when the trustee cleaned up,
they'd collect the drugs. I choose to inspect the booths with a partner.

Just before shift change, I, and Officer Claude Rembry, a well-
liked white male, with an elevated consciousness, inspected the booths
and discovered a small, brown kraft envelope in Booth #2. Slightly, I
opened the flap to discover the contents: top quality, reddish, greenish brown, flowery buds of marijuana. Three of the four officers involved with the booth inspection wrote-up reports. Officer Rembry's
report to Lieutenant James "*Smooth*" Shoulders read:

"*At approximately 2259 this officer and Officer K. Taylor observed a small package and a hand-rolled cigarette. These items
were found in visiting Booth #2. The above mentioned package contained
a greenish brown leafy substance **believed** to be marijuana. The
hand rolled cigarette is **suspected** to contain marijuana also. The
small package was found in the ceiling and the cigarette was found
taped to the bottom of the chair. The material was turned over to
Lt. Shoulders who placed the package in a locked storage container to which only he has keys.*"

Center station Officer Susan Rose, a very light-skinned female,
who later transferred to the Detroit Police Department, also submitted a report, which stated:

"*On February 11, 1986 at approximately 2259 hours in the Andrew C. Baird Detention Center, 7th Floor, Ofc. C. Rembry and Ofc.
K. Taylor searched the civilian visiting area and **observed what
appears** to be a marijuana cigarette and a package containing a
leafy green material believed to be marijuana in visiting Booth #2.*

Ofc. C. Rembry gave the marijuana cigarette to this officer. This officer then notified shift command, Lt. Shoulders and returned suspected marijuana cigarette to Ofc. Rembry."

Of course, I also had to write-up a report, which stated: "*On February 11, 1986 at 2259 hours, an inspection of visiting Booth #2 was conducted by Officer Rembry and Officer Taylor. The inspection revealed that there was a hand-rolled cigarette under a seat in Booth #2. Further inspection of the booth revealed a packet containing a green leafy substance **believed** to be marijuana. Officers Rembry and Y. Tell witnessed the finding. **Suspected** marijuana was T.O.T. Lieutenant Shoulders who secured same in a locked container. Packet of **suspected** marijuana marked by writer and sealed in a brown manila envelope.*"

When officers discover drugs, many of them try to appear naive, and their report writing reflects that (as you can see). We all knew exactly what the contents of the package was (I surely did), but we all had to leave room for speculation. The next day I was told by several officers on the morning shift, that this same white male sergeant, who ordered me to inspect the visitors' booths, had earlier, iinspected them on their shift. To me, this incident appeared to be a setup because of the easy accessibility to the marijuana joint taped under the chair, and also the impromptu call from the sergeant to inspect the booths.

Generally, periodical inspections of the visitors' booths is mandatory for deterring and catching visitors, and stopping them from the practice of causing deputies unnecessary dilemmas. But in this particular incident, the booth inspection proved worthy to *deter* another white male superior's *intended wrath*.

35

Dating At Work:
They Only Come Out At Night

D ATING SOMEONE ON THE JOB CAN BE AN enlightening experience, but more often than not it should be avoided. Not only are you both underfoot all the time, but in many cases a third party at work may also have their eye on the same person you do, thus causing multiple political complications as well. My rule of thumb concerning dating at work is "*don't get ya honey where you get ya money!*" This is especially true in the field of law enforcement. It takes two very special people to date, let alone marry, be together all day and all night without constant squabbling, and downright tragic if one should be taken away forever by making the wrong, split second decision.

You might think that because you are a *dedicated* police officer, where better to find another like you than at work. Granting, however, that the hiring process, like the rest of the prison system, is flawed, you would probably do better not to attempt to judge by what you see in the jail of another person's character. Now you might ask why any administration would turn away someone, who really has a desire and wants to protect civilians? After all, in law enforcement aren't these qualities essential? But some people get the job because of *nepotism*, and others seek it out because it can be a government dole for a minimum of effort.

Then of course there is, in or out of the jail, something called the *Commitment Ambivalence Syndrome* (CAS). CAS victims feel trapped in a pit of indecision as ambivalence causes their emotions and desires to swing back and forth like a pendulum between the candidates for one's affection. Many officers working in the jail suffered from this symptom.

My first inter-Department dating experience was with Officer Keisha Flowers, a sensual, satisfying, spoiled-rotten, archer of the zodiac. In the beginning our chemistry aroused us both, and for awhile I thought Keisha might be the woman for me. Then I found out her real interest was in another man, Officer Fred Steadman. Fred and I attended Mumford High School together from 1969 to 1972. Mumford was the school that gained notoriety and fame when Eddie Murphy wore the school's tee shirt in the "Beverly Hills Cop" movies.

Keisha began working for the Department in the summer of 1985. At 5-foot-2, about 125 pounds, she was petite, an athletic tomboy type, both her personality and physical appearance were alluring. Keisha could be quite charming, with a enticing smile that seemed to surface only when money was plentiful. The first time I met Keisha I asked her out to dinner. She refused, saying she was still grieving over her husband's death. This was quite understandable and I didn't pressure her. Instead I sent her letters in envelopes decorated with red roses and cartoons. I wanted her to know my intentions were sincere. Keisha always made it a point to tell me how nice they were and how much she appreciated them, and I kinda knew she did.

A few months after Keisha and I started socializing, the sheriff's union gave a party at Fandango Hall, which was used primarily for parties, wedding receptions, meetings and cabarets. This was the first union party for both of us. Although we weren't totally committed to getting involved, we were certainly thinking about it. The yearning was there, and I could tell something was eventually going to happen. All the Blacks at the party were dressed up, looking nice and having a good time. Many whites wore blue jeans and hunting shirts, or those V-neck, dime store sweaters (there were very few who knew how to dress appropriately for the occasion).

Blacks congregated on one side of the hall, while whites sat on the other, drinking Bloody Marys, rum and cokes, vodka, Jack Daniels, and, of course, beer, all provided free-of-charge by the union. Most of the Black officers brought exotic drinks like cognacs, Grand Marnier, and wines. The festivities were rumored to be funded by the union with officers' dues, and because many Black officers felt they were being poorly represented, we figured the union was giving a party to pacify us in hopes that we'd temporarily forget about the injustices in the Department.

Everyone took advantage of the free drinks, but I had a little bit too much. I hadn't eaten all day and didn't realize the effect it would have on my stomach. Officers Bill Appel and Dick Berkley, two young white males, who stood at the bar getting drunk all night, dared me to down a Bloody Mary: "Come on Taylor, let me see you drink some of this. This will put some hair on your chest; I guarantee it, buddy." I was a little too far gone with drinking and defending my manhood to refuse: "Well, down it goes. Ugh! Man, that's got to be the nastiest ass drink in the world," I spluttered, just managing not to throw up as the Bloody Mary hit the rum and coke, Grand Marnier, and whatever else was already in my stomach.

Officer Eddie *"Boo-gay"* Wright, who doubled as a disc jockey, was hired to play the music for the party. As usual, just like at my back yard party, Wright had everybody pumped-up and having a good time. As Blacks danced soulfully and naturally to a rhythmic beat, drunk white people dutifully joined in on the dance floor. Whites tried valiantly, but failed to emulate the Black experience of "jammin'." Their uninspired participation on the dance floor and their inability to keep cadence while marching at the police academy gave credence to the theory that many whites have trouble keeping a steady beat. After many of the white officers got drunk, and became overtly ignorant, Black officers sought other Blacks to socialize.

Keisha looked tantalizingly hot that night in a tight, black skirt. When it was time to leave, I was surprised that she asked me if I wouldn't mind taking her, and her girlfriend Carlis home. How could I refuse. So before the party ended, I went outside to warm up my car in the parking lot. The engine wouldn't even turnover in the subzero temperature and it looked like it was about to snow. My car, a diesel, 1981 Cadillac Seville, had been having major alternator problems, and needed a boost to start. Fortunately, a fellow officer came to my rescue by giving me a jump, while Keisha and Carlis were still inside mingling, unaware of my car problems. I was afraid if I told them they wouldn't let me give them a ride home. It seemed like an eternity finally taking them home through a treacherous snowstorm. And something was wrong with me: I was becoming sick. After dropping Carlis off, I drove to Keisha's apartment, only a couple of miles from the hall. Keisha could see I was losing it, and through her kindness (it could have been a hint), offered to pay for me to stay overnight at a Holiday Inn down the street. "No thank you, I think I can manage. I don't want to stay at no Holiday Inn *unless* you can come stay with me," I complained in a quavering voice. "I would come stay with you if my man wasn't waiting for me to come home," Keisha offered with her sexy smile. That exchange gave me every indication that better things were in store.

We talked a few more minutes before she went inside, and we sealed the night with a tender, loving, long, deep-tonguing, french kiss. It was so good that I remained motionless, relishing every tingling sensation, as she disappeared giving me a wave before closing her apartment door, before I pulled away. I couldn't help but think of the near possibility of staying all night with Keisha at the hotel. In my condition, however, it was just as well it didn't happen. The hankering was there, but throwing-up was too much of a possibility—that would have been disastrous.

This night could have also been a life-threatening disaster. It was extreme cold, something like seven degrees below zero, and mechanical problems nearly stalled my car several times in the middle of the highway. All the way home the headlights kept dimming, and my car couldn't go faster than fifty miles per hour, and I was forced to turn everything electrical off so the engine wouldn't die. I kept hoping a Michigan State trooper wouldn't stop me. The snow was coming down like God and His angels were having a heavenly pillow fight. About a 25 minute drive from the hall, I finally made it home 45 minutes later and immediately jumped in bed with all my clothes on.

Forty minutes later my stomach erupted. I didn't even have time to reach the rest room. *Never* before in my entire life had I been so drunk, so totally sick. That night, I got on my knees and promised God that I would *never* again drink another Bloody Mary, nor rum and coke (except for rum mixed in strawberry daiquiris). I only drank a little, trying to prove my manhood and be accepted, because Officers Appel and Berkley, dared me to drink that nasty Bloody Mary. Waking up in your own vomit makes one despondent. I called-in sick that day. I felt terrible and I had to find a mechanic to check out my car. Keisha called me to find out why I didn't come to work, and said she could hardly sleep for worrying about me all night, and how relieved she was that I made it home safely.

At a second union party in 1987, I brought six good-looking, Black female friends with me. It was getting frustrating seeing the same ol' female faces at work *and* union functions. I got my friends to go with me by confiding that I knew where a lot of single men were going to be that night. Some officers labeled me a Casanova just because I brought six females to the party. Ah, the cool playboy, the *cockswain connoisseur*... nope, that's not me, I had long ago developed a laissez faire, nonchalant attitude about women and sex. White and Black male officers came up to me commenting:

"Damn, Taylor. You sho' got some nice-looking 'chicks' with you. Think you can hook-me-up with one of 'em?"

So we all went over to Officer Jeffrey Oliver's house after the party. Officer Oliver is another Black male, who quit the Sheriff's Department to go work for the Detroit Fire Department. After socializing for an hour, Oliver decided he had fallen in love with the beautiful, voluptuous Patti. An accomplished pianist, Oliver entertained us by playing a few songs and putting an x-rated movie in the VCR. He was trying his best to turn the girls on, but instead it turned them off!

"Jeff, don't you have another movie you can put on for us, baby? I ain't even with this," was the consensus.

Porn flick or not, we all laughed the night away till the wee hours of morning; the birds were chirping when we finally left Oliver's house. I always preferred taking a date, or female friends, to departmental functions. Most male officers came alone, hoping to meet someone gullible enough to go home with them for the night. It was important that I was associated with good-looking female dates and friends, rather than deal with the tedious, humiliating, frustrating search for a one night stand.

The second time Keisha and I went out on a date was to see Eddie Murphy at Pine Knob, an amphitheater for summer concerts that doubles as a ski slope in the winter. Located about 35 miles north of Detroit, Pine Knob at one time allowed patrons to bring food and liquor inside the park, until drunken rowdiness at white rock-n-roll concerts got out of hand. When policy changes prohibited bringing anything in, Pine Knob began selling wine, food, and other drinks on the premises at unreasonably high prices. As a result, Keisha and I got tipsy on the way to the concert.

Wrapped in quilts and blankets, we sat atop one of the hills and watched Eddie Murphy strut and cuss across the stage in tight, black leather pants. We consumed a few more drinks from miniature bottles of Grand Marnier we had snuck in, hidden on our persons. In stitches at Eddie's jokes, we cuddled up to stay warm. "Keisha, you sure know how to make me feel pretty good," I confessed. Her forever-changing moodiness was almost sensuous, she had a great feel for what men liked, and I often told her that. I never denied I was falling in love with her, but I had to consider her track record of broken relationships. Nevertheless, Cupid was really doing a hatchet job on me.

Officers Chuck Stallings and Ronald Mitchum, two Black males from the jail, also attended the Eddie Murphy concert. While taking a walk atop the hills, they spotted Keisha and I, and came over to talk—talking more to Keisha than to me, of course. It was generally regarded that she was Fred's **main squeeze** (you remember Officer Steadman from four pages back), but they also knew Keisha was very independent, confused, and a little fickle. I'm sure they wondered why was she at the concert with me? Stallings and Mitchum also had dates, and eventually on my way to the rest room, got a chance to wander over to their cozy spot on another hill to shoot the breeze with them. I had a brief premonition on whether Stallings and Mitchum would go tell Officer Steadman they had seen Keisha and I together, but at the time Keisha acted like she didn't care, and we had already discussed the matter. It was our night and we were going to enjoy it.

Eddie Murphy's jokes started heating up and he made a "eye-catching" wisecrack about Johnny Carson's divorce settlement of eighty million dollars.

"Every time a woman gets a divorce, what does she want?" Making a tomahawk, chopping motion with his hand, Eddie continued:

"She wants half. Half? Fuck that: that's bullshit! Ain't no woman's pussy on this earth worth no damn eighty million dollars!" The whole crowd roared, and Keisha turned to me and said proudly, "That's a damn lie, my pussy is worth at least twice that much."

Naturally, the guys within earshot all looked at me as if I'd better watch out, and then they looked Keisha up-and-down. I had to laugh along with her sarcasm, because I knew she wasn't lying—her loving was good, and I think it's excellent when a woman has such confidence in herself. I began to pay more attention, however, to Keisha's overconfidence in the power of her money-maker to get her anything.

I often ask women, what is the one attribute of theirs they would pick as their best? Some say legs or eyes, and other's say their minds. Many say their breasts, and a few well-equipped women, full of exuberance and overconfidence, have said, "my loving and whip appeal."

After the Eddie Murphy concert, Keisha and I bought two pounds of shrimp and went to my house. When the shrimp was gone, I took her home and we made love all night long. There was a full sunrise when we finally gained our equilibrium. There were times when Keisha could be a very affectionate woman, and she knew exactly what making love was all about. We were *never* disappointment when our bodies entwined. From that night on, I always wanted me some Keisha—to have a platonic relationship with her was *impossible*.

On our third date, Keisha and I attended a fashion show at Marygrove College. We were both dressed sharp: I had on a double-breasted black suit, a tuxedo shirt, red bow tie and cummerbund, black shoes and socks. Keisha wore a red dress with a bare back, high heels that called attention to her well-proportioned legs and calfs. We were one good looking couple. She admired the dresses shown, and I was just making up my mind to buy her one for her birthday, until she indicated her mind was still on Fred, who at the time was considering a divorce. A musician named Ya Tafari played the keyboards at intermission, and the crowd mingled by a fountain, drinking sparkling champagne flowing from the mouth of a nude Greek stone god. A few people by the fountain toasted each other, while Keisha and I landed a couple of affectionate smooches. After the fashion show, we went over to Keisha's apartment and again made passionate love all night.

The relationship of Officer Steadman and Keisha was well-known throughout the jail, even the inmates knew of their involvement. To avoid detection and spend more time together, Keisha and I sometimes worked double shifts because Fred hated working overtime. I saw signs of their growing mutual admiration: walking and holding hands, and all I could do was hopelessly watch. Then, unexpectedly Keisha increased our time together and asked me to lend her an ear. She had grown impatient of Fred's procrastination and indecision in finalizing his pending divorce, so *they* could get married.

Because of that, Keisha and I grew closer and started seeing each other more regularly. We renewed our infatuation several times over a two-year period. While working the same shift, we'd call each other a lot. Our extended conversations seemed to always be about Fred's waning interest. When not assigned to the same floor we'd visit each other when time or circumstances permitted. Our secret affection had us doing adolescent things: hugging, kissing, caressing, and fondling each other to create friction whenever nosey inmates or officers weren't looking. Keisha gave some of the most pleasing kisses I have ever experienced, and each time we left the station, we'd strategically position ourselves in the corridor so no one could see us. Keisha was always paranoid that inmates or officers would see us being affectionate to one another. She was always afraid that Fred would find out, and it was becoming more difficult to keep our relationship a secret. One day an inmate had the gall to quiz me.

"Officer Taylor, isn't that uhhhhh... you know, what-cha-ina-call-its main squeeze?"

"You dipping ain't you brother. I don't know who you're talking about and really don't care. But is it any of your business?" I replied.

When word of our involvement got around, one day Fred came to my floor assignment in 8-Center and stood outside the sliding door of the visitors' elevator, motioning with his finger for me to come out into the sally port. Once inside the sally port Fred pouted, paced, and angrily shouted like a tyrant:

"Man, I wish you'd stop fucking with my *Bitch*!"

"Look Fred," I rejoined, "I don't have time for this kind of nonsense."

"Look Taylor, that's my *Bitch* and why don't you just stop seeing her. Can't you see that she doesn't want to be bothered with you? She's my woman!"

"Hey brother," I persisted, "You can have her if that makes you feel better. Maybe you need to go talk with her about things, not me."

I never thought of fighting over Keisha—never thought of fighting over *any* woman—and I don't think I ever will. Why do men, especially Black men, go on this ego trip about women when confronting other men? In some cases, Black men will kill over a woman. To me, that's crazy when there are at least seven females to one male in America, and most of the single, eligible Black males are in jail. Black men seek to conquer women: get one-up in the sexual department because Black men have lost the fight for jobs, education, economic affluence and influence. Affirmative action is being discontinued just as it has begun to work. It can be argued that affirmative action has only benefited women (Black, but white especially), more than it has Black men. And this isn't a surprise when you consider that white men are most afraid of fair competition with Black men (consider professional sports, casino gambling, corporations, manufacturing, trading) in this country. White men seem to want to keep not only white women, but every gender and race in bondage to them.

Keisha seemed to be having emotional problems because Fred couldn't make up his mind. PMS may really mean ***Putting up with Mens' Shit***. Keisha sometimes felt guilt about showing me her real emotions. She seemed to be able to forget about her problems, think about Fred, and all the while, still love the hell out of me. Keisha often invited me to her apartment to spend the whole day together. I got to know her two sons, who were very intelligent young Black boys. I commended her many times on being a strong, single Black woman striving to survive against the odds of bringing up kids in these turbulent times.

Her attitude about the Department was that it was just a job and a paycheck, typical of many police officers. As has been true of all of us at one time or another, Keisha was influenced too much by those in power at the Sheriff's Department, and it clearly affected her personality—it went to her head. Jealousy did us a disservice when male rumormongers, who also wanted a chance to experience her loving, told tales. We grew further apart: Keisha remained moody, had endless problems with Fred, and those tenacious, persistent rumors were the cause. We stopped seeing each other. I have often wished we could have continued an acquaintance, but it *never* happened because Keisha could not get beyond her relationship with Fred. I'll *never* forget what Keisha said to me about her encounter with Officer Carl Stone, a Black male, whom she admitted having a "*boning session*" with.

"Yes, I just got tired of him always hounding me, so I just *fucked* his little brains out to get him off my case!"

Keisha felt comfortable enough to tell me anything personal. But that hurt me more than it shocked me, and it also showed me something about Keisha.

"Sweets, every time we make love I always find this warm, certain spot that makes my whole body tingle," I would tell Keisha while we made love.

I couldn't help but say that to her, and she loved to hear it. It got to the point that her personal and private confessions about other men, destroyed our friendship altogether. It was hard for me to hear that she gave her precious body to Officer Stone. I was in fact even more shocked when I found out that most female officers felt Carl was unattractive—yet he still got his shot at Keisha.

Never satisfied, Keisha always wanted "her cake and eat it too," and the best of all worlds, one man just wasn't enough. Keisha reminded me of the character Lola Darling, the "*Skeeza,*" who shunned a commitment and continued to see and make love to three men, in Spike Lee's first movie "*She's Gotta Have It.*" One day I worked the same floor with Officer Stone, and told him what Keisha had said.

"Yeah, man, the other night Keisha told me, 'she fucked your little brains out.' Can you believe that shit? She's got a lot of damn nerve."

Stone flushed over the fact that Keisha confided their sexual encounter to me. Without saying another word, Stone gave me a look like he knew it was true! I never felt either of us had to have the edge, but once I knew about Keisha's and Stone's one nighter, I had to think that she must have said similar things about me to other men.

I sometimes pondered, what was it that Fred did that was so great? Fred was cordial and a conservative, sleek dresser, but he didn't seem very serious, or ambitious, and always bummed rides to and from work. Fred gave a couple of house parties during the time he and Keisha were having problems, and Keisha attended one, looking sizzling hot in a red, leather miniskirt. For over two hours, Fred stayed behind his locked bedroom door, sulking presumably, but with another woman.

My social life with people I worked with at the jail was varied to say the least. Once I took a stocky, attractive Black female friend of mine named Deirdre to one of Fred's parties. She was a complete knockout. After returning from a quick trip to the store, I found several previously indifferent Black male officers, trying to strike up a conversation with Deirdre, but she wasn't interested in any of them.

In July 1986, Keisha, Officer Stephanie Brockley (a Black female), and I went to go see violinist Jean Luc-Ponty at Meadowbrook, another amphitheater about 25 miles north of Detroit. Officer Brockley, very light-skinned, was overweight but very attractive, with a beautiful personality and smile. She had won a couple of beauty contests. Black Officer Jack Overton, had led Brockley to believe he had already purchased tickets to the concert, and that they were going to attend together.

I had already planned to attend the Kool Jazz Festival in Cincinnati the day after the Luc-Ponty concert, but Victor Stafford, one of several Detroit promoters for the festival, had unfortunately decided to run a shady business by not providing prepaid accommodations for annual festival goers (many of them sheriff's deputies). I told him that the deputies who gave him money to attend the festival, would vigorously and aggressively prosecute him if he failed to refund their money. Stafford immediately gave back each deputies' money, but I still didn't have mine. I wondered where the money of those who weren't deputies went? After six straight years of attending the festival in Cincinnati, I finally missed a year because of Stafford's foolishness.

Keisha, Brockley, Overton, and I, had all agreed to meet at my house no later than seven to go to the Jean Luc-Ponty concert. Looking impatiently out my window, waiting for my guests to arrive, Stafford drove-up in a spanking, brand new, white stretch limo. I immediately rushed out the front door and yelled.

"Thanks a lot, I was wondering what you were going to do about my money. Man, we've been doing business for years, and why are you keeping all of those other folks money? You've got a good thing going. Why are you messing it all up?"

"I just can't pay them all back, right now. Eventually, they will all get there money back," Stafford claimed evasively. I had an idea.

"Uh, why don't you let me drive your limo to the Jean Luc-Ponty concert at Meadowbrook. It's not that far away, and I'll give you back some of the festival money for the limo."

"I have to use it to go give other people back their money. I need transportation," Stafford quickly countered.

"Man, you can use my car. Let me use the limo for about six to eight hours and you can make a hundred dollars. I used to chauffeur for Butch Pepperidge, remember. You owe me a favor after doing this bullshit, anyway. I'll meet you somewhere later, around three in the morning. Don't worry, I promise I'll take good care of it." Stafford stared at the sky a few moments and consented.

As so as we finished talking, Keisha drove-up in my driveway, got out of her car, and without saying a word, walked into the house to freshen up. As usual, she was looking good and ready to go. Stafford showed me all the special features of the limo before driving off in my car—a 1981 diesel Seville. Time was of essence, as Keisha and I, awed by the newness of the limo, sat in it and waited impatiently for Brockley and Overton to arrive. It was already approaching 7 p.m., and the concert started at 7:30. I hate being late for anything, but I knew in a limo we could possibly ride the shoulders of a crowded highway, and pass everybody. After all, we were cops, whether state-certified yet or not, we had our sheriff's deputy I.Ds.

My patience was wearing thin when the clock hit 7:15. I went back into the house to get some cups, the phone rang, it was Brockley. She was frustrated and angry.

"Taylor, I'm very sorry, man, but that damn Overton, punk-ass motherfucka, stood me up! I called him around seven o'clock and you won't believe this. He said, one of his friends got shot and his girlfriend developed a bad stomach ache. He could have at least called me or just dropped off my ticket! He's so full of shit!"

"Well, Keisha and I are waiting in the limo, please hurry," I encouraged Brockley.

"Oh yeah! You got a limo? I'm on my way: be there in ten minutes," Brockley promised, and hung up.

At exactly 7:30 p.m. Brockley arrived, looking rather sad and discouraged, but willing to still have a good time. I couldn't complain. Here I was, chauffeuring two nice-looking Black women in this spanking, brand new, white stretch limo. On the way to the concert I made a couple of stops, and Brockley bought and introduced Keisha and I, to a new concoction of cranberry juice, peach Schnapps, and Perrier. It was a refreshing change from my preference, Grand Marnier. Brockley also gave me $50 towards the cost of the limo.

In the vicinity of Meadowbrook we encountered miles of traffic jam. I choose to ride on the shoulder, of course, and after several miles of "*Bogart*," we approached a full parking lot with a locked 10-foot tall chain link gate. A white male Oakland County sheriff's officer came to the driver's window. Before he could say a word, I handed over my sheriff's credentials:

"We need to park this limo inside the fence by the ticket office. I've got Anita Baker in the back seat," I told him. Anita Baker had just performed in Detroit the night before. He *never* looked inside the limo, and immediately summoned a parking lot attendant to remove the lock to let us in. The lot was full to capacity, but the section for limos had room, so I parked right next to the ticket office, whereupon we were approached by a stranger who just gave us three free lawn tickets, and we rushed through the turnstiles to find the lawn full to the tilt. We scanned the area until we found a tight space for the three of us, though the people surrounding it grudgingly made room.

Jean-Luc Ponty played my favorite, "Modern Time Blues," and songs from his albums, "Individual Choice" and "Fables." We had a wondrous time, and after the concert we drove around Detroit for four glorious hours, laughing and joking with one another. This helped Brockley forget about Overton. At about 3:30 a.m. the next morning, I met Stafford as promised in the parking lot of a boarded-up restaurant, waiting in my Seville with a beautiful woman.

"Thanks a lot, we had a ball, man, and please return those other people's money," I reminded Stafford once again. Stafford drove off in his limo, ***never*** to be seen again.

I took advantage of my sheriff's identification one other time at Tina Turner's Private Dancer concert, at Joe Louis arena in 1986. While walking on the overpass over the highway, Saleem, a stocky, Arab male, proposed I buy a ticket from him for face value. He claimed one of his friend got sick and couldn't attend. As we were about to finalize the transaction by the railings atop a long stairway, Rita Miller, a Black female cop on the Detroit Police Department, jumped in between us and flashed her badge.

"You guys are busting for ticket scalping."

Rita's tight shorts contrasted with a cops' image. She blended in perfectly with the crowd. Saleem had already told me "he was selling the ticket for *face value*," or I might have claimed a bust myself and taken the ticket.

"The law is that tickets can't be sold on arena property at all," Rita stressed, and summoned other plain clothes officers on her radio, who then took Saleem to a police station under the arena's stands. I followed, trying to persuade the undercover officers (because *I was* a noncertified Wayne County Sheriff's deputy) not to ticket Saleem, but he was issued a ticket anyway for ticket scalping on Joe Louis Arena's property. I later apologized to Saleem. Whether he believed me, I don't know.

"Don't worry about that damn ticket, I can afford it, it's nothing," Saleem demurred, giving me his business card and heading into the concert, with **my** ticket still in his pocket.

I had memorized the ticket section and seat number, so all I had to do now was just find a way to the first floor of the arena. I had already gained entry under the arena's stands once before, when I followed the police to plead Saleem's case. Near the private booth entrance door, was an elevator that took private booth owners up from the basement to the arena floors. Security guards were checking for I.D's, inconspicuously but seriously. Surprisingly, looking inconspicuous, I walked right past the security guards, stepped on the elevator and got in to see Tina Turner, the prettiest legs in show business, without any trouble, and on the main floor, mind you, with

Saleem, who finally sold me *my* ticket.

Getting back to the ubiquitous and heartbreaking Keisha. I grew despondent as her attention remained fixed on Fred, while superiors and officers continued defaming me. It so happened that Sergeant Phil Hopkins, who supposedly owned some real estate, was also trying to "*hit*" on her. According to Keisha, she rode with him to see some of his houses, to see what they looked like, because she was thinking about moving in to rent one. I had my suspicions that something was going on between them for a long time, and Keisha worked her usual convincing persuasion to convince me that it wasn't so. Hopkins wanted more than just **rent with an option to buy**: he wanted a piece of the action.

Keisha seemed to be impressed with rank, authority, and vulnerability. Judging from her past record and Sergeant Hopkins' intensified "harassment" of me, I'm sure they had discussed her on again, off again relationships with Fred and I. I recall the day when something told me that Hopkins had something up his sleeve. I was just about to go through the cafeteria doors when Hopkins tapped me on my arm and confided.

"Hey Taylor, I've got something to tell you." Hungry but cordial, I stopped and asked.

"Yes, and what is that?"

"Well, I thought you'd like to know that there are a few female officers who are betting each other on you," Hopkins continued, smiling slyly.

"Oh yeah, hum, betting on what?" I inquired. Hopkins nodded conspiratorially:

"They're betting on which one of them can get you in the bed first. Lately, you seem to be the hottest thing going on with the females around here."

In other words, Sergeant Hopkins was attempting to set me up with flattery. My immediate inclination was to believe that Hopkins was in collusion with someone. There was no doubt in my mind that he was up to something. I could only think it was because Hopkins and Keisha were getting closer and I didn't approve of his interference. Hopkins, in his fifties, was rumored to have had eighteen children out of wedlock, and still wasn't married.

I had hoped Keisha would be able to see this as she started working in the Administration Building as an operator for the tele-communications division, among the Department's higher adminis-trators. Thinking I was looking out for Keisha's best interest, I told her what Hopkins had said about my so-called, newly found popular-ity. As the situation between Keisha and I heated-up, Sergeant Hopkins became more petty. I wondered what was Keisha telling him? Hopkins began making three or four rounds a day to my assigned floor, when his norm was one, rarely two. Sometimes he covered himself by sign-ing the logbook twice, when he had been on the floor three or four times. When it was Hopkins' turn to schedule officers for assign-ments, he and some of *his superiors* partnered me with officers, who had reputations as snitches and liars.

I was over at Keisha's apartment one day, when Officer Lamar Reese, another Black male, came over unexpectedly, or so Keisha *said*. They went into the kitchen and left me sitting alone on the living room couch. I overheard them talking and then kissing, a tactic Keisha used to calm her men down. Reese was upset because I was there.

"We're only friends," she said, not even trying for something original. She wanted Reese there because she had made me expend-able. She was manipulating Fred, Reese and me (who knows who else?), even though Fred was still slow to propose marriage. In the summer of 1986, after a year of drama and procrastination, Fred and Keisha rode down to Ohio to give their banns: a proclamation of an intended marriage. They did this in a rather hurried way, without fanfare. None of us at the jail knew about it. Their marriage lasted *only* a month or so, and the annulment to finalize their separation lingered on for *seven* years. While they were married Keisha was involved in a car accident. While she was in the hospital recovering from back injuries, Fred neglected to visit her. Fred must have been thoroughly tired of her sexual prowess, and the many men who craved for her. I guess he figured that all along she must have known what she was doing, and had a solid grasp. For over two years Keisha was on and off again with Fred, falling into the trap of too many tranquil-izers to ease her mind.

"All this medicine isn't good for you," I told Keisha many times, but she took them anyway. "It's necessary for right now; I need it," she would say over and over again. She also became a victim of a vicious rumor of having bisexual tendencies. Her so-called friends vandalized her car, by breaking out the windows and slashing the tires.

After two years of ups-and-downs, Keisha and I started having conversations that turned into heated arguments—sometimes there were angry words. One day I was riding alone on the visitors' elevator, when it stopped at the second floor, where Master Control and the command offices are. Many deputies hated for the elevator to stop on that floor. As the elevator doors opened, Keisha stood there, much to my surprise, giving me an odd, sinister look. We both were going down, but she refused to get on with me. Keisha knew that she had been consorting with the same command officers who were harassing me. While the elevator doors remained open Keisha smirked and taunted me:

"Yes, I'm doing what I want to and you can't do nothing about it!"

"Shut up, you little witch!" I shouted back at her as the elevator doors closed slowly. I *really* wanted to say "you little ***Bitch!***" but knew superiors were probably in earshot. Later that same day while in my station, the very white, male jail Commander Steve Maloney called me on the phone.

"Officer Taylor, I was located near the visitors' elevator on the second floor, when I heard you call the female officer a bad name. I hope you didn't say ***what I think*** you said, because it could cause you some reprimanding or disciplinary action."

"No sir! She rides a broom and that's why I called her a ***witch***. Lately we've been having some problems with our friendship, and right now I'm sort of pissed at her reluctance to give me some time to explain myself. But in no way, sir, did I call her a bad name. No sir, that's just not my style," I barked.

I was surprised a high official would think I'd be stupid enough to say something like that, especially in the presence of people who were targeting me. Commander Maloney and whoever else, probably knew what I ***really*** wanted to say, so Maloney's call ***ranked as harassment***. There were other superiors near the elevator, ***who heard*** *exactly what I said*, but no one else said anything. Perhaps Commander Maloney was chosen as the newest spokesman for the group. An hour after my talk with Maloney, Keisha called and *accused* me of calling her a *B-i-t-c-h*.

"Keisha, now you know I didn't call you a *Bitch*: I called you a *witch*, which is what you are. *You heard exactly what I said*, so don't even try it," I warned her.

The infamous institutional racism of white male jail officials just kept on, centered on building up more propaganda and enough paperwork to demonstrate my incorrigibility with regard to infractions of hunky-dory jail rules. This ultimately became evidence for the *already-reached* conclusion that I didn't have the best interests of the Department at heart.

Keisha even had the gall to accuse me of scratching her name on the lavatory doors and partition walls in the mens' rest room, after her other boyfriend, Officer Lamar Reese, told her that her name was inscribed with some sexist remarks. There was a lot of graffito in the mens' rest rooms *Within The Walls*. There were several limericks and lewd material involving several female and male officers working in the jail. Most of the scrawlings involved racial slurs. I always wondered why a so-called "man" would waste his time engraving derogatory remarks on the stainless steel surface of a walled partition, where only people he worked with everyday would see? Those who write such filth secretly in public places are cowards: mean, corrupt, racist, afraid to meet you face to face.

After my unjust termination from the Sheriff's Department on May 16, 1989, Keisha and I eventually came to talking terms again but things were *never* the same. She dropped by my house unexpectedly a couple of times, but I was either busy or had friends over already. Sometimes I regretted having company because I wanted to see if we could recapture that once loving feeling, but it just wasn't meant to be.

In August 1992, Keisha and her two sons, ten and sixteen years of age, picked me up early one morning to go to Cedar Point, a popular park with all kinds of rides. I love the more thrilling rides: roller coaster, standing roller coaster, Demon Drop, and the twirling track, circled roller coaster, and I urged Keisha and her sons to ride them with me. But they were afraid. Two hours before the park closed, I excused myself and went to get something to eat, while Keisha took her sons to nearby kiddie rides. As I ate my hot dog I looked around but couldn't locate them, so I left to get on the rides I really liked before the park closed. After riding the roller coaster three times, I rode the overhead trolley back to the kiddie area and spotted Keisha and her sons walking below. I yelled down

"Hey, Keisha, I'll be right down. Wait there and I'll walk back towards you." When I reached her, she was pouting and *accusatory*:

"Why did you leave us?"

"Hey, all day y'all didn't want to ride any of the rides I wanted to get on. There wasn't much time left, I didn't see where y'all went, so it was time for me to go get on those rides before the park closed," I answered truthfully, "So I just went to go get on them. I came here to have some fun. Did I do something so bad?" Well, you can imagine how it went from there—Keisha stayed mad and didn't say a word to me all the way home.

About a month later my father died. Three days before the funeral, on a very thunderous, lightning, rainy night, I called Keisha around midnight for comfort and asked her if I could come over and spend the night. At first she suggested "tomorrow night," but finally relented and said "Okay." I told her I'd be there in twenty minutes, grabbed a few things and was out-the-door. All the way to Keisha's apartment were traffic accidents and delays caused by hydroplaning on the water, and flooding under several underpasses on the highway. I could barely see through the blinding downpour. I finally got there after forty harrowing minutes. I rang her doorbell, and when Keisha opened the door, the first comforting words out of her mouth were, "*What took you so long?*"

Once upstairs, and after taking a shower, talking, and some fondling foreplay, she decided to give me what was intended to make me feel somewhat better. Knowing her youngest son was asleep across the hall, Keisha constantly reminded me to be a little quiet, so we didn't have the chance to make the kind of good loving we had in the distant past. It had been years since we had made love.

The next morning when I left her apartment, I forgot to put back on a leather bracelet, engraved with my name, that I had bought while at Cedar Point a month ago, ironically on the day with Keisha and her kids. I had decided sentimentally to put the bracelet on my father's wrist in the casket at the funeral, before his burial. I called Keisha and she promised, to put the bracelet in her car and drop it off Sunday on her way to, or back from a Detroit Lions exhibition game. She sounded sincere about keeping her word.

But she *never* called, *never* came by, not to the funeral, or to my home before or after the funeral. She *never* even sent a sympathy card. I called her a week after the funeral to express my anger, accusing her of all the things we had always fought about, but she just shrugged it off, saying *she forgot*. I told her to keep the bracelet, I didn't *need it* anymore—I had a specific purpose for it—on my father's wrist. After that, I didn't see Keisha again for six months, when she popped-up unexpectedly at my home. Unfortunately a neighbor was helping me cement the foundation and replace the flange of a leaky toilet at the time. For some reason, I fantasized about dogging her and "fucking" her little brains out. This time she claimed "she was just in the neighborhood, visiting a girlfriend of hers," who worked at the sheriff's department. Actually all she wanted to do was use my phone.

Of course there were times when Keisha possessed a kinder heart. While I worked for the Department she had twice given me gifts. Keisha once bought me a wrist watch for Christmas, but when I found out she had given Fred the same one, but a different color wristband, I then sold it to an Officer Henderson, a Black male, who later committed suicide. When she didn't see me wearing the watch for a few days, Keisha asked if perhaps I didn't like it: "I haven't seen you wearing your new watch lately. You do like it, don't you?" I told her I smashed it and tossed it down the elevator shaft. Keisha was the kind of woman who'd make a man say and do things, he later would say he didn't mean. After all the crap I had went through, I felt a need to keep Keisha on edge, *never* letting her size-up how I really felt about her.

The other gift I got from Keisha brought good memories in the form of a homely ceramic coffee mug, picturing a little white boy peering through a candy store window at an innocent-looking, young white girl. The little white girl held a book snugly under one arm while selecting candy from a candy jar. The statement just below the rim read *"Sweet memories are everlasting."* I often sipped coffee, tea, or hot chocolate from that mug and couldn't help but think about our better times, wishing there was a chance to rekindle what we once had, and make more *sweet memories*.

36

Perversion:
Can't Get Enough Sex?

X-rated magazines or pornographic material is strictly prohibited in the jail, and on its floors, but many male officers, especially the white ones, brought these types of sleazy publications in the jail, and on its floors, all the time. But many officers, male or female, had no continence or forbearance, concerning their overly indulgent sexual thoughts or activities. Those non-adhering to morals, lured and enticed inmates, showing them pages of sexy models in their most explicit, sexual positions. Prolonged and continued exposure to such material, drove some inmates to act wild, crazy and loose, and made them much more hornier than they were already.

"Dep, can we tear out some of those pictures?" A few inmates asked, while the deputy was looking for a place to hide the material from command officers or snitches. Thieving inmates never asked and just tore the pictures out. Many inmates took a long gaze at the pictures, and later, when they thought no one was looking, would fantasize by going to masturbate in the privacy of their cell.

"Come on Dep, you know you ain't right! Why don't you let me see that magazine, and let me get one-a-them pictures? Damn! Man, that chick looks good than-a-motherfucka. When I get out of this joint, am gonna knock the bottom out of somebody's daughter's pussy," said Frank Bonner, an elderly Black inmate, as a crowd cluttered around pressing their noses up against the station window to get a better view. Nearly all of them [inmates] said similar things, while continually grabbing and squeezing, their ever-hardening crotches. It's rather sickening for male officers to watch male inmates develop *"hard ons"*

right in front of them, in the seduction of being enthralled and im-
mersed into heavy coition. Not yet convicted, Bonner, was charged
with three counts of kidnapping and harboring several adolescent
children in his basement for weeks.

When sexually alluring photos or pages of nude pictures in magazines
were placed up against the station window, hornier inmates sometimes licked the glass, and acted as though they were performing
cunnilingus (oral sex: licking and sucking the vagina). Regularly, white
male officers loved to bring in a Black porno magazine called *Players*, which was full of Black female models, then the more conven-
tional ones like *Hustler*, *Penthouse* or *Playboy* with a lot of white
models. Their sexual exploration and exploitation of Black females
never ceased. Constant confinement, no female visitors, lack of so-
cialization, and especially sex, made male inmates look at female officers like they were pork chops—same thing for the female inmates
wanting some male officers' pork chops—it was vice-versa for the
androgynous types. There were several rumors involving female and
male officers and superiors, having sex with inmates in closets; particularly one female who aroused them by dancing or perpetrating a
strip tease act. Some inmates had sex with officers and superiors, in
hopes of achieving favors, influential reasons in court, have their
sentences reduced, change in jail residency, but mainly, just to get a
dormant "nut off."

There were a few incidents where officers and coworkers had
harbored inmates in their home. One in particular, involved Ms. Claire
Ott, a nice white lady in her early 50s, who in physical and emotional
comparison was like Nurse Alice Cayruth, and not getting any attention from men. Ott taught self-awareness to inmates, and while a
participant, inmate Walt White, a big Black dude about 6-foot-3-inches
tall, weighing about 260, sweet-talked his way into Ott's tender heart.
Immediately, after White's release, Ott took him into her home, without knowing he was just using her as a front while starting another
crime spree. When officers raided and searched her home, they discovered that White had been staying there for months. Instructor
Ott was charged with "***harboring a criminal***" (The total outcome of
that case unknown).

White male officers even had calendars that were commonly given out by Black establishments on special holidays, with Black female models posing nude. Sneakingly, inmates tore pages out if an officer gave them permission to keep the magazine on the ward for any length of time. Characteristically, when this happened there was total pandemonium, because some inmates literally fought over the magazine, if another was selfish, ignored and disregarded the viewing time of others. Many male shift command officers acted naive, and knew exactly which officers were bringing in such material, yet, *never* bothered to reprimand them.

A great percentage of the inmates looking at the porno material, had multiple charges of C.S.C. (criminal sexual conduct). White male officers, who were not harassed, or scrutinized like Black male officers were, hid their porno magazines in duffle bags carried upon the floors. Pants were always a good hiding place for forbidden publications. Themselves, white and Black male command officers, came on the jail floors, and peered through porno magazines. Occasionally, they looked in the desk or file drawers for porn material, found some, and themselves, drooled at the photos. Instead of issuing reprimands, Sergeant Harold Fingerhut, a white male, always talked about "fucking and sucking a Black woman," and made sexual wisecracks about the models, especially the Black ones.

"Yes! Yes! Yes! I'd love to lick that Black babe's luscious-looking cunt. Boy, she's got one fine bush. Momma! Momma! Momma! She can sit on my face, any day at any time. Wow! Ah yeah," capriciously, Sergeant Fingerhut said, while sticking out his tongue, licking and sucking on his lips. He was a very unattractive man, who had severe acne and social problems to obtain a woman. He was real freaky, and always talked about kinky sex, and licking dry some "chicks" pussy—like most of the white males working in the jail. It seemed that was all they were concerned about when it pertained to sex.

The closest thing to nude pictures that was allowed in the jail, were the swimsuit models in the center folds of Jet magazines, in which most Black male inmates collected, and hung on their cell walls or the inside of their cell doors. This gave them some imagination of a concupiscent society. When the jail librarian, Terry Canady, came on the floors with book selections, *every* center fold picture in Jet was absent. Later, while conducting shakedowns, white male officers tore down those pictures of Jet models. Canady, a small framed white male, about 5-foot-4-inches tall, who weighed about 135 pounds with golden hair, wheeled around a little wooden cart with casters, built with three slanted, wooden shelves on each side. The cart was mainly stored with outdated, uninteresting reading material.

Many of the books in the jail were of little interest to Black inmates, and when it was time to pick from the cart, it took them forever, because most of the time, the best selections were already chosen. Usually, the remaining choices were limited to *The National Geographic*, Harlequin love novels, Westerns, and science fiction books. Generally, these books are read by white people. Of course, there was always literature, material and books on religion. The selection of provided books, rarely showed direction towards a rehabilitation process from an Afrikan-American perspective. Books that enrich vocabularies, restore viability, reveal hidden or talented ability through crafts, trades, or something conducive for knowledgeable living, seemed non-existent.

The infamous, Uncle Toms Tavern was always on the cart, but there were *no* books informing Black prisoners on the new celebration of Kwanzaa. There were *no* autobiographies of Malcolm X, Martin Luther King, Marcus Garvey, or books by Carter G. Woodson, W.E.B DuBois, and Ivan van Sertima on Afrika and its destruction through European history. Missing from the cart were research books by Dr. Nathan Hare from *The Black Think Tank*, on the Black plight in the urban school systems, and Afrikan studies to combat racism in America. There were *no* research books by Haki R. Madhubuti from *Third World Press*, on Black cultural and political movements. *No* books on cultural prose and poetry, Black short stories, or Black inventors. It seemed that all the important and historical books of Black history, were unavailable to Black inmates.

There was *no Final Call*, an Islamic newspaper from Chicago, which has tapped the jail system, and has an enormous resurgence of popularity among Black subscribers in jails across the country. With a high percent of jail population nationally, of Black male inmates, the message is obviously clear—more than any other race on this earth, Black inmates are being targeted by not being able to read critical and important literature to enhance their rehabilitation and awareness. Inmates grew frustrated from their efforts to obtain meaningful reading material. This is a self-esteem issue—reminiscent of slavery days, when "Negroes" or "niggers" were beaten, whipped, faced death or were killed, simply for trying to read, and become more educated.

From 1987 through 1990, departmental expenditures on educational books and materials for inmates was very little, it follows:

"The Wayne County Sheriff Departments, 1987 actual expenditure for books was $1,307, $609 in 1988, in 1989 the amended budget for books was $1,500, and the 1989 projected budget was $1,700, the 1990 department requisition for books was $1,000, and the commission approved $1,100 for the year 1990."

Shoot, I donated that much money in books to the department by myself. Several times over those years, I collected interesting books and magazines from neighbors, and friends who were glad to clear off their dusty shelves full of unused material. I then brought them to the jail. The seeds of good, excellent reading material, enhances and elevates the mind to free lost souls, instead of reading and viewing filth. If you want to grow... ***Read***!

The Department did supply a law library, which was on the southside of the ninth floor. Inmates had to sign a sheet in advance, to get permission to use it. Inmates researched past cases similar to theirs, hoping to find *any* legal angles or loopholes to get some charges dropped, if not all.

For entertainment in the jail, I played Scrabble, drew pictures, typed on my typewriter, or read an interesting book. Playing Scrabble with the inmates, got their minds off the corruptive elements of sex, perversion, and their pending fate. More importantly, playing Scrabble helped enrich their vocabularies.

I *never* felt satisfaction out of buying or viewing porno magazines. My theory is: If I can't have the woman to myself, what's the purpose of looking at a naked photo of a woman I'd never meet personally? Sort of like going to an x-rated bar, and watching women dance naked on top of tables—all this does is create perversity. That's why rape, aggravated assault, muggings, and acts of domestic violence, are escalating problems in America, and a primary reason why everyday women are seriously injured or beaten, and being abused at alarming rates.

A couple of times a month, several officers got together and drove over to Windsor, Ontario, to see women dance naked all night on tables. Several times they asked me to go, but I shunned, saying, "I don't get nothing out of that! It just doesn't turn me on. Now if she was dancing naked at my house, or in my bedroom in front of me, well, that's a different story." (In 1997, prostitution became legal in Windsor.)

Over the years (1985-1999), several sheriff's deputies have been accused of simulating sex acts and displaying indecent and obscene conduct, including receiving lap dances and touching nude dancers, in countless raids of topless bars in Detroit. Those deputies arrested had their police powers removed, and were reassigned to jail security and faced an internal investigation that could lead to disciplinary action. They also received misdemeanor tickets and fines, and some faced a day in court. Many of these vice sweeps came in response to community outrage and complaints of too much violence.

Every time officers thought of prohibited material, Officer Mike Byrd and Sergeant Hopkins always came to mind. They also looked out for each other by trading pornographic movies inside the jail, and sometimes in the command office. One day, Byrd brought in several porno movies for Hopkins to chose from to take home. Between the office door, next to the Master Control station, they spoke.

"You got some Vanessa Del Rio movies... I like her," gleefully, Hopkins said.

He always seemed to want Vanessa Del Rio movies. I heard she could handle five or six men at one time, without taking time out, and satisfy every one of them. She was such a sensually sexy woman, but to many in the jail, a diabolic freak.

"Man, I've got some better ones than that, she ain't nothing compared to this other one," Byrd sounded very assuring, about his knowledge of x-rated movies. He was also astute about music, and his knowledge of porno films was as keen. He was one of Sergeant Phil Hopkins' "boys," and sarge always looked out for Byrd when he clearly violated jail rules. For at least eight months, Hopkins protected Byrd, because almost everyday, Byrd left the jail floors an hour prior to shift change... many times leaving the jail before the sergeants and lieutenants were off duty.

Officers could sign-out for the night in the logbook, because the time-card notebook in the Roll Call room, had already been signed prior to starting the shift. Periodically, several afternoon shift officers who continually worked together, took turns leaving early before the shift ended at 11 p.m. Selfishly, Byrd often bragged about "how easy it was to get away with the infraction." Right after lock down at 10 p.m., sometimes officers flipped a coin to determine who'd leave early (if those same officers routinely worked the same floor). But no matter what floor Byrd worked, and no matter who worked the floor with him, Byrd continually left early. Many times he left way before 10 p.m., never giving other officers the same courtesy and a chance to leave early themselves—that's if they had the guts to!

When officers started seeing the blatant, glaringly obvious favoritism, Byrd was receiving, several voiced disfavor. At times, Sergeant Hopkins started using retaliatory measures by harassing those who complained. A supposedly, knowledgeable, astute aficionado of real estate investments, Hopkins told me about property he owned around Wayne County and Ontario, Canada. At one time, we were cordial speaking buddies, and had numerous conversations about "how Hopkins obtained his pilot's license and his love for flying." We even discussed possible flight patterns, and how frequently Hopkins flew up north. One of our conversations involved this fine Black woman I knew in Canada.

"I've got this friend named Mona, a Jamaican cutie, who lives in London, Ontario, sarge. Man, let me tell you... this girl is fine as wine. I'm sure she has some friends, so lets fly up there one day," I told Hopkins many times, hoping one day we would.

Sergeant Hopkins became very eager when we talked about women, but he continued to procrastinate about arranging a weekend. I even expressed a desire to take some aviation lessons, and Hopkins tried to encourage me, by giving me magazines on "heavy" stuff, like aviation and aircraft technology. Since childhood, to learn how to fly a plane was another one of my first loves. Knowing what I found out later, I thanked God that I *never* went flying with Hopkins, because of the way he betrayed me—he might have attempted a kamikaze run or tried forcing me to jump from the plane without a parachute! Missing somewhere in Canada—not found—called off searches, naw, I didn't need that! Many times, Sergeant Hopkins bragged about playing the bass guitar, for several gigs in groups at the old Twenty Grand, and other nostalgic hot, Black night club spots back in the 1960s, and early 70s. These old spots were the starting points for many hot, singing groups for Motown.

With all the pressures and stress in the jail, adjusting to my mother's illness, my aunt's death, my uncle's illness, constant harassment, dealing with my first cousin's problems of chemical dependency, everything seemed insurmountable. But I kept battling the odds to overcome the obstacles. Also knowing that Keisha, was frequently consorted with Sergeant Hopkins and Officer Steadman (and whoever else), made me distrustful and at odds with her. Keisha wouldn't give me any quality time, and kept refusing me a chance for meaningful redemption. As the pettiness and harassment of the shift command officers seemed to escalate, Hopkins' demeanor became stern and forthright, whenever I was in his midst.

Sergeant Hopkins was an intricate, ever-connected part of the "*Black nexus*" of white male jail officials' staged puppet show, who with insinuated propaganda, were targeting me and other Black officers. Working for the Department was nothing but constant exposure to an *ongoing supply* of minion, peon reinforcements, and a ever-battling war involving numerous innuendoes, for prolonged confliction. Denunciatory rhetoric from the *perverted minds* of loyal superiors and white male jail officials, who *never* came down off their high pinnacles, and took great pride in systematically putting Black officers in insubordinate positions. They only acknowledged our qualms through written rebuttals, which often showed pent-up anger and a sometimes sarcastic... but, righteous point of view.

37

The Lottery: Legal Gambling: Where Does The Money Go?

I N THE SECLUDED SECRECY OF CLOSETS, ROOMS, and gyms on the jail floors, some officers just paid a few days before and nearly strapped of funds, gambled frequently, because they needed extra money to pay for additional expenses. Religiously, some played lottery games hoping to ease financial crunches, especially those with a large family to support. Of course, it's always a joy to hit the jackpot considering the sheriff's department meager wages. Seeing the long stacks of losing lottery tickets many officers bought, produced instant debates about "if the lottery was so worthwhile, why are urban and minority children, Black neighborhoods and its schools suffering and neglected so much?"

Yet, several Detroit schools, mainly elementary and junior high, are forced to close their doors every school year because of money shortages. These schools are the beginning of educational goals for many Black children in the inner city. For decades, citizens of Michigan and around the nation were told that state lotteries were instituted, and necessary to have a solid impact on keeping school systems' educational needs productive. Even today, lottery officials continue to tell the nation that profits are earmarked for worthy causes, such as education, and the appropriate means and programs would be legislated to achieve it. Though lottery profits are considered only a small percentage of state school budgets, schools became more dependent on this unstable source of money. What a travesty!

Not since 1972, when Michigan Governor William Milliken opposed a lottery, has there been any opposition of an electoral process for citizens to vote on whether there should be one. But 73 percent of Michigan voters disagreed with Milliken and voted it in anyway. It has been nearly thirty years since this underlying, burdensome taxation has been in existence in Michigan, and citizens should have a vote on whether there should be the necessity of a lottery.

In the mid-1970s, the late former mayor Coleman A. Young, tried desperately to get casino gambling in Detroit, but failed to convince its citizens to vote for it—instead, citizens were tricked into voting for proposals that raised their taxes. In 1988, there was a futile attempt by Detroit proponents to cast casino gambling on a ballot. Casino gambling opponents opposed the idea because they believed it would definitely increase crime and further damage the city's already tarnished image. City organizers fighting for legal gambling argued the venture would create some 10,000 jobs for the city. On June 2, 1993, Detroit voters for the fourth time in seventeen years, voted down casino gambling, and whether it should be authorized by Detroit's city council.

Voters in Michigan and across the country should have another say-so in the lottery scheme. It would be very interesting to see "what percentage of voters would approve a lottery?" Seeing the funds used inappropriately, and the manipulative corruption it breeds, surely most voters would think differently, if the lottery issue was placed before them on a ballot. Still, the question remains, where has all that money gone?

Rarely, do citizens see a printing of the proportionate budget, telling them "where money has been distributed?" Nor do state, city, county, and townships, see how much money was sent to this school or that school, and other usages? Where does all the money go? Even if that *"manipulated data"* was furnished, citizens can rest assured the statistics would be misleading, and a reputable state controlled audit is definitely out of the question.

For centuries, lotteries thrived worldwide. The kings of England allowed American colonies to use lotteries to raise money in the 1600s. In the 1700s, lotteries helped finance the American Revolution. State-run lotteries continued well into the 1800s, then partly, because of continued fraud and corruption, they ended abruptly, not to be resumed until the 1960s. In 1963, the state of New Hampshire approved a lottery to raise money for education, and in 1966, New York state approved a lottery. The New Hampshire lottery had only two drawings per year; while New York had twelve. But back then there was a very low chance of winning, and little excitement in playing. Initially, the lotteries didn't make as much profit as participating states had hoped for.

In 1732, a quote from Henry Fielding concerning the lottery said, "*A lottery is a taxation, upon all the __fools__ in creation.*" In 1966, New York State Governor Nelson Rockefeller, branded the lottery the "*__most retrogressive__ taxation you can get.*" But despite Rockefeller's obvious disapproval, New Yorkers voted the lottery in by a margin of 61 percent, and in 1992, spent over $1.5 billion on tickets. In 1984, California Governor George Deukmejian said, "*It is wrong for the state to go out, push and urge people to gamble.*" But California's voters still approved the lottery by a 58% margin. In 1986, Floridians voted 64 percent for a state-run lottery, despite Governor Bob Graham's contention that, "*government should not be in the business of pandering to __people's worst instincts__.*"

In 1993, there were 34 states with government manipulated lotteries. The first million-dollar lottery prize was in 1971. Daily drawings began in 1972. Instant games began in Massachusetts in 1974... instant games were implemented to encourage winners to buy more tickets. Since 1975, players were permitted to pick their own numbers. All these significant changes gave lotteries major publicity and interest rose. Michigan was among the billion-dollar-plus lottery states. One Michigan budget counted on $502.5 million in lottery revenue.

There's no question that state lottery expenditures were mainly used to fund an already depleting and dependent governmental fund, not to help urban inner city schools. The lottery acts like a tax (*voluntary but heavily promoted*) that takes a bigger percentage from the poor than the more affluent. This again, proves the lottery's claim is particularly a farce, and shows lottery officials' insensitivity towards humanitarian issues involving poor communities, whose educational systems remain in political shambles, and are left "out in the cold."

Welfare reform will definitely, and significantly, affect the poor, especially, single-headed, Black female families. That's not the only irony, the lottery was not the only way the State Treasury fed on the defunct wages of the poor. The disparity of winners in the city and the suburbs is alarmingly gapping. In 1991, lottery radio advertisements were played continually, and mainly on Black radio stations that claimed, "two-thirds of all Michigan adults have played the Michigan State Lottery," and "fifty-three percent of the lottery's 7.3 billion is spent for kindergarten to middle aged brackets of young school children."

The commercials were virtually absent from the air of several white radio stations in Detroit's tri-county area (Wayne, Macomb, Oakland), or not played as much as on Black radio stations. This bombardment of continuous lottery advertising promotes a fantasy of wealth, luxury, encourages people to dream, and hope for *success through luck*, while taking high risks to an instant problem-free life. The millions of dollars lost, and the remote odds of winning are rarely mentioned. Instead of providing commercials of lottery statistics over the radio, why not *show and tell* the citizens of Michigan the number of people who play and lose? why the constant neglect for lottery officials to publish statistics of "where that money goes?" why not state and publish what the lottery's main method of chosen distribution targets are? in the newspaper for everyone to read?

But instead, everyday, papers, pamphlets, and other printed material are sold in stores, with psychic predictions of possible winnings with number associations with names, articles, and zodiac correlation variables. Again, these are other underlying psyches to get people to play. In the *Detroit News* and *Detroit Free Press*, the two major newspapers of the city, winning numbers are published from a month back, to remind losers of "what they should have played," instead of "where the billions of dollars are being appropriated?"

Black radio stations continue to give air time to "Lottery Mania," despite the continued deterioration of poor, urban Black, and other people of color neighborhoods. Black radio stations show a financial desperation to survive themselves by providing often misleading lottery commercials. When lottery winnings are unclaimed over a period of one year, the prize is *supposedly*, sent to school funding. There must be a lot of people in the suburbs, who don't pick up their money because their school systems' seem to remain intact, despite st⁻

budget restraints and fiscal catastrophes.

National network television newscasters often comment on the outlandish statistics, involving lottery ticket sales in some states. On April 18, 1991, the California lottery hit $117 million. Lottery officials claimed, "at one period computers stored 1,300 tickets sold per second." Drawn on July 7, 1993, the "Powerball" lottery drawing in conjunction with several states had a $110 million dollar pot, and had only one winner. This kind of media hype, just makes the poor, naive players attempt to win, forgetting responsibilities, and spend needed money, forgoing necessities. Who wouldn't be tempted or enticed to try winning millions of that magnitude? In the long run, the practice of gambling becomes a sickening habit as devious as using crack cocaine, or the end results of children continually playing years of video games, and a very depressing one when your numbers *never* win! Food for thought... is it better for a person to gamble, or to buy and use drugs? Both are leading causes to harmful and destructive addictions.

Putting your faith in state legalized gambling, raises another alarming question. Why can't urban city dwellers have their own lottery? to fund their own businesses and neighborhood developments? Like the Indian tribes in northern Michigan. When the economy of white and Greek restaurant entrepreneurs in Greektown was threatened, the first thing they wanted was to get state legislation passed to get Indian casinos—legal gambling to help their situation and attract customers. Mind you, the white man owes the American Indians and Afrikan-Americans quite a lot for their historical travesties committed against them. Through casino gambling, the Indians got their *Reparations*, while Blacks after over 400 years of oppression are still waiting for theirs.

Many Detroit ministers, clergymen, bishops, priests, and non-profit organizations became enraged at the thought of casino gambling, mainly because it would affect church tithes and contributions even more drastically. Yes, the religious sector must survive, but ￢-versa, casino gambling has created newly built water systems in ￢ies. Indian tribes in Northern Michigan, 400 miles away from ￢d reservations into thriving enterprises. Davenport, Iowa, ￢n into its economy... there are some successes.

In the fall of 1992, acquisitions to have a state-ran Indian gambling casino in Greektown, was endorsed by both union presidents of the sheriff's department, and Detroit Police Department. Both cited, "jobs are a deterrent to crime..." a very lame, politically motivated statement, considering the many types of criminality gambling breeds. Both union presidents knew the jails would fill up even more with gambling in the city, and the unions would benefit from new recruits, more union dues, and many moonlighting opportunities for its members. Many Detroit citizens were shocked that top ranked police officers gave their endorsement and support to gambling. Surely, that statement was a conflict of interest, and geared specifically to keep the jobs for law enforcement officers, because gambling in the midst of downtown would definitely, need more police protection, be beneficial for hiring more correction officers in the institutionalized setting, and would increase law enforcement agencies pockets.

On May 20, 1993, a long-standing, Wayne County Prosecutor, warned: "Casino gambling in Detroit would invite a tripling of the city's crime rate if voters opt to legalize casino gambling. Can you imagine a Detroit with three and a half times as much crime as we have now?" He also cited a study of Atlantic City that showed serious crimes increased by 250 percent since casinos opened there in 1978.

Trying to establish gambling casinos is an obvious sign that a city is in bad economic condition and local governments want an *unrealistic quick fix*. In the past, citizens of Detroit were quite aware of this, and turned down four attempts by local government and business leaders to make casino gambling legal in Detroit and Highland Park. To many Detroit citizens, donating a small part of Greektown to a Michigan Indian tribe is the shiftiest, most absurd plan to achieve a respectable tax base.

Prematurely, on November 11, 1993, after days of radio advertising for an estimated 4,000-plus job openings for a Indian ran casino in Greektown—it attracted 10,000 applicants to react and stand in line for hours in anticipation of a favorable decision by Michigan's governor and the U.S. Interior Secretary. Indian tribes in Michigan and across the nation began running gambling operations in the mid-1980s, to *help relieve* desperate poverty, drug addiction, and alcoholism.

Working for the lottery commission can also affect future aspirations. On November 7, 1990, another old alumnus of mine from Mumford High School, lost the election for a position as Wayne County Commissioner—many believed he lost because he had previously worked for the lottery commission. Surely his appointment, the lottery's continuing allocations to other sources, and public upheaval had some impact on the vote's final outcome. He had to be aware of the thoughts of citizens about lottery mismanagement.

One of his endorsements was "the first Black to work on the lottery commission." Not falling for it, knowledgeable Black voters didn't heed to that, and being the son of a state representative, wasn't enough to convince voters, while Commissioner Michael Mitchell was reelected. Both candidates were old Mumford High School alumnus... the same school I attended.

Many times, I had some "hell-of-a" hunches, and became disappointed, and regretted I didn't play some lottery numbers. The most noticeable was when the Department *unjustly* terminated me on Tuesday, May 16, 1989. Three days later, my badge number, "**2317**," came out straight. I felt that it was a gift from God—the "***highest official***." But as usual, I choose not to play, though I had thought about playing it several times. I kept saying, "One day, I'm going to play my badge number," which should've been the most obvious number to play, especially, after all I had been through. It was God's way of saying, "Here's some money you deserve," but since I was such a procrastinator about playing the lottery, and believed deeply, about its underlying, damaging affect on the Black community as a whole, I didn't play but maybe four or five times a year, if that... so my chances of winning were virtually nil. I was sick for two weeks for not playing "**2317**."

Still, I never felt I was hurting a child's education by refusing to play the lottery. If citizens believe that playing the lottery supplements education, again, I must ask, why are people of color neighborhoods decaying at alarming rates? Why do schools continue to close? Why are teachers' salaries low compared to suburban teachers? Why are urban cities' schools in America having so many budget and internal problems? Why are the majority of training equipment, books, and supplies so outdated and obsolete? Why is the infrastructure, and landscape surrounding many inner city schools looking like prairie or desert land, instead of a bustling educational haven? Surveying the majority of the suburban and adult college landscapes, there's an obvious, significant difference.

I have some more important, pertinent questions about the misuse of lottery revenues. Why are classroom sizes staying over capacity requirements? Doesn't this affect effective learning? Why are so many teachers disgusted, underpaid, and outnumbered? Why is the lack of security for schools understaffed and ineffective? And why are the average grade levels, in important classes: math and science, so low? and the dropout rates so staggering? The underlying, *Trickle Down Syndrome's*, damaging affects of irresponsible, parental guidance is also affected by the lottery—when parents religiously play the lottery and neglect the needs of their children.

Male officers always circulated betting pool sheets around the jail, for football, hockey, and basketball games. Sometimes they even betted on what male officer would fuck a certain female? Sort-a-like when Sergeant Phil Hopkins told me that, "certain females were betting on who could get me in bed first." I wondered if Officer Keisha Flowers won that bet!

Every year when college basketball's, NCAA *"March Madness"* tournament arrived, copies of the round pairings were given to sport fanatic male officers, who wanted to enter a betting pool. To enter this contest every participant had to pay ten dollars, and if no one picked a champion, whoever had the best winning percentage after all the games were played, won all the money. Many times when the betting sheet was passed around to officers, it seemed like I always got it last, after all the choice box selections were already taken. This obviously cut down my odds of winning. I *never* wagered in the betting pool, but before the University of Michigan won the NCAA tournament in 1988," I posted my newspaper sheet of winners on the Roll Call's bulletin board, for daily review and criticism of others.

To everyone's surprise, just before the tournament started, the coach, unceremoniously left the team for another coaching job at Arizona State. The newly appointed coach, won all of the games in the tournament... the rest is history. For the first few rounds, everyone in the jail rooted for Michigan, though it was sentimental, no one really thought it was possible for the Michigan Wolverines to reach the Finals. But I predicted it, by posting it, beforehand.

In 1988, Fred Steadman, the officer who courted Keisha, bet $50 with me on the Detroit Piston's, seventh game loss to the Los Angeles Lakers, for the NBA championship. This was the year when the NBA's defensive, rebounding specialist, cross-dresser, colored-hair phenomenon, Dennis Rodman, was blamed for the loss, because he attempted an errant jumper with about 13 seconds still left on the clock. Many thought Rodman should've given up the ball to a guard (Isiah Thomas or Joe Dumars), to set up for a better shot.

On the day of the seventh game, I had an eerie feeling that the Lakers would prevail—they won by three points. Everyone in the jail wanted the Detroit Pistons to win, but I, a devoted Pistons fan, just had a hunch. While undressing after shift change in the locker room, minding my own business and talking with other officers about the game, Fred, came over to my aisle of lockers, and without provocation.

"Taylor, I'll bet your stupid ass. How about betting fifty dollars? Think you can handle it? Man, you must be crazy because the Pistons are gonna win tonight, baby! Why don't you just put your money where your mouth is!"

"Yeah, I want them to win also, but I just don't think they will tonight. Not a seventh game in L.A. Naw, I don't think so," I said, while still pulling off my raiments.

"Well, you've got a bet brother," Fred insisted, and we shook hands to solidify the bet in front of many officers. When the Pistons lost, I felt sad for the city of Detroit, but I also knew I had won $50 from Fred. I got happy real quick thinking about that! After losing the game and fifty dollars, Fred became extinct, unreachable, and antisocial. I wouldn't see Fred, unless I waited to catch him by the lobby door after the shift, or called him at his guard station while on duty, because Fred wouldn't call me. When I finally caught up with Fred, he acted very boisterous, and typical of ignorant people—a real "*nigga.*" When I asked Fred for my money, he broke into a tantrum and "went off" on me.

"Man, why don't you stop bothering me about that damn money.

I'll pay you when I can, so stop bugging me about that shit!"

"Look my man, you don't have to holler at me, I didn't make the bet, nor did I approach you with it. You thought you had a sure thing, and you lost, and now you can't take the heat... so pay up," pathetically, I expressed.

This was typical of several officers working in the jail, many were so phoney and irresponsibly inept. Several officers in the locker room overheard Fred's forced bet with me, and vowed *never* to bet or ever lend him money, because now, they knew of his reluctance to pay up. Fred's tiring shenanigans, and uncalled for attitude, lingered on for weeks. After three weeks of trying useless twits to embarrass him among other officers, I just gave up and relinquished the fifty dollars, and forgot about the indebtedness.

I had believed in Fred's troth, but his word was "*not worth its weight in gold*." It would've been fine with me to settle it in another fashion, but departmental regulations prohibited such actions against fellow officers. When people make bets with others, they expect honesty and integrity, *especially those they work with*. But more important than that—a man's word, *should* be a man's word. *Enough said*!

Notes and References

Chapter Two

- Jack Knight, "County jail reform goals set," <u>Detroit Free Press</u>, 12 January 1972, Sec. A, p. 12.
- Joan Ryzak, "Westland opposes site plan for new Wayne County jail," <u>Detroit News</u>, 11 January 1972, Sec. B, p. 1.
- Kevin Brown, "Warden confronts new job," <u>Plymouth Observer</u>, 16 December 1993, Sec. A, pgs. 1 & 4.
- Ronald L. Russell, "New corrections unit, jail are urged for Wayne County," <u>Detroit News</u>, 4 April 1972, Sec. A, p. 17.
- Russell, "County to vote on new jail," <u>Detroit News</u>, 19 September 1972 Sec. B, p. 1.
- Russell, "Taxes considered for jail and capital improvements," <u>Detroit News</u>, 26 May 1972, Sec. B, p. 1.
- Russell, "Wayne jail levy loses," <u>Detroit News</u>, 8 November 1972, Sec. C, p. 3.
- Russell, "Plan for Wayne jail jolted," <u>Detroit News</u>, 14 December 1972, Sec. B, p. 1.
- Said Deep, "Judge says Ficano can't fire deputies," <u>Detroit News</u>, 21 April 1993, Sec. B, pgs. 1-2.
- James Graham, "Hoffa joins Lucas to back millage for jail," <u>Detroit News</u>, 19 October 1972, Sec. B, p. 11.
- Michael Brogan, "2 in jail suit seek fees," <u>Detroit News</u>, 9 May 1972, Sec. A, p. 13.
- Stephen Cain, "U. of D. ordered to halt jail advice on lawyers," <u>Detroit News</u>, 26 February 1972, Sec. A, p. 2.
- Judy Diebolt, "Judge Tells Jail To Let Inmates Register To Vote," <u>Detroit Free Press</u>, 5 October 1972, Sec. A, p. 14.
- Michael Graham, "U.S. Indicts 2 Deputies In Beating at Jail Here," <u>Detroit Free Press</u>, 6 October 1972, Sec. A, p. 3.
- John Gill, "Judges accused of meddling on jail bond vote," <u>Detroit News</u>, 5 October 1972, Sec. A, p. 20.
- Hugh McDiarmid, "It's a cold welcome for William Lucas," <u>Detroit Free Press</u>, 27 March 1993, Sec. A, p. 3.

Chapter Three

- Shawn Lewis, "Detroit council OK's juvenile jail downtown," <u>Detroit News</u>, 7 December 1995, Sec. C, p. 4.
- Reuters and Michele Chandler, "Black urban teens' unemployment nearly 50%," <u>Detroit Free Press</u>, 6 June 1992, Sec. A, p. 9.
- Haki R. Madhubuti, <u>Black Men: Obsolete, Single, Dangerous? The Afrikan American Family in Transition</u> (Illinois: Third World Press, 1990), pgs. 67-68.
- Robert Blauner, <u>Racial Oppression in America</u> (New York: Harper & Row, 1972).

Chapter Four

- Brenda Ingersoll and Tarek Hamada, "Despite boycott, store owners say tensions are easing," <u>Detroit News</u>, 26 April 1991, Sec. B, pgs. 1-2.
- Brenda J. Gilchrist, "Simmering Distrust: Merchants blame poverty, not race, <u>Detroit Free Press</u>, 22 February 1993, Sec. A, pgs. 1 & 5.
- John D. McClain, "Detroit ranks high in home affordability," <u>Detroit News</u>, 22 May 1991, Sec. C, pgs. 1-2.
- Angie Cannon, "City's public housing called nation's worst," <u>Detroit News</u>, 6 March 1991, Sec. A, pgs. 1 & 5.
- Yolanda W. Woodlee, "Census: 36,000 Detroit homes vacant but usable," <u>Detroit News</u>, 21 April 1991, Sec. A, pgs. 1 & 10.
- National News Briefs, <u>The Final Call</u>, Vol. 17, No. 9, 23 December 1997, p. 8.
- "Fewer Farms And Black Farmers: Census Bureau," <u>Jet</u>, 5 December 1994, Vol. 85, No. 5, p. 36.
- Dan Gillmor, "Black views shared widely," <u>Detroit Free Press</u>, 14 June 1993, Sec. A, pgs. 1 & 6.
- Clarence Lusane and contributions by Dennis Desmond, <u>Pipe Dream Blues: Racism & The War on Drugs</u> (Massachusetts, South End Press, 1991), p. 102.
- William Kleinknecht, "In city, no car often means no job," <u>Detroit Free Press</u>, 5 November 1990, Sec. A, pgs. 1 & 8.
- William Raspberry (Washington Post columnist), "Racism a fact, but not always the culprit," <u>Detroit News</u>, 22 May 1991, Sec. A, p. 13.
- George Wilson, "Injustice... Down on the Farm," <u>Michigan Citizen</u>, Vol. XIX, No. 24, 11-17 May 1997, Sec. A, pgs. 1 & 7.

Chapter Five

- Appendix A, Court Orders Affecting the Wayne County Jail.

Chapter Six

- Lusane and Desmond, p. 92.
- Betty DeRamus, "Ex-drug lord must prove himself first," <u>Detroit News</u>, 14 August 1990, Sec. B, p. 1.
- Carl S. Taylor, "Dangerous Society," <u>Michigan State University Press</u>, East Lansing, MI, 1989, p. 99.

Chapter Nine

- Madhubuti, p. 200.

Chapter Eleven

- Robert Byrd, "High school suicide—27% had thoughts," <u>Detroit Free Press</u>, 20 September 1991, Sec. A, p. 4.
- Health Note, "Suicide increases among American youth," <u>The Final Call</u>, 10 May 1995, p. 28.
- Christopher Sullivan (Associated Press), "Jailed youths are killing themselves at troubling rate," <u>Detroit News</u>, 12 March 1995, Sec. A, p. 2.
- Melinda Wilson, "Cop kills estranged wife, himself," <u>Detroit News</u>, 16 May 1995, Sec. B, pgs. 1 & 4.
- Gary Heinlein and Nicole Jihad, "Cops twice as likely to kill themselves," <u>Detroit News</u>, 16 May 1995, Sec. A, p. 4.
- Nancy Abner, "An attempted suicide is usually a cry for help, a last-ditch effort to reach out to humanity," <u>Detroit News</u>, 27 January 1972, Sec. E, p. 13.
- "3 Guilty In Slaying in County Jail Cell," <u>Detroit Free Press</u>, 15 November 1972, Sec. A, p. 3.
- "3 convicted in slaying of jail inmate," <u>Detroit News</u>, 15 November 1972, Sec. A, p. 8.
- Robert E. Roach, "County ordered to hire more guards for jail," <u>Detroit News</u>, 30 July 1972, Sec. A, p. 8.
- Bobby E. Wright, Ph.D., <u>The Psychopathic Racial Personality and Other</u> Essays (Illinois: Third World Press, 1977), pgs. 17-19.

Chapter Eleven (cont.)

- Did You Know? "Typist's letters exposed major political scandal," <u>Detroit News</u>, 19 April 1995, Sec. B, p. 3.
- Jim Schutze, "A preventable jail suicide?," <u>Detroit Free Press</u>, 8 August 1972, Sec. B, p. 1.

Chapter Twelve

- Evan Ramstad, "FBI bombards cult with sound and light," <u>Detroit Free Press</u>, 27 March 1993, Sec. A, p. 4.
- David Ritz, <u>Divided Soul: The Life of Marvin Gaye</u> (New York: McGraw-Hill Book Company edition published in 1985, and PaperJacks edition published in May 1986), pgs. 130-131.
- Deborah Culp, "The New York Experience," <u>Complete Neighborhood News</u>, Vol. 1, No. 12, April 1991, p. 5.
- Donald Muhammad, "Curtis Mayfield's 'New World Order'," <u>The Final Call</u>, 12 November 1996, p. 38.

Chapter Thirteen

- "What You Might Be Missing in Entertainment," <u>The Plain Truth: A Magazine of Understanding</u>, July 1990, pgs. 3-6.
- Carol Teegardin, "How to lower volume of viewing time," <u>Detroit Free Press</u>, 24 July 1991, Sec. F, p. 1 (Sources: Doug Snow, program director of Eastwood Clinic, a drug and alcohol rehabilitation center in Royal Oak, Michigan; Francis Haman, a drug and alcohol rehabilitation therapist with the Eastwood Clinic in Troy, Michigan).
- Mike McQueen, "Now playing: 'The Big Snooze'. At county jailhouses, the curtain falls on flicks featuring violence," <u>Detroit Free Press</u>, 8 August 1995, Sec. B, pgs. 1 & 3.
- Valarie Basheda, "Official wants violent videos banned at jail," <u>Detroit News</u>, 11 June 1995, Sec. C, p. 5.
- R.Z. Sheppard, "A Natural Selection," <u>Time</u>, July 23, 1990, p. 74.
- Madhubuti, pgs. 78-79.
- Dr. Nathan Hare and Robert Chrisman, <u>Contemporary Black Thought</u>: The Best From the Black Scholar (Indianapolis/New York: The Bobbs-Merrill Co., Inc., 1973), p. 224.

Chapter Fourteen

- As We See It, "Bail Bonding is a Blot On the System of Justice," <u>Detroit Free Press</u>, 27 June 1972, Sec. A, p. 6.
- "Judges Urge Liberalized Bail Rules," <u>Detroit Free Press</u>, 22 June 1972, Sec. C, p. 8.
- Bonnie DeSimone, "Sheriff's deputy accused of embezzling $12,000," <u>Detroit News</u>, 13 February 1991, Sec. B, p. 4.

Chapter Fifteen

- Madhubuti, pgs. 67-68.

Chapter Sixteen

- Hare and Chrisman, pgs. 225-226.

Chapter Seventeen

- A.L. Flagg, "Asthma Jumps Among Blacks," <u>Black Enterprise</u>, February 1991, p. 22.
- "AAAI, NIAID, and NHLBI Join Ranks to Train Minorities in Asthma Research," <u>Press Release on February 8, 1993</u>. First National Conference on Asthma Management, October 12-13, 1992, Sponsored by NAEP Coordinating Committee.
- Erin Marcus, "Asthma's Grip: Millions Gasp For Breath as Serious Attacks Soar And Deaths Nearly Double," <u>Washington Post Health</u>, 4 August 1992.
- John Gallagher, "Detroit buildings making workers sick, survey finds," <u>Detroit Free Press</u>, 6 June 1992, Sec. A, pgs. 9-10.
- Valarie Basheda, "Prisoners face ban on smoking," <u>Detroit News</u>, 14 March 1995, Sec. B, pgs. 1 & 4.
- Jerry Schwartz, "Smoke in workplace targeted," <u>Detroit Free Press</u>, 28 June 1991, Sec. A, p. 3.
- Becky Beaupre and Mike Wowk, "Mysterious illness kills 3 prisoners at Jackson," <u>Detroit News</u>, 1 September 1993, Sec, A, pgs. 1 & 6.
- Ken Miller, "Polluted indoor air called a $60 billion problem," <u>Detroit News</u>, 2 November 1993, Sec. A, p. 2.

Chapter Seventeen (cont.)

- Associated Press and Washington Post, "OSHA is told to change its work habits," <u>Detroit News</u>, 16 May 1995, Sec. A, p. 5.
- Emilia Askari, "Law to touch everyone in U.S.," <u>Detroit Free Press</u>, 15 November 1990, Sec. A, pgs. 1 & 16.

Chapter Nineteen

- "<u>Amazing Grace</u>," John Newton, American Melody from Carrell & Clayton's Virginia Harmony, 1831, and arranged by Norman Johnson.
- Leonard W. Ingraham, <u>Slavery in the United States</u> (New York: Franklin Watts, Inc. 1968), pgs. 24-25.
- Mark Hornbeck, "Engler riled by prisoners' religious wants," <u>Detroit News</u>, 14 March 1995, Sec. A, pgs. 1 & 8.

Chapter Twenty

- Thomas J. Bray and Robert H. Giles, "Disorder in the Court," <u>Detroit News</u>, 16 May 1995, Sec. A, p. 6.
- Appendix A, Court Orders Affecting the Wayne County Jail.

Chapter Twenty-eight

- Lori Sharn, "Getting MADD makes roads safer," <u>Detroit News</u>, 31 December 1991, Sec. A, p. 2.
- Chris Christoff, "Law would get drunks off road at 1st offense," <u>Detroit Free Press</u>, 25 September 1990, Sec. A, pgs. 1 & 11.
- Jim Mitzelfeld, "Engler signs tougher drunken-driving laws," <u>Detroit News</u>, 9 August 1991, Sec. B, p. 1.

Chapter Twenty-nine

- Bill Kole (Associated Press), "Prison wiretap bill fuels debate," <u>Detroit News</u>, 31 May 1993, Sec. B, p. 9.
- Tom Greenwood, "Windows enhance workers' morale," <u>Detroit News</u>, 28 June 1993, Sec. E, p. 2.

Chapter Thirty

- Dave Farrell and Dwight E.M. Angell, "Hospital owes IRS $1.2 million," Detroit News, 15 March 1991, Sec. A, pgs. 1 & 6.
- Jim Doggett, Back to Barnesville: Home Remedies (Michigan: Stake N' Rake, Inc. 1977), p. 63.
- Tammy Joyner, "Ouch! Headaches cost billions," Detroit News, 1 September 1993, Sec. A, pgs. 1 & 8.
- J.R. Clairborne, "Migranes, depression linked, study finds," Detroit News, 5 July 1994, Sec. A, p. 2.
- Blue Cross and Blue Shield of Michigan, Michigan Public School Retirees' Newsletter, "Pain Pills: There Is a Grain of Difference," February 1991, Vol. 36, pgs. 4-5.
- The Old Farmer's Almanac

Chapter Thirty-one

- Interview with Vernice Davis-Anthony, Former Assistant Wayne County Executive, Native Detroiter (Sherman Eaton: Publisher), 1990 (month unknown), p. 11.
- Jack Kresnak, "Juvenile justice slows," Detroit Free Press, 23 November 1995, Sec. B, pgs. 1 & 4.
- Kresnak, "Argument escalates into gunfire; teens join a crime trend. Serious crimes by youths up sharply," Detroit Free Press, 18 March 1995, Sec. A, pgs. 3 & 6.
- Kresnak, "State to send teen criminals to jails outside Michigan," Detroit Free Press, 4 May 1995, Sec. B, pgs. 1 & 6.
- John Flesher, "Report says U.S. has highest inmate rate," Detroit Free Press and Associated Press.
- Elizabeth Atkins, "Answers sought to high rate of blacks in prison," Detroit News, 14 September 1994, Sec. A, p. 2.
- Atkins, "Male-female stats don't add up for blacks," Detroit News, 14 September 1994, Sec. B, pgs. 1 & 6.
- "News About Doing Time," Detroit Free Press, 9 May 1995, Sec. A, p. 4.
- "More than 1 Mil. in U.S. Prisons; More Blacks Locked Up Than Whites," Jet, 14 November 1994, Vol. 87, p. 18.
- Toni Watson, "Aging and ill inmates putting a strain on the prison systems," Detroit News, 4 April 1995, Sec. A, pgs. 5 & 7.

Chapter Thirty-one (cont.)

- Rosalind Muhammad and Richard Muhammad, "More prisoners, more profits: Black males hot commodity for corrections industry," The Final Call, 20 December 1995, Vol. 15, no. 4, pgs. 3, 8-9.
- Cal Thomas, "We've invested too much in prisons, not enough in virtue," Detroit Free Press, 3 August 1994, Sec. A, p. 13.
- Associated Press, "Numbers up at state, federal levels," El Dorado News-Times, 4 November 1995, Sec. A, p. 5.
- Michael J. Sniffen (Associated Press), "Nearly 2.7% of U. S. adults in corrections system," Detroit News, 28 August 1995, Sec. A, p. 2.
- Sniffen (Associated Press), "Prison population soars since '86: Report: 1 of every 167 Americans an inmate in '95," Detroit News, 19 August 1996, Sec. A, p. 5.
- "Doing Time: Our Women in Prison," Essence, May 1994, pgs. 83-86.
- Lusane and Desmond, pgs. 71-72.
- Dawson Bell, "Engler budget would increase prison spending," Detroit Free Press, 17 March 1993, Sec. B, p. 3.
- Bell, "5 prisons needed now, Engler says," Detroit Free Press, 13 November 1997, Sec. A, pgs. 1 & 16.
- Mark Hornbeck and Kenneth Cole, "Prison spending to soar in 1994," Detroit News, 1 September 1993, Sec. B, pgs. 1 & 6.
- Robert Musial, "Sheriffs play let's make a deal to fill surplus jail cells, Detroit Free Press and Associated Press, 29 November 1990, Sec. B, p. 1.
- "Jail Overcrowding... or not?," All Points Bulletin, July/August 1990, Vol. V., No. 5, pgs. 1 & 11.
- Daniel Pesta (Capital News Service), "Overcrowding forces jailers to consider alternatives," Michigan Citizen, 9-15 November 1997, Sec. A, pgs. 1 & 8.
- Eric Freedman, "Lawsuits go after 9 inmates for $37,000," Detroit News, 17 February 1991, Sec. C, pgs. 1 & 2.

Chapter Thirty-two

- Vivian S. Toy, "Union, Ficano at odds over job appointees," <u>Detroit News</u>, 13 March 1992, Sec. F, p. 9.
- Jon Jeter, "County commissioner to challenge Ficano: Kelley accuses sheriff of mismanagement," <u>Detroit Free Press</u>, 18 March 1992, Sec. A, p. 14.
- Jim Tittsworth, "Sheriff Ficano's speech at union rally is seen as breaking code of police neutrality," <u>Detroit News</u>, 21 July 1995, Sec. A, p. 10.
- Bonnie DeSimone, "Unions draw battle lines in effort to dump Ficano," <u>Detroit News</u>, 22 May 1992, Sec. B, p. 1.

Chapter Thirty-four

- <u>Awake!</u>: Is Your God Alive?, "**BOREDOM** Can Cause Stress and Depression," December 22, 1989, p. 12.

Chapter Thirty-six

- Suzette Hackney, "2 deputies arrested in raid of topless bar," <u>Detroit Free Press</u>, 26 February 1999, Sec. B, p. 7.

Chapter Thirty-seven

- George Weeks, "Exploiting the wages of weakness," <u>Detroit News</u>, 4 March 1990, Sec. C, p. 3.
- John Diamond, "Odds are gambling will keep on growing," <u>Detroit News</u>, 2 June 1991, Sec. A, p. 10.
- "Lotteries: Are You Being Cheated?," <u>The Plain Truth</u>: <u>A Magazine of Understanding</u>, November/December 1989, pgs. 14-15.
- Wayne County Prosecutor John D. O'Hair's statement, "Crime and gambling," <u>Detroit News</u>, 21 May 1993, Sec. B, p. 4.
- <u>Awake!</u>: Gambling: A Growing Addiction, "Gambling: The Addiction of the '90's," September 22, 1995, pgs. 3-5.
- Bill McDonough (Little Rock, Arkansas), "Gambling," <u>Good News... Up Words ....for a Change</u>," A Newsletter for Family and Friends of the College Avenue Church of Christ, August 1996, Vol. 3, No. 8, p. 8.
- Lori Montgomery, "Indian gambling legalized: It may clear path for Detroit casino," <u>Detroit Free Press</u>, 21 August 1993, Sec. A, pgs. 1 & 9.

Yes! I want to purchase ____ copies of the book *WITHIN THE WALLS*. Enclosed is my check or money order for $21.95 for each book ordered, $3.00 shipping and handling included for each book. (And in Michigan, add 6% sales tax.) Please mail payment and coupon to:

Ora's Publishing, L.L.C.
P.O. Box 47438
Oak Park, MI 48237

The book(s) will most likely be delivered promptly to you within two weeks, however, please allow 2 - 4 weeks for delivery.

NAME: _____

ADDRESS: _____

CITY: _____ STATE: _____ ZIP: _____

HOME PHONE: (_____)_____

WORK PHONE: (_____)_____

FAX: (_____)_____ E-MAIL:_____